Very truly Yours
Thos. W. Knox

OVERLAND THROUGH ASIA.

PICTURES OF

SIBERIAN, CHINESE, AND TARTAR LIFE.

TRAVELS AND ADVENTURES IN KAMCHATKA, SIBERIA, CHINA, MONGOLIA, CHINESE TARTARY, AND EUROPEAN RUSSIA, WITH FULL ACCOUNTS OF THE SIBERIAN EXILES, THEIR TREATMENT, CONDITION, AND MODE OF LIFE, A DESCRIPTION OF THE AMOOR RIVER, AND THE SIBERIAN SHORES OF THE FROZEN OCEAN.

WITH AN APPROPRIATE MAP,

AND

NEARLY 200 ILLUSTRATIONS.

BY

THOMAS W. KNOX.

AUTHOR OF "CAMP FIRE AND COTTON FIELD."

HARTFORD, CONN.:

AMERICAN PUBLISHING COMPANY.

BLISS & CO., NEWARK, N. J.; R. W. BLISS & CO., TOLEDO, OHIO.

F. G. GILMAN & CO., CHICAGO, ILL.; NETTLETON & CO., CINCINNATI, OHIO.

F. A. HUTCHINSON & CO., ST. LOUIS, MO.; GEO. M. SMITH & CO., BOSTON, MASS.

H. H. BANCROFT AND COMPANY, SAN FRANCISCO, CAL.

1871.

WILLIAM H. LOCKWOOD,
Electrotyper,
HARTFORD, CONN.

PREFACE.

FOURTEEN years ago Major Perry McD. Collins traversed Northern Asia, and wrote an account of his journey, entitled "A Voyage Down the Amoor." With the exception of that volume no other work on this little known region has appeared from the pen of an American writer. In view of this fact, the author of "Overland Through Asia" indulges the hope that his book will not be considered a superfluous addition to the literature of his country.

The journey herein recorded was undertaken partly as a pleasure trip, partly as a journalistic enterprise, and partly in the interest of the company that attempted to carry out the plans of Major Collins to make an electric connection between Europe and the United States by way of Asia and Bering's Straits. In the service of the Russo-American Telegraph Company, it may not be improper to state that the author's official duties were so few, and his pleasures so numerous, as to leave the kindest recollections of the many persons connected with the enterprise.

Portions of this book have appeared in Harper's, Putnam's, The Atlantic, The Galaxy, and the Overland Monthlies, and in Frank Leslie's Illustrated Newspaper. They have been received with such favor as to encourage their reproduction wherever they could be introduced in the narrative of the journey. The largest part of the book has been written from a carefully recorded journal, and is now in print for the first time. The illustrations have been made from photographs and pencil sketches, and in all cases great care has been exercised to represent correctly the costumes of the country. To

Frederick Whymper, Esq., artist of the Telegraph Expedition, and to August Hoffman, (Photographer,) of Irkutsk, Eastern Siberia, the author is specially indebted.

The orthography of geographical names is after the Russian model. The author hopes it will not be difficult to convince his countrymen that the shortest form of spelling is the best, especially when it represents the pronunciation more accurately than does the old method. A frontier justice once remarked, when a lawyer ridiculed his way of writing ordinary words, that a man was not properly educated who could spell a word in only one way. On the same broad principle I will not quarrel with those who insist upon retaining an extra letter in Bering and Ohotsk and two superfluous letters in Kamchatka.

Among those not mentioned in the volume, thanks are due to Frederick Macrellish, Esq., of San Francisco, Hon. F. F. Low of Sacramento, Alfred Whymper, Esq., of London, and the many gentlemen connected with the Telegraph Expedition. There are dozens and hundreds of individuals in Siberia and elsewhere, of all grades and conditions in life, who have placed me under numberless obligations. Wherever I traveled the most uniform courtesy was shown me, and though conscious that few of those dozens and hundreds will ever read these lines, I should consider myself ungrateful did I fail to acknowledge their kindness to a wandering American.

T. W. K.

Astor House, N. Y., Sept. 15, 1870.

LIST OF ILLUSTRATIONS
BY
FAY & COX
15 NASSAU ST.
N.Y.

CHAPTER XXX.

PAGE.

CHAPTER XXXI.

CHAPTER XXXII.

CHAPTER XXXIII.

CHAPTER XXXIV.

CHAPTER XXXV.

CHAPTER XLII.

PAGE.

CHAPTER XLIII.

CHAPTER XLIV.

CHAPTER XLV.

CHAPTER XLVI.

CHAPTER XLVII.

CHAPTER XLVIII.

CHAPTER I.

IT is said that an old sailor looking at the first ocean steamer, exclaimed, "There's an end to seamanship." More correctly he might have predicted the end of the romance of ocean travel. Steam abridges time and space to such a degree that the world grows rapidly prosaic. Countries once distant and little known are at this day near and familiar. Railways on land and steamships on the ocean, will transport us, at frequent and regular intervals, around the entire globe. From New York to San Francisco and thence to our antipodes in Japan and China, one may travel in defiance of propitious breezes formerly so essential to an ocean voyage. The same untiring power that bears us thither will bring us home again by way of Suez and Gibraltar to any desired port on the Atlantic coast. Scarcely more than a hundred days will be required for such a voyage, a dozen changes of conveyance and a land travel of less than a single week.

The tour of the world thus performed might be found monotonous. Its most salient features beyond the overland journey from the Atlantic to the Pacific, would be the study of the ocean in breeze or gale or storm, a knowledge of steamship life, and a revelation of the peculiarities of men and women when cribbed, cabined, and confined in a floating prison. Next to matrimony there is nothing better than a few months at sea for developing the realities of human character in either sex. I have sometimes fancied that the Greek temple over whose door "Know thyself" was written, was really the passage office of some Black Ball clipper line of ancient days. Man is generally desirous of the company of his fellow man or woman, but on a long sea voyage he is in danger of having too much of it. He has the alternative of shutting himself in his room and appearing only at meal times, but as solitude has few charms, and cabins are badly ventilated, seclusion is accompanied by ennui and headache in about equal proportions.

CHARACTER DEVELOPED.

Wishing to make a journey round the world, I did not look favorably upon the ocean route. The proportions of water and land were much like the relative quantities of sack and bread in Falstaff's hotel bill. Whether on the Atlantic or the Pacific, the Indian, or the Arctic, the appearance of Ocean's blue expanse is very much the same. It is water and sky in one place, and sky and water in another. You may vary the monotony by seeing ships or shipping seas, but such occurrences are not peculiar to any one ocean. Desiring a reasonable amount of land travel, I selected the route that included Asiatic and European Russia. My passport properly endorsed at the Russian embassy, authorized me to enter the empire by the way of the Amoor river.

A few days before the time fixed for my departure, I visited a Wall street banking house, and asked if I could obtain a letter of credit to be used in foreign travel.

"Certainly sir," was the response.

"Will it be available in Asia?"

"Yes, sir. You can use it in China, India, or Australia, at your pleasure."

"Can I use it in Irkutsk?"

"Where, sir?"

"In Irkutsk."

"Really, I can't say; what *is* Irkutsk?"

"It is the capital of Eastern Siberia."

The person with whom I conversed, changed from gay to grave, and from lively to severe. With calm dignity he remarked, "I am unable to say, if our letters can be used at the place you mention. They are good all over the civilized world, but I don't know anything about Irkutsk. Never heard of the place before."

I bowed myself out of the establishment, with a fresh conviction of the unknown character of the country whither I was bound. I obtained a letter of credit at the opposition shop, but without a guarantee of its availability in Northern Asia.

In a foggy atmosphere on the morning of March 21, 1866, I rode through muddy streets to the dock of the Pacific Mail Steamship Company. There was a large party to see us off, the passengers having about three times their number of friends. There were tears, kisses, embraces, choking sighs, which ne'er might be repeated; blessings and benedictions among the serious many, and gleeful words of farewell among the hilarious few. One party of half a dozen became merry over too much champagne, and when the steward's bell sounded its warning, there was confusion on the subject of identity. One stout gentleman who protested that he *would* go to sea, was led ashore much against his will.

After leaving the dock, I found my cabin room-mate a gaunt, sallow-visaged person, who seemed perfectly at home on a steamer. On my mentioning the subject of sea-sickness, he eyed me curiously and then ventured an opinion.

"I see," said he, "you are of bilious temperament and will be very ill. As for myself, I have been a dozen times over the route and am rarely affected by the ship's motion."

Then he gave me some kind advice touching my conduct when I should feel the symptoms of approaching *mal du mer*.

I thanked him and sought the deck. An hour after we passed Sandy Hook, my new acquaintance succumbed to the evils that afflict landsmen who go down to the sea in ships. Without any qualm of stomach or conscience, I returned the advice he had proffered me. I did not suffer a moment from the marine malady during that voyage, or any subsequent one.*

The voyage from New York to San Francisco has been so often 'done' and is so well watered, that I shall not describe it in detail. Most of the passengers on the steamer were old Californians and assisted in endeavoring to make the time pass pleasantly. There was plenty of whist-playing, story telling, reading, singing, flirtation, and a very large amount of sleeping. So far as I knew, nobody quarreled or manifested any disposition to be riotous. There was one passenger, a heavy, burly Englishman, whose sole occupation was in drinking "arf and arf." He took it on rising, then another drink before breakfast, then another between his steak and his buttered roll, and so on every half hour until midnight, when he swallowed a double dose and went to bed. He had a large quantity in care of the baggage master, and every day or two he would get up a few dozen pint bottles of pale ale and an equal quantity of porter. He emptied a bottle of each into a pitcher and swallowed the whole as easily as an ordinary man would take down a dose of peppermint. The empty bottles were thrown overboard, and the captain said that if this man were a frequent passenger there would be danger of a reef of bottles in the ocean all the way from New York

---

* A few years ago a friend gave me a prescription which he said would prevent sea-sickness. I present it here as he wrote it.

"The night before going to sea, I take a blue pill (5 to 10 grains) in order to carry the bile from the liver into the stomach. When I rise on the following morning, a dose of citrate of magnesia or some kindred substance finishes my preparation. I take my breakfast and all other meals afterward as if nothing had happened."

I have used this prescription in my own case with success, and have known it to benefit others.

to Aspinwall. I never saw his equal for swallowing malt liquors. To quote from Shakspeare, with a slight alteration:

> "He was a man, take him for half and half,
> I ne'er shall look upon his like again."

ASPINWALL TO PANAMA.

We had six hours at Aspinwall, a city that could be done in fifteen minutes, but were allowed no time on shore at Panama. It was late at night when we left the latter port. The waters were beautifully phosphorescent, and when disturbed by our motion they flashed and glittered like a river of stars. Looking over the stern one could half imagine our track a path of fire, and the bay, ruffled by a gentle breeze, a waving sheet of light. The Pacific did not belie its name. More than half the way to San Francisco we steamed as calmly and with as little motion as upon a narrow lake. Sometimes there was no sensation to indicate we were moving at all.

SLIGHTLY MONOTONOUS.

Even varied by glimpses of the Mexican coast, the occasional appearance of a whale with its column of water thrown high into the air, and the sportive action of schools of porpoises which is constantly met with, the passage was slightly monotonous. On the twenty-third day from New York we ended the voyage at San Francisco.

On arriving in California I was surprised at the number of old acquaintances I encountered. When leaving New York I could think of only two or three persons I knew in San Francisco, but I met at least a dozen before being on shore twelve hours. Through these individuals, I became known to many others, by a rapidity of introduction almost bewildering. Californians are among the most genial and hospitable people in America, and there is no part of our republic where a stranger receives a kinder and more cordial greeting. There is no Eastern iciness of manner, or dignified indifference at San Francisco. Residents of the Pacific coast have told me that when visiting their old homes they feel as if dropped into a refrigerator. After learning the customs of the Occident, one can fully appreciate the sensations of a returned Californian.

MONTGOMERY STREET IN HOLIDAY DRESS.

Montgomery street, the great avenue of San Francisco, is not surpassed any where on the continent in the variety of physiognomy it presents. There are men from all parts of America, and there is no lack of European representatives. China has many delegates, and Japan also claims a place. There are merchants of all grades and conditions, and professional and unprofessional men of every variety, with a long array of miscellaneous characters. Commerce, mining, agriculture, and manufactures, are all represented. At the wharves there are ships of all nations. A traveler would find little difficulty, if he so willed it, in sailing away to Greenland's icy mountains or India's coral strand. The cosmopolitan character of San Francisco is the first thing that impresses a visitor. Almost from one stand-point he may see the church, the synagogue, and the pagoda. The mosque is by no means impossible in the future.

SAN FRANCISCO, 1848.

In 1848, San Francisco was a village of little importance. The city commenced in '49, and fifteen years later it claimed a population of a hundred and twenty thousand.* No one

* I made many notes with a view to publishing two or three chapters upon California. I have relinquished this design, partly on account of the un-Siberian

who looks at this city, would suppose it still in its minority. The architecture is substantial and elegant; the hotels vie with those of New York in expense and luxury; the streets present both good and bad pavements and are well gridironed with railways; houses, stores, shops, wharves, all indicate a permanent and prosperous community. There are gas-works

CHINESE DINNER.

and foundries and factories, as in older communities. There are the Mission Mills, making the warmest blankets in the world, from the wool of the California sheep. There are the

---

character of the Golden State, and partly because much that I had written is covered by the excellent book "Beyond the Mississippi," by Albert D. Richardson, my friend and associate for several years. The particulars of his death by assassination are familiar to many readers.

fruit and market gardens whose products have a Brobdignagian character. There are the immense stores of wine from California vineyards that are already competing with those of France and Germany. There are—I may as well stop now, since I cannot tell half the story in the limits of this chapter.

During my stay in California, I visited the principal gold, copper, and quicksilver mines in the state, not omitting the famous or infamous Mariposa tract. In company with Mr. Burlingame and General Van Valkenburg, our ministers to China and Japan, I made an excursion to the Yosemite Valley, and the Big Tree Grove. With the same gentlemen I went over the then completed portion of the railway which now unites the Atlantic with the Pacific coast, and attended the banquet given by the Chinese merchants of San Francisco to the ambassadors on the eve of their departure. A Chinese dinner, served with Chinese customs;—it was a prelude to the Asiatic life toward which my journey led me.

I arrived in San Francisco on the thirteenth of April and expected to sail for Asia within a month. One thing after another delayed us, until we began to fear that we should never get away. For more than six weeks the time of departure was kept a few days ahead and regularly postponed. First, happened the failure of a contractor; next, the non-arrival of a ship; next, the purchase of supplies; and so on through a long list of hindrances. In the beginning I was vexed, but soon learned complacency and gave myself no uneasiness. Patience is an admirable quality in mankind, and can be very well practiced when one is waiting for a ship to go to sea.

On the twenty-third of June we were notified to be on board at five o'clock in the evening, and to send heavy baggage before that hour. The vessel which was to receive us, lay two or three hundred yards from the wharf, in order to prevent the possible desertion of the crew. Punctual to the hour, I left the hotel and drove to the place of embarkation. My trunk, valise, and sundry boxes had gone in the forenoon, so that my only remaining effects were a satchel, a bundle of newspapers, a dog, and a bouquet. The weight of these combined articles was of little consequence, but I positively declare that I never handled a more inconvenient lot of baggage. While I was descending a perpendicular ladder to a small boat, some one abruptly asked if that lot of baggage had been cleared at the custom house. Think of walking through a custom house with my portable property! Happily the question did not come from an official.

It required at least an hour to get everything in readiness after we were on board. Then followed the leave taking of friends who had come to see us off and utter their wishes for a prosperous voyage and safe return. The anchor rose slowly from the muddy bottom; steam was put upon the engines, and the propeller whirling in the water, set us in motion. The gang-way steps were raised and the rail severed our connection with America.

It was night as we glided past the hills of San Francisco, spangled with a thousand lights, and left them growing fainter in the distance. Steaming through the Golden Gate we were soon on the open Pacific commencing a voyage of nearly four thousand miles. We felt the motion of the waves and became fully aware that we were at sea. The shore grew indistinct and then disappeared; the last visible objects being the lights at the entrance of the bay. Gradually their rays grew dim, and when daylight came, there were only sky and water around us.

"Far upon the unknown deep,
With the billows circling round
Where the tireless sea-birds sweep;
Outward bound.

Nothing but a speck we seem,
In the waste of waters round,
Floating, floating like a dream;
Outward bound."

CHAPTER II.

THE G. S. Wright, on which we were embarked, was a screw steamer of two hundred tons burthen, a sort of pocket edition of the new boats of the Cunard line. She carried the flag and the person of Colonel Charles S. Bulkley, Engineer in Chief of the Russo-American Telegraph Expedition. She could sail or steam at the pleasure of her captain, provided circumstances were favorable. Compared with ocean steamers in general, she was a very small affair and displayed a great deal of activity. She could roll or pitch to a disagreeable extent, and continued her motion night and day. I often wished the eight-hour labor system applied to her, but my wishing was of no use.

Besides Colonel Bulkley, the party in the cabin consisted of Captain Patterson, Mr. Covert, Mr. Anossoff, and myself. Mr. Covert was the engineer of the steamer, and amused us at times with accounts of his captivity on the Alabama after the destruction of the Hatteras. Captain Patterson was an ancient mariner who had sailed the stormy seas from his boyhood, beginning on a whale-ship and working his way from the fore-castle to the quarter deck. Mr. Anossoff was a Russian gentleman who joined us at San Francisco, in the capacity of commissioner from his government to the Telegraph Company. For our quintette there was a cabin six feet by twelve, and each person had a sleeping room to himself.

Colonel Bulkley planned the cabin of the Wright, and I shall always consider it a misfortune that the Engineer-in-Chief was only five feet seven in his boots rather than six feet and over like myself. The cabin roof was high enough for the colonel, but too low for me. Under the skylight was the only place below deck where I could stand erect. The sleeping rooms were too short for me, and before I could lie at full length in my berth, it was necessary to pull away a partition near my head. The space thus gained was taken from a closet containing a few trifles, such as jugs of whiskey, and cans of powder. Fortunately no fire reached the combustibles at any time, or this book might not have appeared.

OVER SIX FEET.

There was a forward cabin occupied by the chief clerk, the draughtsman, the interpreter, and the artist of the expedition, with the first and second officers of the vessel. Sailors, firemen, cook and cabin boys all included, there were forty-five persons on board. Everybody in the complement being masculine, we did not have a single flirtation during the voyage.

I never sailed on a more active ship than the Wright. In ordinary seas, walking was a matter of difficulty, and when the wind freshened to a gale locomotion ceased to be a pastime. Frequently I wedged myself into my berth with books and cigar boxes. On the first day out, my dog (for I traveled with a dog) was utterly bewildered, and evidently thought himself where he did not belong. After falling a dozen times upon his side, he succeeded in learning to keep his feet. The carpenter gave him a box for a sleeping room, but the space was so large that his body did not fill it. On the second day from port he took the bit of carpet that formed his bed and used it as a wedge to keep him in position. From that time he had no trouble, though he was not fairly on his sea legs for nearly a week.

Sometimes at dinner our soup poured into our laps and seemed engaged in reconstructing the laws of gravitation. The table furniture was very uneasy, and it was no uncommon occurrence for a tea cup or a tumbler to jump from its proper place and turn a somersault before stopping. We had no severe storm on the voyage, though constantly in expectation of one.

In 1865 the Wright experienced heavy gales with little interruption for twelve days. She lost her chimney with part of her sails, and lay for sixteen hours in the trough of the sea. The waves broke over her without hindrance and drenched every part of the ship. Covert gave an amusing account of the breaking of a box of soap one night during the storm. In the morning the cabin, with all it contained, was thoroughly lathered, as if preparing for a colossal shave.

Half way across the ocean we were followed by sea-birds that, curiously enough, were always thickest at meal times. Gulls kept with us the first two days and then disappeared, their places being taken by boobies. The gull is a pretty and graceful bird, somewhat resembling the pigeon in shape and agility. The booby has a little resemblance to the duck, but his bill is sharp pointed and curved like a hawk's. Beechey and one or two others speak of encountering the Albatross in the North Pacific, but their statements are disputed by mariners of the present day. The Albatross is peculiar to the south as the gull to the north. Gulls and boobies dart into the water when any thing is thrown overboard, and show great dexterity in catching whatever is edible. At night they are said to sleep on the waves, and occasionally we disturbed them at their rest.

STEAMSHIP WRIGHT IN A STORM.

One day we caught a booby by means of a hook and line, and found him unable to fly from the deck. It is said that nearly all sea-birds can rise only from the water. We detained our prize long enough to attach a medal to his neck and send him away with our date, location, and name. If kept an hour or more on the deck of a ship these birds become sea-

A SEA-SICK BOOBY.

sick, and manifest their illness just as an able-bodied landsman exhibits an attack of marine malady. Strange they should be so affected when they are all their lives riding over the tossing waves.

About thirty miles from San Francisco are the Farralone Islands, a favorite resort of sea-birds. There they assemble in immense numbers, particularly at the commencement of their breeding season.

Parties go from San Francisco to gather sea-birds eggs at these islands, and for some weeks they supply the market. These eggs are largely used in pastry, omelettes, and other things, where their character can be disguised, but they are far inferior to hens' eggs for ordinary uses.

There were no islands in any part of our course, and we found but a single shoal marked on the chart. We passed far to the north of the newly discovered Brooks Island, and kept southward of the Aleutian chain. Since my return to America I have read the account of a curious discovery on an island of the North Pacific. In 1816, the ship Canton, belonging to the East India Company, sailed from Sitka and was supposed to have foundered at sea. Nothing was heard of her until 1867, when a portion of her wreck was found upon a coral island of the Sybille group. The remaining timbers were in excellent preservation, and the place where the crew had encamped was readily discernible. The frame of the main hatchway had been cast up whole, and a large tree was growing through it. The quarter board bearing the word "Canton," lay near it, and revealed the name of the lost ship. No writing or inscription to reveal the fate of her crew, could be found anywhere.

WRECK OF THE SHIP CANTON.

On Friday, July thirteenth, we crossed the meridian of 180° from London, or half around the world. We dropped a day from our reckoning according to the marine custom, and appeared in our Sunday dress on the morrow. Had we been sailing eastward, a day would have been added to our calendar. A naval officer once told me that he sailed eastward over this meridian on Sunday. On the following morning the chaplain was surprised to receive orders to hold divine service. He obeyed promptly, but could not understand the situation. With a puzzled look he said to an officer—

"This part of the ocean must be better than any other or we would not have Sunday so often."

Sir Francis Drake, who sailed around the world in the time of Queen Elizabeth, did not observe this rule of the navigator, and found on reaching England that he had a day too much. In the Marquesas Islands the early missionaries who came from the Indies made the mistake of keeping Sunday on Saturday. Their followers preserve this chronology, while later converts have the correct one. The result is, there are two Sabbaths among the Christian inhabitants of the cannibal islands. The boy who desired two Sundays a week in order to have more resting time, might be accommodated by becoming a Marquesas colonist.

On the day we crossed this meridian we were three hundred miles from the nearest Aleutian Islands, and about eight hundred from Kamchatka.

The boobies continued around us, but were less numerous than a week or ten days earlier. If they had any trouble with their reckoning, I did not ascertain it. A day later we saw three "fur seal" playing happily in the water. We hailed the first and asked his longitude, but he made no reply. I never knew before that the seal ventured so far from land. Yet his movements are as carefully governed as those of the sea-birds, and though many days in the open water he never forgets the direct course to his favorite haunts. How marvelous the instinct that guides with unerring certainty over the trackless waters!

A few ducks made their appearance and manifested a feeling of nostalgia. Mother Carey's chickens, little birds resembling swallows, began to flit around us, skimming closely along the waves. There is a fiction among the sailors that nobody ever saw one of these birds alight or found its nest. Whoever harms one is certain to bring misfortune upon himself and possibly his companions. A prudent traveler would be careful not to offend this or any other nautical superstition. In case of subsequent danger the sailors might remember his misdeed and leave him to make his own rescue.

Nearing the Asiatic coast we saw many whales. One afternoon, about cigar time, a huge fellow appeared half a mile distant. His blowing sounded like the exhaust of a western steamboat, and sent up a respectable fountain of spray.

Covert pronounced him a high pressure affair, with horizontal engines and carrying ninety pounds to the inch.

After sporting awhile in the misty distance, the whale came near us. It was almost calm and we could see him without glasses. He rose and disappeared at intervals of a minute, and as he moved along he rippled the surface like a subsoil plough on a gigantic scale. After ten or twelve small dives, he threw his tail in air and went down for ten minutes or more. When he reappeared he was two or three hundred yards from his diving place.

Once he disappeared in this way and came up within ten feet of our bows. Had he risen beneath us the shock would have been severe for both ship and whale. After this manoeuvre he went leisurely around us, keeping about a hundred yards away.

"He is working his engines on the slow bell," said our engineer, "and keeps his helm hard-a-port."

We brought out our rifles to try this new game, though the practice was as much a trial of skill as the traditional 'barn at ten paces.' Several shots were fired, but I did not see any thing drop. The sport was amusing to all concerned; at any rate the whale did n't seem to mind it, and we were delighted at the fun. When his survey was finished he braced his helm to starboard, opened his throttle valves and went away to windward.

We estimated his length at a hundred and twenty feet, and thought he might register 'A 1,' at the proper office. Captain Patterson called him a 'bow head,' good for a hundred barrels of oil and a large quantity of bone. The Colonel proposed engaging him to tow us into port. Covert wished his blubber piled in our coal bunkers; the artist sketched him, and the draughtsman thought of putting him on a Mercator's projection. For my part I have written the little I know of his life and experiences, but it is very little. I cannot even say where he lodges, whose hats he wears, when his notes fall due, or whether he ever took a cobbler or the whooping cough.

Of course this incident led to stories concerning whales. Captain Patterson told about the destruction of the ship Essex by a sperm whale thirty or more years ago. The Colonel described the whale fishery as practiced by the Kamchadales and Aleutians. These natives have harpoons with short lines

ALEUTIANS CATCHING WHALES.

to which they attach bladders or skin bags filled with air. A great many boats surround a whale and stick him with as many harpoons as possible. If successful, they will so encumber him that his strength is not equal to the buoyancy of the bladders, and in this condition he is finished with a lance. A great feast is sure to follow his capture, and every interested native indulges in whale-steak to his stomach's content.

The day before we came in sight of land, my dog repeatedly placed his fore feet upon the rail and sniffed the wind blowing from the coast. His inhalations were long and earnest, like those of a tobacco smoking Comanche. In her previous voyage the Wright carried a mastiff answering to the name of Rover. The colonel said that whenever they approached land, though long before it was in sight, Rover would put his paws on the bulwarks and direct his nose toward the shore. His demonstrations were invariably accurate, and showed him to possess the instinct of a pilot, whatever his lack of training. He did not enjoy the ocean and was always delighted to see land.

In 1865 an Esquimaux dog was domiciled on the barque Golden Gate, on her voyage from Norton Sound to Kamchatka. He ran in all parts of the vessel, and made himself agreeable to every one on board. At Petropavlovsk a Kamchadale dog became a passenger for San Francisco. Immediately on being loosed he took possession aft and drove the Esquimaux forward. During the whole passage he retained his place on the quarter deck and in the cabin. Occasionally he went forward for a promenade, but he never allowed the other dog to go abaft the mainmast. The Esquimaux endeavored to establish amicable relations, but the Kamchadale rejected all friendly overtures.

I heard of a dog on one of the Honolulu packets that took his turn at duty with the regularity of a sailor, coming on deck when his watch was called and retiring with it to the forecastle. When the sails flapped from any cause and the clouds indicated a sudden shower, the dog gave warning with a bark—on the sea. I ventured to ask my informant if the animal stood the dog watch, but the question did not receive a definite answer.

What a wonderful thing is the science of navigation. One measures the sun's height at meridian; looks at a chronometer; consults a book of mystical figures; makes a little slate work like a school-boy's problem; and he knows his position at sea. Twelve o'clock, if there be neither fog nor cloud, is the most important hour of a nautical day. A few minutes before noon the captain is on deck with his quadrant. The first officer is similarly provided, as he is supposed to keep a log and practice-book of his own. Ambitious students of navigation are sure to appear at that time. On the Wright we turned out four instruments, with twice as many hands to hold them. A minute before twelve, *conticuere omnes.*

"Eight bells."

"Eight bells, sir."

The four instruments are briefly fixed on the sun and the horizon, the readings of the scale are noted, and the quartette descend to the practice of mathematics. A few minutes later we have the result.

"Latitude 52° 8′ North, Longitude 161° 14′ East. Distance in last twenty-four hours two hundred forty-six miles."

The chart is unrolled, and a few measurements with dividers, rule and pencil, end in the registry of our exact position. Unlike the countryman on Broadway or a doubting politician the day before election, we do know where we are. The compass, the chronometer, the quadrant; what would be the watery world without them!

On the twenty-fourth of July we were just a month at sea. In all that time we had spoken no ship nor had any glimpse of land, unless I except a trifle in a flower pot. The captain made his reckoning at noon, and added to the reading—

"Seventy-five miles from the entrance of Avatcha Bay. We ought to see land before sunset."

About four in the afternoon we discovered the coast just where the captain said we should find it. The mountains that serve to guide one toward Avatcha Bay were exactly in the direction marked on our chart. To all appearances we were not a furlong from our estimated position. How easily may the navigator's art appear like magic to the ignorant and superstitious.

The breeze was light, and we stood in very slowly toward the shore. By sunset we could see the full outline of the coast of Kamchatka for a distance of fifty or sixty miles. The general coast line formed the concavity of a small arc of a circle. As it was too late to enter before dark, and we did not expect the light would be burning, we furled all our sails and lay to until morning.

By daybreak we were under steam, and at five o'clock I came on deck to make my first acquaintance with Asia. We were about twenty miles from the shore, and the general appearance of the land reminded me of the Rocky Mountains from Denver or the Sierra Nevadas from the vicinity of Stockton. On the north of the horizon was a group of four or five mountains, while directly in front there were three separate peaks, of which one was volcanic. Most of these mountains were conical and sharp, and although it was July, nearly every summit was covered with snow. Between and among these high peaks there were many smaller mountains, but no less steep and pointed. As one sees it from the ocean, Kamchatka appears more like a desolate than a habitable country.

It requires very good eyesight to discover the entrance of Avatcha Bay at a distance of eight or ten miles, but the landmarks are of such excellent character that one can approach without hesitation. The passage is more than a mile wide. Guarding it on the right is a hill nearly three hundred feet high, and standing almost perpendicular above the water. At the left is a rock of lesser height, terminating a tongue or ridge of land. On the hill is a light-house and signal station with a flag staff. Formerly the light was only exhibited when a ship was expected or seen, but in 1866, orders were given for its maintainance every night during the summer months.

Years ago, on the coast of New Hampshire, a man from the interior was appointed light keeper. The day he assumed his position was his first on the sea-shore. Very soon there were complaints that his lights did not burn after midnight. On being called to account by his superior, he explained—

"Well, I thought all the ships ought to be in by midnight, and I wanted to save the ile."

CHAPTER III.

AS one leaves the Pacific and enters Avatcha Bay he passes high rocks and cliffs, washed at their base by the waves. The loud-sounding ocean working steadily against the solid walls, has worn caverns and dark passages, haunted by thousands of screaming and fluttering sea-birds. The bay is circular and about twenty miles in diameter; except at the place of entrance it is enclosed with hills and mountains that give it the appearance of a highland lake. All over it there is excellent anchorage for ships of every class, while around its sides are several little harbors, like miniature copies of the bay.

At Petropavlovsk we hoped to find the Russian ship of war, Variag, and the barque Clara Bell, which sailed from San Francisco six weeks before us. As we entered the bay, all eyes were turned toward the little harbor. "There is the Russian," said three or four voices at once, as the tall masts and wide spars of a corvette came in sight. "The Clara Bell, the Clara Bell—no, it's a brig," was our exclamation at the appearance of a vessel behind the Variag.

"There's another, a barque certainly,—no, it's a brig, too," uttered the colonel with an emphasis of disgust. Evidently his barque was on the sea.

Rounding the shoal we moved toward the fort, the Russian corvette greeting us with "Hail Columbia" out of compliment to our nationality. We carried the American flag at the quarter and the Russian naval ensign at the fore as a courtesy to the ship that awaited us. As we cast anchor just outside the little inner harbor, the Russian band continued playing Hail Columbia, but our engineer played the mischief with the music by letting off steam. As soon as we were at rest a boat from the corvette touched our side, and a subordinate officer announced that his captain would speedily visit us. Very soon came the Captain of The Port or Collector of Customs, and after him the American merchants residing in the town. Our gangway which we closed at San Francisco was now opened, and we once more communicated with the world.

Petropavlovsk (Port of Saints Peter and Paul) is situated in lat. 53° 1′ North, long. 158° 43′ East, and is the principal place in Kamchatka. It stands on the side of a hill sloping into the northern shore of Avatcha Bay, or rather into a little harbor opening into the bay. Fronting this harbor is a long peninsula that hides the town from all parts of the bay except those near the sea. The harbor is well sheltered from winds and furnishes excellent anchorage. It is divided into an inner and an outer harbor by means of a sand spit that extends from the main land toward the peninsula, leaving an opening about three hundred yards in width. The inner harbor is a neat little basin about a thousand yards in diameter and nearly circular in shape.

Some of the mountains that serve as landmarks to the approaching mariner, are visible from the town, and others can be seen by climbing the hills in the vicinity. Wuluchinski is to the southward and not volcanic, while Avatcha and Korianski, to the north and east, were smoking with a dignified air, like a pair of Turks after a champagne supper. Eruptions of these volcanoes occur every few years, and during the most violent ones ashes and stones are thrown to a considerable distance. Captain King witnessed an eruption of Avatcha in 1779, and says that stones fell at Petropavlovsk, twenty-five miles away, and the ashes covered the deck of his ship. Mr. Pierce, an old resident of Kamchatka, gave me a graphic description of an eruption in 1861. It was preceded by an earthquake, which overturned crockery on the tables, and demolished several ovens. For a week or more earthquakes of a less violent character occurred hourly.

Besides the Variag we found in port the Russian brig Poorga and the Prussian brig Danzig, the latter having an American captain, crew, hull, masts, and rigging. Two old hulks were rotting in the mud, and an unseaworthy schooner lay on the beach with one side turned upward as if in agony. "There be land rats and water rats," according to Shakspeare. Some of the latter dwelt in this bluff-bowed schooner and peered curiously from the crevices in her sides.

The majority of our visitors made their calls very brief. After their departure, I went on shore with Mr. Hunter, an American resident of Petropavlovsk. In every house I visited I was pressed to take *petnatzet copla* (fifteen drops,) the universal name there for something stimulating. The drops might be American whisky, French brandy, Dutch gin, or Russian vodka. David Crockett said a true gentleman is one who turns his back while you pour whisky into your tumbler. The etiquette of Kamchatka does not permit the host to count the drops taken by his guest.

BREACH OF ETIQUETTE.

Take a log village in the backwoods of Michigan or Minnesota, and transport it to a quiet spot by a well sheltered harbor of Lilliputian size. Cover the roofs of some buildings with iron, shingles or boards from other regions. Cover the balance with thatch of long grass, and erect chimneys that just peer above the ridge poles. Scatter these buildings on a hillside next the water; arrange three-fourths of them in a single street, and leave the rest to drop wherever they like. Of course those in the higgledy-piggledy position must be of the poorest class, but you can make a few exceptions. Whitewash the inner walls of half the buildings, and use paper or cloth to hide the nakedness of the other half.

This will make a fair counterfeit of Petropavlovsk. Inside each house place a brick stove or oven, four or five feet square and six feet high. Locate this stove to present a side to each of two or three rooms. In each side make an aperture two inches square that can be opened or closed at will. The amount of heat to warm the rooms is regulated by means of the apertures.

Furnish the houses with plain chairs, tables, and an occasional but rare piano. Make the doors very low and the entries narrow. Put a picture of a saint in the principal room of every house, and adorn the walls with a few engravings. Make a garden near each house, and let a few miscellaneous gardens cling to the hillside and strive to climb it. Don't forget to build a church, or you will fail to represent a Russian town.

Petropavlovsk has no vehicle of any kind except a single hand cart. Consequently the street is not gashed with wheel ruts.

We were invited to 'assist' at a wedding that happened in the evening after our arrival. The ceremony was to begin at five o'clock, and was a double affair, two sisters being the brides. A Russian wedding requires a master of ceremonies to look after the affair from beginning to end. I was told it was the custom in Siberia (but not in European Russia) for this person to pay all expenses of the wedding, including the indispensable dinner and its fixtures. Such a position is not to be desired by a man of limited cash, especially if the leading characters are inclined to extravagance. Think of being the conductor of a diamond wedding in New York or Boston, and then paying the bills!

The steward of the Variag told me he was invited to conduct a wedding shortly after his arrival at Petropavlovsk. Thinking it an honor of which he would hereafter be proud, he accepted the invitation. Much to his surprise on the next day he was required to pay the cost of the entertainment.

UNEXPECTED HONORS.

The master of ceremonies of the wedding under consideration was Mr. Phillipeus, a Russian gentleman engaged in the fur trade. The father of the brides was his customer, and doubtless the cost of the wedding was made up in subsequent dealings. As the party emerged from the house and moved toward the church, I could see that Phillipeus was the central figure. He had a bride on each arm, and each bride was clinging to her prospective husband. The women were in white and the men in holiday dress.

Behind the front rank were a dozen or more groomsmen and bridesmaids. Behind these were the members of the families and the invited relatives, so that the cortége stretched to a considerable length. Each of the groomsmen wore a bow of colored ribbon on his left arm and a smaller one in the button hole. The children of the families—quite a troop of juveniles—brought up the rear.

The church is of logs, like the other buildings. It is old, unpainted, and shaped like a cross, lacking one of the arms. The doors are large and clumsy, and the entrance is through a vestibule or hall. The roof had been recently painted a brilliant red at the expense of the Variag's officers. On the inside, the church has an antiquated appearance, but presents such an air of solidity as if inviting the earthquakes to come and see it.

There were no seats in the building, nor are there seats of any kind in the edifices of the same character in any part of Russia. It is the theory of the Eastern Church that all are equal before God. In His service no distinction is made; autocrat and subject, noble and peasant, stand or kneel in the same manner while worshipping at His altars.

As we entered, we found the wedding party standing in the center of the church; the spectators were grouped nearer the door, the ladies occupying the front. With the thermometer at seventy-two, I found the upright position a fatiguing one, and would have been glad to send for a camp stool. Colonel Bulkley had undertaken to escort a lady, and as he stood in a conspicuous place, his uniform buttoned to the very chin and the perspiration pouring from his face, the ceremony appeared to have little charm for him.

The service began under the direction of two priests, each dressed in a long robe extending to his feet, and wearing a chapeau like a bell-crowned hat without a brim. "The short one," said a friend near me, pointing to a little, round, fat, oily man of God, "will get very drunk when he has the opportunity. Watch him to-night and see how he leaves the dinner party."

Priests of the Greek Church wear their hair very long, frequently below the shoulders, and parted in the middle, and do not shave the beard. Unlike those of the Catholic Church, they marry and have homes and families, engaging in secular occupations which do not interfere with their religious duties.

During the evening after the wedding, I was introduced to "the pope's wife;" and learned that Russian priests are called popes. As the only pope then familiar to my thoughts is considered very much a bachelor, I was rather taken aback at this bit of information. The drink-loving priest was head of a goodly sized family, and resided in a comfortable and well furnished dwelling.

RUSSIAN MARRIAGE.

At the wedding there was much recitation by the priests, reading from the ritual of the Church, swinging of censers, singing by the chorus of male voices, chanting and intonation, and responses by the victims. There were frequent signs of the cross with bowing or kneeling. A ring was used, and afterwards two crowns were held over the heads of the bride and bridegroom. The fatigue of holding these crowns was considerable, and required that those who performed the service should be relieved once by other bridesmen. After a time the crowns were placed on the heads they had been held over. Wearing these crowns and preceded by the priests, the pair walked three times round the altar in memory of the Holy Trinity, while a portion of the service was chanted. Then the crowns were removed and kissed by each of the marrying pair, the bridegroom first performing the osculation. A cup of water was held by the priest, first to the bridegroom and then to the bride, each of whom drank a small portion. After this the first couple retired to a little chapel and the second passed through the ordeal. The preliminary ceremony occupied about twenty minutes, and the same time was consumed by each couple.

There is no divorce in Russia, so that the union was one for life till death. Before the parties left the church they received congratulations. There was much hand-shaking, and among the women there were decorous kisses. Our party regretted that the custom of bride kissing as practiced in America does not prevail in Kamchatka.

When the affair was ended, the whole cortége returned to the house whence it came, the children carrying pictures of the Virgin and saints, and holding lighted candles before them. The employment of lamps and tapers is universal in the Russian churches, the little flame being a representation of spiritual existence and a symbol of the continued life of the soul. The Russians have adapted this idea so completely that there is no marriage, betrothal, consecration, or burial, in fact no religious ceremony whatever without the use of lamp or taper.

In the house of every adherent to the orthodox Russian faith there is a picture of the Virgin or a saint; sometimes holy pictures are in every room of the house. I have seen them in the cabins of steamboats, and in tents and other temporary structures. No Russian enters a dwelling, however humble, without removing his hat, out of respect to the holy pictures, and this custom extends to shops, hotels, in fact to every place where people dwell or transact business. During the earlier part of my travels in Russia, I was unaware of this custom, and fear that I sometimes offended it.

I have been told that superstitious thieves hang veils or kerchiefs before the picture in rooms where they depredate. Enthusiastic lovers occasionally observe the same precaution. Only the eyes of the image need be covered, and secrecy may be obtained by turning the picture to the wall.

The evening began with a reception and congratulations to the married couples. Then we had tea and cakes, and then came the dinner. The party was like the African giant imported in two ships, for it was found impossible to crowd all the guests into one house. Tables were set in two houses and in the open yard between them.

The Russians have a custom of taking a little lunch just before they begin dinner. This lunch is upon a side table in the dining room, and consists of cordial, spirits or bitters, with morsels of herring, caviar, and dried meat or fish. It performs the same office as the American cocktail, but is oftener taken, is more popular and more respectable. After the lunch we sat down to dinner. Fish formed the first course and soup the second. Then we had roast beef and vegetables, followed by veal cutlets. The feast closed with cake and jelly, and was thoroughly washed down with a dozen kinds of beverages that cheer *and* inebriate.

The fat priest was at table and took his lunch early. His first course was a glass of something liquid, and he drank a dozen times before the soup was brought. Early in the dinner I saw him gesturing toward me.

"He wants to take a glass with you," said some one at my side.

I poured out some wine, and after a little trouble in touching glasses we drank each other's health.

Not five minutes later he repeated his gestures. To satisfy him I filled a glass with sherry, as there was no champagne handy at the moment, and again went through the clinking process. As my glass was large I put it down after sipping a few drops, but the old fellow objected. Draining and inverting his glass, he held it as one might suspend a rat by the tail, and motioned me to do the same. Luckily he soon after conceived a fondness for one of the Wright's officers, and the twain fell to drinking. The officer, assisted by three men, went on board late at night, and was reported attempting to wash his face in a tar-bucket and dry it with a chain cable. About midnight the priest was taken home on a shutter.

RUSSIAN POPE AT HOME.

There were toasts in a large number, with a great deal of cheering, drinking, and smoking. About ten o'clock the dinner ended, and arrangements were made for a dance. Dancing was not among my accomplishments, and I retired to the ship, satisfied that on my first day in Asia I had been treated very kindly—and very often.

For two days more the wedding festivities continued, etiquette requiring the parties to visit all who attended the dinner. On the third day the hilarity ceased, and the happy couples were left to enjoy the honeymoon with its promise of matrimonial bliss. May they have many years of it.

CHAPTER IV.

THE name of Kamchatka is generally associated with snow-fields, glaciers, frozen mountains, and ice-bound shores. Its winters are long and severe; snow falls to a great depth, and ice attains a thickness proportioned to the climate. But the summers, though short, are sufficiently hot to make up for the cold of winter. Vegetation is wonderfully rapid, the grasses, trees and plants growing as much in a hundred days as in six months of a New England summer. Hardly has the snow disappeared before the trees put forth their buds and blossoms, and the hillsides are in all the verdure of an American spring. Men tell me they have seen in a single week the snows disappear, ice break in the streams, the grass spring up, and the trees beginning to bud. Nature adapts herself to all her conditions. In the Arctic as in the Torrid zone she fixes her compensations and makes her laws for the best good of her children.

It was midsummer when we reached Kamchatka, and the heat was like that of August in Richmond or Baltimore. The thermometer ranged from sixty-five to eighty. Long walks on land were out of question, unless one possessed the power of a salamander. The shore of the bay was the best place for a promenade, and we amused ourselves watching the salmon fishers at work.

Salmon form the principal food of the Kamchadales and their dogs. The fishing season in Avatcha Bay lasts about six weeks, and at its close the salmon leave the bay and ascend the streams, where they are caught by the interior natives. In the bay they are taken in seines dragged along the shore, and the number of fish caught annually is almost beyond computation.

Some years ago the fishery failed, and more than half the dogs in Kamchatka starved. The following year there was a bountiful supply, which the priests of Petropavlovsk commemorated by erecting a cross near the entrance of the harbor. The supply is always larger after a scarcity than in ordinary seasons.

The fish designed for preservation are split and dried in the sun. The odor of a fish drying establishment reminded me of the smells in certain quarters of New York in summer, or of Cairo, Illinois, after an unusual flood has subsided. One of our officers said he counted three hundred and twenty distinct and different smells in walking half a mile.

In 1865 one of the merchants started the enterprise of curing salmon for the Sandwich Island market. He told me he paid three roubles, (about three greenback dollars,) a hundred (in number) for the fresh fish, delivered at his establishment. Evidently he found the speculation profitable, as he repeated it the following year.

A SCALY BRIDGE.

When the salmon ascend the rivers they furnish food to men and animals. The natives catch them in nets and with spears, while dogs, bears, and wolves use their teeth in fishing. Bears are expert in this amusement, and where their game is plenty they eat only the heads and backs. The fish are very abundant in the rivers, and no great skill is required in their capture. Men with an air of veracity told me they had seen streams in the interior of Kamchatka so filled with salmon that one could cross on them as on a corduroy bridge! The story has a piscatorial sound, but it *may* be true.

House gardening on a limited scale is the principal agriculture of Kamchatka. Fifty years ago, Admiral Ricord introduced the cultivation of rye, wheat, and barley with considerable success, but the inhabitants do not take kindly to it. The government brings rye flour from the Amoor river and sells it to the people at cost, and in case of distress it issues rations from its magazines.

When I asked why there was no culture of grain in Kamchatka, they replied: "What is the necessity of it? We can buy it at cost of the government, and need not trouble ourselves about making our own flour."

There is not a sawmill on the peninsula. Boards and plank are cut by hand or brought from California. I slept two nights in a room ceiled with red-wood and pine from San Francisco.

On my second evening in Asia I passed several hours at the governor's house. The party talked, smoked, and drank tea until midnight, and then closed the entertainment with a substantial supper. An interesting and novel feature of the affair was the Russian manner of making tea. The infusion had a better flavor than any I had previously drank. This is due partly to the superior quality of the leaf, and partly to the manner of its preparation.

The "samovar" or tea-urn is an indispensable article in a Russian household, and is found in nearly every dwelling from the Baltic to Bering's Sea. "Samovar" comes from two Greek words, meaning 'to boil itself.' The article is nothing but a portable furnace; a brazen urn with a cylinder two or three inches in diameter passing through it from top to bottom. The cylinder being filled with coals, the water in the urn is quickly heated, and remains boiling hot as long as the fire continues. An imperial order abolishing samovars throughout all the Russias, would produce more sorrow and indignation than the expulsion of roast beef from the English bill of fare. The number of cups it will contain is the measure of a samovar.

Tea pots are of porcelain or earthenware. The tea pot is rinsed and warmed with hot water before receiving the dry leaf. Boiling water is poured upon the tea, and when the pot is full it is placed on the top of the samovar. There it is kept hot but not boiled, and in five or six minutes the tea is ready. Cups and saucers are not employed by the Russians, but tumblers are generally used for tea drinking, and in the best houses, where it can be afforded, they are held in silver sockets like those in soda shops. Only loaf sugar is used in sweetening tea. When lemons can be had they are employed to give flavor, a thin slice, neither rolled nor pressed, being floated on the surface of the tea. The Russians take tea in the morning, after dinner, after lunch, before bed-time, in the evening, at odd intervals in the day or night, and they drink a great deal of it between drinks.

RUSSIAN TEA SERVICE.

In rambling about Petropavlovsk I found the hills covered with luxuriant grass, sometimes reaching to my knees. Two or three miles inland the grass was waist high on ground covered with snow six weeks before. Among the flowers I recognized the violet and larkspur, the former in great abundance. Earlier in the summer the hills were literally carpeted with flowers. I could not learn that any skilled botanist had ever visited Kamchatka and classified its flora. Among the arboreal productions the alder and birch were the most numerous. Pine, larch, and spruce grow on the Kamchatka river, and the timber from them is brought to Avatcha from the mouth of that stream.

The commercial value of Kamchatka is entirely in its fur trade. The peninsula has no agricultural, manufacturing, or mining interest, and were it not for the animals that lend their skins to keep us warm, the merchant would find no charms in that region. The fur coming from Kamchatka was the cause of the Russian discovery and conquest. For many years the trade was conducted by individual merchants from Siberia. The Russian American Company attempted to control it early in the present century, and drove many competitors from the fields. It received the most determined opposition from American merchants, and in 1860 it abandoned Petropavlovsk, its business there being profitless.

In 1866 I found the fur trade of Kamchatka in the control of three merchants: W. H. Boardman, of Boston, J. W. Fluger, of Hamburg, and Alexander Phillipeus, of St. Petersburg. All of them had houses in Petropavlovsk, and each had from one to half a dozen agencies or branches elsewhere. To judge by appearances, Mr. Boardman had the lion's share of the trade. This gentleman's father began the Northwest traffic sometime in the last century, and left it as an inheritance about 1828. His son continued the business until bought off by the Hudson Bay Company, when he turned his attention to Kamchatka. Personally he has never visited the Pacific Ocean.

Mr. Fluger had been only two years in Kamchatka, and was doing a miscellaneous business. Boardman's agent confined himself to the fur trade, but Fluger was up to anything. He salted salmon for market, sent a schooner every year into the Arctic Ocean for walrus teeth and mammoth tusks, bought furs, sold goods, kept a dog team, was attentive to the ladies, and would have run for Congress had it been possible. He had in his store about half a cord of walrus teeth piled against a back entrance like stove wood.

Phillipeus was a roving blade. He kept an agent at Petropavlovsk and came there in person once a year. In February he left St. Petersburg for London, whence he took the Red Sea route to Japan. There he chartered a brig to visit Kamchatka and land him at Ayan, on the Ohotsk Sea. From Ayan he went to Yakutsk, and from that place through Irkutsk to St. Petersburg, where he arrived about three hundred and fifty days after his departure. I met him in the Russian capital just as he had completed the sixth journey of this kind and was about to commence the seventh. If he were a Jew he should be called the wandering Jew.

Trade is conducted on the barter principle, furs being low and goods high. The risks are great, transport is costly, and money is a long time invested before it returns. The palmy days of the fur trade are over; the product has greatly diminished, and competition has reduced the percentage of profit on the little that remains.

CHANGE FOR A DOLLAR

There was a time in the memory of man when furs formed the currency of Kamchatka. Their employment as cash is not unknown at present, although Russian money is in general circulation.

There is a story of a traveler who paid his hotel bill in a country town in Minnesota and received a beaver skin in change. The landlord explained that it was legal tender for a dollar. Concealing this novel cash under his coat, the traveler sauntered into a neighboring store.

"Is it true," he asked carelessly, "that a beaver skin is legal tender for a dollar?"

"Yes, sir," said the merchant; "anybody will take it."

"Will you be so kind, then," was the traveler's request, "as to give me change for a dollar bill?"

"Certainly," answered the merchant, taking the beaver skin and returning four muskrat skins, current at twenty-five cents each.

The sable is the principal fur sought by the merchants in Kamchatka, or trapped by the natives. The animal is caught in a variety of ways, man's ingenuity being taxed to capture him. The 'yessak,' or 'poll-tax' of the natives is payable in sable fur, at the rate of a skin for every four persons. The governor makes a yearly journey through the peninsula to collect the tax, and is supposed to visit all the villages. The merchants go and do likewise for trading purposes.

Mr. George S. Cushing, who was long the agent of Mr. Boardman in Kamchatka, estimated the product of sable fur at about six thousand skins annually. Sometimes it exceeds and sometimes falls below that figure. About a thousand foxes, a few sea otters and silver foxes, and a good many bears, may be added, more for number than value. Silver foxes and otters are scarce, while common foxes and bears are of little account. A black fox is worth a great deal of money, but one may find a white crow almost as readily.

Bears are abundant, but their skins are not articles of export. The beasts are brown or black, and grow to a disagreeable size. Bear hunting is an amusement of the country, very pleasant and exciting until the bear turns and becomes the hunter. Then there is no fun in it, if he succeeds in his pursuit. A gentleman in Kamchatka gave me a bearskin more than six feet long, and declared that it was not unusually large. I am very glad there was no live bear in it when it came into my possession.

There is a story of a man in California who followed the track of a grizzly bear a day and a half. He abandoned it because, as he explained, "it was getting a little too fresh."

One day, about two years before my visit, a cow suddenly entered Petropavlovsk with a live bear on her back. The bear escaped unhurt, leaving the cow pretty well scratched. After that event she preferred to graze in or near the town, and never brought home another bear.

COW AND BEAR.

Kamchatka without dogs would be like Hamlet without Hamlet. While crossing the Pacific my *compagnons du voyage* made many suggestions touching my first experience in Kamchatka. "You won't sleep any the first night in port. The dogs will howl you out of your seven senses." This was the frequent remark of the engineer, corroborated by others. On arriving, we were disappointed to find less than a hundred dogs at Petropavlovsk, as the rest of the canines belonging there were spending vacation in the country. About fifteen hundred were owned in the town.

Very few Kamchadale dogs can bark, but they will howl oftener, longer, and louder than any 'yaller dog' that ever went to a cur pound or became sausage meat. The few in Petropavlovsk made much of their ability, and were especially vocal at sunset, near their feeding time. Occasionally during the night they try their throats and keep up a hailing and answering chorus, calculated to draw a great many oaths from profane strangers.

In 1865 Colonel Bulkley carried one of these animals to California. The dog lifted up his voice on the waters very often, and received a great deal of rope's ending in consequence. At San Francisco Mr. Covert took him home, and attempted his domestication. 'Norcum,' (for that was the brute's name,) created an enmity between Covert and all who lived within hearing distance, and many were the threats of canicide. Covert used to rise two or three times every night and argue, with a club, to induce Norcum to be silent. While I was at San Francisco, Mr. Mumford, one of the Telegraph Company's directors, conceived a fondness for the dog, and took him to the Occidental Hotel.

On the first day of his hotel life we tied Norcum on the balcony in front of Mumford's room, about forty feet from the ground. Scarcely had we gone to dinner when he jumped from the balcony and hung by his chain, with his hind feet resting upon a cornice.

A howling wilderness is nothing to the noise he made before his rescue, and he gathered and amused a large crowd with his performance. He passed the night in the western basement of the hotel, and spoiled the sleep of a dozen or more persons who lodged near him. When we left San Francisco, Norcum was residing in the baggage-room at the Occidental, under special care of the porters, who employed a great deal of muscle in teaching him that silence was a golden virtue.

The Kamchadale dogs are of the same breed as those used

by the Esquimaux, but are said to possess more strength and endurance. The best Asiatic dogs are among the Koriaks, near Penjiusk Gulf, the difference being due to climate and the care taken in breeding them. Dogs are the sole reliance

A KAMCHATKA TEAM.

for winter travel in Kamchatka, and every resident considers it his duty to own a team. They are driven in odd numbers, all the way from three to twenty-one. The most intelligent and best trained dog acts as a leader, the others being harnessed in pairs. No reins are used, the voice of the driver being sufficient to guide them.

Dogs are fed almost entirely upon fish. They receive their rations daily at sunset, and it is always desirable that each driver should feed his own team. The day before starting on a journey, the dog receives a half ration only, and he is kept on this slender diet as long as the journey lasts. Sometimes when hungry they gnaw their reindeer skin harnesses, and sometimes they do it as a pastime. Once formed, the habit is not easy to break.

Two kinds of sledges are used, one for travel and the other for transporting freight. The former is light and just large enough for one person with a little baggage. The driver sits with his feet hanging over the side, and clings to a bow that rises in front. In one hand he holds an iron-pointed staff, with which he retards the vehicle in descending hills, or brings it to a halt. A traveling sledge weighs about twenty-five pounds, but a freight sledge is much heavier.

A good team will travel from forty to sixty miles a day with favorable roads. Sometimes a hundred a day may be accomplished, but very rarely. Once an express traveled from Petropavlovsk to Bolcheretsk, a hundred and twenty-five miles, in twenty-three hours, without change of dogs.

Wolves have an inconvenient fondness for dog meat, and occasionally attack travelers. A gentleman told me that a wolf once sprang from the bushes, seized and dragged away one of his dogs, and did not detain the team three minutes. The dogs are cowardly in their dispositions, and will not fight unless they have large odds in their favor. A pack of them will attack and kill a single strange dog, but would not disturb a number equaling their own.

Most of the Russian settlers buy their dogs from the natives who breed them. Dogs trained to harness are worth from ten to forty roubles (dollars) each, according to their quality. Leaders bring high prices on account of their superior docility and the labor of training them. Epidemics are frequent among dogs and carry off great numbers of them. Hydrophobia is a common occurrence.

The Russian inhabitants of Kamchatka are mostly descended from Cossacks and exiles. There is a fair but not undue proportion of half breeds, the natural result of marriage between natives and immigrants. There are about four hundred Russians at Petropavlovsk, and the same number at each of two other points. The aboriginal population is about six thousand, including a few hundred dwellers on the Kurile Islands.

No exiles have been sent to Kamchatka since 1830. One

old man who had been forty years a colonist was living at Avatcha in 1866. He was at liberty to return to Europe, but preferred remaining.

In 1771 occurred the first voyage from Kamchatka to a foreign port, and curiously enough, it was performed under the Polish flag. A number of exiles, headed by a Pole named Benyowski, seized a small vessel and put to sea. Touching at Japan and Loo Choo to obtain water and provisions, the party reached the Portuguese colony of Macao in safety. There were no nautical instruments or charts on the ship, and the successful result of the voyage was more accidental than otherwise.

Close by the harbor of Petropavlovsk there is a monument to the memory of the ill-fated and intrepid navigator, La Perouse. It bears no inscription, and was evidently built in haste. There is a story that a French ship once arrived in Avatcha Bay on a voyage of discovery. Her captain asked the governor if there was anything to commemorate the visit of La Perouse.

"Certainly," was the reply; "I will show it to you in the morning."

During the night the monument was hastily constructed of wood and sheet iron, and fixed in the position to which the governor led his delighted guest.

Captain Clerke, successor to Captain Cook, of Sandwich Island memory, died while his ships were in Avatcha Bay, and was buried at Petropavlovsk. A monument that formerly marked his grave has disappeared. Captain Lund and Colonel Bulkley arranged to erect a durable memorial in its place. We prepared an inscription in English and Russian, and for temporary purposes fixed a small tablet on the designated spot. Americans and Russians formed the party that listened to the brief tribute which one of our number paid to the memory of the great navigator.

In the autumn of 1854, a combined English and French fleet of six ships suffered a severe repulse from several land batteries and the guns of a Russian frigate in the harbor.

Twice beaten off, their commanders determined an assault. They landed a strong force of sailors and marines, that attempted to take the town in the rear, but the Kamchadale sharpshooters created a panic, and drove the assailants over a steeply sloping cliff two hundred feet high.

REPULSE OF THE ASSAILANTS.

Naturally the natives are proud of their success in this battle, and mention it to every visitor. The English Admiral committed suicide early in the attack. The fleet retired to San Francisco, and returned in the following year prepared to capture the town at all hazards, but Petropavlovsk had been abandoned by the Russians, who retired beyond the hills. An American remained in charge of a trading establishment, and hoisted his national colors over it. The allies burned the government property and destroyed the batteries.

There were five or six hundred dogs in town when the fleet entered the bay. Their violent howling held the allies aloof a whole day, under the impression that a garrison should be very large to have so many watch-dogs.

CHAPTER V.

THE first project for making discoveries in the ocean east of Kamchatka was formed by Peter the Great. Danish, German, and English navigators and *savans* were sent to the eastern coast of Asia to conduct explorations in the desired quarter, but very little was accomplished in the lifetime of the great czar. His successors carried out his plans.

In June, 1741, Vitus Bering, the first navigator of the straits which bear his name, sailed from Avatcha Bay. Passing south of the islands of the Aleutian chain, Bering steered to the eastward, and at length discovered the American continent. "On the 16th of July," says Steller, the naturalist and historian of the expedition, "we saw a mountain whose height was so great as to be visible at the distance of sixteen Dutch miles. The coast of the continent was much broken and indented with bays and harbors."

The nearest point of land was named Cape St. Elias, as it was discovered on St. Elias' day. The high mountain received the name of the saint, and has clung to it ever since.

When Bering discovered Russian America he had no thought it would one day be sold to the United States, and there is nothing to show that he ever corresponded with Mr. Seward about it. He sailed a short distance along its coast, visited various islands, and then steered for Kamchatka.

The commander was confined to his cabin by illness, and the crew suffered severely from scurvy. "At one period," says Steller, "only ten persons were capable of duty, and they were too weak to furl the sails, so that the ship was left to the mercy of the elements. Not only the sick died, but those who pretended to be healthy fainted and fell down dead when relieved from their posts."

In this condition the navigators were drifted upon a rocky island, where their ship went to pieces, but not until all had landed. Many of the crew died soon after going on shore, but the transfer from the ship appeared to diminish the ravages of the scurvy. Commander Bering died on the 8th of December, and was buried in the trench where he lay. The island where he perished bears his name, but his grave is unmarked. An iron monument to his memory was recently erected at Petropavlovsk.

No human dwellers were found on the island. Foxes were numerous and had no fear of the shipwrecked mariners. "We killed many of them," Steller adds, "with our hatchets and knives. They annoyed us greatly, and we were unable to keep them from entering our shelters and stealing our clothing and food." The survivors built a small vessel from the wreck, and succeeded in reaching Avatcha in the following summer. "We were given up for dead," says the historian, "and the property we left in Kamchatka had been appropriated by strangers."

The reports concerning the abundance of fur-bearing animals on Bering's Island and elsewhere, induced private parties to go in search of profit. Various expeditions were fitted out in ships of clumsy construction and bad sailing qualities. The timbers were fastened with wooden pins and leathern thongs, and the crevices were caulked with moss. Occasionally the cordage was made from reindeer skins, and the sails from the same material. Many ships were wrecked, but this did not frighten adventurous merchants.

Few of these voyages were pushed farther than the Aleutian islands. The natives were hostile and killed a fair proportion of the Russian explorers. In 1781 a few merchants of Kamchatka arranged a company with a view to developing commerce in Russian America. They equipped several ships, formed a settlement at Kodiak and conducted an extensive and profitable business. Their agents treated the natives with great cruelty, and so bad was their conduct that the emperor Paul revoked their privileges.

A new company was formed and chartered in July, 1779, under the title of the Russian-American Company. It succeeded the old concern, and absorbed it into its organization.

The Russian-American Company had its chief office in St. Petersburg, where the Directors formed a kind of high court of appeal. It was authorized to explore and place under control of the crown all the territories of North-Western America not belonging to any other government. It was required to deal kindly with the natives, and endeavor to convert them to the religion of the empire. It had the administration of the country and a commercial monopoly through its whole extent. All other merchants were to be excluded, no matter what their nationality. At one time so great was the jealousy of the Company's officers that no foreign ship was allowed within twenty miles of the coast.

The Imperial Government required that the chief officer of the company should be commissioned in the service of the crown, and detailed to the control of the American Territory. His residence was at Sitka, to which the principal post was removed from Kodiak. In the early history of the Company there were many encounters with the natives, the severest battle taking place on the present site of Sitka. The natives had a fort there, and were only driven from it after a long and obstinate fight. The first colony that settled at Sitka was driven away, and all traces of the Russian occupation were destroyed. After a few years of conflict, peace was declared, and trade became prosperous. The Company occupied Russian America and the Aleutian Islands, and pushed its traffic to the Arctic Ocean. It established posts on the Kurile Islands, in Kamchatka, and along the coast of the Ohotsk Sea. It built churches, employed priests, and was quite successful in converting the natives to Christianity.

Having a monopoly of trade and being the law giver to the natives, the Company had things in pretty much its own way. The governor at Sitka was the autocrat of all the American

Russians. There was no appeal from his decision except to the Directory at St. Petersburg, which was about as accessible as the moon. The natives were reduced to a condition of slavery; they were compelled to devote the best part of their time to the company's labor, and the accounts were so managed as to keep them always in debt.

Alexander Baranoff was the first governor, and continued more than twenty years in power. He managed affairs to his own taste, paying little regard to the wishes of the Directory, or even of the Emperor, when they conflicted with his own. The Russians in the company's employ were *Promushleniks*, or adventurers, enlisted in Siberia for a term of years. They were soldiers, sailors, hunters, fishermen, or mechanics, according to the needs of the service. Their condition was little better than that of the natives they held in subjection. The territory was divided into districts, each under an officer who reported to the Chief at Sitka.

The Directory was not troubled so long as profits were large, but the government had suspicions that the Company's reign was oppressive. An exploring expedition under Admiral Krusenstern visited the North Pacific in 1805; the reports of the Admiral exposed many abuses and led to changes. A more rigid supervision followed, and produced much good. The government insisted upon appointing officers of integrity and humanity to the chief place at Sitka.

For many years the Company prospered. In 1812 it founded the colony of Ross, on the coast of California, and a few years later prepared to dispute the right of the Spanish Governor to occupy that region. The natives were everywhere peaceable, and the dividends satisfied the stockholders. The slaughter of the fur-bearing animals was injudiciously conducted, and led to a great decrease of revenue. The last dividend of importance (12 per cent.) was in 1853. After that year misfortune seemed to follow the Company. Its trade was greatly reduced, partly by the diminished fur production and partly by the illicit traffic of independent vessels along the coast. Several ships were lost, one in 1865, with a valuable cargo of furs. In 1866 the Company's stock, from a nominal value of 150, had fallen to about 80, and the Company was even obliged to accept an annual subsidy of 200,000 roubles from the Government. So late as February, 1867, it received a loan of 1,000,000 roubles from the Imperial Bank. Probably a few years more would have seen the total extinction of the Company, and the reversion of all its rights and expenses to the Crown.

In 1866 the fleet of the Russian-American Company comprised two sea steamers, six ships, two brigs, one schooner, and several smaller craft for coasting and inland service. During the Crimean war the Company's property was made neutral on condition of its taking no part in hostilities. Two of its ships were captured and burned for an alleged violation of neutrality.

The Company leased a portion of its territory to the Hudson Bay Company, and allowed it to establish hunting and trading posts. A strip of land bordering the ocean was thus in English hands, and gave access to a wide region beyond the Coast Mountains. Not content with what was leased, the Hudson Bay Company deliberately seized a locality on the Yukon river when it had no right. It built Fort Yukon and secured much of the interior trade of Russian America.

When our Secretary of State purchased the Emperor's title to the western coast of America, there were various opinions respecting the sagacity of the transaction. No one could say what was the intrinsic value of the country, either actual or prospective. The Company never gave much attention to scientific matters.

The Russian government had made some explorations to ascertain the character and extent of the rivers, mountains, plains, and swamps that form the country. In 1841 Lieutenant Zagoyskin commenced an examination of the country bordering the rivers, and continued it for two years. He traced the course of the Kuskokvim and the lower portions of the Yukon, or Kvikpak. His observations were chiefly confined to the rivers and the country immediately bordering

VIEW OF SITKA

them. He made no discoveries of agricultural or mineral wealth. Fish and deer-meat, with berries, formed the food of the natives, while furs were their only articles of trade.

Russian America is of great extent, superficially. It is agreeably diversified with mountains, hills, rolling country, and table land, with a liberal amount of *pereval* or undulating swamp. In the northern portion there is timber scattered along the rivers and on the mountain slopes; but the trees and their quantity are alike small. In the southern parts there are forests of large trees, that will be valuable when Oregon and Washington are exhausted. Along the coast there are many bays and harbors, easy of access and well sheltered. Sitka has a magnificent harbor, never frozen or obstructed with ice.

Gold is known to exist in several localities. A few placer mines have been opened on the Stikeen river, but no one knows the extent of the auriferous beds, in the absence of all 'prospecting' data. I do not believe gold mining will ever be found profitable in Russian America. The winters are long and cold, and the snows are deep. The working season is very short, and in many localities on the mainland 'ground ice' is permanent at slight depths. Veins of copper have been found near the Yukon, but so far none that would pay for developing.

Building stone is abundant, and so is ice. Neither is of much value in commerce.

The fur trade was the chief source of the Company's revenue. The principal fur-bearing animals are the otter, seal, beaver, marten, mink, fox, and a few others. There is a little trade in walrus teeth, mammoth tusks, whalebone, and oil. The rivers abound in fish, of which large quantities are annually salted and sent to the Pacific markets. The fisheries along the coast are valuable and of the same character as those on the banks of Newfoundland.

Agriculture is limited to a few garden vegetables. There are no fruit trees, and no attempts have thus far been made to introduce them.

The number of native inhabitants is unknown, as no census has ever been taken. I have heard it estimated all the way from twenty to sixty thousand. The island and sea coast inhabitants are of the Esquimaux type, while those of the interior are allied to the North American Indians. The explorers for the Western Union Telegraph Company found them friendly, but not inclined to labor. Some of the natives left their hunting at its busiest season to assist an exploring party in distress.

The change of rulers will prove a misfortune to the aboriginal. Very wisely the Russian American Company prohibited intoxicating liquors in all dealings with the natives. The contraband stuff could only be obtained from independent trading ships, chiefly American. With the opening of the country to our commerce, whisky has been abundant and accessible to everybody. The native population will rapidly diminish, and its decrease will be accompanied by a falling off in the fur product. Our government should rigidly continue the prohibitory law as enforced by the Russian officials.

The sale of his American property was an excellent transaction on the part of the Emperor. The country brought no revenue worth the name, and threatened to be an expensive ornament in coming years. It required a sea voyage to reach it, and was upon a continent which Russia does not aspire to control. It had no strategic importance in the Muscovite policy, and was better out of the empire than in it.

The purchase by ourselves may or may not prove a financial success. Thus far its developments have not been promising. When the country has been thoroughly examined, it is possible we may find stores of now unknown wealth. Politically the acquisition is more important. The possession of a large part of the Pacific coast, indented with many bays and harbors, is a matter of moment in view of our national ambition. The American eagle can scream louder since its cage has been enlarged, and if any man attempts to haul down that noble bird, scoop him from the spot.

CHAPTER VI.

COLONEL BULKLEY determined to sail on the 6th of August for Anadyr Bay, and ordered the Variag to proceed to the Amoor by way of Ghijiga. Early in the morning the corvette changed her moorings and shook a reef from her telescopic smoke stack, and at nine o'clock I bade adieu to the Wright and went on board the Variag, to which I was welcomed by Capt. Lund, according to the Russian custom, and quartered in the room specially designed for the use of the Admiral. The ladies were on the nearest point of the beach, and just before our departure the Captain and most of his officers paid them a farewell visit. Seizing the tow line of the Danzig, which we were to take to sea, we steamed from the harbor into the Pacific, followed by the cheers of all on board the Wright and the waving of ladies' handkerchiefs till lost in the distance. We desired to pass the fourth, or Amphitrite, channel of the Kurile Islands; the weather was so thick that we could not see a ship's length in any direction, and all night men stood with axes ready to cut the Danzig's tow line in case any sudden danger should appear. The fog lifted just as we neared the channel, and we had a clear view on all sides.

We cast off the Danzig when fairly out of the Pacific. During the two days the Variag had her in tow we maintained communication by means of a log line and a junk bottle carefully sealed. Casting our bottle on the waters, we allowed it to drift along side the Danzig, where it could be fished up and opened. Answers were returned in the same mail pouch.

One response was in liquid form, and savored of gin cocktail, fabricated by the American captain.

An hour after dropping the Danzig we stopped our engines and prepared to run under sail. The whole crew was called on deck to hoist out the screw, a mass of copper weighing twenty-five thousand pounds, and set in a frame raised or lowered like a window sash. With strong ropes and the power of three hundred men, the frame and its contents were lifted out of water, and the Variag became a sailing ship. The Russian government is more economical than our own in running ships of war. Whenever possible, sails are used instead of steam. A few years ago a Russian Admiral was transferred from active to retired service because he burned too much coal.

The Variag was 2100 tons burthen, and carried seventeen guns, with a crew of 306 men. She was of the fleet that visited New York in 1863, and her officers recounted many pleasant reminiscences of their stay in the United States. While wintering in Japanese waters she was assigned to assist the telegraph enterprise, and reported as soon as possible at Petropavlovsk; but the only service demanded was to proceed to the mouth of the Amoor by way of Ghijiga and Ohotsk.

The officers of the Variag were, a captain, a commander, four lieutenants, six sub-lieutenants, an officer of marines with a cadet, a lieutenant of naval artillery, two sailing masters, two engineers, a surgeon, a paymaster, and a priest. As near as I could ascertain, their pay, including allowances, was about three-fourths that of American officers of similar grades. They received three times as much at sea as when awaiting orders, and this fact led them to seek constant service. In the ward room they read, wrote, talked, smoked, and could play any games of amusement except cards. Card playing is strictly forbidden by the Russian naval regulations.

The sailors on the corvette were robust and powerful fellows, with appetites to frighten a hotel keeper. Russian sailors from the interior of the empire are very liable to scurvy. Those from Finland are the best for long voyages. Captain Lund once told me the experience of a Russian expedition of five ships upon a long cruise. One ship was manned by Finlanders, and the others carried sailors from the interior. The Finlanders were not attacked with scurvy, but the rest suffered severely.

"All the Russians," said the captain, "make good sailors, but those from the maritime provinces are the best seamen."

Early in the voyage it was interesting to see the men at dinner. Their table utensils were wooden spoons and tubs, at the rate of ten spoons and one tub to every ten men. A piece of canvas upon the deck received the tub, which generally contained soup. With their hats off, the men dined leisurely and amicably. Soup and bread were the staple articles of food. Cabbage soup (*schee*) is the national diet of Russia, from the peasant up to the autocrat. Several times on the voyage we had soup on the captain's table from the supply prepared for the crew, and I can testify to its excellence. The food of the sailors was carefully inspected before being served. When the soup was ready, the cook took a bowl of it, with a slice of bread and a clean spoon, and delivered the whole to the boatswain. From the boatswain it went to the officer of the deck, and from him to the chief officer, who delivered it to the captain. The captain carefully examined and tasted the soup. If unobjectionable, the bowl was returned to the galley and the dinner served at once.

A sailor's ration in the Russian navy is more than sufficient for an ordinary appetite and digestion. The grog ration is allowed, and the boatswain's call to liquid refreshment is longer and shriller than for any other duty. At the grog tub the sailor stands with uncovered head while performing the ceremonial abhorred of Good Templars. As of old in our navy, grog is stopped as a punishment. The drink ration can be entirely commuted and the food ration one half, but not more. Many sailors on the Variag practiced total abstinence at sea, and as the grog had been purchased in Japan at very high cost, the commutation money was considerable.

Commutation is regulated according to the price of the articles where the ship was last supplied.

I was told that the sailor's pay, including ordinary allowances, is about a hundred roubles a year. The sum is not munificent, but probably the Muscovite mariner is no more economical than the American one. In his liberty on shore he will get as drunk as the oft quoted 'boiled owl.' *En passant* I protest against the comparison, as it is a slander upon the owl.

At Petropavlovsk there was an amusing fraternization between the crews of the Variag and the Wright. The American sailors were scattered among the Russians in the proportion of one to six. Neither understood a word of the other's language, and the mouth and eye were obliged to perform the duties of the ear. The flowing bowl was the manual of conversation between the Russians and their new friends. The Americans attempted to drink against fearful odds, and the result was unfortunate. They returned sadly intoxicated and were unfit for social or nautical duties until the next day.

When the Variag was at New York in 1863, many of her sailors were entrapped by bounty-brokers. When sailors were missing after liberty on shore, a search through the proper channels revealed them converted into American soldiers, much against their will. Usually they were found at New York, but occasionally a man reached the front before he was rescued. Some returned to the ship dressed as zouaves, others as artillerists; some in the yellow of cavalry, and so on through our various uniforms. Of course they were greatly jeered by their comrades.

Everyone conversant with Russian history knows that Peter the Great went to England, and afterward to Holland, to study ship building. He introduced naval construction from those countries, and brought from Holland the men to manage his first ships and teach his subjects the art of navigation. As a result of his enterprise, the principal parts of a Russian ship have English or Dutch names, some words being changed a little to adapt them to Russian pronunciation.

The Dutch navigators exerted great influence upon the nautical language of Russia. To illustrate this Captain Lund said: "A Dutch pilot or captain could come on my ship and his orders in his own language would be understood by my crew. I mean simply the words of command, without explanations. On the other hand, a Dutch crew could understand my orders without suspecting they were Russian."

Sitting among the officers in the ward-room, I endeavored to accustom my ear to the sound of the Russian language and learn to repeat the most needed phrases. I soon acquired the alphabet, and could count up to any extent; I could spell Russian words much as a schoolboy goes through his 'first reader' exercise, but was unable to attain rapid enunciation. I could never get over the impression that the Muscovite type had been set up by a drunken printer who could n't read. The R's looked the wrong way, the L's stood bottom upward, H's became N's, and C's were S's, and lower case and small caps were generally mixed up. The perplexities of Russian youth must be greater than ours, as they have thirty-six letters in their alphabet and every one of them must be learned. A brief study of Slavonic verbs and nouns convinced me they could never be acquired grammatically in the short time I proposed remaining in Russia, and so I gave them up.

What a hindrance to a traveler and literal man of the world is this confusion of tongues! There is no human being who can make himself verbally understood everywhere on this little globe. In the Russian empire alone there are more than a hundred spoken languages and dialects. The emperor, with all his erudition, has many subjects with whom he is unable to converse. What a misfortune to mankind that the Tower of Babel was ever commenced! The architect who planned it should receive the execration of all posterity.

The apartment I occupied was of goodly size, and contained a large writing desk. My bed was parallel to the keel, and hung so that it could swing when the ship rolled. Previous to my embarkation the room was the receptacle of a quantity of chronometers, sextants, charts, and other nautical apparatus. There were seventeen chronometers in one box, and a few others lay around loose. I never had as much time at my command before or since. Twice a day an officer came to wind these chronometers and note their variation. There were marine instruments enough in that room to supply a dozen sea-captains, but if the entire lot had been loan'd me, I never could have ascertained the ship's position without asking somebody who knew it.

PLENTY OF TIME.

The partition separating me from the ward-room was built after the completion of the ship, and had a way of creaking like a thousand or more squeaky boots in simultaneous action. Every time we rolled, each board rubbed against its neighbor and waked the echoes of the cabin. The first time I slept in the room the partition seemed talking in Russian, and I distinctly remember that it named a majority of the cities and many noble families throughout the empire. After the first night it was powerless to disturb me. I thought it possible that on leaving the ship I might be in the condition of the woman whose husband, a fearful snorer, was suddenly called from home. The lady passed several sleepless nights, until she hit upon the expedient of calling a servant with the coffee mill. The vigorous grinding of that household utensil had the effect of a powerful opiate.

At eight o'clock every morning, Yakuff, (the Russian for Jacob,) brought me a pitcher of water. When my toilet was over, he appeared with a cup of tea and a few cakes. We conversed in the beginning with a sign language, until I picked up enough Russian to ask for tea, water, bread, and other necessary things. At eleven we had breakfast in the

RUSSIAN OFFICERS AT MESS.

captain's cabin, where we discussed steaks, cutlets, tea, and cigars, until nearly noon. Dinner at six o'clock was opened with the never failing zakushka, or lunch, the universal preparative of the empire, and closed with tea and cigars. At eight o'clock tea was served again. After it, any one who chose could partake of the cup which cheers and inebriates.

One morning during my voyage a sailor died. The ocean burial occurred on the following day, and was conducted according to the ceremonial of the Eastern Church. At the appointed time, I went with Captain Lund to the place of worship, between decks. The corpse was in a canvas coffin, its head and breast being visible. The coffin, partially covered with the naval ensign, lay on a wide plank about two feet above the deck. At its head the priest was reading the burial service, while near him there was a group of sailors forming the choir. Captain Lund and several officers stood at the foot of the coffin, each holding a burning taper.

The service lasted about twenty minutes, and consisted of reading by the priest and responses by the choir. The censer was repeatedly swung, as in Catholic ceremonials, the priest bowing at the same time toward the sacred picture. Simultaneously all the candles were extinguished, and then several men advanced and kissed a small cross lying upon the coffin. The priest read a few lines from a written paper and placed it with the cross on the breast of the corpse. The coffin was then closed and carried upon the plank to the stern of the ship.

After a final chant by the choir, one end of the plank was lifted, and a single splash in the water showed where the body went down. During the service the flag floated at half mast. It was soon lowered amid appropriate music, which ended the burial at sea.

On the third day after leaving the Pacific we were shrouded in fog, but with it we had a fine southerly breeze that carried us rapidly on our course. The fog was so dense that we obtained no observation for four days, but so accurate was the sailing master's computation that the difference between our observed and estimated positions was less than two miles.

When the fog rose we were fairly in Ghijiga Bay, a body of water shaped like a narrow V. Sharp eyes looking ahead discovered a vessel at anchor, and all hoped it was the Clara Bell. As we approached she developed into a barque, and gave us comfort, till her flag completed our delight. We threw the lead and began looking for anchorage.

Nine, eight, seven fathoms were successively reported, and for some minutes the depth remained at six and a half. A mile from the Clara Bell we dropped anchor, the ship trembling from stem to stern as the huge chain ran through the hawse-hole. We were at the end of a nine days voyage.

CHAPTER VII.

WE were fifteen miles from the mouth of Ghijiga river, the shoals forbidding nearer approach. The tide rises twenty-two feet in Ghijiga Bay, and to reach the light-house and settlement near the river, even with small boats, it is necessary to go with the tide. We learned that Major Abasa, of the Telegraph service, was at the light-house awaiting our arrival, and that we must start before midnight to reach the landing at the proper time.

Captain Lund ordered a huge box filled with provisions and other table ware, and threw in a few bottles of wine as ballast. I was too old a traveler to neglect my blankets and rubber coat, and found that Anossoff was as cautious as myself.

We prolonged our tea-drinking to ten o'clock and then started. Descending the ship's side was no easy matter. It was at least three feet from the bottom of the gang-way ladder to the water, and the boat was dancing on the chopping sea like a pea on a hot shovel. Captain Lund descended first, followed by Anossoff. Then I made my effort, and behind me was a grim Cossack. Just as I reached the lowest step a wave swung the boat from the ship and left me hanging over the water. The Cossack, unmindful of things below, was backing steadily toward my head. I could not think of the Russian phrase for the occasion and was in some dilemma how to act. I shouted 'Look out', with such emphasis that the man understood me and halted with his heavy boots about two inches above my face. Clinging to the side ropes and watching my opportunity, I jumped at the right moment and happily hit the boat. The Cossack jumped into the lap of a sailor and received a variety of epithets for his carelessness. There are fourteen ways in the Russian language of calling a man a —— fool, and I think all of them were used.

Wind and tide opposed each other and tossed us rather uncomfortably. The waves breaking over the bow saturated

ASCENDING THE BAY.

the Cossack and sprinkled some of the sailors. At the stern we managed to protect ourselves, though we caught occasionally a few drops of spray. Wrapped in my overcoat and holding a bear-skin on my knees, I studied the summer night in that high northern latitude. At midnight it seemed like day break, and I half imagined we had wrongly calculated the hours and were later than we supposed. Between sunset and sunrise the twilight crept along the horizon from Occident to Orient. Further north the inhabitants of the Arctic circle were enjoying the light of their long summer day. What a contrast to the bleak night of cold and darkness that stretches with faint glimmerings of dawn through nearly half the year.

The shores of the bay were high perpendicular banks, sharply cut like the bluffs at Vicksburg. There are several head-lands, but none project far enough to form harbors behind them. The bottom furnishes good anchoring ground, but the bay is quite open to southerly winds.

Captain Lund dropped his chin to his breast and slept soundly. Anossoff raised his coat collar and drew in his head like a tortoise returning into his shell, but with all his efforts he did not sleep. I was wakeful and found that time dragged slowly. The light-house had no light and needed none, as the darkness was far from profound. In approaching the mouth of the river we discovered a cluster of buildings, and close at hand two beacons, like crosses, marking the direction of the channel.

There was a little surf breaking along the beach as our keel touched the ground. Our blankets came dripping from the bottom of the boat, and my satchel had taken water enough to spoil my paper collars and a dozen cigars. My greatest calamity on that night was the sudden and persistent stoppage of my watch. An occurrence of little moment in New York or London was decidedly unpleasant when no trusty watchmaker lived within four thousand miles.

Major Abasa and the Ispravnik of Ghijiga escorted us from the landing to their quarters, where we soon warmed ourselves with hot tea, and I took opportunity and a couple of bear-skins and went to sleep. Late in the day we had a dinner of soup, pork and peas, reindeer meat, and berry pudding. The deer's flesh was sweet and tender, with a flavor like that of the American elk.

In this part of Siberia there are many wide plains (*tundras*) covered with moss and destitute of trees. The blueberry grows there, but is less abundant than the "maroska," a berry that I never saw in America. It is yellow when ripe, has an acid flavor, and resembles the raspberry in shape and size. We ate the maroska in as many forms as it could be prepared, and they told us that it grew in Scotland, Scandinavia, and Northern Russia.

The ordinary residents at the mouth of Ghijiga river were the pilot and his family, with three or four Cossacks to row boats on the bay. The natives of the vicinity came there occasionally, but none were permanent citizens. The arrival of the Variag and Clara Bell gave unusual activity to the settlement, and the Ispravnik might have returned a large population had he imitated the practice of those western towns that take their census during the stay of a railway train or a steamboat. There was once, according to a rural historian, an aspiring politician in Tennessee who wanted to go to Congress. There were not inhabitants enough in his district to send him, and so he placed a couple of his friends at the railway station to take the names of passengers as they visited the refreshment saloon and entered or left the depot. In a short time the requisite constituency was secured and sworn

TAKING THE CENSUS.

to, so that the aspirant for official honor accomplished the wish of his heart.

The light-house on the promontory is a hexagonal edifice ten feet in diameter and height; it is of logs and has a flat top covered with dirt, whereon to kindle a fire. The interior is entered by a low door, and I found it floored with two sticks of wood and a mud puddle. One could reach the top by climbing a sloping pole notched like an American fence-post. The pilot resides at the foot of the bluff, and is expected to visit this beacon daily. A cannon, old enough to have served at Pultava, stands near the light-house, in a condition of utter helplessness.

LIGHT-HOUSE AT GHIJIGA.

The houses were furnished quite primitively. Beds were of bearskins and blankets, and the floor was the only bedstead. There were rustic tables of hewn boards, and benches without backs. In a storehouse there was a Fairbanks' scale, somewhat worn and rusty, and I found a tuneless melodeon from Boston and a coffee mill from New York.

The town of Ghijiga is on the bank of the river, twelve miles from the light-house, and the route thither was overland or by water, at one's choice. Overland there was a footpath crossing a hill and a wet tundra. The journey by water was upon the Ghijiga river; five versts of rowing and thirteen of towing by men or dogs. As it was impossible to hire a horse, I repudiated the overland route altogether, and tried a brief journey on the river, but could not reach the town and return in time for certain engagements. Ghijiga has a population of less than three hundred, and closely resembles Petropavlovsk. Two or three foreign merchants go there annually with goods to exchange for furs which the Russian traders gather. The inhabitants are Russians or half breeds, the former predominating. The half breeds are said to possess all the vices of both races with the virtues of neither.

Mr. Bilzukavitch, the Ispravnik of Ghijiga, was a native of Poland, and governed seventy-two thousand square miles of territory, with a population of sixteen hundred taxed males. His military force comprised thirty Cossacks with five muskets, of which three were unserviceable. The native tribes included in the district of Ghijiga are the Koriaks and Chukchees; the Koriaks readily pay tribute and acknowledge the Russian authority, but the Chukchees are not yet fairly subdued. They were long in open war with the Russians, and though peace is now established, many of them are not tributary. Those who visit the Russian towns are compelled to pay tribute and become Imperial subjects before selling or purchasing goods. The Ispravnik is an artist of unusual merit, as evinced by an album of his sketches illustrating life in Northern Siberia. Some of them appeared like steel engravings, and testified to the skill and patience of the man who made them.

On my second day at Ghijiga I tried a river journey with a dog team. The bottom of the boat was on the 'dug-out' principle, and the sides were two planks meeting in sharp and high points at the ends. I had a seat on some bearskins on the plank flooring, and found it reasonably comfortable. One man steered the boat, another in the bow managed the towline, and a third, who walked on land, drove the dogs. We had seven canines—three pairs and a leader—pulling upon a deerskin towline fastened to a thole-pin. It was the duty of the man in the bow to regulate the towline according to circumstances. The dogs were unaccustomed to their driver, and balky in consequence. Two of them refused to pull when we started, and remained obstinate until persuaded

TOWED BY DOGS

with sticks. The driver used neither reins nor whip, but liberally employed the drift wood along the banks. Clubs were trumps in that day's driving. The team was turned to the left by a guttural sound that no paper and ink can describe, and to the right by a rapid repetition of the word 'ca.'

Occasionally the path changed from one bank to the opposite. At such times we seated the dogs in the bow of the boat and ferried them over the river. In the boat they were generally quiet, though inclined to bite each other's legs at convenient opportunities. One muddy dog shook himself over me; I forgave him, but his driver did not, the innocent brute receiving several blows for making his toilet in presence of passengers.

The Koriaks have a habit of sacrificing dogs to obtain a fortunate fishery. The animals are hung on limbs of trees, and the sacrifice always includes the best. Major Abasa urged them to give only their worthless dogs to the evil spirit, assuring them the fishery would result just as well, and they promised to try the experiment. Dogs were scarce and expensive in consequence of a recent canine epidemic. Only a day before our arrival three dogs developed hydrophobia and were killed.

The salmon fishery was very poor in 1866, and the inhabitants of the Ghijiga district were relying upon catching seals in the autumn. At Kolymsk, on the Kolyma river, the authorities require every man to catch one-tenth more than enough for his own use. This surplus is placed in a public storehouse and issued in case of famine. It is the rule to keep a three years supply always at hand. Several seasons of scarcity led to the adoption of the plan.

We were frequently visited by the natives from a Koriak village near the light-house. Their dress was of deer skin, and comprised a kotlanka, or frock, pantaloons, and boots, or leggings. Winter garments are of deer skin with its hair remaining, but summer clothing is of dressed skins alone. These natives appear below the ordinary stature, and their legs seemed to me very small. Ethnologists are divided concerning the origin of the Koriaks, some assigning them to the Mongol race and others to the Esquimaux. The Koriaks express no opinion on the disputed point, and have none.

Both sexes dress alike, and wear ornaments of beads in their ears. They have a curious custom of shaving the back part of the head, *a la moine.* Fashion is as arbitrary among the Koriaks as in Paris or New York, and dictates the cut of garments and the style of hair dressing with unyielding severity.

Like savages everywhere, these natives manifest a fondness for civilized attire. A party visited the Clara Bell and obtained some American clothing. One man sported a cast-off suit, in which he appeared as uneasy as an organ grinder's monkey in a new coat. Another wore a sailor's jacket from the Variag, and sported the number '19' with manifest pride. A third had a fatigue cap, bearing the letters 'U. S.' in heavy brass, the rest of his costume being thoroughly aboriginal. One old fellow had converted an empty meat can into a hat, without removing the printed label "stewed beef." I gave him a pair of dilapidated gloves, which he donned at once.

The Koriaks are of two kinds, wandering and settled. The wanderers have great numbers of reindeer, and lead a migratory life in finding pasturage for their herds. The settled Koriaks are those who have lost their deer and been forced to locate where they can subsist by fishing. The former are kind and hospitable; the latter generally the reverse. Poverty has made them selfish, as it has made many a white man. All are honest to a degree unusual among savages. When Major Abasa traveled among them in the winter of 1865, they sometimes refused compensation for their services, and were scrupulously careful to guard the property of their guests. Once the Major purposely left some trivial articles. The next day a native brought them forward, and was greatly astonished when pay was offered for his trouble.

"This is your property," was the response; "we could not keep it in our tents, and it was our duty to bring it to you."

The wandering Koriaks estimate property in deer as our

Indians count in horses. It is only among the thousands that wealth is eminently respectable. Some Koriaks own ten or twelve thousand deer, and one fortunate native is the possessor of forty thousand in his own name, (O-gik-a-mu-tik.) Though the wealthiest of his tribe, he does not drive fast horses, and never aspired to a seat in Congress. How much he has missed of real life!

Reindeer form the circulating medium, and all values are expressed in this four-footed currency. The animal supplies nearly every want. They eat his meat and pick his bones, and not only devour the meat, but the stomach, entrails, and their contents. When they stew the mass of meat and half digested moss, the stench is disgusting. Captain Kennan told me that when he arrived among the Koriaks the peculiar odor made him ill, and he slept out of doors with the thermometer at – 35° rather than enter a tent where cooking was in progress.

The Koriaks build their summer dwellings of light poles covered with skin, or bark. Their winter habitations are of logs covered with earth and partly sunk into the ground, the crevices being filled with moss. The summer dwellings are called *balagans*, and the winter ones *yourts*, but the latter name is generally applied to both. A winter yourt has a hole in the top, which serves for both chimney and door. The ladder for the descent is a hewn stick, with holes for one's feet, and leans directly over the fire. Whatever the outside temperature, the yourt is suffocatingly hot within, and no fresh air can enter except through the top. When a large fire is burn-

KORIAK YOURT.

ing and a thick volume of smoke pours out, the descent is very disagreeable. Russians and other white men, even after long practice, never attempt it without a shudder.

The yourt is generally circular or oblong, and its size is proportioned to the family of the owner. The fire is in the center, and the sleeping apartments are ranged around the walls. These apartments, called 'polags,' are about six feet square and four or five high, partitioned with light poles and skin curtains. Owing to the high temperature the natives sleep entirely naked. Sometimes in the coldest nights their clothing is hung out of doors to rid it of certain parasites not unknown in civilization. Benumbed with frost, the insects lose their hold and fall into the snow, to the great comfort of those who nursed and fed them. The body of a Koriak, considered as a microcosm, is remarkably well inhabited.

Captain Kennan gave me a graphic description of the Koriak marriage ceremonial. The lover must labor for the loved one's father, not less than one nor more than five years. No courtship is allowed during this period, and the young man must run the risk of his love being returned. The term of service is fixed by agreement between the stern parent and the youth.

At an appointed day the family and friends are assembled in a yourt, the old women being bridesmaids. The bride is placed in one polag and the bridegroom in the next. At a given signal a race commences, the bride leading. Each must enter every polag, and the man must catch his prize in a specified way before she makes the circuit of the yourt.

The bridesmaids, armed with long switches, offer every assistance to the woman and equal hindrance to the man. For her they lift the curtains of the polags, but hold them down against her pursuer and pound him with their switches. Unless she stops voluntarily it is utterly impossible to overtake her within the circuit. If she is not overtaken the engagement is 'off,' and the man must retire or serve again for the privilege of another love chase. Generally the pursuit is successful; the lover doubtless knows the temper of the lovee before becoming her father's apprentice. But coquettes are not unknown in Koriakdom, and the pursuing youths are sometimes left in the lurch—or the polags.

Should the lover overtake the maiden before making the circuit, both remain seven days and nights in a polag. Their food is given them under the curtain during that period, and they cannot emerge for any purpose whatever. The bridesmaids then perform a brief but touching ceremonial, and the twain are pronounced one flesh.

Northeast of Ghijiga is the country of the Chukchees, a people formerly hostile to the Koriaks. The feuds are not entirely settled, but the ill feeling has diminished and both parties maintain a dignified reserve. The Chukchees are hunters and traders, and have large herds of reindeer but very few dogs. They are the most warlike of these northern races, and long held the Russians at bay. They go far from shore with their *baydaras*, or seal skin boats, visiting islands along the coast, and frequently crossing to North America. Their voyages are of a mercantile character, the Chukchee buying at the Russian towns and selling his goods among the Esquimaux.

At Ghijiga I made a short voyage in a baydara. The frame appeared very fragile, and the seal skin covering displayed several leaks. I was unwilling to risk myself twenty feet from land, but after putting me ashore the Koriak boatman pulled fearlessly into the bay.

The Chukchee trader has a crew of his own race to paddle his light canoe. Occasionally the baydaras are caught in storms and must be lightened. I have the authority of Major Abasa that in such case the merchant keeps his cargo and throws overboard his crew. Goods and furs are costly, but men are cheap and easily replaced. The crew is entirely reconciled to the state of affairs, and drowns itself with that resignation known only to pagans.

"But," I asked, "do not the men object to this kind of jettison?"

"I believe not," was the major's reply; "they are only

discharging their duty to their employer. They go over the side just as they would step from an over-laden sledge."

I next inquired if the trader did not first throw out the men to whom he was most indebted; but could not obtain information on that point. It is probable that with an eye to business he disposes promptly of his creditors and keeps debtors to the last. What a magnificent system of squaring accounts!

DISCHARGING A DECK LOAD.

The Chukchees have mingled much with whalemen along Anadyr Bay and the Arctic Ocean, and readily adopt the white man's vices. They drink whisky without fear, and will get very drunk if permitted. When Captain Macrae's telegraph party landed at the mouth of the Anadyr the natives supposed the provision barrels were full of whisky, and became very importunate for something to drink. The captain made a mixture of red pepper and vinegar, which he palmed off as the desired article. All were pleased with it, and the hotter it was the better.

One native complained that its great heat burned the skin from his throat before he could swallow enough to secure intoxication. The fame of this whisky was wide-spread. Captain Kennan said he heard at Anadyrsk and elsewhere of its wonderful strength, and was greatly amused when he arrived at Macrae's and heard the whole story.

Many of these natives have learned English from whalemen and speak enough to be understood. Gov. Bilzukavitch visited Anadyrsk in the spring of 1866, and met there a Chukchee chief. Neither spoke the other's language, and so the governor called his Koriak servant. The same dilemma occurred, as each was ignorant of the other's vernacular. There was an awkward pause until it was discovered that both Koriak and Chukchee could speak English. Business then proceeded without difficulty.

Among the Chukchees a deer can be purchased for a pound of tobacco, but the price increases as one travels southward. With the Koriaks it is four or five roubles, at Ohotsk ten or fifteen, and on the banks of the Amoor not often less than fifty. South of the Amoor the reindeer is not a native. I am inclined to discredit many stories of the wonderful swiftness of this animal. He sometimes performs remarkable journeys, but ordinarily he is outstripped by a good dog team. Reindeer have the advantage of finding their food under the snow, while provision for dogs must be carried on the sledge When turned out in winter, the deer digs beneath the snow and seeks his food without troubling his master. The American sailors when they have liberty on shore in these northern regions, invariably indulge in reindeer rides, to the disgust of the animals and

REINDEER RIDE.

their owners. The deer generally comes to a halt in the first twenty yards, and nothing less than building a fire beneath him can move him from his tracks.

There is a peculiar mushroom in Northeastern Siberia spotted like a leopard and surmounted with a small hood. It grows in other parts of Russia, where it is poisonous, but among the Koriaks it is simply intoxicating. When one finds a mushroom of this kind he can sell it for three or four reindeer. So powerful is this fungus that the fortunate native who eats it remains drunk for several days. By a process of transmission which I will not describe, as it might offend fastidious persons, half a dozen individuals may successively enjoy the effects of a single mushroom, each of them in a less degree than his predecessor.

Like savages everywhere, these northern natives are greatly pleased with pictures and study them attentively. I heard that several copies of American illustrated papers were circulating among the Chukchees, who handled them with great care. There is a superstitious reverence for pictures mingled with childlike curiosity. People possessing no written language find the pictorial representations of the civilized world the nearest approach to savage hieroglyphics.

The telegraph was an object of great wonder to all the natives. In Ghijiga a few hundred yards of wire were put up in the spring of 1866. Crowds gathered to see the curiosity, and many messages were exchanged to prove that the machine really spoke. At Anadyrsk Captain Kennan arranged a small battery and held in his pocket the key that controlled the circuit. Then the marvel began. The instrument told when persons entered or left the room, when any thing was taken from the table without permission, or any impropriety committed. Even covered with a piece of deer skin, it could see distinctly. With the human tendency to ascribe to the devil anything not understood, these natives looked upon the telegraph as supernatural. As it showed no desire to harm them, they exhibited no fear but abundance of respect.

The Chukchees and Koriaks are creditable workers in

metals and ivory. I saw animal representations rudely but well cut in ivory, and spear-heads that would do credit to any blacksmith. Their hunting knives, made from hoop-iron, are well fashioned, and some of the handles are tastefully inlaid with copper, brass, and silver. In trimming their garments they are very skillful, and cut bits of deerskin into various fantastic shapes.

At Ghijiga I bought a kotlanka, intending to wear it in my winter travel. Its sleeves were purposely very long, and the hood had a wide fringe of dogskin to shield the face. I could never put the thing on with ease, and ultimately sold it to a curiosity hunter. Gloves and mittens, lined with squirrel skin, are made at Ghijiga, and worn in all the region within a thousand miles.

A great hindrance to winter travel in Northeastern Siberia is the prevalence of *poorgas*, or snow storms with wind. On the bleak tundras where there is no shelter, the poorgas sweep with pitiless severity. Some last but a few hours, with the thermometer ten or twenty degrees below zero. Sometimes the wind takes up whole masses of snow and forms drifts several feet deep in a few moments. Travelers, dogs, and sledges are frequently buried out of sight, and remain in the snow till the storm is over.

Dogs begin to howl at the approach of a poorga, long before men can see any indication of it. They display a tendency to burrow in the snow if the wind is cold and violent. Poorgas do not occur at regular intervals, but are most prevalent in February and March.

A few years ago a party of Koriaks crossing the great tundra north of Kamchatka encountered a severe storm. It was of unusual violence, and soon compelled a halt. Dogs and men burrowed into the snow to wait the end of the gale. Unfortunately they halted in a wide hollow that, unperceived by the party, filled with a deep drift. The snow contains so much air that it is not difficult to breathe in it at a considerable depth, and the accumulation of a few feet is not alarming. Hour after hour passed, and the place grew darker, till two men of the party thought it well to look outside. Digging to the surface, the depth proved much greater than expected.

Quite exhausted with their labor, they gained the open air, and found the storm had not ceased. Alarmed for their companions they tried to reach them, but the hole where they ascended was completely filled. The snow drifted rapidly, and they were obliged to change their position often to keep near the surface. When the poorga ended they estimated it had left fifty feet of snow in that spot.

Again endeavoring to rescue their companions, and in their weak condition finding it impossible, they sought the nearest camp. In the following summer the remains of men and dogs were found where the melting snow left them. They had huddled close together, and probably perished from suffocation.

CHAPTER VIII.

WE remained four days at Ghijiga and then sailed for Ohotsk. For two days we steamed to get well out of the bay, and then stopped the engines and depended upon canvas. A boy who once offered a dog for sale was asked the breed of the pup.

"He *was* a pointer," replied the youth; "but father cut off his ears and tail last week and made a bull-dog of him."

Lowering the chimney and hoisting the screw, the Variag became a sailing ship, though her steaming propensities remained, just as the artificial bull-dog undoubtedly retained the pointer instinct. The ship had an advantage over the animal in her ability to resume her old character at pleasure.

On the fourth day, during a calm, we were surrounded by sea-gulls like those near San Francisco. We made deep sea soundings and obtained specimens of the bottom from depths of two or three hundred fathoms. Near the entrance of Ghijiga Bay we brought up coral from eighty fathoms of water, and refuted the theory that coral grows only in the tropics and at a depth of less than two hundred feet. The specimens were both white and red, resembling the moss-like sprigs often seen in museums. The temperature of the water was 47° Fahrenheit. Captain Lund told me coral had been found in the Ohotsk sea in latitude 55° in a bed of considerable extent.

Every day when calm we made soundings, which were carefully recorded for the use of Russian chart makers. Once we found that the temperature of the bottom at a depth of two hundred fathoms, was at the freezing point of water.

The doctor proposed that a bottle of champagne should be cooled in the marine refrigerator. The bottle was attached to the lead and thrown overboard.

"I send champagne to Neptune," said the doctor. "He drink him and he be happy."

When the lead returned to the surface it came alone. Neptune drank the champagne and retained the bottle as a souvenir.

One day the sailors caught a gull and painted it red. When the bird was released he greatly alarmed his companions, and as long as we could see them they shunned his society. At least eighty miles from land we had a dozen sparrows around us at once. A small hawk seized one of these birds and seated himself on a spar for the purpose of breakfasting. A fowling piece brought him to the deck, where we examined and pronounced him of the genus *Falco*, species *NISUS*, or in plain English, a sparrow hawk. During the day we saw three varieties of small birds, one of them resembling the American robin. The sailors caught two in their hands, and released them without injury.

Approaching Ohotsk a fog bank shut out the land for an hour or two, and when it lifted we discovered the harbor. A small sand-bar intervened between the ocean and the town, but did not intercept the view. As at Petropavlovsk, the church was the most prominent object and formed an excellent landmark. With my glass I surveyed the line of coast where the surf was breaking, but was long unable to discover an entering place. The Ohota river is the only harbor, and entirely inaccessible to a ship like the Variag.

Descending the ship's side after we anchored, I jumped when the boat was falling and went down five or six feet before alighting. Both hands were blistered as the gang-way ropes passed through them. Keeping the beacons carefully in line, we rolled over the bar on the top of a high wave, and then followed the river channel to the landing.

Many years ago Ohotsk was the most important Russian port on the waters leading to the Pacific. Supplies for Kamchatka and Russian America were brought overland from Yakutsk and shipped to Petropavlovsk, Sitka, and other points under Russian control. Many ships for the Pacific Ocean and Ohotsk sea were built there. I was shown the spot where Bering's vessel was constructed, with its cordage and extra sails of deerskin, and its caulking of moss. Billings' expedition in a ship called Russia's Glory, was organized here for an exploration of the Arctic ocean. At one time the Government had foundries and workshops at Ohotsk. The shallowness of water on the bar was a great disadvantage, as ships drawing more than twelve feet were unable to enter. Twenty years ago the government abandoned Ohotsk for Ayan, and when the Amoor was opened it gave up the latter place. The population, formerly exceeding two thousand, is now less than two hundred.

We landed on a gravelly beach, where we were met by a crowd of Cossacks and "Lamuti." The almond-shaped eyes and high cheek bones of the latter betray their Mongolian origin. As I walked among them each hailed me with '*sdrastveteh*,' the Russian for 'good-morning.' I endeavored to reply with the same word, but my pronunciation was far from accurate. Near these natives there were several Yakuts and Tunguze, with physiognomies unlike the others. The Russian empire contains more races of men than any rival government, and we frequently find the population of a single locality made up from two or more branches of the human family. In this little town with not more than ten or twelve dozens of inhabitants, there were representatives of the Slavonic, the Tartar, and the Mongolian races.

We found Captain Mahood, of the Telegraph service, in a quiet residence, where he had passed the summer in comparitive idleness. He had devoted himself to exploring the country around Ohotsk and studying the Russian language. "We don't expect to starve at present," said the captain; "Providence sends us fish, the emperor sends us flour, and the merchants furnish tea and sugar. We have lived so long

7*

on a simple bill of fare that we are almost unfitted for any other."

We had a lunch of dried fish, tea, whisky, and cigars, and soon after went to take tea at a house where most of the Variag's officers were assembled. The house was the property of three brothers, who conducted the entire commerce of Ohotsk. The floor of the room where we were feasted was of hewn plank, fastened with enormous nails, and appeared able to resist anything short of an earthquake. The windows were double to keep out the winter's cold, but on that occasion they displayed a profusion of flower pots. The walls were papered, and many pictures were hung upon them. Every part of the room was scrupulously clean.

WAGON RIDE WITH DOGS.

Three ladies were seated on a sofa, and a fourth occupied a chair near them. The three were the wives of the merchant brothers, and the fourth a visiting friend. One with black eyes and hair was dressed tastefully and even elaborately. The eldest, who acted as hostess, was in black, and her ease in receiving visitors would have done credit to a society dame in St. Petersburg. By way of commencement we had tea and *nalifka*, the latter a kind of currant wine of local manufacture and very well flavored. They gave us corned beef and bread, each person taking his plate upon his knee as at an American pic-nic, and after two or three courses of edibles we had coffee and cigarettes, the latter from a manufactory at Yakutsk. According to Russian etiquette each of us thanked the hostess for her courtesy.

Out in the broad street there were many dogs lying idle in the sunshine or biting each other. A small wagon with a team of nine dogs carried a quantity of tea and sugar from the Variag's boats to a warehouse. When the work was finished I took a ride on the wagon, and was carried at good speed. I enjoyed the excursion until the vehicle upset and left me sprawling on the gravel with two or three bruises and a prejudice against that kind of traveling. By the time I gained my feet the dogs were disappearing in the distance, and fairly running away from the driver. Possibly they are running yet.

An old weather beaten church and equally old barracks are near each other, an appropriate arrangement in a country where church and state are united. The military garrison includes thirty Cossacks, who are under the orders of the Ispravnik. They row the pilot boat when needed, travel on courier or other service, guard the warehouses, and when not wanted by government labor and get drunk for themselves. The governor was a native of Poland, and it struck me as a curious fact that the ispravniks of Kamchatka, Ghijiga, and Ohotsk were Poles.

Cows and dogs are the only stock maintained at Ohotsk. The former live on grass in summer, and on hay and fish in winter. Though repeatedly told that cows and horses in Northeastern Siberia would eat dried fish with avidity, I was inclined to skepticism. Captain Mahood told me he had seen them eating fish in winter and appearing to thrive on it. What was more singular, he had seen a cow eating fresh salmon in summer when the hills were covered with grass.

There is a story that Cuvier in a fit of illness, once imagined His Satanic Majesty standing before him.

"Ah!" said the great naturalist, "horns, hoofs; graniverous; need n't fear him."

I wonder if Cuvier knew the taste of the cows at Ohotsk?

No ship had visited Ohotsk for nearly a year before our arrival, though half a dozen whalers had passed in sight. A steamer goes annually from the Amoor with a supply of flour and salt on government account. The mail comes once a year, so that the postmaster has very little to do for three hundred and sixty-four days. Sometimes the mail misses, and then people must wait another twelvemonth for their letters. What a nice residence it would be for a young man whose sweetheart at a distance writes him every day. He would get three hundred and sixty-five letters at once, and in the case of a missing mail, seven hundred and thirty of them.

YEARLY MAIL.

Bears are quite numerous around Ohotsk, and their dispositions do not savor of gentleness. Only a few days before our visit a native was partly devoured within two miles of town.

Many of the dogs are shrewd enough to catch their own fish, but have not learned how to cure them for winter use. When at Ohotsk I went to the bank of the river as the tide was coming in, and watched the dogs at their work. Wading on the sand bars and mud flats till the water was almost over their backs, they stood like statues for several minutes. Waiting till a salmon was fairly within reach, a dog would snap at him with such accuracy of aim that he rarely missed.

I kept my eye on a shaggy brute that stood with little more

than his head out of water. His eyes were in a fixed position, and for twelve or fifteen minutes he did not move a muscle. Suddenly his head disappeared, and after a brief struggle he came to shore with a ten-pound salmon in his jaws. None of the cows are skilled in salmon catching.

DOGS FISHING.

Two or three years ago a mail carrier from Ayan to Yakutsk was visited by a bear during a night halt. The mail bag was lying by a tree a few steps from the Cossack, and near the bank of a brook. The bear seized and opened the pouch, regardless of the government seal on the outside. After turning the letter package several times in his paws, he tossed it into the brook. The Cossack discharged his pistol to frighten the bear, and then fished the letters from the water. It is proper to say the package was addressed to an officer somewhat famous for his bear-hunting proclivities.

When we left Ohotsk at the close of day, we took Captain Mahood and the governor to dine with us, and when our guests departed we hoisted anchor and steamed away. Captain Lund burned a blue light as a farewell signal, and we could see an answering fire on shore. Our course lay directly southward, and when our light was extinguished we were barely visible through the distance and gloom.

"But true to our course, though our shadow grow dark,
We'll trim our broad sail as before;
And stand by the rudder that governs the bark,
Nor ask how we look from the shore."

CHAPTER IX.

ON the Ohotsk Sea we had calms with light winds, and made very slow progress. One day while the men were exercising at the guns, the look out reported a sail. We were just crossing the course from Ayan to Ghijiga, and were in the Danzig's track. The strange vessel shortened sail and stood to meet us, and before long we were satisfied it was our old acquaintance. At sunset we were several miles apart and nearing very slowly. The night was one of the finest I ever witnessed at sea; the moon full and not a cloud visible, and the wind carrying us four or five miles an hour. The brig was lying to, and we passed close under her stern, shortening our sail as we approached her. Everybody was on deck and curious to learn the news.

"SDRASTVETEH," shouted Captain Lund when we were in hearing distance.

"SDRASTVETEH," responded the clear voice of Phillipeus; and then followed the history of the Danzig's voyage.

"We had a good voyage to Ayan, and staid there four days. We are five days out, and passed through a heavy gale on the second day. Going to Ghijiga."

Then we replied with the story of our cruise and asked for news from Europe.

"War in progress—France and Austria against Prussia, Italy, and Russia. No particulars."

By this time the ships were separated and our conversation ended. It was conducted in Russian, but I knew enough of the language to comprehend what was said. There was a universal "eh!" of astonishment as the important sentence was completed.

Here were momentous tidings; France and Russia taking part in a war that was not begun when I left America. A French fleet was in Japanese waters and might be watching for us. It had two ships, either of them stronger than the Variag.

As the Danzig disappeared we went below. "I hoped to go home at the end of this voyage," said the captain as we seated around his table; "but we must now remain in the Pacific. War has come and may give us glory or the grave; possibly both."

For an hour we discussed the intelligence and the probabilities of its truth. As we separated, Captain Lund repeated with emphasis his opinion that the news was false.

"I do not believe it," said he; "but I must prepare for any emergency."

In the wardroom the officers were exultant over the prospect of promotion and prize money. The next day the men were exercised at the guns, and for the rest of the voyage they could not complain of ennui. The deck was cleared of all superfluous rubbish, and we were ready for a battle. The shotted case for the signal books was made ready, and other little preparations attended to. I seemed carried back to my days of war, and had vivid recollections of being stormed at with shot and shell.

From Ohotsk to the mouth of the Amoor is a direct course of about four hundred miles. A light draught steamer would have made short work of it, but we drew too much water to enter the northern passage. So we were forced to sail through La Perouse Straits and up the Gulf of Tartary to De Castries Bay. The voyage was more than twelve hundred miles in length, and had several turnings. It was like going from New York to Philadelphia through Harrisburg, or from Paris to London through Brussels and Edinboro'.

A good wind came to our relief and took us rapidly through La Perouse straits. There is a high rock in the middle of the passage covered with sea-lions, like those near San Francisco. In nearly all weather the roaring of these creatures can be heard, and is a very good substitute for a fog-bell. I am not aware that any government allows a subsidy to the sea-lions.

We saw the northern coast of Japan and the southern end of Sakhalin, both faint and shadowy in the fog and distance. The wind freshened to a gale, and we made twelve knots an hour under double reefed mainsails and topsails. In the narrow straits we escaped the heavy waves encountered at sea in a similar breeze. Turning at right angles in the Gulf of Tartary, we began to roll until walking was no easy matter. The wind abated so that by night we shook out our reefs and spread the royals and to'gallant sails to keep up our speed.

As we approached De Castries the question of war was again discussed.

"If I find only one French ship there," said the captain, "I shall proceed. If there are two I cannot fight them, and must run to San Francisco or some other neutral port."

Just then San Francisco was the last place I desired to visit, but I knew I must abide the fortunes of war. We talked of the possibility of convincing a French captain that we were engaged in an international enterprise, and therefore not subject to capture. Anossoff joined me in arranging a plan to cover contingencies.

As we approached De Castries we could see the spars of a large ship over the islands at the entrance of the harbor. A moment later she was announced.

"A corvette, with steam up."

She displayed her flag—an English one. As we dropped anchor in the harbor a boat came to us, and an officer mounted the side and descended to the cabin. The ship proved to be the British Corvette Scylla, just ready to sail for Japan. Escaping her we did not encounter Charybdis. The mission of the Scylla was entirely pacific, and her officer informed us there had been war between Prussia and Austria, but at last accounts all Europe was at peace. The war of 1866 was finished long before I knew of its commencement.

De Castries Bay is on the Gulf of Tartary, a hundred and thirty-five miles from Nicolayevsk. La Perouse discovered and surveyed it in 1787, and named it in honor of the French Minister of Marine. It is in Lat. 51° 28' N., Lon. 140° 49' E., and affords good and safe anchorage. Near the entrance are several islands, which protect ships anchored behind them. The largest of these islands is occupied as a warehouse and coal depot, and has an observatory and signal station visible from the Gulf. The town is small, containing altogether less than fifty buildings. It is a kind of ocean port to Nicolayevsk and the Amoor river, but the settlement was never a flourishing one.

Twelve miles from the landing is the end of Lake Keezee, which opens into the Amoor a hundred and fifty miles from its mouth. It was formerly the custom to send couriers by way of Lake Keezee and the Amoor to Nicolayevsk to notify consigners and officials of the arrival of ships. Now the telegraph is in operation and supercedes the courier.

In 1855 an English fleet visited De Castries in pursuit of some Russian vessels known to have ascended the Gulf. When the fleet came in sight there were four Russian ships in port, and a few shots were exchanged, none of them taking effect. During a heavy fog in the following night and day the Russians escaped and ascended the Straits of Tartary toward the Amoor. The Aurora, the largest of these ships, threw away her guns, anchors, and every heavy article, and succeeded in entering the Amoor. The English lay near De Castries, and could not understand where the Russians had gone, as the southern entrance of the Amoor was then unknown to geographers.

We reached this port on the morning of September eleventh. The Variag could go no further owing to her draft of water, but fortunately the Morje, a gunboat of the Siberian fleet, was to sail for Nicolayevsk at noon, and we were happily disappointed in our expectations of waiting several days at De

Castries. About eleven o'clock I left the Variag and accompanied Captain Lund, the doctor, and Mr. Anassoff into the boat dancing at the side ladder. Half an hour after we boarded the Morje she was under way, and we saw the officers and men of the corvette waving us farewell.

The Morje drew eight feet of water, and was admirably adapted to the sea coast service. There were several vessels of this class in the Siberian fleet, and their special duty was to visit the ports of Kamchatka, North Eastern Siberia, and Manjouria, and act as tow boats along the Straits of Tartary. The officers commanding them are sent from Russia, and generally remain ten years in this service. At the end of that time, if they wish to retire they can do so and receive half-pay for the rest of their lives. This privilege is not granted to officers in other squadrons, and is given on the Siberian station in consequence of the severer duties and the distance from the centers of civilization.

In its military service the government makes inducements of pay and promotion to young officers who go to Siberia. I frequently met officers who told me they had sought appointments in the Asiatic department in preference to any other. The pay and allowances are better than in European Russia, promotion is more rapid, and the necessities of life are generally less costly. Duties are more onerous and privations are greater, but these drawbacks are of little consequence to an enterprising and ambitious soldier.

The Morje had no accommodations for passengers, and the addition to her complement was something serious. Captain Lund, the doctor, Mr. Anassoff, and myself were guests of her captain. The cabin was given to us to arrange as best we could. My proposal to sleep under the table was laughed at as impracticable. I knew what I was about, having done the same thing years before on Mississippi steamers. When you must sleep on the floor where people may walk about, always get under the table if possible. You run less risk of receiving boot heels in your mouth and eyes, and whole acres of brogans in your ribs.

The navigation of the Straits of Tartary is very intricate, the water being shallow and the channel tortuous. From

TEACHINGS OF EXPERIENCE.

De Castries to Cape Catherine there is no difficulty, but beyond the cape the channel winds like the course of the Ohio, and at many points bends quite abruptly. The government has surveyed and buoyed it with considerable care, so that a good pilot can take a light draught steamer from De Castries to Nicolayevsk in twelve or fifteen hours. Sailing ships are greatly retarded by head winds and calms, and often spend weeks on the voyage. In 1857 Major Collins was nineteen days on the barque Bering from one of these ports to the other.

In the straits we passed four vessels, one of them thirty days from De Castries and only half through the worst of the passage. The water shoals so rapidly in some places that it is necessary to sound on both sides of the ship at once. Vessels drawing less than ten feet can pass to the Ohotsk sea around the northern end of Sakhalin island, but the channel is even more crooked than the southern one.

We anchored at sunset, and did not move till daybreak.

At the hour of sunset, on this vessel as on the corvette, we had the evening chant of the service of the Eastern church. While it was in progress a sentinel on duty over the cabin held his musket in his left hand and made the sign of the cross with his right. Soldier and Christian at the same moment, he observed the outward ceremonial of both. The crew, with uncovered heads, stood upon the deck and chanted the prayer. As the prayer was uttered the national flag, lowered from the mast, seemed, like those beneath it, to bow in adoration of the Being who holds the waters in the hollow of His hand, and guides and controls the universe.

While passing the straits of Tartary we observed a mirage of great beauty, that pictured the shores of Sakhalin like a tropical scene. We seemed to distinguish cocoa and palm trees, dark forests and waving fields of cane, along the rocky shores, that were really below the horizon. Then there were castles, with lofty walls and frowning battlements, cloud-capped towers, gorgeous palaces, and solemn temples, rising among the fields and forests, and overarched with curious combinations of rainbow hues. The mirage frequently occurs in this region, but I was told it rarely attained such beauty as on that occasion.

Sakhalin island, which separates the Gulf of Tartary from the Ohotsk sea, extends through nine degrees of latitude and belongs partly to Russia and partly to Japan. The Japanese have settlements in the Southern portion, engaging in trade with the natives and catching and curing fish. The natives are of Tunguze origin, like those of the lower Amoor, and subsist mainly upon fish. The Russians have settlements at Cape Dui, where there is excellent coal in veins eighteen feet thick and quite near the coast. Russia desired the entire island, but the Japanese positively refuse to negotiate. Some years ago the Siberian authorities established a colony near the Southern extremity, but its existence was brief.

At three o'clock in the afternoon of September eleventh we entered the mouth of the Amoor, the great river of Asiatic Russia. The entrance is between two Capes or headlands, seven miles apart and two or three hundred feet high. The southern one, near which we passed, is called Cape Pronge, and has a Gilyack village at its base. Below this cape the hills border the Gulf and frequently show precipitous sides. The shallow water at their base renders the land undesirable for settlement. The timber is small and indicates the severity of the cold seasons. In their narrowest part the Straits are eight miles wide and frozen in winter. The natives have a secure bridge of ice for at least four months of the year. De Castries Bay is generally filled with ice and unsafe for vessels from October to March.

From the time we entered the Gulf of Tartary the water changed its color, growing steadily dirtier until we reached the Amoor. At the mouth of the river I found it a weak tea complexion, like the Ohio at its middle stage, and was told that it varied through all the shades common to rivers according to its height and the circumstances of season. I doubt if it ever assumes the hue of the Missouri or the Sacramento, though it is by no means impossible.

Passing Cape Pronge and looking up the river, a background of hills and mountains made a fine landscape with beautiful lights and shadows from the afternoon sun. The channel is marked with stakes and buoys and with beacons along the shore. The pilots when steering frequently turned their backs to the bow of the steamer and watched the beacons over the stern. As we approached Nicolayevsk there was a mirage that made the ships in port appear as if anchored in the town itself.

We passed Chinyrack, the fortress that guards the river, and is surrounded, as if for concealment, with a grove of trees. Along the bank above Chinyrack there are warehouses of various kinds, all belonging to government. Soon after dark we anchored before the town, and below several other vessels. My sea travel was ended till I should reach Atlantic waters.

CHAPTER X.

AT Nicolayevsk it is half a mile from the anchorage to the shore. A sand spit projects from the lower end of the town and furnishes a site for government workshops and foundries. Above this tongue of land the water is shallow and allows only light draft and flat bottomed boats to come to the piers. All sea-going vessels remain in mid-stream, where they are discharged by lighters. There is deeper water both above and below the town, and I was told that a change of site had been meditated. The selection of the spot where Nicolayevsk stands was owing to the advantages of the sand spit as a protection to river boats.

After dining on the Morje we went on shore, and landed at a flight of wooden steps in the side of a pier. The piers of Nicolayevsk are constructed with 'cribs' about twenty feet apart and strong timbers connecting them. The flooring was about six feet above water, and wide enough for two teams to pass.

Turning to the left at the end of the pier, we found a plank sidewalk ascending a sloping road in the hillside. The pier reminded me of Boston or New York, but it lacked the huge warehouses and cheerful hackmen to render the similarity complete. "This is Natchez, Mississippi," I said as we moved up the hill, "and this is Cairo, Illinois," as my feet struck the plank sidewalk. The sloping road came to an end sooner than at Natchez, and the sidewalk did not reveal any pitfalls like those in Cairo a few years ago. The bluff where the city stands is about fifty feet high, and the ascent of the road so gentle that one must be very weak to find it fatiguing.

The officers who came on shore with me went to the club rooms to pass the evening. I sought the residence of Mr. H. G. O. Chase, the Commercial Agent of the United States, and representative of the house of Boardman. I found him living very comfortably in bachelor quarters that contained a library and other luxuries of civilization. In his sitting-room there was a map of the Russian empire and one of Boston, and there were lithographs and steel engravings, exhibiting the good taste of the owner.

Rising early the next morning, I began a study of the town. Nicolayevsk was founded in 1853 in the interest of the Russian government, but nominally as a trading post of the Russian American Company. Very soon it became a military post, and its importance increased with the commencement of hostilities between Russia and the Western powers in 1854. Foundries were established, fortifications built, warehouses erected, and docks laid out from time to time, until the place has attained a respectable size. Its population in 1866 was about five thousand, with plenty of houses for all residents.

Nicolayevsk is emphatically a government town, five-sixths of the inhabitants being directly or indirectly in the emperor's employ. "What is this building?" I asked, pointing to a neat house on the principal street. "The residence of the Admiral," was the reply.

"And this?"

"That is the Chancellerie."

"And this?"

"The office of the Captain of the Port."

So I questioned till three-fourths the larger and better establishments had been indicated. Nearly all were in some way connected with government. Many of the inhabitants are employed in the machine shops, others in the arsenals and warehouses, and a goodly number engage in soldiering. The multitude of whisky shops induces the belief that the verb 'to soldier' is conjugated in all its moods and tenses.

The best part of the town is along its front, where there is a wide and well made street called 'the Prospect.'

The best houses are on the Prospect, and include the residences of the chief officials and the merchants. On the back streets is the '*Slobodka*,' or poorer part of the town. Here the laborers of every kind have their dwellings, and here the *lafka* is most to be found. Lafkas are chiefly devoted to liquor selling, and are as numerous in proportion to the population as beer-shops in Chicago. I explored the '*slobodka*,' but did not find it attractive. Dogs were as plentiful and as dubious in breed and character as in the Sixth Ward or near Castle Garden.

The church occupies a prominent position in the foreground of the town, and, like nearly all edifices at Nicolayevsk, is built of logs. Back of it is the chancellerie, or military and civil office, with a flag-staff and semaphore for signalling vessels in the harbor. Of other public buildings I might name the naval office, police office, telegraph house, and a dozen others.

On the morning after my arrival I called on Admiral Fulyelm, the governor of the Maritime Provinces of Eastern Siberia. The region he controls includes Kamchatka and all the seacoast down to Corea, and has an area of nearly seven hundred and fifty thousand square miles. He had been only a few months in command, and was busily at work regulating his department. He spoke English fluently, and was well acquainted with America and American affairs. During my voyage on the Variag I heard much of the charming manners of Madame Fulyelm, and regretted to learn she was spending the summer in the country.

The machine shops, foundries, and dock-yard are described in Russian by the single word 'port.' I visited the port of Nicolayevsk and found it more extensive than one might expect in this new region. There were machines for rolling, planing, cutting, casting, drilling, hammering, punching, and otherwise treating and maltreating iron. There were shops for sawing, planing, polishing, turning, and twisting all sorts of wood, and there were other shops where copper and brass could take any coppery or brassy shape desired. To sum up the port in a few words, its managers can make or repair marine and other engines, and produce any desired wood-work for house building or ship repairing. They build ships and equip them with machinery ready for sea.

The establishment is under the direct supervision of Mr. Woods, an American citizen of Scotch birth. Mr. Elliott, a Massachusetts Yankee, and Mr. Laney, an Englishman, are connected with the affair. Mr. Elliott had become a permanent fixture by marrying a Russian woman and purchasing a commodious house The three men appeared to take great pride in what they had accomplished in perfecting the port.

It was a little curious to see at the mouth of the Amoor a steam fire engine from the Amoskeag Works at Manchester, N. H. The engine was labelled 'Amoor' in Russian characters, and appeared to be well treated. A house was assigned it, and watchmen were constantly on duty. The whole town being of wood it is highly important that the engine should act promptly in case of fire. The supply of hose was ample for all emergencies.

Several heavy guns were shown me, which were hauled overland from the Ural Mountains during the Crimean war and brought in boats down the Amoor. The expense of transporting them must have been enormous, their journey by roads to the head of the river being fully three thousand miles.

I spent a morning with Mr. Chase in calling upon several foreign merchants and their families. The most prominent of the merchants is Mr. Ludorf, a German, who went there in 1856, and has transacted a heavy business on the Amoor and in Japan and China. Mrs. Ludorf followed her husband in 1858, and was the first foreign lady to enter Nicolayevsk.

The most interesting topic to Mr. Chase and the ladies was that of cooks. Within two weeks there had been much trouble with the *chefs de cuisine*, and every housekeeper was in deep grief. Servants are the universal discomfort from the banks of the Hudson to those of the Amoor. Man to be happy must return to the primitive stages of society before cooks and housemaids were invented.

The hills around Nicolayevsk are covered with forests of small pines. Timber for house building purposes is rafted from points on the Amoor where trees are larger. Formerly the town was in the midst of a forest, but the vicinity is now pretty well cleared. Going back from the river, the streets begin grandly, and promise a great deal they do not perform. For one or two squares they are good, the third square is passable, the fourth is full of stumps, and when you reach the fifth and sixth, there is little street to be found. I never saw a better illustration of the road that commenced with a double row of shade trees, and steadily diminished in character until it became a squirrel-track and ran up a tree. There is very little agriculture in the vicinity, the soil and climate being unfavorable. The chief supply of vegetables comes from the settlements on the south bank of the river up to Lake Keezee, and along the shores of the lake. All the ordinary garden vegetables are raised, and in some localities they attain goodly size.

Every morning there was a lively scene at the river's edge in front of the town. Peasants from the farming settlements were there with articles for sale, and a vigorous chaffering was in progress. There were soldiers in grey coats, sailors from the ships in the harbor, laborers in clothing more or less shabby, and a fair sprinkling of aboriginals. To an American freshly arrived the natives were quite a study. They were of the Mongol type, their complexions dark, hair black, eyes obliquely set, noses flat, and cheek bones high. Most of them had the hair plaited in a queue after the Chinese fashion. Some wore boots of untanned skin, and a few had adopted those of Russian make. They generally wear blouses or frocks after the Chinese pattern, and the most of them could be readily taken for shabby Celestials.

Their hats were of two kinds, some of felt and turned up at the sides, and others of decorated birch bark shaped like a parasol. These hats were an excellent protection against sun and rain, but could hardly be trusted in a high wind. All these men were inveterate smokers, and carried their pipes and tobacco pouches at their waists. Most had sheath knives attached to belts, and some carried flint, steel, and tinder. They formed picturesque groups, some talking with purchasers and others collected around fires or near their piles of fish.

As I stood on the bank, a Gilyak boat came near me with a full cargo of salmon. The boat was built very high at bow and stern, and its bottom was a single plank, greatly curved. It was propelled by a woman manipulating a pair of oars with blades shaped like spoon-bowls, beaten flat, which she pulled alternately with a kind of 'hand-over-hand' process. This mode of rowing is universal among the Gilyaks, but does not prevail with other natives along the Amoor.

BOAT LOAD OF SALMON.

Whenever I approached a group of Gilyaks I was promptly hailed with '*reba! reba!*' (fish! fish!) I shook my head and uttered *nierte* (no,) and our conversation ceased. The salmon were in piles along the shore or lying in the native boats. Fishing was not a monopoly of the Gilyaks, as I saw several Russians engaged in the business. They appeared on the best terms with their aboriginal neighbors.

Salmon are abundant in the Amoor and as much a necessity of life as in Northern Siberia. They are not as good as in Kamchatka, and I believe it is the rule that the salmon deteriorates as one goes toward the south. Possibly the quality of the Amoor salmon is owing to the time the fish remain in the brackish waters of the Straits of Tartary. The fishing season is the only busy portion of the year with the natives.

The town is supplied with water by carts like those used in many places along our Western rivers. For convenience

AN EFFECTIVE PROTEST.

in filling the driver goes into the stream until the water is pretty well up his horse's sides. A bucket attached to a long handle is used for dipping, and moves very leisurely. I saw one driver go so far from shore that his horse protested in dumb but expressive show. The animal turned and walked to land, over-setting the cart and spilling the driver into the water. There was a volley of Russian epithets, but the horse did not observe them.

At a photographic establishment I purchased several views of the city and surrounding region. I sought a watch dealer in the hope of replacing my broken time piece, but was unsuccessful. I finally succeeded in purchasing a cheap watch of so curious workmanship that it ran itself out and utterly stopped within a week.

One evening in the public garden a military band furnished creditable music, and I was told that it was formed by selecting men from the ranks, most of whom had never played a single note on any instrument. Writers on Russia twenty years ago said that men were frequently assigned to work they had never seen performed. If men were wanted for any government service a draft was made, just as for filling the army, and when the recruits arrived they were distributed. One was detailed for a blacksmith, and straightway went to his anvil and began. Another was told to be a machinist, and received his tools. He seated himself at his bench, watched his neighbor at work, and commenced with little delay. Another became a glass-blower, another a lapidary, another a musician, and so on through all the trades.

I have heard that an Ohio colonel in our late war had a fondness for never being outdone by rivals. One day his chaplain told him that a work of grace was going on in the army. "Fifteen men," said he, "were baptized last Sunday in Colonel Blank's regiment, and the reformation is still going on." Without replying the colonel called his adjutant.

"Captain," was the command, "detail twenty men for baptism at once. I won't be outdone by any other —— regiment in the army."

Near the river there are several large buildings, formerly belonging to the Amoor Company, an institution that closed its affairs in the summer of 1866. After the opening of the Amoor this company was formed in St. Petersburg with a paid up or guaranteed capital of nearly half a million pounds sterling. Its object was the control of trade on the Amoor and its tributaries, and the general development of commerce in Northern Asia.

It began operations in 1858, but was unfortunate from the beginning. In 1859 it sent out three ships, two of which were lost between De Castries and Nicolayevsk. Each of them had valuable cargoes, and the iron and machinery for two river steamers. The third ship arrived safely, and a steamer which she brought was put together during the winter. It struck a rock and sunk on its first voyage up the river. The misfortunes of the company in following years did not come quite as thick, but their number was ample.

The company's dividends were invariably Hibernian. It lost money from the beginning, and after spending two and a half million dollars, closed its affairs and went up in a balloon.

The Russian government has been disappointed in the result of opening the Amoor. Ten years ago it was thought a great commerce would spring up, but the result has been otherwise. There can be no traffic where there are no people to trade with, and when the Amoor was opened the country was little better than a wilderness. The natives were not a mercantile community. There was only one Manjour city on the bank of the Amoor, and for some time its people were not allowed to trade with Russians. Even when it was opened it had no important commerce, as it was far removed from the silk, tea, or porcelain districts of China. Plainly the dependence must be upon colonization.

The Amoor was peopled under government patronage, many settlers coming from the Trans-Baikal province, and others from European Russia. Nearly all were poor and brought very little money to their new homes. Many were Cossacks and soldiers, and not reconciled to hard labor. During the first two years of their residence the Amoor colonists were supplied with flour at government expense, but after that it was expected they could support themselves. Most of the colonies were half military in their character, being composed of Cossacks, with their families. On the lower part of the Amoor, outside the military posts, the settlers were peasants.

Flour was carried from St. Petersburg to the Amoor to supply the garrison and the newly arrived settlers. The production is not yet sufficient for the population, and when I was at Nicolayevsk I saw flour just landed from Cronstadt. The settlers had generally reached the self-sustaining point, but they did not produce enough to feed the military and naval force. Until they do this the Amoor will be unprofitable.

On the upper Amoor flour was formerly brought from the Trans-Baikal province to supply the settlements down to Habarofka. In 1866 there was a short crop in that province and a good one on the upper Amoor. A large quantity of wheat and rye,—I was told fifty thousand bushels,—was taken to the Trans-Baikal and sold there. On the whole the Amoor country is very good for agriculture, and will sustain itself in time.

The import trade is chiefly in American and German hands, and comprises miscellaneous goods, of which they told me at least fifty per cent. were wines and intoxicating liquors! The Russian emperor should make intemperance a penal offence and issue an edict against it.

A Boston house was the first foreign one opened here, and then came a German one. Others followed, principally from America, the Sandwich Islands, Hamburg, and Bremen. Most of the Americans have retired from the field, two were closing when I was at the Amoor, and Mr. Boardman's was the only house in full operation. There were three German establishments, and another of a German-American character.

All the cereals can be grown on the Amoor, and the yield is said to be very good. When its production is developed, wheat can be exported to China and the Sandwich Islands at a good profit. Until 1864 the government prohibited the export of timber, although it had inexhaustible quantities growing on the Amoor and its tributaries. I saw at Nicolayevsk and elsewhere oak and ash of excellent quality. The former was not as tough as New England oak, but the ash could hardly be excelled anywhere, and I was surprised to learn that no one had attempted its export to California, where good timber for wagons and similar work is altogether wanting. Pine trees are large, straight, tough, and good-fibred. They ought to compete in Chinese ports with pine lumber from elsewhere.

There is a peculiar kind of oak, the Maackia, suitable for cabinet work. Some exports of wool, hides, and tallow have been made, but none of importance. One cargo of ice has been sent to China, but it melted on the way from improper packing. A Hong Kong merchant once ordered a cargo of hams from the Amoor, and when he received it and opened the barrels he found they contained nothing but bones. As the bone market was low at that time he did not repeat his order.

NOTHING BUT BONES.

Flax and hemp will grow here, and might become profitable exports. There is excellent grazing land and no lack of pasturage, but at present bears make fearful havoc among the cattle and sheep. In some localities tigers are numerous, particularly among the Buryea Mountains, where the Cossacks make a profession of hunting them. The tiger is not likely to become an article of commerce, but on the contrary is calculated to retard civilization.

With increased agriculture, pork can be raised and cured, and the Russians might find it to their advantage to introduce Indian corn, now almost unknown on the Amoor. At present hogs on the lower Amoor subsist largely on fish, and the pork has a very unpleasant flavor. The steward of the Variag told me that in 1865, when at De Castries, he had two small pigs from Japan. A vessel just from the Amoor had a large hog which had been purchased at Nicolayevsk.

The captain of the ship offered his hog for the two pigs, on the plea that he wished to keep them during his voyage. As the hog was three times the weight of the pigs the steward gladly accepted the proposal, and wondered how a man who made so absurd a trade could be captain of a ship. On killing his prize he found the pork so fishy in flavor that nobody could eat it. The whole hog went literally to the dogs.

Nicolayevsk is a free port of entry, and there are no duties upon merchandise anywhere in Siberia east of Lake Baikal. Since the opening of commerce, in 1865, the number of ships arriving annually varies from six or eight to nearly forty. In 1866 there were twenty-three vessels on government, and fifteen on private account. The government vessels brought flour, salt, lead, iron, machinery, telegraph material, army and navy equipments, and a thousand and one articles included under the head of 'government stores.' The private ones, (three of them American,) brought miscellaneous cargoes for the mercantile community. There were no wrecks in that year, or at any rate, none up to the time of my departure.

At the Amoor I first began to hear those stories of peculation that greet every traveler in Russia. According to my informants there were many deficiencies in official departments, and very often losses were ascribed to 'leakage,' 'breakage,' and damage of different kinds. "Did you ever hear," said a gentleman to me, "of rats devouring window-glass, or of anchors and boiler iron blowing away in the wind?" However startling such phenomena, he declared they had been known at Nicolayevsk and elsewhere in the empire. I think if all the truth were revealed we might learn of equally strange occurrences in America during the late war.

The Russians have explored very thoroughly the coast of Manjouria in search of good harbors. Below De Castries the first of importance is Barracouta Bay, in Latitude 49°. The government made a settlement there in 1853, but subsequently abandoned it for Olga Bay, six degrees further south. Vladivostok, or Dominion of the East, was occupied in 1857, and a naval station commenced. A few years later, Posyet was founded near the head of the Corean peninsula, and is now growing rapidly. It has one of the finest harbors on the Japan Sea, completely sheltered, easily defended, and affording superior facilities for repairing ships of war or commerce. It is free from ice the entire year, and has a little cove or bay that could be converted into a dry dock at small expense.

In 1865 Posyet was visited by ten merchant vessels; it exported fifteen thousand poods of *beche de mer*, the little fish formerly the monopoly of the Feejees, and of which John Chinaman is very fond. It exported ten thousand poods of bean cake, and eleven times that quantity of a peculiar sea-grass eaten by the Celestials. Ginseng root was also an article of commerce between Posyet and Shanghae. Russia appears in earnest about the development of the Manjourian coast, and is making many efforts for that object. The telegraph is completed from Nicolayevsk to the new seaport, and a post route has been established along the Ousuree.

From San Francisco to the mouth of the Amoor I did not see a wheeled vehicle, with the exception of a hand cart and a dog wagon. At Nicolayevsk there were horses, carts, and carriages, and I had my first experience of a horse harnessed with the Russian yoke. The theory of the yoke is, that it keeps the shafts away from the animal's sides, and enables him to exert more strength than when closely hedged. I cannot give a positive opinion on this point, but believe the Russians are correct. The yoke standing high above the horse's head and touching him nowhere, has a curious appearance when first seen. I never could get over the idea while looking at a dray in motion, that the horse was endeavoring to walk through an arched gateway and taking it along with him.

The shafts were wide apart and attached by straps to the horse's collar. All the tension came through the shafts, and these were strengthened by ropes that extended to the ends of the forward axle. Harnesses had a shabby, 'fixed up' appearance, with a good deal of rope in their composition. Why they did not go to pieces or crumble to nothing, like the deacon's One Horse Shay, was a mystery.

Before leaving Nicolayevsk I enjoyed a ride in one of its private carriages. The vehicle was open, its floor quite low, and the wheels small. We had two horses, one between the shafts and wearing the inevitable yoke. The other was outside, and attached to an iron single-tree over the forward wheel. Three horses can be driven abreast on this kind of carriage.

The shaft horse trotted, while the other galloped, holding his head very low and turned outward. This is due to a check rein, which keeps him in a position hardly natural. The orthodox mode in Russia is to have the shaft horse trotting while the other runs as described; the difference in the motion gives an attractive and dashy appearance to the turnout. Existence would be incomplete to a Russian without an equipage, and if he cannot own one he keeps it on hire. The gayety of Russian cities in winter and summer is largely due to the number of private vehicles in constant motion through the streets.

CHAPTER XI.

I ARRANGED to ascend the Amoor on the steamer Ingodah, which was appointed to start on the eighteenth of September. My friend Anossoff remained at Nicolayevsk during the winter, instead of proceeding to Irkutsk as I had fondly hoped. I found a *compagnon du voyage* in Captain Borasdine, of General Korsackoff's staff. In a drenching rain on the afternoon of the seventeenth, we carried our baggage to the Ingodah, which lay half a mile from shore. We reached the steamer after about twenty minutes pulling in a whale-boat and shipping a barrel of water through the carelessness of an oarsman.

At Nicolayevsk the Amoor is about a mile and a half wide, with a depth of twenty to thirty-five feet in the channel. I asked a resident what he thought the average rapidity of the current in front of the town.

"When you look at it or float with it," said he, "I think it is about three and a half miles. If you go against it you find it not an inch less than five miles."

The rowers had no light task to stem the rapid stream, and I think it was about like the Mississippi at Memphis.

The boat was to leave early in the morning. I took a farewell dinner with Mr. Chase, and at ten o'clock received a note from Borasdine announcing his readiness to go to the steamer. Anossoff, Chase, and half a dozen others assembled to see us off, and after waking the echoes and watchmen on the pier, we secured a skiff and reached the Ingodah. The rain was over, and stars were peeping through occasional loop-holes in the clouds.

'Seeing off' consumed much time and more champagne. As we left the house I observed Chase and Anossoff each putting a bottle in his pocket, and remarking the excellent character of their ballast. From the quantity that revealed itself afterward the two bottles must have multiplied, or other persons in the party were equally provided. To send off a friend in Russia requires an amount of health-drinking rarely witnessed in New York or Boston. If the journey is by land the wayfarer is escorted a short distance on his route, sometimes to the edge of the town, and sometimes to the first station. Adieus are uttered over champagne, tea, lunch —and champagne. It was nearly daybreak when our friends gave us the last hand-shake and went over the side. Watching till their boat disappeared in the gloom, I sought the cabin, and found the table covered with a beggarly array of empty bottles and a confused mass of fragmentary edibles. I retired to sleep, while the cabin boy cleared away the wreck.

SEEING OFF.

The sun rose before our captain. When I followed their example we were still at anchor and our boilers cold as a refusal to a beggar. Late in the morning the captain appeared; about nine o'clock fire was kindled in the furnace, and a little past ten we were under way. As our anchor rose and the wheel began to move, most of the deck passengers turned in the direction of the church and devoutly made the sign of the cross. As we slowly stemmed the current the houses of Nicolayevsk and the shipping in its front, the smoking foundries, and the pine-covered hills, faded from view, and with my face to the westward I was fairly afloat on the Amoor.

The Ingodah was a plain, unvarnished boat, a hundred and ten feet long, and about fifteen feet beam. Her hull was of boiler iron, her bottom flat, and her prow sharp and perpendicular. Her iron, wood work, and engines were brought in a sailing ship to the Amoor and there put together. She had two cabins forward and one aft, all below deck. There was a small hold for storing baggage and freight, but the most of the latter was piled on deck. The pilot house was over the forward cabin, and contained a large wheel, two men, and a chart of the river. The rudder was about the size of a barn door, and required the strength of two men to control it. Had she ever refused to obey her helm she would have shown an example of remarkable obstinacy.

Over the after cabin there was a cook-house, where dwelt a shabby and unwholesome cuisinier. Between the wheels was a bridge, occupied by the captain when starting or stopping the boat; the engines, of thirty horse power, were below deck, under this bridge. The cabins, without state rooms, occupied the whole width of the boat. Wide seats with cushions extended around the cabins, and served as beds at night. Each passenger carried his own bedding and was his own chambermaid. The furniture consisted of a fixed table, two feet by ten, a dozen stools, a picture of a saint, a mirror, and a boy, the latter article not always at hand.

The cabins were unclean, and reminded me of the general condition of transports during our late war. Can any philosopher explain why boats in the service of government are nearly always dirty?

The personnel of the boat consisted of a captain, mate, engineer, two pilots, and eight or ten men. The captain and mate were in uniform when we left port, but within two hours they appeared in ordinary suits of grey. The crew were deck hands, roustabouts, or firemen, by turns, and when we took wood most of the male deck passengers were required to assist.

On American steamboats the after cabin is the aristocratic one; on the Amoor the case is reversed. The steerage passengers lived, moved, and had their being and baggage aft the engine, while their betters were forward. This arrangement gave the steerage the benefit of all cinders and smoke, unless the wind was abeam or astern.

Steam navigation on the Amoor dates from 1854. In that year two wooden boats, the Shilka and the Argoon, were constructed on the Shilka river, preparatory to the grand expedition of General Mouravieff. Their timber was cut in the forests of the Shilka, and their engines were constructed at Petrovsky-Zavod. The Argoon was the first to descend, leaving Shilikinsk on the 27th of May, 1854, and bringing the Governor General and his staff. It was accompanied by fifty barges and a great many rafts loaded with military forces to occupy the Amoor, and with provisions for the Pacific fleet. The Shilka descended a few months later. She was running in 1866, but the Argoon, the pioneer, existed less than a decade. In 1866 there were twenty-two steamers on the Amoor, all but four belonging to the government.

The government boats are engaged in transporting freight, supplies, soldiers, and military stores generally, and carrying the mail. They carry passengers and private freight at fixed rates, but do not give insurance against fire or accidents of navigation. Passengers contract with the captain or steward for subsistence while on board. Deck passengers generally support themselves, but can buy provisions on the boat if they wish. The steward may keep wines and other beverages for sale by the bottle, but he cannot maintain a bar. He has various little speculations of his own and does not feed his customers liberally. On the Ingodah the steward purchased eggs at every village, and expected to sell them at a large profit in Nicolayevsk. When we left him he had at least ten bushels on hand, but he never furnished eggs to us unless we paid extra for them.

One cabin was assigned to Borasdine and myself, save at meal times, when two other passengers were present. One end of it was filled with the mail, of which there were eight bags, each as large as a Saratoga trunk and as difficult to handle. The Russian government performs an 'express' service and transports freight by mail; it receives parcels in any part of the empire and agrees to deliver them in any other part desired. From Nicolayevsk to St. Petersburg the charges are twenty-five copecks (cents) a pound, the distance being seven thousand miles. It gives receipts for the articles, and will insure them at a charge of two per cent. on their value.

Goods of any kind can be sent by post through Russia just as by express in America. Captain Lund sent a package containing fifty sable skins to his brother in Cronstadt, and another with a silk dress pattern to a lady in St. Petersburg. In the mail on the Ingodah there were twelve hundred pounds of sable fur sent by Mr. Chase to his agent in St. Petersburg. Money to any amount can be remitted, and its delivery insured. I have known twenty thousand roubles sent on a single order.

Parcels for transportation by post must be carefully and securely packed. Furs, silks, clothing, and all things of that class are enveloped in repeated layers of oil cloth and canvas to exclude water and guard against abrasion. Light articles, like bonnets, must be packed with abundance of paper filling them to their proper shape, and very securely boxed. A Siberian lady once told me that a friend in St. Petersburg sent her a lot of bonnets, laces, and other finery purchased at great expense. She waited a long time with feminine anxiety, and was delighted when told her box was at the post office. What was her disappointment to find the articles had been packed in a light case which was completely smashed. She never made use of any part of its contents.

In crossing Siberian rivers the mail is sometimes wet, and it is a good precaution to make packages waterproof. A package of letters for New York from Nicolayevsk I enveloped in canvas, by advice of Russian friends, and it went through unharmed.

SCENES ON THE AMOOR.

The post wagons are changed at every station, and the mail while being transferred is not handled with care. Frail articles must be boxed so that no tossing will injure them. My lady friend told me of a bride who ordered her trousseau from St. Petersburg and prepared for a magnificent wedding. The precious property arrived forty-eight hours before the time fixed for the ceremony. Moving accidents by flood and field had occurred. The bridal paraphernalia was soaked, crushed, and reduced to a mass that no one could resolve into its original elements. The wedding was postponed and a new supply of goods ordered.

The mail is always in charge of a postillion, who is generally a Cossack, and his duty is much like that of a mail agent in other countries. He delivers and receives the sacks of matter at the post offices, and guards them on the road. During our voyage on the Ingodah there was no supervision over the mail bags after they were deposited in our cabin. I passed many hours in their companionship, and if Borasdine and I had chosen to rifle them we could have done so at our leisure. Possibly an escape from the penalties of the law would have been less easy.

Our cook was an elderly personage, with thin hair, a yellow beard, and a much neglected toilet. On the first morning I saw him at his ablutions, and was not altogether pleased with his manner. He took a half-tumbler of water in his mouth and then squirted the fluid over his hands, rubbing them meanwhile with invisible soap. He was quite skillful, but I could never relish his dinners if I had seen him any time within six hours. His general appearance was that of having slept in a gutter without being shaken afterwards.

The day of our departure from Nicolayevsk was like the best of our Indian summer. There was but little wind, the faintest breath coming now and then from the hills on the southern bank. The air was of a genial warmth, the sky free from clouds and only faintly dimmed with the haze around the horizon. The forest was in the mellow tints of autumn, and the wide expanse of foliferous trees, dotted at frequent intervals with the evergreen pine, rivalled the October hues of our New England landscape. Hills and low mountains rose on both banks of the river and made a beautiful picture. The hills, covered with forest from base to summit, sloped gently to the water's edge or retreated here and there behind bits of green meadow. In the distance was a background of blue mountains glowing in sunshine or dark in shadow, and varying in outline as we moved slowly along. The river was ruffled only by the ripples of the current or the motion of our boat through the water. Just a year earlier I descended the Saint Lawrence from Lake Ontario to Quebec. I saw nothing on the great Canadian river that equaled the scenery of my first day's voyage on the Amoor.

Soon after leaving Nicolayevsk we met several loads of hay floating with the current to a market at the town. On the meadows along the river the grass is luxuriant, and hay requires only the labor of cutting and curing. During the day we passed several points where haymaking was in progress. Cutting was performed with an instrument resembling the short scythe used in America for cutting bushes. After it was dried, the hay was brought to the river bank on dray-like carts. An American hay wagon would have accomplished twice as much with equal labor.

The hay is like New England hay from natural meadows, and is delivered at Nicolayevsk for six or eight dollars a ton. Cattle and horses thrive upon it, if I may judge by the condition of the stock I saw. For its transportation two flat-bottomed boats are employed, and held about twelve feet apart by timbers. A floor on these timbers and over the boats serves to keep the hay dry. Men are stationed at both ends of the boats, and when once in the stream there is little to do beside floating with the current. A mile distant one of these barges appears like a haystack which an accident has set adrift.

We saw many Gilyak boats descending the river with the current or struggling to ascend it. The Gilyaks form the native population in this region and occupy thirty-nine villages with about two thousand inhabitants. The villages are on both banks from the mouth of the river to Mariensk, and out of the reach of all inundations. Distance lends enchantment to the view of their houses, which will not bear close inspection.

Some of the houses might contain a half dozen families of ordinary size, and were well adapted to the climate. While we took wood at a Gilyak village I embraced the opportunity

A GILYAK VILLAGE.

to visit the aboriginals. The village contained a dozen dwellings and several fish-houses. The buildings were of logs or poles, split in halves or used whole, and were roofed with poles covered with a thatch of long grass to exclude rain and cold. Some of the dwelling houses had the solid earth for floors, while others had floorings of hewn planks.

The store houses were elevated on posts like those of an American 'corn barn,' and were wider and lower than the dwellings. Each storehouse had a platform in front where canoes, fishing nets, and other portable property were stowed.

These buildings were the receptacles of dried fish for the winter use of dogs and their owners. The elevation of the floor serves to protect the contents from dogs and wild animals. I was told that no locks were used and that theft was a crime unknown.

The dwellings were generally divided into two apartments; one a sort of ante room and receptacle of house-keeping goods, and the other the place of residence. Pots, kettles, knives, and wooden pans were the principal articles of household use I discovered. At the storehouses there were several fish-baskets of birch or willow twigs. A Gilyak gentleman does not permit fire carried into or out of his house, not even in a pipe. This is not owing to his fear of conflagrations, but to a superstition that such an occurrence may bring him ill luck in hunting or fishing.

It was in the season of curing fish, and the stench that greeted my nostrils was by no means delightful. Visits to dwellings or magazines would have been much easier had I possessed a sponge saturated with cologne water. Fish were in various stages of preparation, some just hung upon poles, while others were nearly ready for the magazine. The manner of preparation is much the same as in Kamchatka, save that the largest fish are skinned before being cut into strips. The poorest qualities go to the dogs, and the best are reserved for bipeds.

Though the natives do the most of the fishing on the Amoor, they do not have a monopoly of it, as some of the Russians indulge in the sport. One old fellow that I saw had a boat so full of salmon that there was no room for more. Now and then a fish went overboard, causing an expression on the boatman's face as if he were suffering from a dose of astonishment and toothache drops in equal proportions.

There were dogs everywhere, some lying around loose, and others tied to posts under the storehouses. Some walked about and manifested an unpleasant desire to taste the calves of my legs. All barked, growled, and whined in a chorus like a Pawnee concert. There were big dogs and little dogs, white, black, grey, brown, and yellow dogs, and not one friendly. They did not appear courageous, but I was not altogether certain of their dispositions. Their owners sought to quiet them, but they refused comfort.

These dogs had some peculiarities of those in Kamchatka, but their blood was evidently much debased; they appeared to be a mixture of Kamchadale, greyhound, bull dog, and cur, the latter predominating. They are used for hunting at all seasons, and for towing boats in summer and dragging sledges in winter. I was told that since the Russian settlement of the Amoor the Gilyak dogs have degenerated, in consequence of too much familiarity with Muscovite canines. Nicolayevsk appeared quite cosmopolitan in the matter of dogs, and it was impossible to say what breed was most numerous. One day I saw nineteen in a single group and no two alike.

ABOUT FULL.

Near the entrance of the village an old man was repairing his nets, which were stretched along a fence. He did not regard us as we scrutinized his jacket of blue cotton, and he made no response to a question which Borasdine asked. Further along were two women putting fish upon poles for drying, and a third was engaged in skinning a large salmon. The women did not look up from their work, and were not inclined to amiability. They had Mongol features, complexion, eyes, and hair, the latter thick and black. Some of the men wear it plaited into queues, and others let it grow pretty much at will. Each woman I saw had it braided in two queues, which hung over her shoulders. In their ears they wore long pendants, and their dresses were generally arranged with taste.

When recalled by the steam whistle we left the village and took a short route down a steep bank to the boat. In descending, my feet passed from under me, and I had the pleasure of sliding about ten yards before stopping. Had it not been for a Cossack who happened in my way I should have entered the Amoor after the manner of an otter, and afforded much amusement to the spectators, though comparatively little to myself. The sliding attracted no special attention as it was supposed to be the American custom, and I did not deem it prudent to make an explanation lest the story might bring discredit to my nationality.

CHAPTER XII.

I HAD a curiosity to examine the ancient monuments at Tyr, opposite the mouth of the Amgoon river, but we passed them in the night without stopping. There are several traditions concerning their origin. The most authentic story gives them an age of six or seven hundred years. They are ascribed to an emperor of the Yuen dynasty who visited the mouth of the Amoor and commemorated his journey by building the 'Monastery of Eternal Repose.' The ruined walls of this monastery are visible, and the shape of the building can be easily traced. In some places the walls are eight or ten feet high.

Mr. Collins visited the spot in 1857 and made sketches of the monuments. He describes them situated on a cliff a hundred and fifty feet high, from which there is a magnificent view east and west of the Amoor and the mountains around it. Toward the south there are dark forests and mountain ridges, some of them rough and broken. To the north is the mouth of the Amgoon, with a delta of numerous islands covered with forest, while in the northwest the valley of the river is visible for a long distance. Back from the cliff is a table-land several miles in width.

This table-land is covered with oak, aspen, and fir trees, and has a rich undergrowth of grass and flowers. On a point of the cliff there are two monuments. A third is about four hundred yards away. One is a marble shaft on a granite pedestal; a second is entirely granite, and the third partly granite and partly porphyry. The first and third bear inscriptions in Chinese, Mongol, and Thibetan. One inscription announces that the emperor Yuen founded the Monastery of Eternal Repose, and the others record a prayer of the Thibetans. Archimandrate Avvakum, a learned Russian, who deciphered the inscriptions, says the Thibetan prayer *Om-mani-badme-khum* is given in three languages.*

The lowest of the monuments is five and the tallest eight feet in height. Near them are several flat stones with grooves in their surface, which lead to the supposition of their employment for sacrificial purposes. Mr. Chase told me at Nicolayevsk that he thought one of the monuments was used as an altar when the monastery flourished. There are no historical data regarding the ruins beyond those found on the stones.

Many of the Russians and Chinese believe the site was selected by Genghis Khan, and the monastery commemorated one of his triumphs. The natives look upon the spot with veneration, and frequently go there to practice their mysterious rites.

Before leaving Nicolayevsk I asked the captain of the Ingodah how fast his boat could steam. "Oh!" said he, "ten or twelve versts an hour." Accustomed to our habit of ex-

---

* Abbe Huc in his 'Recollections of a journey through Thibet and Tartary,' says:—

"The Thibetans are eminently religious. There exists at Lassa a touching custom which we are in some sort jealous of finding among infidels. In the evening as soon as the light declines, the Thibetans, men, women, and children, cease from all business and assemble in the principal parts of the city and in the public squares. When the groups are formed, every one sits down on the ground and begins slowly to chant his prayers in an undertone, and this religious concert produces an immense and solemn harmony throughout the city. The first time we heard it we could not help making a sorrowful comparison between this pagan town, where all prayed in common, with the cities of the civilized world, where people would blush to make the sign of the cross in public.

The prayer chanted in these evening meetings varies according to the season of the year; that which they recite to the rosary is always the same, and is only composed of six syllables, *om-mani-badme-khum*. This formula, called briefly the *mani*, is not only heard from every mouth, but is everywhere written in the streets, in the interior of the houses, on every flag and streamer floating over the buildings, printed in the Landzee, Tartar, and Thibetan characters. The Lamas assert that the doctrine contained in these words is immense, and that the whole life of man is not sufficient to measure its depth and extent."

aggerating the powers of a steamer, I expected no more than eight or nine versts. I was surprised to find we really made twelve to fifteen versts an hour. Ten thousand miles from St. Louis and New Orleans I at last found what I sought for several years—a steamboat captain who understated the speed of his boat! Justice to the man requires the explanation that he did not own her.

My second day on the Amoor was much like the first in the general features of the scenery. Hills and mountains

ON THE AMOOR.

on either hand; meadows bounding one bank or the other at frequent intervals; islands dotted here and there with pleasing irregularity, or stretching for many miles along the valley; forests of different trees, and each with its own particular hue; a canopy of hazy sky meeting ranges of misty peaks in the distance; these formed the scene. Some one asks if all the tongues in the world can tell how the birds sing and the lilacs smell. Equally difficult is it to describe with pen upon paper the beauties of that Amoor scenery. Each bend of the stream gave us a new picture. It was the unrolling of a magnificent panorama such as no man has yet painted. And what can I say? There was mountain, meadow, forest, island, field, cliff, and valley; there were the red leaves of the autumn maple, the yellow of the birch, the deep green of pine and hemlock, the verdure of the grass, the wide river winding to reach the sea, and we slowly stemming its current. How powerless are words to describe a scene like this!

The passengers of our boat were of less varied character than those on a Mississippi steamer. There were two Russian merchants, who joined us at meal times in the cabin but slept in the after part of the boat. One was owner of a gold mine two hundred miles north of Nicolayevsk, and a general dealer in everything along the Amoor. He had wandered over Mongolia and Northern China in the interest of commerce, and I greatly regretted my inability to talk with him and learn of the regions he had visited. He was among the first to penetrate the Celestial Empire under the late commercial treaty, and traveled so far that he was twice arrested by local authorities. He knew every fair from Leipsic to Peking, and had been an industrious commercial traveler through all Northern Asia.

Once, below Sansin, on the Songaree river, he was attacked by thieves where he had halted for the night. With a single exception his crew was composed of Chinese, and these ran away at the first alarm. With his only Russian companion he attempted to defend his property, but the odds were too great, especially as his gun could not be found. He was made prisoner and compelled to witness the plundering of his cargo. Every thing valuable being taken, the thieves left him.

In the morning he proceeded down the stream. Not caring to engage another crew, he floated with the current and shared with his Russian servant the labor of steering. The next night he was robbed again, and the robbers, angry at finding so little to steal, did not leave him his boat. After much difficulty he reached a native village and procured an old skiff. With this he finished his journey unmolested.

There were fifteen or twenty deck passengers, a fair proportion being women and children. Among the latter was a black eyed girl of fifteen, in a calico dress and wearing a shawl pinned around a pretty face. On Sunday morning she appeared in neat apparel and was evidently desirous of being seen. There were two old men dressed in coarse cloth of a 'butternut' hue, that reminded me of Arkansas and Tennessee. The morning we started one of them was seated on the deck counting a pile of copper coin with great care. Two, three, four times he told it off, piece by piece, and then folded it carefully in the corner of his kerchief. In all he had less than a rouble, but he preserved it as if it were a million.

CASH ACCOUNT.

The baggage of the deck passengers consisted of boxes and household furniture in general, not omitting the ever-present samovar. This baggage was piled on the deck and was the reclining place of its owners by day. In the night they had the privilege of the after cabin, where they slept on the seats and floor.

'Wooding up' was not performed with American alacrity. To bring the steamer to land she was anchored thirty feet from shore, and two men in a skiff carried a line to the bank and made it fast. With this line and the anchor the boat was warped within ten feet of the shore, another line keeping the stern in position. An ordinary plank a foot wide made the connection with the solid earth. These boats have no guards and cannot overhang the land like our Western craft.

Wood was generally piled fifty, a hundred, or five hundred feet from the landing place, wherever most convenient to the owner. No one seems to think of placing it near the water's edge as with us; they told me that this had been done formerly, and the freshets had carried the wood away. The peasants, warned by their loss, are determined to keep on the safe side.

When all was ready the deck hands went very leisurely to work. Each carried a piece of rope which he looped around a few sticks of wood as a boy secures his bundle of school books. The rope was then slung upon the shoulder, the wood hanging over the back of the carrier and occasionally coming loose from its fastenings. No man showed any sign of hurrying, but all acted as if there were nothing in the world as cheap as time. One day I watched the wooding operation from beginning to end. It took an hour and a half and twelve men to bring about four cords of wood on board. There was but one man displaying any activity, and *he* was falling from the plank into the river.

WOODING UP.

The Russian measure of wood is the *sajene* (fathom,) and a sajene of wood is a pile a fathom long, wide, and high. The Russian marine fathom measures six feet like our own, but the land fathom is seven feet. It is by the land fathom that everything on solid earth is measured. A stick seven feet long is somewhat inconvenient, and therefore they cut wood half a fathom in length.

We landed our first freight at Nova Mihalofski, a Russian village on the southern bank of the river. The village was small and the houses were far from palatial. The inhabitants live by agriculture in summer, sending their produce to Nicolayevsk, and by supplying horses for the postal service in winter. I observed here and at other villages an example of Russian economy. Not able to purchase whole panes of window glass the peasants use fragments of glass of any shape they can get. These are set in pieces of birch bark cut to the proper form and the edges held by wax or putty. The bark is then fastened to the window sash much as a piece of mosquito netting is fixed in a frame.

Near Springfield, Missouri, I once passed a night in a farmer's house. The dwelling had no windows, and when we breakfasted we were obliged to keep the door open to give us light, though the thermometer was at zero, with a strong wind blowing. "I have lived in this house seventeen years," said the owner; "have a good farm and own four niggers." But he could not afford the expense of a window, even of the Siberian kind!

Ten or fifteen miles above this village we reached Mihalofski, containing a hundred houses and three or four hundred inhabitants. From the river this town appeared quite pretty and thriving; the houses were substantially built, and many had flower gardens in front and neat fences around them. Between the town and the river there were market gardens in flourishing condition, bearing most of the vegetables in common use through the north. The town is along a ridge of easy ascent, and most of the dwellings are thirty or forty feet above the river. Its fields and gardens extend back from the river wherever the land is fertile and easiest cleared of the forest. On the opposite side of the river there are meadows where the peasants engage in hay cutting. The general appearance of the place was like that of an ordinary village on the lower St. Lawrence, though there were many points of difference.

In several rye fields the grain had been cut and stacked. Near our landing was a mill, where a man, a boy, and a horse were manufacturing meal at the rate of seven poods or 280 pounds a day. The whole machinery was on the most primitive scale.

Entering the house of the mill-owner I found the principal apartment quite neat and well arranged, its walls being whitewashed and decorated with cheap lithographs and wood-cuts. Among the latter were several from the Illustrated London News and *L'Illustration Universelle.* The sleeping room was fitted with bunks like those on steamboats, though somewhat wider. There was very little clothing on the beds, but several sheepskin coats and coverlids were hanging on a fence in front of the house.

Borasdine had business at the telegraph station, whither I accompanied him. The operator furnished a blank for the despatch, and when it was written and paid for he gave a receipt. The receipt stated the hour and minute when the despatch was taken, the name of the sender, the place where sent, the number of words, and the amount paid. This form is invariably adhered to in the Siberian telegraph service.

The telegraph on the lower Amoor was built under the supervision of Colonel Romanoff and was not completed at the time of my visit. It commenced at Nicolayevsk and followed the south bank of the Amoor to Habarofka at the mouth of the Ousuree. At Mariensk there was a branch to De Castries, and from Habarofka the line extended along the Ousuree and over the mountains to Posyet and Vladivostok. From Habarofka it was to follow the north bank of the Amoor to the Shilka, to join the line from Irkutsk and St. Petersburg. Arrangements have been made recently to lay a cable from Posyet to Hakodadi in Japan, and thence to Shanghae and other parts of China. When the cable proposed by Major Collins is laid across the Pacific Ocean, and the break in the

Amoor line is closed up, the telegraph circuit around the globe will be complete.

The telegraph is operated on the Morse system with instruments of Prussian manufacture. Compared to our American instruments the Prussian ones are quite clumsy, though they did not appear so in the hands of the operators. The signal key was at least four times as large as ours, and could endure any amount of rough handling. The other machinery was on a corresponding scale.

A merchant who knew Mr. Borasdine invited us to his house, where he brought a lunch of bread, cheese, butter, and milk for our entertainment. Salted cucumbers were added, and the repast ended with tea. In the principal room there was a Connecticut clock in one corner. and the windows were filled with flowers, among which were the morning glory, aster, and verbena. Several engravings adorned the walls, most of them printed at Berlin. We purchased a loaf of sugar, and were shown a bear-skin seven feet long without ears and tail. The original and first legitimate owner of the skin was killed within a mile of town.

In addition to his commerce and farming, this merchant was superintendent of a school where several Gilyak boys were educated. It was then vacation, and the boys were engaged in catching their winter supply of fish. At the merchant's invitation we visited the school buildings.

The study room was much like a backwoods schoolroom in America, having rude benches and desks, but with everything clean and well made. The copy-books exhibited fair specimens of penmanship. On a desk lay a well worn reading book containing a dozen of Æsop's fables translated into Russian and profusely illustrated. It corresponded to an American 'Second Reader.'

There was a dormitory containing eight beds, and there was a wash-room, a dining-room, and a kitchen, the latter separate from the main building. Close at hand was a forge where the boys learned to work in iron, and a carpenter shop with a full set of tools and a turning lathe. The superintendent showed me several articles made by the pupils, including wooden spoons, forks, bowls, and cups, and he gave me for a souvenir a seal cut in pewter, bearing the word 'Fulyhelm' in Russian letters, and having a neatly turned handle.

The school is in operation ten months of each year. The superintendent said the children of the Russian peasants could attend if they wished, but very few did so. The teacher was a subordinate priest of the Eastern church. The expense of the establishment was paid by Government, with the design of making the boys useful in educating the Gilyaks.

The Gilyaks of the lower Amoor are pagans, and the attempts to Christianize them have not been very successful thus far. Their religion consists in the worship of idols and animals, and their priests or *shamans* correspond to the 'medicine man' of the American Indians. Among animals they revere the tiger, and I was told no instance was known of their killing one. The remains of a man killed by a tiger are buried without ceremony, but in the funerals of other persons the Gilyaks follow very nearly the Chinese custom. The bear is also sacred, but his sanctity does not preserve him from being killed.

BEAR IN PROCESSION.

In hunting this beast they endeavor to capture him alive; once taken and securely bound he is placed in a cage in the middle of a village, and there fattened upon fish. On fete-days he is led, or rather dragged, in procession, and of course is thoroughly muzzled and bound. Finally a great day arrives on which Bruin takes a prominent part in the festival by being killed. There are many superstitious ceremonies carefully observed on such occasions. The ears, jawbones, and skull of the bear are hung upon trees to ward off evil spirits, and the flesh is eaten, as it is supposed to make all who partake of it both fortunate and courageous.

I did not have the pleasure of witnessing any of these ursine festivals, but I saw several bear cages and looked upon a bear while he lunched on cold salmon. If the bear were more gentle in his manners he might become a household pet among the Gilyaks; but at present he is not in favor, especially where there are small children.

Ermines were formerly domesticated for catching rats, the high price of cats confining their possession to the wealthy. Cats have a half-religious character and are treated with great respect. Since the advent of the Russians the supply is very good. Before they came the Manjour merchants used to bring only male cats that could not trouble themselves about posterity. The price was sometimes a hundred roubles for a single mouser, and by curtailing the supply the Manjours kept the market good.

The Gilyaks, like nearly all the natives of Northern Asia, are addicted to Shamanism. The shaman combines the double function of priest and doctor, ministering to the physical and spiritual being at the same time. When a man is taken sick he is supposed to be attacked by an evil spirit and the shaman is called to practice exorcism. There is a distinct spirit for every disease and he must be propitiated in a particular manner. While practicing his profession the shaman contorts his body and dances like one insane, and howls worse than a dozen Kamchadale dogs. He is dressed in a fantastic manner and beats a tambourine during his performance. To accommodate himself to the different spirits he modulates his voice, changes the character of his dance, and alters his costume. Both doctor and patient are generally decked with wood-shavings while the work is going on.

Sometimes an effigy of the sick person is prepared, and the spirit is charmed from the man of flesh to the one of straw. The shaman induces him to take up lodgings in this effigy, and the success of his persuasion is apparent when the in-

PRACTICE OF MEDICINE.

valid recovers. If the patient dies the shaman declares that the spirit was one over which he had no control, but he does not hesitate to take pay for his services.

A Russian traveler who witnessed one of these exorcisms said that the shaman howled so fearfully that two Chinese merchants who were present out of curiosity fled in very terror. The gentleman managed to endure it to the end, but did not sleep well for a week afterward.

The Gilyaks believe in both good and evil spirits, but as the former do only good it is not thought necessary to pay them any attention. All the efforts are to induce the evil spirits not to act. They are supposed to have power over hunting, fishing, household affairs, and the health and well-being of animals and men.

The shamans possess great power over their superstitious subjects, and their commands are rarely refused. I heard of an instance wherein a native caught a fine sable and preserved the skin as a trophy. Very soon a man in the village fell ill. The shaman after practicing his art announced that the spirit commanded the sable skin to be worn by the doctor himself. The valuable fur was given up without hesitation. A Russian traveler stopping one night in a Gilyak house discovered in the morning that his sledge was missing, and was gravely told that the spirit had taken it.

In 1814 the small pox raged in one of the tribes living on the Kolyma river, and the deaths from it were numerous. The shamans practiced all their mysteries and invoked the spirits, but they could not stop the disease. Finally, after new invocations, they declared the evil spirits could not be appeased without the death of Kotschen, a chief of the tribe. This chief was so generally loved and respected that the people refused to obey the shamans. But as the malady made new progress, Kotschen magnanimously came forward and was stabbed by his own son.

In general the shamans are held in check by the belief that should they abuse their power they will be long and severely punished after death. This punishment is supposed to occur in a locality specially devoted to bad shamans. A good shaman who has performed wonderful cures receives after death a magnificent tomb to his memory.

The Russians think that with educated Gilyaks they can succeed in winning the natives to Christianity, especially when the missionaries are skilled in the useful arts of civilized life. Hence the school in Mihalofski, and it has so far succeeded well in the instruction of the boys. Russian and Gilyak children were working in the gardens in perfect harmony, and there was every indication of good feeling between natives and settlers.

CHAPTER XIII.

ON leaving Mihalofski we took the merchant and two priests and dropped them fifteen miles above, at a village where a church was being dedicated. The people were in their holiday costume and evidently awaited the priests. The church was pointed out, nestling in the forest just back of the river bank. It seemed more than large enough for the wants of the people, and was the second structure of the kind in a settlement ten years old. I have been told, but I presume not with literal truth, that a church is the first building erected in a Russian colony.

At night we ran until the setting of the moon, and then anchored. It is the custom to anchor or tie up at night unless there is a good moon or very clear starlight. An hour after we anchored the stars became so bright that we proceeded and ran until daylight, reaching Mariensk at two in the morning. I had designed calling upon two gentlemen and a lady at Mariensk, but it is not the fashion in Russia to make visits between midnight and daybreak. Borasdine had the claim of old acquaintance and waked a friend for a little talk.

This town is at the entrance of Keezee lake, and next to Nicolayevsk is the oldest Russian settlement on the lower Amoor. It was founded by the Russian American Company in the same year with Nicolayevsk, and was a trading post until the military occupation of the river. Difficulties of navigation have diminished its military importance, the principal rendezvous of this region being transferred to Sofyesk.

On an island opposite Mariensk is the trace of a fortification built by Stepanoff, a Russian adventurer who descended the Amoor in 1654. Stepanoff passed the winter at this point, and fortified himself to be secure against the natives. He seems to have engaged in a general business of filibustering on joint account of himself and his government. In the winter of his residence at this fortress he collected nearly five thousand sable skins as a tribute to his emperor—and himself.

Morning found us at Sofyesk taking a fresh supply of wood. This town was founded a few years ago, and has a decided appearance of newness. There is a wagon road along the shore of Keezee lake and across the hills to De Castries Bay. Light draft steamboats can go within twelve miles of De Castries. Surveys have been made with the design of connecting Keezee Lake and the Gulf of Tartary by a canal. A railway has also been proposed, but neither enterprise will be undertaken for many years. I passed an hour with the post commander, who had just received a pile of papers only two months from St. Petersburg, the mail having arrived the day before.

MANJOUR MERCHANT.

The steamer Telegraph lay at the landing when we arrived; among her passengers was a Manjour merchant, who possessed an intelligent face, quite in contrast with the sleepy Gilyaks. He wore the Manjour dress, consisting of wide trowsers and a long robe reaching to his heels; his shoes and hat were Chinese, and his robe was held at the waist with a silk cord. His hair was braided in the Chinese fashion, and he sported a long mustache but no beard.

A few versts above Sofyesk we met a Manjour merchant

evidently on a trading expedition. He had a boat about twenty-five feet long by eight wide, with a single mast carrying a square sail. His boat was full of boxes and bales and had a crew of four men. A small skiff was towed astern and another alongside. These Manjour merchants are quite enterprising, and engage in traffic for small profits and large risks when better terms are not attainable. Before the Russian occupation all the trade of the lower Amoor was in Manjour hands. Boats annually descended from San-Sin and Igoon bringing supplies for native use. Sometimes a merchant would spend five or six months making his round journey.

The merchants visited the villages on the route and bargained their goods for furs. There was an annual fair at the Gilyak village of Pul, below Mariensk, and this was made the center of commerce. The fair lasted ten days, and during that time Pul was a miniature Nijne Novgorod. Manjour and Chinese merchants met Japanese from the island of Sakhalin, Tunguse from the coast of the Ohotsk Sea, and others from the head waters of the Zeya and Amgoon. There were Gilyaks from the lower Amoor and various tribes of natives from the coast of Manjouria.

A dozen languages were spoken, and traffic was conducted in a patois of all the dialects. Cloth, powder, lead, knives, and brandy were exchanged for skins and furs. A gentleman who attended one of these fairs told me that the scene was full of interest and abounded in amusing incidents. Of late years the navigation of the Amoor has discontinued the fair of Pul. The Manjour traders still descend the river, but they are not as numerous as of yore.

With a good glass from the deck of the steamer I watched the native process of catching salmon. The fishing stations are generally, though not always, near the villages. The natives use gill nets and seines in some localities, and scoop nets in others. Sometimes they build a fence at right angles to the shore, and extend it twenty or thirty yards into the stream. This fence is fish-proof, except in a few places where holes are purposely left.

The natives lie in wait with skiffs and hand-nets and catch the salmon as they attempt to pass these holes. I watched a Gilyak taking fish in this way, and think he dipped them up at the rate of two a minute; when the fish are running well a skiff can be filled in a short time. Sometimes pens of wicker work are fixed to enclose the fish after they pass the holes in the fence. The salmon in this case has a practical illustration of life in general: easy to get into trouble but difficult to get out of it.

GILYAK MAN.

For catching sturgeon they use a circular net five feet across at the opening, and shaped like a shallow bag. One side of the mouth is fitted with corks and the other with weights of lead or iron. Two canoes in mid stream hold this net between them at right angles to the current. The sturgeon descending the river enters the trap, and the net proceeds of the enterprise are divided between the fishermen.

It requires vision or a guide to find a fishing station, but the sense of smell is quite sufficient to discover where salmon are dressed and cured. The offal from the fish creates an unpleasant stench and no effort is made to clear it away. The natives and their dogs do not consider the scent disagreeable and have no occasion to consult the tastes or smell of others. The first time I visited one of their fish-curing places I thought of the western city that had, after a freshet, 'forty-five distinct and different odors beside several wards to hear from.'

Above Mariensk the Amoor valley is often ten or twenty miles mide, enclosing whole labyrinths of islands, some of great extent. These islands are generally well out of water and not liable to overflow. Very few have the temporary appearance of the islands of the lower Mississippi. Here and there were small islands of slight elevation and covered with cottonwoods, precisely like those growing between Memphis and Cairo.

GILYAK WOMAN.

The banks of this part of the Amoor do not wash like the alluvial lands along the Mississippi and Missouri, but are more like the shores of the Ohio. They are generally covered with grass or bushes down to the edge of the water. There are no shifting sand-bars to perplex the pilot, but the channel remains with little change from year to year. I saw very little drift wood and heard no mention of snags. The general features of the scenery were much like those below Mihalofski.

The numerous islands and the labyrinth of channels often permit boats to pass each other without their captains knowing it. One day we saw a faint line of smoke across an island three or four miles wide; watching it closely I found it

NIGHT SCENE—GROUP OF PEASANTS.

was in motion and evidently came from a descending steamboat. On another occasion we missed in these channels a boat our captain was desirous of hailing. Once while General Monravieff was ascending the river he was passed by a courier who was bringing him important despatches.

The pilot steers with a chart of the river before him, and relies partly upon his experience and partly upon the delineated route. Sometimes channels used at high water are not navigable when the river is low, and some are favorable for descent but not for ascent. In general the pilotage is far more facile than on the Mississippi, and accidents are not frequent.

The peasants always came to the bank where we stopped, no matter what the hour. At one place where we took wood at night there was a picturesque group of twenty-five or thirty gathered around a fire; men and women talking, laughing, smoking, and watching the crew at work. The light of the fire poured full upon a few figures and brought them into strong relief, while others were half hidden in shadow. Of the men some wore coats of sheepskin, others Cossack coats of grey cloth; some had caps of faded cloth, and others Tartar caps of black sheepskin. Red beards, white beards, black beards, and smooth faces were played upon by the dancing flames. The women were in hoopless dresses, and held shawls over their heads in place of bonnets.

A hundred versts above Sofyesk the scenery changed. The mountains on the south bank receded from the river and were more broken and destitute of trees. Wide strips of lowland covered with forest intervened between the mountains and the shore. On the north the general character of the country remained. I observed a mountain, wooded to the top and sloping regularly, that had a curious formation at its summit. It was a perpendicular shaft resembling Bunker Hill Monument, and rising from the highest point of the mountain; it appeared of perfect symmetry, and seemed more like a work of art than of nature. On the same mountain, half way down its side, was a mass of rock with towers and buttresses that likened it to a cathedral. These formations were specially curious, as there were no more of the kind in the vicinity. Borasdine observed the rocks soon after I discovered them, and at first thought they were ancient monuments.

There were many birds along the shore. Very often we dispersed flocks of ducks and sent them flying over islands and forests to places of safety. Snipe were numerous, and so were several kinds of wading and swimming birds. Very often we saw high in air the wild geese of Siberia flying to the southward in those triangular squadrons that they form everywhere over the world. These birds winter in the south of China, Siam, and India, while they pass the summer north of the range of the Yablonoi mountains.

The birds of the Amoor belong generally to the species found in the same latitudes of Europe and America, but there are some birds of passage that are natives of Southern Asia, Japan, the Philippine Islands, and even South Africa and Australia. Seven-tenths of the birds of the Amoor are found in Europe, two-tenths in Siberia, and one-tenth in regions further south. Some birds belong more properly to America, such as the Canada woodcock and the water ouzel; and there are several birds common to the east and west coasts of the Pacific. The naturalists who came here at the Russian occupation found two Australian birds on the Amoor, two from tropical and sub-tropical Africa, and one from Southern Asia.

The number of stationary birds is not great, in consequence of the excessive cold in winter. Mr. Maack enumerates thirty-nine species that dwell here the entire year. They include eagles, hawks, jays, magpies, crows, grouse, owls, woodpeckers, and some others. The birds of passage generally arrive at the end of April or during May, and leave in September or October.

It is a curious fact that they come later to Nicolayevsk than to the town of Yakutsk, nine degrees further north. This is due to differences of climate and the configuration of the country. The lower Amoor is remarkable for its large quantities of snow, and at Nicolayevsk it remains on the ground till the end of May. South of the lower Amoor are the Shanalin mountains, which arrest the progress of birds. On the upper Amoor and in Trans-Baikal very little snow falls, and there are no mountains of great height.

The day after leaving Sofyesk I observed a native propelling a boat by pulling both oars together. On my expressing surprise my companion said:

"We have passed the country of the Gilyaks who pull their oars alternately, and entered that of the Mangoons and Goldees. The manner of rowing distinguishes the Gilyaks from all others."

The Mangoons, Goldees, and Gilyaks differ in much the same way that the tribes of American Indians are different. They are all of Tungusian or Mongolian stock, and have many traits and words in common. Their features have the same general characteristics and their languages are as much alike as those of a Cheyenne and Comanche. Each people has its peculiar customs, such as the style of dress, the mode of constructing a house, or rowing a boat. All are pagans and indulge in Shamanism, but each tribe has forms of its own. All are fishers and hunters, their principal support being derived from the river.

The Goldee boat was so much like a Gilyak one that I could see no difference. There was no opportunity to examine it closely, as we passed at a distance of two or three hundred feet.

Besides their boats of wood the Goldees make canoes of birch bark, quite broad in the middle and coming to a point at both ends. In general appearance these canoes resemble those of the Penobscot and Canadian Indians. The native sits in the middle of his canoe and propels himself with a double-bladed oar, which he dips into the water with regular alternations from one side to the other. The canoes are flat bottomed and very easy to overturn. A canoe is designed to carry but one man, though two can be taken in an emergency. When a native sitting in one of them spears a fish he moves only his arm and keeps his body motionless.

At the Russian village of Gorin there was an Ispravnik who had charge of a district containing nineteen villages with about fifteen hundred inhabitants. At Gorin the river is two or three miles wide, and makes a graceful bend. We landed near a pile of ash logs awaiting shipment to Nicolayevsk. The Ispravnik was kind enough to give me the model of a Goldee canoe about eighteen inches long and complete in all particulars. It was made by one Anaka Katonovitch, chief of an ancient Goldee family, and authorized by the emperor of China to wear the uniform of a mandarin. The canoe was neatly formed, and reflected favorably upon the skill of its designer. I boxed it carefully and sent it to Nicolayevsk for shipment to America.

The Ispravnik controlled the district between Habarofka and Sofyesk on both banks of the river, his power extending over native and Russian alike. He said that this part of the Amoor valley was very fertile, the yield of wheat and rye being fifteen times the seed. The principal articles cultivated were wheat, rye, hemp, and garden vegetables, and he thought the grain product of 1866 in his district would be thirty thousand poods of wheat and the same of rye. With a population of fifteen hundred in a new country, this result was very good.

The Goldees do not engage in agriculture as a business. Now and then there was a small garden, but it was of very little importance. Since the Russian occupation the natives have changed their allegiance from China to the 'White Czar,' as they call the Muscovite emperor. Formerly they were much oppressed by the Manjour officials, who displayed great rapacity in collecting tribute. It was no unusual occurrence for a native to be tied up and whipped to compel him to bring out all his treasures. The Goldees call the Manjours 'rats,' in consequence of their greediness and destructive powers.

The Goldees are superior to the Gilyaks in numbers and intelligence, and the Manjours of Igoon and vicinity are in turn superior to the Goldees. The Chinese are more civilized than the Manjours, and call the latter 'dogs.' The Manjours take revenge by applying the epithet to the Goldees, and these transfer it to Mangoons and Gilyaks. The Mangoons are not in large numbers, and live along the river between the Gilyaks and Goldees. Many of the Russian officials include them with the latter, and the captain of the Ingodah was almost unaware of their existence.

A peculiar kind of fence employed by the Russian settlers on this part of the Amoor attracted my attention. Stakes were driven into the ground a foot apart and seven feet high. Willow sticks were then woven between these stakes in a sort of basket work. The fence was impervious to any thing larger than a rat, and no sensible man would attempt climbing it, unless pursued by a bull or a sheriff, as the upper ends of the sticks were very sharp and about as convenient to sit upon as a row of harrow-teeth.

It reminded me of a fence in an American village where I once lived, that an enterprising fruit-grower had put around his orchard,—a structure of upright pickets, and each picket armed with a nail in the top. One night four individuals bent on stealing apples, were confronted by the owner and a bull-dog and forced to surrender or leap the fence. Three of them were "treed" by the dog; the fourth sprang over the fence, but left the seat of his trousers and the rear section of his shirt, the latter bearing in indelible ink the name of the wearer. The circumstantial evidence was so strong against him that he did not attempt an alibi, and he was unable to sit down for nearly a fortnight.

CHAPTER XIV.

I TOOK the first opportunity to enter a Goldee house and study the customs of the people. A Goldee dwelling for permanent habitation has four walls and a roof. The sides and ends are of hewn boards or small poles made into a close fence, which is generally double and has a space six or eight inches wide filled with grass and leaves. Inside and out the dwelling is plastered with mud, and the roofs are thatch or bark held in place by poles and stones. Sometimes they are entirely of poles. The doors are of hewn plank, and can be fastened on the inside.

The dwellings are from fifteen to forty feet square, according to the size of the family. In one I found a grandfather and his descendants; thirty persons at least. There are usually two windows, made of fish skin or thin paper over lattices. Some windows were closed with mats that could be rolled up or lowered at will.

The fire-place has a deep pan or kettle fixed over it, and there is room for a pot suspended from a rafter. Around the room is a divan, or low bench of boards or wicker work, serving as a sofa by day and a bed at night. When dogs are kept in the house a portion of the divan belongs to them, and among the Mangoons there is a table in the center specially reserved for feeding the dogs.

I found the floors of clay, smooth and hard. Near the fire-place a little fire of charcoal is kept constantly burning in a shallow hole. Pipes are lighted at this fire, and small things can be warmed over it. Household articles were hung upon the rafters and cross beams, and there was generally a closet for table ware and other valuables. The cross-beams were sufficiently close to afford stowage room for considerable property. Fish-nets, sledges, and canoes were the most bulky articles I saw there.

Part of one wall was reserved for religious purposes, and covered with bear-skulls and bones, horse-hair, wooden idols, and pieces of colored cloth. Occasionally there were badly-painted pictures, purchased from the Chinese at enormous prices. Sometimes poles shaped like small idols are fixed before the houses.

A Goldee house is warmed by means of wooden pipes under the divan and passing out under ground to a chimney ten or fifteen feet from the building. Great economy is shown in using fuel and great care against conflagrations. I was not able to stand erect in any Goldee houses I entered.

Like all people of the Mongolian race, the natives pretended to have little curiosity. When we landed at their villages many continued their occupations and paid no attention to strangers. Above Gorin a Goldee gentleman took me into his house, where a woman placed a mat on the divan and motioned me to a seat. The man tendered me a piece of dried fish, which I ate out of courtesy to my hosts. Several children gathered to look at me, but retired on a gesture from *pater familias*. I am not able to say if the fact that my eyes were attracted to a pretty girl of seventeen had anything to do with the dispersal of the group. Curiosity dwells in Mongol breasts, but the Asiatics, like our Indians, consider its exhibition in bad taste.

Outside this man's house there were many scaffoldings for drying fish. A tame eagle was fastened with a long chain to one of the scaffolds; he was supposed to keep other birds away and was a pet of his owner. There were many dogs walking or lying around loose, while others were tied to the posts that supported the scaffolds.

The dogs of the Goldees are very intelligent. One morning Mr. Maack missed his pots which he had left the night before full of meat. After some search they were found in the woods near the village, overturned and empty. Several dogs were prowling about and had evidently committed the theft. Fearing to be interrupted at their meal they carried the pots where they could eat at leisure.

While steaming up the river I frequently saw temporary dwellings of poles and bark like our Indian wigwams. These were at the fishing stations upon sand bars or low islands. The afternoon following our departure from Gorin I counted about thirty huts, or *yourts*, on one island, and more than fifty boats on the river.

For half a mile the scene was animated and interesting. Some boats were near the shore, their inmates hauling seines or paddling up or down the stream. In one heavily laden boat there was one man steering with a paddle. Four men towed the craft against the current, and behind it was another drawn by six dogs. Out in the river were small skiffs and canoes in couples, engaged in holding nets across the direction of the current. The paddles were struck regularly and slowly to prevent drifting down the stream.

TEN MILES AN HOUR.

One boat with two men rowing and another steering attempted a race with the steamer and fairly passed us, though we were making ten miles an hour. All these natives are very skillful in managing their boats.

When we passed near a boat we were greeted with '*Mendow, mendow*,' the Mongol word of welcome. Sometimes we were hailed with the Russian salutation of '*sdrastveteh.*' In one boat I saw a Goldee belle dressed with considerable taste and wearing a ring in the cartilage of her nose. How powerful are the mandates of Fashion! This damsel would scorn to wear her pendants after the manner of Paris and New York, while the ladies of Broadway and the Boulevards would equally reject the Goldee custom.

The natives of this part of the Amoor have a three-pronged spear like a Neptune's trident, and handle it with much dexterity. The spear-head is attached to a long line, and when a fish is struck the handle is withdrawn. The fish runs out the line, which is either held in the hand or attached to a bladder floating on the water.

Ropes and nets are made from hemp and the common sting nettle, the latter being preferred. The nettle-stalks are soaked in water and then dried and pounded till the fibres separate. Ropes and cords are equal to those of civilized manufacture, though sometimes not quite as smooth. Thread for sewing and embroidery comes from China, and is purchased of Manjour traders.

The night after we left Gorin the boat took wood at the village of Doloe. It was midnight when we arrived, and as I walked through the village nearly all the inhabitants were sleeping. The only perambulating resident was very drunk and manifested a desire to embrace me, but as I did not know his language and could not claim relationship I declined the honor. Near the river there was a large building for government stores and a smaller one for the men guarding it. A few hundred yards distant there was a Goldee village, and for want of something better Borasdine proposed that we should call on one of its inhabitants. We took a Russian peasant to guide and introduce us, our credentials and passports having been left on the steamer.

As we approached the first house we were greeted by at least a dozen dogs. They barked on all keys and our guide thought it judicious to provide himself with a stick; but I must do the brutes the justice to say that they made no attempt at dentistry upon our legs. Some of them were large enough to consume ten pounds of beef at a sitting, and some too small for any but ornamental purposes.

The door was not locked and the peasant entered without warning, while we stood outside among the dogs. Our guide aroused the chief of the establishment and made a light; a strip of birch bark was used, and it took a good deal of blowing on the fire coals before a flame was produced. When we entered we found the proprietor standing in a short garment and rubbing his oblique eyes to get himself thoroughly awake. Near the place he had vacated, the lady of the house was huddled under a coverlid about as large as a postage stamp, and did not appear encumbered with much clothing. Three or four others had waked and made some attempt to cover themselves. At least a dozen remained asleep and lay in a charming condition of nudity. The Goldee houses are heated to a high degree, and their inmates sleep without clothing. The delay in admitting us was to permit the head of the house to dress in reception costume, which he did by putting on his shirt.

After wishing this aboriginal a long and happy life, and thanking him for his courtesy, we departed. I bumped my head against the rafters both in entering and leaving, and found considerable difference between the temperature in the house and out of it. The peasant offered to guide us to visit more Goldees, but we returned to the boat and retired to sleep.

The Russian peasants and the natives live in perfect harmony and are of mutual advantage and assistance. The peasant furnishes the native with salt, flour, and other things, while the latter catches fish enough for both. Each has a peaceable disposition, and I was told that quarrels were of rare occurrence.

The Chinese call the natives *Yu-pi-ta-tze*, which in English means 'wearers of fish-skins.' I saw many garments of fish-skins, most of them for summer use. The operation of preparing them is quite simple. The skins are dried and after-

A GOLDEE HOUSE

ward pounded, the blows making them flexible and removing the scales. This done they are ready to be sewn into garments.

A coat of this material embroidered and otherwise decorated is far from ugly, and sheds water like India rubber. Fish-skins are used in making sails for boats and for the windows of houses. A Russian who had worn a Goldee coat said it was both warm and waterproof, and he suggested that it would be well to adopt fish-skin garments in America.

The Goldees and Mangoons practice Shamanism in its general features, and have a few customs peculiar to themselves. At a Goldee village I saw a man wearing a wooden representation of an arm, and learned that it is the practice to wear amulets to cure disease, the amulet being shaped like the part affected. A lame person carries a small leg of wood, an individual suffering from dyspepsia a little stomach, and so on through a variety of disorders. A hypochondriac who thought himself afflicted all over had covered himself with these wooden devices, and looked like a museum of anatomy on its travels. I thought the custom not unknown in America, as I had seen ladies in New York wearing hearts of coral and other substances on their watch-chains. Evidently the fashion comes from l'Amour.

THE HYPOCHONDRIAC.

The morning after leaving Doloe we had a rain-storm with high wind that blew us on a lee shore. The river was four or five miles wide where the gale caught us, and the banks on both sides were low. The islands in this part of the river were numerous and extensive. At one place there are three channels, each a mile and a half wide and all navigable. From one bank to the other straight across the islands is a distance of nineteen miles.

The wind and weather prevented our making much progress on that day; as the night was cloudy we tied up near a Russian village and economised the darkness by taking wood. At a peasant's house near the landing four white-headed children were taking their suppers of bread and soup under the supervision of their mother. Light was furnished from an apparatus like a fishing jack attached to the wall; every few minutes the woman fed it with a splinter of pine wood. Very few of the peasants on the Amoor can afford the expense of candles, and as they rarely have fire-places they must burn pine splinters in this way.

Along the Amoor nearly every peasant house contains hundreds, and I think thousands, of cockroaches. They are quiet in the day but do not fail to make themselves known at night. The table where these children were eating swarmed with them, and I can safely say there were five dozen on a space three feet square. They ran everywhere about the premises except into the fire. Walls, beds, tables, and floors were plentifully covered with these disagreeable insects. The Russians do not appear to mind them, and probably any one residing in that region would soon be accustomed to their presence. Occasionally they are found in bread and soup, and do not improve the flavor.

Life on the steamboat was a trifle monotonous, but I found something new daily. Our steward (who is called *Boofetchee* in Russian) brought me water for washing when I rose in the morning, and the samovar with tea when I was dressed. Borasdine rose about the time I did and joined me at tea. Then we had breakfast of beef and bread with potatoes about eleven or twelve o'clock, and dinner at six.

The intervals between meals were variously filled. I watched the land, talked with Borasdine, read, wrote, smoked, and contemplated the steward, but never imagined him a disguised angel. I looked at the steerage passengers and the crew, and think their faces are pretty well fixed in memory.

Had I only been able to converse in Russian I should have found much more enjoyment. As for the cook it is needless to say that I never penetrated the mysteries of his realm. Little games of cards were played daily by all save myself; I used to look on occasionally but never learned the games.

One of the Russian games at cards is called poker, and is not much unlike that seductive amusement so familiar to the United States. Whence it came I could not ascertain, but it was probably taken there by some enterprising American. Some years ago a western actor who was able to play Hamlet, Richelieu, Richard III., Claude Melnotte, and draw-poker, made his way to Australia, where he delighted the natives with his dramatic genius. But though he drew crowded houses his cash box was empty, as the treasurer stole the most of the receipts. He did not discharge him as there was little prospect of finding a better man in that country; but he taught him draw-poker, borrowed five dollars to start the game, and then every morning won from the treasurer the money taken at the door on the previous night.

As we approached the Ousuree there was a superior magnificence in the forest. The trees on the southern bank grew to an enormous size in comparison with those lower down the river. Naturalists say that within a short distance in this region may be found all the trees peculiar to the Amoor. Some of them are three or four feet in diameter and very tall and straight. The elm and larch attain the greatest size, while the ash and oak are but little inferior. The cork-tree is two feet through, and the maackia—a species of oak with a brown, firm wood—grows to the diameter of a foot or more.

In summer the foliage is so dense that the sun's rays hardly penetrate, and there is a thick 'chapparel' that makes locomotion difficult. Just below the Ousuree the settlers had removed the under growth over a small space and left the trees appearing taller than ever. In a great deal of travel I have never seen a finer forest than on this part of the Amoor. I do not remember anything on the lower Mississippi that could surpass it.

Tigers and leopards abound in these forests, and bears are more numerous than agreeable. Occasionally one of these animals dines upon a Goldee, but the custom is not in favor with the natives. It is considered remarkable that the Bengal tiger, belonging properly to a region nearer the equator, should range so far north. On some of its excursions it reaches 53° North Latitude, and feeds upon reindeer and sables. The valley of the Amoor is the only place in the world outside of a menagerie where all these animals are found together. The tropical ones go farther north and the Arctic ones farther south than elsewhere.

It is the same with the vegetable kingdom. The mahogany and cork tree grow here, and the bark of the latter is largely used by the natives. On the slopes of the mountains a few miles away are the Siberian pine, the Ayan spruce, and here and there a larch tree. Cedars and fir trees are abundant and grow to a great size. The whole appearance of the region is one of luxuriance and fertility.

The mouth of the Ousuree is a mile wide, and the stream is said to be magnificent through its whole length. Its sources are in Latitude 44°, and its length is about five hundred miles. While I was at Nicolayevsk Admiral Fulyelm said to me:

"I have just returned from a voyage on the Ousuree. It is one of the loveliest rivers I ever saw. The valley bears such a resemblance to a settled country with alternate parks and open country that I almost looked to see some grand old mansion at every bend of the stream."

A little past noon we sighted the town and military post of Habarofka at the mouth of the Ousuree. It stands on a promontory overlooking both rivers, and presents a pleasing appearance from the Amoor. The portion first visible included the telegraph office and storehouses, near which a small steamer was at anchor. A Manjour trading boat was at the bank, its crew resting on shore; a piece of canvas had been spread on the ground and the men were lounging upon it. One grave old personage, evidently the owner of the boat, waved his hand toward us in a dignified manner, but we could not understand his meaning.

Coming to shore we narrowly missed running over a Gol-dee boat that crossed our track. Our wheel almost touched the stern of the craft as we passed it, but the occupants appeared no wise alarmed. Two women were rowing and a man steering, while a man and a boy were idle in the bow. A baby, strapped into a shallow cradle, lay in the bottom of the boat near the steersman. The young Mongol was holding his thumb in his mouth and appeared content with his position.

The town was in a condition of rawness like a western city in its second year; there was one principal street and several smaller ones, regularly laid out. As in all the Russian settlements on the Amoor the houses were of logs and substantially built. Passing up the principal street we found a store, where we purchased a quantity of canned fruit, meats, and pickles.

These articles were from Boston, New York, and Baltimore, and had American labels. The pictures of peaches, strawberries, and other fruits printed on the labels were a great convenience to the Russian clerk who served us. He could not read English, but understood pictorial representations. On the boat we gave the cans to the steward, to be opened when we ordered. The pictures were especially adapted to this youth as he read no language whatever, including his own.

"NONE FOR JOE."

On one occasion a quantity of devilled turkey was put up in cans and sent to the Amoor, and the label was beautified with a picture of His Satanic Majesty holding a turkey on the end of a fork. The natives supposed that the devil was in the cans and refused to touch them. The supply was sent back to Nicolayevsk, where it was eaten by the American merchants.

Accompanying Borasdine I called upon the officer in command. We were ushered through two or three small rooms into the principal apartment, which contained a piano of French manufacture. Three or four officers and as many ladies enabled us to pass an hour very pleasantly till the steam whistle recalled us, but we did not leave until two hours after going on board. Two or three men had been allowed on shore and were making themselves comfortable in a *lafka*. Two others went for them, but as they did not return within an hour the police went to search for both parties. When all were brought to the steamer it was difficult to say if the last were not first—in intoxication.

Several passengers left us at Habarofka, among them the black eyed girl that attracted the eyes of one or two passengers in the cabin; as we departed she stood on the bank and waved us an adieu. In the freight taken at this point there were fifteen chairs of local manufacture; they were piled in the cabin and did not leave us much space, when we considered the number and size of the fleas. On my first night on the Ingodah the fleas did not disturb me as I came after visiting hours and was not introduced. On all subsequent nights they were persevering and relentless; I was bitten until portions of my body appeared as if recovering from a Polynesian tattoo. They used to get inside my under clothing by some mysterious way and when there they walked up and down like sentries on duty and bit at every other step. It was impossible to flee from them, and they appointed their breakfasts and lunches at times most inconvenient to myself.

If I were Emperor of Russia I would issue a special edict expelling fleas from my dominions and ordering that the labor expended in scratching should be devoted to agriculture or the mechanic arts. I suggested that the engines should be removed from the Ingodah and a treadmill erected for the fleas to propel the boat. There have been exhibitions where fleas were trained to draw microscopic coaches and perform other fantastic tricks; but whatever their ability I would wager that the insects on that steamboat could not be outdone in industry by any other fleas in the world.

One of my standard amusements was to have a grand hunt for these lively insects just before going to bed, and I have no doubt that the exercise assisted to keep me in good health. I used to remove my clothing, which I turned inside out and shook very carefully. Then I bathed from head to foot in some villainous brandy that no respectable flea would or could endure; after this ablution was ended, I donned my garments, wrapped in my blanket, and proceeded to dream that I was a hen with thirteen chickens, and doomed to tear up an acre of ground for their support.

CHAPTER XV.

WHEN I rose in the morning after leaving Habarofka the steward was ready with his usual pitcher of water and basin. In Siberia they have a novel way of performing ablutions. They rarely furnish a wash-bowl, but in place of it bring a large basin of brass or other metal. If you wish to wash hands or face the basin is placed where you can lean over it. A servant pours from a pitcher into your hands, and if you are skillful you catch enough water to moisten your face. Frequently the peasants have a water-can attached to the wall of the house in some out-of-the-way locality. The can has a valve in the bottom opened from below like a trap-door in a roof. By lifting a brass pin that projects from this valve one can fill his hands with water without the aid of a servant.

While I was arranging my toilet the steward pointed out of the cabin window and uttered the single word "Kitie"—emphasizing the last syllable. I looked where he directed and had my first view of the Chinese empire.

"Kitie" is the Russian name of China, and is identical with the Cathay of Marco Polo and other early travelers. I could not see any difference between Kitie on one hand and Russia on the other; there were trees and bushes, grass and sand, just as on the opposite shore. In the region immediately above the Ousuree there are no mountains visible from the river, but only the low banks on either hand covered with trees and bushes. Here and there were open spaces appearing as if cleared for cultivation. With occasional sand bars and low islands, and the banks frequently broken and shelving, the resemblance to the lower Mississippi was almost perfect.

Mr. Maack says of this region:

"In the early part of the year when the yellow blossoms of the Lonicera chrysantha fill the air with their fragrance, when the syringas bloom and the Hylonecon bedecks large tracts with a bright golden hue, when corydales, violets, and pasque flowers are open, the forests near the Ousuree may bear comparison in variety of richness and coloring with the open woods of the prairie country. Later in the year, the scarcity of flowers is compensated by the richness of the herbage, and after a shower of rain delicious perfumes are wafted towards us from the tops of the walnut and cork trees."

A little past noon we touched at the Russian village of Petrovsky. At this place the river was rapidly washing the banks, and I was told that during three years nearly four hundred feet in front of the village had been carried away. The single row of houses forming the settlement stands with a narrow street between it and the edge of the bank. The whole population, men, women, and children, turned out to meet us. The day was cool and the men were generally in their sheepskin coats. The women wore gowns of coarse cloth of different colors, and each had a shawl over her head. Some wore coats of sheepskin like those of the men, and several were barefooted. Two women walked into the river and stood with utter nonchalance where the water was fifteen inches deep. I immersed my thermometer and found it indicated 51°.

Walking on shore I was nearly overturned by a small hog running between my legs. The brute, with a dozen of his companions, had pretty much his own way at Petrovsky, and after this introduction I was careful about my steps. These hogs are modelled something like blockade runners: with great length, narrow beam, and light draft. They are capable of high speed, and would make excellent time if pursued by a bull-dog or pursuing a swill-bucket.

A peasant told us there were wild geese in a pond near by,

and as the boat remained an hour or more to take wood, Borasdine and I improvised a hunting excursion. It proved in every sense a wild-goose chase, as the birds flew away be-

RECEPTION AT PETROVSKY.

fore we were in shooting distance. Not wishing to return empty-handed we purchased two geese a few hundred yards from the village, and assumed an air of great dignity as we approached the boat. We subsequently ascertained that the same geese were offered to the steward for half the price we paid.

Just above Petrovsky we passed the steamer Amoor, which left Nicolayevsk a week before us with three barges in tow. With such a heavy load her progress was very slow. Barges on the Amoor river are generally built of iron, and nearly as large as the steamers. They are not towed alongside as on the Mississippi, but astern. The rope from the steamer to the first barge is about two hundred feet long, and the barges follow each other at similar distances. Looking at this steamer struggling against the current and impeded by the barges, brought to mind Pope's needless Alexandrine:

"That, like a wounded snake, drags its slow length along."

Each barge has a crew, subordinate, of course, to the captain of the tow-boat. This crew steers the barge in accordance with the course of the steamer, looks after its welfare, and watches over the freight on board. In case it fastens on a sand bar the crew remains with it, and sometimes has the pleasure of wintering there. The barge is decked like a ship, and has two or three hatchways for receiving and discharging freight. Over each hatchway is a derrick that appears at a distance not unlike a mast.

Above Petrovsky the banks generally retain their level character on the Russian side. Cliffs and hills frequently extend to the water on the Chinese shore, most of the land being covered with forests of foliferous trees. Some of the mountains are furrowed along their sides as regularly as if turned with a gigantic plow. Near the villages of Ettoo and Dyrki the cliffs are precipitous and several hundred feet high; at their base the water is deep and the current very strong. On the north shore the plain is generally free from tall trees, but has a dense growth of grass and bushes. Sand-banks are frequent, and the islands are large and numerous.

This region is much frequented during the fishing season, and the huts of the natives, their canoes and drying scaffolds are quite numerous. There are but few fixed villages, the country not being desirable for permanent habitation. Near one village there was a gently sloping hillside about a mile square with a forest of oak so scattered that it had a close resemblance to an American apple-orchard.

The treaty between Russia and China, fixing the boundaries between the two empires, contains a strange oversight. Dated on the 14th of November, 1860, it says:

"Henceforth the eastern frontier between the two empires shall commence from the junction of the rivers Shilka and Argoon, and will follow the course of the River Amoor to the junction of the river Ousuree with the latter. The land on the left bank (to the north) of the River Amoor belongs to the empire of Russia, and the territory on the right bank (to the south) to the junction of the River Ousuree, to the empire of China."

The treaty further establishes the boundaries from the

mouth of the Ousuree to the sea of Japan, and along the western region toward Central Asia. It provides for commissioners to examine the frontier line.

It declares that trade shall be free of duty along the entire line, and removes all commercial restrictions. It gives the merchants of Kiachta the right of going to Pekin, Oorga, and Kalgan; allows a Russian consulate at Oorga, and permits Russian merchants to travel anywhere in China. It annuls former treaties, and establishes a postal arrangement between Pekin and Kiachta.

I presume the oversight in the treaty was on the part of the Chinese, as the Russians are too shrewd in diplomacy to omit any point of advantage. Nothing is said about the land in the Amoor. "The land on the north bank is Russian, and on the south bank Chinese." What is to be the nationality of the islands in the river? Some of them are large enough to hold a population of importance, or be used as the sites of fortifications. There are duchies and principalities in Europe of less territorial extent than some islands of the Amoor.

When Russia desires them she will doubtless extend her protection, and I observed during my voyage that several islands were occupied by Russian settlers for hay-cutting and other purposes. Why could not an enterprising man of destiny like the grey-eyed Walker or unhappy Maximilian penetrate the Amoor and found a new government on an island that nobody owns? Quite likely his adventure would result like the conquests of Mexico and Nicaragua, but this probability should not cause a man of noble blood to hesitate.

Below the Ousuree the Russian villages were generally on the south bank of the river, but after passing that stream I found them all on the north side. The villages tributary to China consisted only of the settlements of Goldees and Mangoons, or their temporary fishing stations. The Chinese empire contains much territory still open to colonization, and I imagine that it would be to the interest of the Celestial government to scatter its population more evenly over its dominions. Possibly it does not wish to send its subjects into regions that may hereafter fall into the hands of the emperor of Russia. There is a great deal of land in Manjouria adapted to agriculture, richly timbered and watered, but containing a very small population. Millions of people could find homes where there are now but a few thousands.

A Russian village and military post seventeen miles below the mouth of the Songaree is named Michael Semenof, in honor of the Governor General of Eastern Siberia. We landed before the commandant's house, where two iron guns pointed over the river in the direction of China. However threatening they appeared I was informed they were unserviceable for purposes of war, and only employed in firing salutes. A military force was maintained there, and doubtless kept a sharp watch over the Chinese frontier.

The soldiers appeared under good sanitary regulations, and the quarters of the Commandant indicated an appreciation of the comforts of life. The peasants that gathered on the bank were better dressed than those of Petrovsky and other villages. The town is on a plain covered with a scattered growth of oaks. Below this place the wood furnished us was generally ash or poplar; here it was oak, somewhat gnarly and crooked, but very good for steamboat fuel. One design of the colonization of the Amoor is to furnish a regular supply of wood to the government steamers. The peasants cut the wood and bring it to the bank of the river. Private steamers pay cash for what they purchase; the captains of the government boats gives vouchers for the wood they take, and these vouchers are redeemed at the end of the season of navigation. About sixty thousand roubles worth of wood is consumed annually by government, and twelve thousand on private account.

While the boat took wood Borasdine and I resumed our hunting, he carrying a shot-gun and I an opera glass; with this division of labor we managed to bag a single snipe and kill another, which was lost in the river. My opera glass was of assistance in finding the birds in the grass; they were quite abundant almost within rifle-shot of town, and it seemed strange that the officers of the post did not devote their leisure to snipe hunting.

Our snipe was cooked for dinner, and equalled any I ever saw at Delmonico's. We had a wild goose at the same meal, and after a careful trial I can pronounce the Siberian goose an edible bird. He is not less cunning than wild geese elsewhere, but with all his adroitness he frequently falls into the hands of man and graces his dinner table.

ARMED AND EQUIPPED.

On the northern horizon, twenty or thirty miles from Michael Semenof, there is a range of high and rugged mountains. As we left the town, near the close of day, the clouds broke in the west and the sunshine lighted up these mountains and seemed to lift them above their real position. With the red and golden colors of the clouds; the lights and shadows of the mountains; the yellow forests of autumn, and the green plains near the river; the stillness broken only by our own motion or the rippling of the river, the scene was 'most fair to look upon.' I have never seen sunsets more beautiful than those of the Amoor.

I rose early in the morning to look at the mouth of the Songaree. Under a cloudy moon I could distinguish little beyond the outline of the land and the long low water line where the Amoor and Songaree sweep at right angles from their respective valleys. Even though it was not daylight I could distinguish the line of separation, or union, between the waters of the two streams, just as one can observe it where the Missouri and Mississippi unite above Saint Louis. I would have given much to see this place in full daylight, but the fates willed it otherwise.

This river is destined at some time to play an important part in Russian and Chinese diplomacy. At present it is entirely controlled by China, but it appears on all the late maps of Eastern Siberia with such minuteness as to indicate that the Russians expect to obtain it before long. Formerly the Chinese claimed the Songaree as the real Amoor, and based their argument on the fact that it follows the general course of the united stream and carried a volume of water as large as the other. They have now abandoned this claim, which the Russians are entirely willing to concede. Once the fact established that the Songaree is the real Amoor, the Russians would turn to the treaty which gives them "all the land north of the Amoor." Their next step would be to occupy the best part of Manjouria, which would be theirs by the treaty.

By far the larger portion of Manjouria is drained by the Songaree and its tributaries. The sources of this river are in the Shanalin mountains, that separate Corea from Manjouria, and are ten or twelve thousand feet high. They resemble the Sierra Nevadas in having a lake twelve miles in circumference as high in air as Lake Tahoe. The affluents of the Songaree run through a plateau in some places densely wooded while in others it has wide belts of prairie and marshy ground. A large part of the valley consists of low, fertile lands, through which the river winds with very few impediments to navigation.

Very little is known concerning the valley, but it is said to be pretty well peopled and to produce abundantly. M. De la Bruniere when traveling to the country of the Gilyaks in 1845, crossed this valley, and found a dense population along the river, but a smaller one farther inland. The principal cities are Kirin and Sansin on the main stream, and Sit-si-gar on the Nonni, one of its tributaries. The Songaree is navigable to Kirin, about thirteen hundred versts from the Amoor,

12*

and it is thought the Nonni can be ascended to Sit-si-gar. The three cities have each a population of about a hundred thousand.

According to the treaty of 1860 Russian merchants with proper passports may enter Chinese territory, but no more than two hundred can congregate in one locality. Russian merchants have been to all the cities in Manjouria, but the difficulties of travel are not small. The Chinese authorities are jealous of foreigners, and restrict their movements as much as possible.

The Russians desire to open the Songaree to commerce, but the Chinese prefer seclusion. A month before my visit a party ascended the river to ascertain its resources. A gentleman told me the Chinese used every means except actual force to hinder the progress of the steamer and prevent the explorers seeing much of the country. Whenever any one went on shore the people crowded around in such numbers that nothing else could be seen. Almost the whole result of the expedition was to ascertain that the river was navigable and its banks well peopled.

In the dim light of morning I saw some houses at the junction of the rivers, and learned they were formerly the quarters of a Manjour guard. Until 1864 a military force, with two or three war junks, was kept at the mouth of the Songaree to prevent Russian boats ascending. Mr. Maximowicz, the naturalist, endeavored in 1859 to explore the river as far as the mouth of the Nonni. Though his passport was correct, the Manjour guard ordered him to stop, and when he insisted upon proceeding the Celestial raised his matchlock. Maximowicz exhibited a rifle and revolver and forced a passage.

He was not molested until within forty miles of San-Sin, when the natives came out with flails, but prudently held aloof on seeing the firearms in the boat. Finding he could not safely proceed, the gentleman turned about when only twenty-five miles below the city.

After passing the Songaree I found a flat country with wide

prairies on either side of the river. In the forest primeval the trees were dense and large, and where no trees grew the grass was luxuriant. The banks were alluvial and evidently washed by the river during times of freshet. There were many islands, but the windings of the river were more regular than farther down. I saw no native villages and only two or three fishing stations. Those acquainted with the river say its banks have fewer inhabitants there than in any other portion.

On the Russian shore there were only the villages established by government, but notwithstanding its lack of population, the country was beautiful. With towns, plantations, and sugar-mills, it would greatly resemble the region between Baton Rouge and New Orleans. I could perceive that the volume of the river was much diminished above its junction with the Songaree.

At long and rare intervals snags were visible, but not in the navigable channel. We took soundings with a seven foot pole attached to a rope fastened to the rail of the boat. A man threw the pole as if he were spearing fish, and watched the depth to which it descended. The depth of water was shouted in a monotonous drawl. "*Sheiste; sheiste polivinnay; sem; sem polivinnay;*" and so on through the various quantities indicated. I thought the manner more convenient than that in use on some of our western rivers.

While smoking a cigar on the bridge I was roused by the cry of "*tigre! tigre!*" from Borasdine. I looked to where he pointed on the Chinese shore and could see an animal moving slowly through the grass. It may have been a tiger, and so it was pronounced by the Russians who saw it; I have never looked upon a real tiger outside of a menagerie, and am not qualified to give an opinion. I brought my opera glass and Borasdine his rifle, but the beast did not again show himself. Provoked by this glimpse my companions retired to the cabin and made a theoretical combat with the animal until dinner time.

The day was made memorable by a decent dinner; the

special reason for it was the fact that Borasdine had presented our caterer with an old coat. I regretted I could not afford to reduce my wardrobe, else we would have secured another comfortable repast. Both steward and cook were somewhat negligently clad, and possibly a spare garment or two might have opened their hearts and larders.

Of course the sight of the tiger led to stories about his kindred, and we whiled away a portion of the evening in narrating incidents of a more or less personal character. An officer, who was temporarily our fellow-passenger, on his way to one of the Cossack posts, a few miles above, gave an account of his experience with a tiger on the Ousuree.

I was out (said he) on a survey that we were making on behalf of the government to establish the boundary between Russia and China. The country was then less known than now; there were no settlements along the river, and with the exception of the villages of the natives, thirty or forty miles apart, the whole country was a wilderness. At one village we were warned that a large tiger had within a month killed two men and attacked a third, who was saved only by the sudden and unexpected appearance of a party of friends. We prepared our rifles and pistols, to avoid the possibility of their missing fire in case of an encounter with the man-stealing beast. Rather reluctantly some of the natives consented to serve us as guides to the next village. We generally found them ready enough to assist us, as we paid pretty liberally for their services, and made love to all the young women that the villages contained. With an eye to a successful campaign, I laid in a liberal supply of trinkets to please these aboriginals, and found that they served their purposes admirably. So the natives were almost universally kind to us, and their reluctance to accompany us on this occasion showed the great fear they entertained of the tiger.

We were camped on the bank of the Ousuree, about ten miles from the village, and passed the night without disturbance. In the morning, while we were preparing for breakfast, one of the natives went a few hundred yards away, to a little pond near, where he thought it possible to spear some salmon. He waded out till he was immersed to his waist, and then with his spear raised, stood motionless as a statue for several minutes. Suddenly he darted the spear into the water and drew out a large salmon, which he threw to the shore, and then resumed his stationary position. In twenty minutes he took three or four salmon, and then started to return to camp. Just as he climbed the bank and had gathered his fish, a large tiger darted from the underbrush near by, and sprung upon him as a cat would spring upon a mouse.

Stopping not a moment, the tiger ran up the hillside and disappeared. I was looking toward the river just as the tiger sprang upon him, and so were two of the natives; we all uttered a cry of astonishment, and were struck motionless for an instant, though only for an instant. The unfortunate man did not struggle with the beast, and as the latter did not stop to do more than seize him, I suspected that the fright and suddenness of the attack had caused a fainting fit. I and my Russian companion seized our rifles, and the natives their spears, and started in pursuit.

We tracked the tiger through the underbrush, partly by the marks left by his feet, but mainly by the drops of blood that had fallen from his victim. Going over a ridge, we lost the trail, and though we spread out and searched very carefully, it was nearly an hour before we could resume the pursuit. Every minute seemed an age, as we well knew that the tiger would thus gain time to devour his prey. Probably I was less agitated than the natives, but I freely and gladly admit that I have never had my nerves more unstrung than on that occasion, though I have been in much greater peril. We searched through several clumps of bushes, and examined several thickets, in the hope of finding where the tiger had concealed himself. The natives approached all these thickets with fear and trembling, so that most of the searching was done by the Russian members of the party.

Just as we were beating around a little clump of bushes,

fifteen or twenty yards across, my companion on the other side shouted:

"Look out; the tiger is preparing to spring upon you."

Instantly I cocked my rifle and fired into the bushes; they were so dense that I could hardly discern the outline of the beast, who had me in full view, and was crouching preparatory to making a leap. I called to my friend to shoot, as the density of the thicket made it very probable that my fire would be lost, by the ball glancing among the shrubbery. But my friend was in the same predicament, and I quickly formed a plan of operations.

We were both good shots, and I thought our safety lay in killing the beast as he rose in the air. Aiming at his head, I stepped slowly backward, and shouted to my friend to cover the tiger and shoot as he sprang. All this occurred in less time than I tell of it. Hardly had I stepped two paces backward when the tiger leaped toward me. As he rose, his throat was exposed for a moment, and I planted a bullet in his breast. Simultaneously a ball from the other rifle struck his side. We fired so closely together that neither of us heard the report of the other's weapon. The tiger gave a roar of agony, and despite the wounds he received, either of which would have been fatal, he completed his spring so

GENERAL ACTIVITY.

nearly that he caught me by the foot and inflicted a wound that lamed me for several months, and left permanent scars.

The natives, hearing the report of our rifles, came to our assistance, and so great was their reverence for the tiger, that they prostrated themselves before his quivering body, and muttered some words which I could not understand.

Though assured that the beast was dead, they hesitated to enter the thicket to search for the body of their companion, and it was only on my leading the way that they entered it.

We found the remains of the poor native somewhat mutilated, though less so than I expected. There was no trace of suffering upon his features, and I was confirmed in my theory that he fainted the moment he was seized, and was not conscious afterward. His friends insisted upon burying the body where they found it, and said it was their custom to do so. They piled logs above the grave, and after the observance of certain pagan rites, to secure the repose of the deceased, they signified their readiness to proceed.

The tiger was one of the largest of his kind. I had his skin carefully removed, and sent it with my official report to St. Petersburg. A Chinese mandarin who met me near Lake Hinka offered me a high price for the skin, but I declined his offer, in order to show our Emperor what his Siberian possessions contained.

CHAPTER XVI.

ON the morning of September 28th we arrived at Ekaterin-Nikolskoi, a flourishing settlement, said to contain nearly three hundred houses. It stood on a plateau forty feet above the river, and was the best appearing village I had seen since leaving Habarofka. The people that gathered on the bank were comfortably clad and evidently well fed, but I could not help wondering how so many could leave their labor to look at a steamboat. The country was considered excellent for agriculture, yielding abundantly all the grains that had been tried.

On the Amoor the country below Gorin belongs to the Maritime province, which has its capital at Nicolayevsk. Above Gorin is the Province of The Amoor, controlled by the governor at Blagoveshchensk. In the Maritime Province the settlers are generally of the civilian or peasant class, while in the Amoor Province they are mostly Cossacks. The latter depend more upon themselves than the former, and I was told that this was one cause of their prosperity. Many peasants in the Maritime Province do not raise enough flour for their own use, and rely upon government when there is a deficiency.

It is my opinion that the Emperor does too much for some of his subjects in the eastern part of his dominions. In Kamchatka and along the coast of the Ohotsk sea the people are supplied with flour at a low price or for nothing, a ship coming annually to bring it. It has been demonstrated that agriculture is possible in Kamchatka. When I asked why rye was not raised there, one reply was: "We get our flour from government, and have no occasion to make it." Now if the government would furnish the proper facilities for commencing agriculture, and then throw the inhabitants on their own resources, I think it would make a decided change for the better. A self-reliant population is always the best.

Some of the colonists on the Amoor went there of their own accord, induced by liberal donations of land and materials, while others were moved by official orders. In Siberia the government can transfer a population at its will. A whole village may be commanded to move ten, a hundred, or a thousand miles, and it has only to obey. The people gather their property, take their flocks and herds, and move where commanded. They are reimbursed for losses in changing their residence, and the expense of new houses is borne by government. A community may be moved from one place to another, and the settlers find themselves surrounded by their former neighbors.

The Cossacks are moved oftener than the peasants, as they are more directly subject to orders. I found the Cossack villages on the Amoor were generally laid out with military precision, the streets where the ground permitted being straight as sunbeams, and the houses of equal size. Usually each house had a small yard or flower garden in its front, but it was not always carefully tended. Every village has a chief or headman, who assigns each man his location and watches over the general good of his people. When Cossacks are demanded for government service the headman makes the selection, and all cases of insubordination or dispute are regulated by him.

A Cossack is half soldier and half citizen. He owes a certain amount of service to the government, and is required to labor for it a given number of days in the year. He may be called to travel as escort to the mail or to an officer, to watch over public property, to row a boat, construct a house, or perform any other duty in his power. In case of war he becomes a soldier and is sent wherever required. As a servant of government he receives rations for himself and family, but I believe he is not paid in money. The time belonging to himself he can devote to agriculture or any other employment he chooses.

The Cossacks reside with their families, and some of them acquire considerable property. A Russian officer told me there were many wealthy Cossacks along the Argoon river on the boundary between Russia and China. They trade across the frontier, and own large droves of cattle, horses, and sheep. Some of their houses are spacious and fitted with considerable attempt at luxury. The Amoor settlements are at present too young to possess much wealth.

Soon after leaving Ekaterin-Nikolskoi we entered the Buryea or Hingan mountains. This chain extends across the valley of the Amoor at nearly right angles, and the river flows through it in a single narrow defile. The mountains first reach the river on the northern bank, the Chinese shore continuing low for thirteen miles higher up. There are no islands, and the river, narrowed to about half a mile, flows with a rapid current. In some places it runs five miles an hour, and its depth is from fifty to a hundred feet. The mountains come to the river on either bank, sometimes in precipitous cliffs, but generally in regular slopes.

Their elevation is about a thousand feet, and they are covered to their summits with dense forests of foliferous and coniferous trees. Occasionally the slopes are rocky or covered with loose debris that does not give clinging room to the trees. The undergrowth is dense, and everything indicates a good vegetation.

The mountains are of mica-schist, clay-slate, and rocks of similar origin resting upon an axis of granite. Porphyry has been found in one locality. According to the geologists there are indications of gold and other precious metals, and I would not be surprised if a thorough exploration led to valuable discoveries.

As the boat struggled against the current in this mountain passage I spent most of the time on deck. The tortuous course of the river added much to the scenic effect. Almost every minute the picture changed. Hill, forest, cliff, and valley assumed different aspects as we wound our sinuous way up the defile. Here and there were tiny cascades breaking over the steep rocks to the edge of the river, and occasionally a little meadow peeped out from the mountain valleys. Some features of the scenery reminded me of the Highlands of the Hudson, or the Mississippi above Lake Pepin. At times we seemed completely enclosed in a lake from which there was no escape save by climbing the hills. Frequently it was impossible to discover any trace of an opening half a mile in our front. Had we been ascending an unexplored river I should have half expected to find it issuing like a huge spring from the base of a high mountain.

The Russian villages in these mountains are located in the valleys of streams flowing to the Amoor. In one bend we found a solitary house newly-erected and waiting its occupants who should keep the post-station in winter. We sent a Cossack ashore in a skiff at this point, and he came near falling into the river while descending the steps at the steamer's side. While returning from the bank one of the men in the skiff broke an oar and fell overboard, which obliged us to back the steamer nearly half a mile down the river to pick him up. The unlucky individual was arrayed in the only suit of clothes he possessed, and was hung up to dry in the engine room.

A mile above this landing place we passed two Manjour boats ascending the stream. These boats were each about twenty feet long, sitting low in the water with the bow more elevated than the stern, and had a mast in the center for carrying a small sail. In the first boat I counted six men, four pushing with poles, one steering, and the sixth, evidently the proprietor, lying at ease on the baggage. Where the nature of the ground permits the crew walk along the shore and tow the boat.

The men were in cotton garments and conical hats, and their queues of hair hung like ships pennants in a dead calm, or the tails of a group of scared dogs. They seemed to enjoy themselves, and were laughing merrily as we went past them. They waved their hands up the stream as if urging us to go ahead and say they were coming. The one reclining was a venerable personage, with a thin beard fringing a sedate visage, into which he drew long whiffs and comfort from a Chinese pipe.

These boats were doubtless from Kirin or San-Sin, on their way to Igoon. The voyage must be a tedious one to any but a Mongol, much like the navigation of the Mississippi before the days of steamboats. In spite of the great advantages to commerce, the Manjours resisted to the last the introduction of steam on the Amoor just as they now oppose it on the Songaree.

MANJOUR BOAT.

In the language of the natives along its banks the Amoor has several names. The Chinese formerly called the Songaree 'Ku-tong,' and considered the lower Amoor a part of that stream. Above the Songaree the Amoor was called 'Sakhalin-Oula,' (black water,) by the Manjours and Chinese. The Goldees named it 'Mongo,' and the Gilyaks called it 'Mamoo.' The name Amoor was given by the Russians, and is considered a corruption of the Gilyak word. When Mr. Collins descended, in 1857, the natives near Igoon did not or would not understand him when he spoke of the Amoor. They called the river 'Sakhalin,' a name which the Russians gave to the long island at the mouth of the Amoor. As the Mongolian maps do not reach the outside world I presume the Russian names are most likely to endure with geographers.

The upper part of the defile of the Buryea Mountains is wider and has more meadows than the lower portion. On one of these meadows, where there is a considerable extent of arable land, we found the village of Raddevski, named in honor of the naturalist Raddy, who explored this region. The resources here were excellent, if I may judge by the quantity and quality of edibles offered to our steward. The people of both sexes flocked to the landing with vegetables, bread, chickens, butter, and other good things in much larger quantity than we desired. There was a liberal supply of pigs and chickens, with many wild geese and ducks. We bought a pig and kept him on board three or four days. He squealed without cessation, until our captain considered him a bore, and ordered him killed and roasted.

Pigs were generally carried in bags or in the arms of their owners. One day a woman brought a thirty pound pig suspended over her shoulder. The noise and kicking of the brute did not disturb her, and she held him as unconcernedly as if he were an infant. Finding no market for her property, she turned it loose and allowed it to take its own way home. Milk was almost invariably brought in bottles, and eggs in boxes or baskets. Eggs were sold by the dizaine (ten,) and not as with us by the dozen.

At Raddevski several kinds of berries were offered us, but only the blackberry and whortleberry were familiar to my eyes. One berry, of which I vainly tried to catch the Russian name, was of oblong shape, three-fourths an inch in length, and had the taste of a sweet grape. It was said to grow on a climbing vine. Cedar nuts were offered in large quantities, but I did not purchase.

Here, as elsewhere on the lower Amoor, men and women labor together in the fields and engage equally in marketing at the boats. I was much amused in watching the commercial transactions between the peasants and our steward. I could not understand what was said, but the conversation in loud tones and with many words had much the appearance of an altercation. Several times I looked around expecting to see blows, but the excitement was confined to the vocal organs alone.

The passage of the Amoor through the Buryea mountains is nearly a hundred miles in length. Toward the upper end the mountains are more precipitous and a few peaks rise high above the others, like The Sentinels in Yosemite valley. The last cliff before one reaches the level country is known as Cape Sverbef, a bold promontory that projects into the river and is nearly a thousand feet high. Not far from this cliff is a flat-topped mountain remarkable for several crevices on its northern side, from which currents of cold air steadily issue. Ice forms around these fissures in midsummer, and a thermometer suspended in one of them fell in an hour to 30° Fahrenheit.

An hour after passing the mountains I saw a dozen conical huts on the Chinese shore and a few dusky natives lounging in front of them. They reminded me of the lodges of our noble red men as I saw them west of the Missouri several years before. Instead of being Cheyennes or Sioux they proved to be Birars, a tribe of wandering Tunguse who inhabit this region. Their dwellings were of light poles covered with birch bark. One of the native gentlemen was near the bank of the river in the attitude of an orator, but not properly dressed for a public occasion. His only garments were a hat and a string of beads, and he was accompanied by a couple of young ladies in the same picturesque costume, minus the hat and beads.

These Tungusians lead a nomadic life. Above the mouth of the Zeya there are two other tribes of similar character, the Managres and Orochons. The principal difference between them is that the former keep the horse and the latter the reindeer. The Birars have no beasts of burden except a very few horses.

None of these people live in permanent houses, but move about wherever attracted by fishing or the chase. During spring and summer they generally live on the banks of the river, where they catch and cure fish. Their scaffoldings and storehouses were like those ot the natives already described, and during their migrations are left without guards and universally respected. Their fish are dried for winter use, and they sell the roe of the sturgeon to the Russians for making caviar.

My first acquaintance with caviar was at Nicolayevsk, and I soon learned to like it. It is generally eaten with bread, and forms an important ingredient in the Russian lunch. On the Volga its preparation engages a great many men, and the caviar from that river is found through the whole empire. Along the Amoor the business is in its infancy, the production thus far being for local consumption. I think if some enterprising American would establish the preparation of caviar on the Hudson where the sturgeon is abundant, he could make a handsome profit in shipping it to Russia.

The roe is taken from the fish and carefully washed. The membrane that holds the eggs together is then broken, and after a second washing the substance is ready for salting. One kind for long carriage and preservation is partially dried and then packed and sealed in tin cans. The other is put in kegs, without pressing, and cannot be kept a long time.

In the autumn and winter the natives are hunters. They chase elk and deer for their flesh, and sables, martens, and squirrels for their furs. Squirrels are especially abundant, and a good hunter will frequently kill a thousand in a single season. The Siberian squirrel of commerce comes from this region by way of Irkutsk and St. Petersburg. The natives hunt the bear and are occasionally hunted by him.

At one landing a Birar exhibited an elk skin which he wished to exchange for tobacco, and was quite delighted when I gave him a small quantity of the latter. He showed me a scar on his arm where a bear had bitten him two or three years before. The marks of the teeth and the places where the flesh was torn could be easily seen, but I was unable to learn the particulars of his adventure.

These Tungusians are rather small in stature, and their arms and legs are thin. Their features are broad, their mouths large and lips narrow, and their hair is black and smooth, the men having very little beard. Their clothing is of the skins of elk and deer, with some garments of cotton cloth of Chinese manufacture. Most of the men I saw wore a belt at the waist, to which several articles of daily use were attached.

At each Russian settlement above the mountains I observed a large post painted in the official colors and supporting a board inscribed with the name of the village. It was fixed close to the landing place, and evidently designed for the convenience of strangers. One of my exercises in learning the language of the country was to spell the names on these signs. I found I could usually spell much faster if I knew beforehand the name of a village. It was like having a Bohn's translation of a Latin exercise.

At the village of Inyakentief I saw the first modern fortification since leaving Nicolayevsk,—a simple lunette without cannon but with several hundred cannon shot somewhat rusty with age. The governor of this village was a prince by title, and evidently controlled his subjects very well. I saw Madame the princess, but did not have the pleasure of her acquaintance. She was dressed in a costume of which crinoline, silk, and ribbons were component parts, contrasting sharply with the coarse garments of the peasant women.

This village had recently sold a large quantity of wheat and rye to the government. It had the best church I had seen since leaving Nicolayevsk, and its general appearance was prosperous. Among the women that came to the boat was one who recognized Borasdine as an old acquaintance. She hastened back to her house and brought him two loaves of bread made from wheat of that year's growth. As a token of friendship he gave her a piece of sugar weighing a pound or two and a glass of bad brandy that brought many tears to her eyes. I think she was at least fifteen minutes drinking the fiery liquid, which she sipped as one would take a compound of cayenne pepper and boiling water. The worst 'tanglefoot' or 'forty-rod' from Cincinnati or St. Louis would have been nectar by the side of that brandy.

The country for a hundred miles or more above the Buryea mountains was generally level. Here and there were hills and ridges, and in the background on the south a few mountains were visible. There were many islands which, with the banks of alluvium, were evidently cut by the river in high freshets. Where the beach sloped to the water there was a little driftwood, and I could see occasional logs resting upon islands and sand bars.

When taken in a tumbler the water of the Amoor appeared perfectly clear, but in the river it had a brownish tinge. There were no snags and no floating timber. I never fancied an iron boat for river travel owing to the ease of puncturing it. On the Mississippi or Missouri it would be far from safe, but on the Amoor there are fewer perils of navigation. More boats have been lost there from carelessness or ignorance than from accidents really unavoidable. The Amoor is much like what the Mississippi would be with all its snags removed and its channel made permanent.

While among the islands I saw a small flotilla of boats in line across a channel, and after watching them through a glass discovered they were hauling a net. There were ten or twelve summer huts on the point of an island, and the boats were at least twice as many. A dozen men on shore were hauling a net that appeared well filled with fish. I do not think a single native looked up as we passed. Possibly they have a rule there not to attend to outside matters when exercising their professions.

CHAPTER XVII.

THE second day above the mountains we passed a region of wide prairie stretching far to the north and bearing a dense growth of rank grass and bushes, with a few clumps of trees. On the Chinese side there were hills that sloped gently to the river's edge or left a strip of meadow between them and the water. Many hills were covered with a thin forest of oaks and very little underbrush. At a distance the ground appeared as if carefully trimmed for occupation, especially as it had a few open places like fields. In the sere and yellow leaf of autumn these groves were charming, and I presume they are equally so in the fresh verdure of summer.

If by some magic the Amoor could be transferred to America, and change its mouth from the Gulf of Tartary to the Bay of New York, a multitude of fine mansions would soon rise on its banks.

Among the islands that stud this portion of the river we passed the steamer Constantine with two barges in tow. She left Nicolayevsk twelve days before us, and her impediments made her journey a slow one. Her barges were laden with material for the Amoor telegraph, then under construction. About the same time we met the Nicolai towing a barge with a quantity of cattle destined for the garrison at the mouth of the river. The Nicolai was the property of a merchant (Mr. Ludorf) at Nicolayevsk.

The village of Poyarkof, where we stopped for wood, impressed me very favorably. It was carefully laid out, and its single street had a wide and deep ditch on each side, crossed by little bridges. The houses were well built and had an air of neatness, while all the fences were substantial. Very few persons visited the boat, most of the inhabitants being at work in the fields. We walked through the settlement, and were shown specimens of wheat and rye grown in the vicinity. Four or five men, directed by a priest, were building a church, and two others were cutting plank near by with a primitive 'up-and-down' saw. The officer controlling the village was temporarily absent with the farm laborers. All around there were proofs of his energy and industry.

This village was one of the military colonies of the Province of the Amoor. When in proper hands the military settlement is preferable to any other, as the men are more accustomed to obeying orders and work in greater harmony than the peasants. What is most needed is an efficient and energetic chief to each village, who has and deserves the confidence of his people. With enough of the *fortiter in re* to repress any developments of laziness and prevent intemperance, such a man can do much for the government and himself.

If His Imperial Majesty will take nine-tenths of his present military force on the Amoor, place it in villages, allow the men to send for their families, and put the villages in the hands of proper chiefs under a general superintendent, he will take a long step toward making the new region self-sustaining. We have ample proof in America that an army is an expensive luxury, and the cost of maintaining it is proportioned to its strength. The verb 'to soldier' has a double meaning in English, and will bear translation. On distant stations like the Amoor, the military force could be safely reduced to a small figure in time of peace. Less play and more work would be better for the country and the men.

As we proceeded up the river there was another change of the native population. The tents of the Birars disappeared, and we entered the region of the Manjours and Chinese. The captain called my attention to the first Manjour village we passed. The dwellings were one story high, their walls being of wood with a plastering of mud. The chimneys were on the outside like those of the Goldees already described, and the roofs of the houses were thatched with straw.

The Manjour villages are noticeable for the gardens in and around them. Each house that I saw had a vegetable garden that appeared well cultivated. In the corner of nearly every garden I observed a small building like a sentry box. In some doubt as to its use, I asked information of my Russian friends, and learned it was a temple where the family idols are kept and the owners go to offer their prayers.

A PRIVATE TEMPLE.

Near each village was a grove which enclosed a public temple on the plan of a church in civilized countries. The temple was generally a square house, built with more care and neatness than the private dwellings. On entering, one found himself in a kind of ante-room, separated from the main apartment by a pink curtain. This curtain has religious inscriptions in Chinese and Manjour. In the inner apartment there are pictures of Chinese deities, with a few hideous idols carved in wood. A table in front of the pictures receives the offerings of worshippers.

The Manjours appear very fond of surrounding their temples with trees, and this is particularly noticeable on account of the scarcity of wood in this region. Timber comes from points higher up the Amoor, where it is cut and rafted down. Small trees and bushes are used as fuel and always with the strictest economy. The grove around the temple is held sacred, as among the Druids in England, and I presume a native would suffer long from cold before cutting a consecrated tree.

Along the river near the first village several boats were moored or drawn on the bank out of reach of the water. A few men and women stood looking at us, and some of them shouted '*mendow*' when we were directly opposite their position. Of course we returned their salutation.

Unlike the aboriginals lower down the river, the Manjours till the soil and make it their chief dependence. I saw many fields where the grain was uncut, and others where it had been reaped and stacked. The stacks were so numerous in proportion to the population that there must be a large surplus each year. Evidently there is no part of the Amoor valley more fertile than this. Horses and cattle were grazing in the meadows and looked up as we steamed along. We passed a dozen horses drinking from the river, and set them scampering with our whistle.

The horse is used here for carrying light loads, but with heavy burdens the ox finds preference. Along the Chinese shore I frequently saw clumsy carts moving at a snail-like pace between the villages. Each cart had its wheels fixed on an axle that generally turned with them. Frequently there was a lack of grease, and the screeching of the vehicle was rather unpleasant to tender nerves.

Near the village we met a Manjour boat, evidently the property of a merchant. The difference between going with and against the current was apparent by comparing the progress of this boat with the one I saw in the Buryea mountains. One struggled laboriously against the stream, but the other had nothing to do beyond keeping where the water ran swiftest. This one carried a small flag, and was deeply laden with merchandise. The crew was dozing and the man at the helm did not appear more than half awake.

Villages were passed in rapid succession, and the density of the population was in agreeable contrast to the desolation of many parts of the lower Amoor. It was a panorama of houses, temples, groves, and fields, with a surrounding of rich meadows and gentle hills. There was a range of low mountains in the background, but on the Russian shore the flat prairie continued.

In the middle of the afternoon we passed the town of Yah-tou-kat-zou, situated on the Chinese shore where the river makes a bend toward the north and east. It had nothing of special interest, but its gardens were more extensive and more numerous than in the villages below. Just above it there was a bay forming a neat harbor containing several boats and barges. When the Chinese controlled the Amoor they occupied this bay as a dock-yard and naval station. Had my visit been ten or twelve years earlier I should have seen several war junks anchored here. When the Russians obtained the river the Chinese transferred their navy to the Songaree.

From this ancient navy yard the villages stretched in a nearly continuous line along the southern bank, and were quite frequent on the northern one. We saw three Manjour women picking berries on the Russian shore. One carried a baby over her shoulders much after the manner of the American Indians. These women wore garments of blue cotton shaped much like the gowns of the Russian peasants. Near them a boat was moving along the shore, carrying a crew consisting of a man, a boy, and a dog. The boat, laden with hay, was evidently destined for ‘cows and a market.’ Near it was another boat rowed by two men, carrying six women and a quantity of vegetables. Some of the women were sorting the vegetables, and all watched our boat with interest. From the laughter as we passed I concluded the remarks on our appearance were not complimentary.

The scene on this part of the river was picturesque. There were many boats, from the little canoe or ‘dug-out,’ propelled by one man, up to the barge holding several tons of merchandise. The one-man boats were managed with a double-bladed oar, such as I have already described. Nearly every boat that carried a mast had a flag or streamer attached to it, and some had dragons’ heads on their bows. Would Lindley

Murray permit me to say that I saw one barge manned by ten women?

Though subsisting mainly by agriculture and pastoral pursuits, the Manjours devote considerable time to fishing. One fishing implement bore a faint resemblance to a hand-cart, as it had an axle with two small wheels and long handles. A

FISHING IMPLEMENTS.

frame over the axle sustained a pole, to which a net was fastened. The machine could be pushed into the water and the net lowered to any position suitable for entrapping fish.

Occasionally I saw a native seated on the top of a tripod about ten feet high, placed at the edge of the river. Here he fished with pole, net, or spear, according to circumstances. He always appeared to me as if left there during a freshet and waiting for the river to rise and let him off.

At one place two boys were seated cross-legged near the water and fishing with long poles. They were so intent in looking at us that they did not observe the swell of the steamer until thoroughly drenched by it. As they stood dripping on the sand they laughed good-naturedly at the occurrence, and soon seated themselves again at their employment.

Late in the afternoon I saw a village larger than all the others, lying in a bend of the river, stretching three or four miles along the bank and a less distance away from it. This was Igoon, the principal place of the Chinese on the Amoor, and once possessing considerable power. Originally the fort and town of Igoon were on the left bank of the river, four miles below the present site. The location was changed in 1690, and when the new town was founded it grew quite rapidly. For a long time it was a sort of Botany Bay for Pekin, and its early residents were mostly exiles. At present its population is variously estimated from twenty to fifty thousand. The Chinese do not give any information on this point, and the Russian figures concerning it are based upon estimates.

Igoon was formerly the capital of the Chinese 'Province of the Amoor,' but is now destitute of that honor. The seat of government was removed about twenty years ago to Sit-si-gar.

As we approached Igoon I could see below it many herds of cattle and horses driven by mounted men. There was every appearance of agricultural prosperity. It was near the end of harvest, and most of the grain was stacked in the fields. Here and there were laborers at work, and I could see many people on the bank fronting the river. Around the city were groves enclosing the temples which held the shrines consecrated to Mongol worship, as the cross is reverenced by the followers of the Christian faith.

The city had a sombre look, as all the houses were black. The buildings were of wood plastered with mud, and nearly all of one story. Over the temples in the city there were flag-staffs, but with no banners hanging from them or on the outer walls. The governor's house and the arsenals were similarly provided with tall poles rising from the roofs, but here as elsewhere no flags were visible.

Along the beach there were many rafts of logs beside numerous boats either drawn on shore or moored to posts or stakes. Fishermen and boys were sitting cross-legged near the water, and the inattention of several caused their drenching by our swell. Idle men stood on the bank above the beach, nearly all smoking their little brass pipes with apparent unconcern. Men and women, principally the latter, were carrying water from the river in buckets, which they balanced from the ends of a neck-yoke.

We dropped anchor and threw a line that was made fast by a young Manjour. On shore we met several residents, who greeted us civilly and addressed the captain in Russian. Most of the Manjour merchants have learned enough Russian to make a general conversation, especially in transacting business.

I was introduced as an American who had come a long distance purposely to see Igoon. The governor was absent, so that it was not possible to call on him. We were shown to a temple near at hand, a building fifteen feet by thirty, with a red curtain at the door and a thick carpet of matting over a brick pavement. The altar was veiled, but its covering was lifted to allow me to read, if I could, the inscription upon it. It stood close to the entrance, like the screen near the door of a New York bar-room. There were several pictures on the walls, a few idols, and some lanterns painted in gaudy colors. Outside there were paintings over the door, some representing Chinese landscapes. The windows were of lattice work, the roof had a dragon's head at each end of the ridge, and a mosaic pavement extended like a sidewalk around the entire building.

Our guide, who lived near, invited us to his house. We entered it through his office, which contained a table, three or four chairs, and a few account books. Out of this we walked into a large apartment used for lounging by day and sleeping at night. Its principal furniture was a wide divan at one side, where the bed clothing of three or four persons was rolled into neat bundles. It turned out on inquiry that the man lived in two houses, the principal part of his family being domiciled several squares away. As time pressed we did not stop longer than to thank him for his attention.

The streets of Igoon reminded me of New York under the contract system four or five years ago. We walked through one street upon a narrow log fixed in the mud, and steadied ourselves against a high fence. On a larger thoroughfare there were some dry spots, but as there were two logs to walk upon we balanced very well. Chinese streets rarely have sidewalks, and every pedestrian must care for himself the best way he can. The rains the week before my visit had reduced the public ways to a disagreeable condition. Were I to describe the measurement of the Broadway of Igoon, I should say its length was two miles, more or less, its width fifty feet, and its depth two feet.

Our captain carried a sword cane which confused him a little as the lower part occasionally stuck in the mud and came off. This exposition of weapons he evidently wished to avoid. On the principal street I found several stores, and, true to the instinct of the American abroad, stopped to buy something. The stores had the front open to the street, so that one could stand before the counter and make his purchases without entering. The first store I saw had six or seven clerks and very little else, and as I did not wish a Chinese clerk I moved to another shop.

For the articles purchased I paid only five times their actual value, as I afterward learned. The merchants and their employees appeared to talk Russian quite fluently, and were earnest in urging me to buy. One of them imitated the tactics of Chatham street, and became very voluble over things I did not want.

Holding up an article he praised its good qualities and named its price.

"Five roubles; very good; five roubles."

I shook my head.

"Four roubles; yes; good; four roubles."

Again I made a negation.

"Three roubles; very good; yes."

I continued shaking my head as he fell to two and a half, two, and finally to one rouble. I left him at that figure, or it is possible he would have gone still lower.

"They are great rascals," said Borasdine as we walked away. "They ask ten times the real price and hope to cheat you in some way. It is difficult to buy anything here for its actual value."

We went through more streets and more mud, passing butchers' shops where savage dogs growled with that amiable tone peculiar to butcher dogs everywhere. We passed tea shops, shoe shops, drug stores, and other establishments, each with a liberal number of clerks. Labor must be cheap, profits large, or business brisk, to enable the merchants to maintain so many employees.

At the end of a long street we came to the guard-house, near the entrance of the military quarters. We entered the dirty barrack, but saw nothing particularly interesting. I attempted to go inside the room where the instruments of punishment were kept, but the guard stood in the way and would not move. The soldiers in this establishment had evidently partaken of a beverage stronger than tea, as they were inclined to too much familiarity. One patted me on the shoulder and pressed my hand affectionately, indulging the while in snatches of Chinese songs.

In the prison were two or three unfortunates with their feet shackled so as to prevent their stepping more than four inches at a time. While we stood there a gaily dressed officer rode past us on a magnificent horse, reminding me of an American militia hero on training day. We looked at the fence of palisades, and stepped under the gateway leading to the government quarter. Over the gate was a small room like the drawbridge room in a castle of the middle ages. Twenty men could be lodged there to throw arrows, hot water, or Chinese perfumery on the invading foe.

A Manjour acquaintance of our captain invited us to visit his house. We entered through the kitchen, where there was a man frying a kind of 'twisted doughnut' in vegetable oil. The flour he used was ground in the Manjour mills, and lacked the fineness of European or American flour. Judging by the quantity of food visible the family must have been a large one.

The head of the household proclaimed himself a Tartar,

and said he was the proprietor of four wives. I smoked a cigar with him, and during our interview Borasdine hinted that we would like to inspect his harem. After a little decorous hesitation, he led us across an open and muddy courtyard to a house where a dozen women were in the confusion of preparing and eating supper. With four wives one must have a proportionate number of servants and retainers, else he cannot maintain 'style.'

Such a scene of confusion I never saw before in one man's family. There were twelve or fifteen children of different ages and sexes, and not one silent. Some were at table, some quarreling, some going to sleep, and some waking. Two women were in serious dispute, and the Tartar words poured out freely. The room was hot, stifling, and filled with as many odors as the city of Cologne, and we were glad to escape into the open air as soon as possible. I did not envy that Mongol gentleman his domestic bliss, and am inclined to think he considered it no joke to be as much married as he was.

I did not see any pretty women at Igoon, but learned afterward that they exist there. The Manjour style of hair-dressing attracts the eye of a stranger. The men plait the hair after the Chinese manner, shaving the fore part of the head. The women wind theirs in a peculiar knot, in about the position of the French chignon. They pierce this knot with two long pins like knitting needles, and trim it with bright ribbons and real or artificial flowers. The fashion is becoming, and, excluding the needles, I would not be surprised to see it in vogue in Western civilization within half a dozen years.

The men wore long blue coats of cotton or silk, generally the former, loose linen trousers, fastened at the knee or made into leggings, and Chinese shoes or boots of skin. The women dress in pantaletts and blue cotton gowns with short, loose sleeves, above which they wear at times a silk cape or mantle. They have ear rings, bracelets, and finger rings in profusion, and frequently display considerable taste in their adornment.

It was nearly sunset when we landed at Igoon, and when we finished our visit to the Tartar family the stars were out. The delay of the boat was entirely to give me a view of a Chinese-Manjour city. Darkness put an end to sight-seeing,

A CHINESE FAMILY PICTURE.

and so we hastened to the steamer, followed by a large crowd of natives.

We took three or four Manjour merchants as passengers to Blagoveshchensk. One of them spent the evening in our cabin, but would neither drink alcoholic beverages nor smoke. This appeared rather odd among a people who smoke persistently and continually. Men, women, and children are addicted to the practice, and the amount of tobacco they burn is enormous.

CHAPTER XVIII.

AT daylight on the morning after leaving Igoon, we were passing the mouth of the Zeya, a river half a mile wide, flowing with a strong current. It was along this river that the first white men who saw the Amoor found their way. It is said to be practicable for steam navigation three or four hundred miles from its mouth. At present four or five thousand peasants are settled along the Zeya, with excellent agricultural prospects. As I came on deck rubbing my half-opened eyes, I saw a well-built town on the Russian shore.

"Blagoveshchensk," said the steward, as he waved his arm in that direction.

I well knew that the capital of the Province of the Amoor was just above the mouth of the Zeya. It stands on a prairie fifteen or twenty feet above the river, and when approached from the south its appearance is pleasing. The houses are large and well built, and each has plenty of space around it. Some of them have flower gardens in front, and a public park was well advanced toward completion at the time of my arrival.

A wharf extended into the river at an angle of forty degrees with the shore. The steamer Korsackoff was moored at this wharf, with a barge nearly her own size. The Ingodah tied to the bank just below the wharf, and was welcomed by the usual crowd of soldiers and citizens, with a fair number of Manjours from the other bank.

On landing, I called upon Colonel Pedeshenk, the governor of the Province, and delivered my letters of introduction. The Colonel invited me to dine with him that day, and stated that several officers of his command would be present. After this visit and a few others, I went with Captain Borasdine to attend the funeral of the late Major General Bussy. This gentleman was five years governor of the Province of the Amoor, and resigned in 1866 on account of ill-health. He died on his way to St. Petersburg, and the news of his death reached Blagoveshchensk three days before my arrival. I happened to reach the town on the morning appointed for the funeral service.

The church was crowded, everybody standing, according to the custom prevailing in Russia. Colonel Pedeshenk and his officers were in full uniform, and almost all present held lighted candles. Five or six priests, with an Archbishop, conducted the ceremonies. The services consisted of a ritual, read and intoned by the priests, with chanting by the choir of male voices. The Archbishop was in full robes belonging to his position, and his long gray beard and reverend face gave him a patriarchal appearance. When the ceremony was finished the congregation opened to the right and left to permit the governor and officers to pass out first. From beginning to end the service lasted about an hour.

Colonel Pedeshenk had been governor but a few months, and awaited confirmation in his position. Having served long on the staff of General Bussy, he was disposed to follow in the footsteps of his predecessor and carry out his plans for developing the resources of his district.

At the appointed hour I went to dine at the governor's, where I found eight or ten officers and the young wife of Colonel Pedeshenk. We spent a half-hour on the balcony, where there was a charming view of the river and the Chinese shore with its background of mountains. The governor's house was more like a mansion in a venerable town than in a settlement less than ten years old. The reception hall would have made a good ball-room anywhere out of the large cities.

The charming young madame did not speak English but was fluent in French. She was from Irkutsk, and had spent several years in the schools and society of St. Petersburg. She had many reminiscences of the capital, and declared herself delighted with her home on the Amoor. After dinner we retired to the balcony for prosaic tea drinking and a poetical study of the glories of an autumn sunset behind the hills of Manjouria.

There was no hotel in the town, and I had wondered where I should lodge. Before I had been half an hour on shore, I was invited by Dr. Snider, the surgeon in chief of the province, to make my home at his house. The doctor spoke English fluently, and told me he learned it from a young American at Ayan several years before. He was ten years in government service at Ayan, and met there many of my countrymen. Once he contemplated emigrating to New Bedford at the urgent solicitation of a whaling captain who frequently came to the Ohotsk sea.

Dr. Snider was from the German provinces of Russia, and his wife, a sister of Admiral Fulyelm, was born in Sweden. They usually conversed in German but addressed their children in Russian. They had a Swedish housemaid who spoke her own language in the family and only used Russian when she could not do otherwise. Madame Snider told me her children spoke Swedish and Russian with ease, and understood German very well. They intended having a French or English governess in course of time.

"I speak," said the doctor, "German with my wife, Swedish to the housemaid, Russian to my other servants, French with some of the officers, English with occasional travelers, and a little Chinese and Manjour with the natives over the river."

Blagoveshchensk has a pretty situation, and I should greatly prefer it to Nicolayevsk for permanent habitation. In the middle of the Amoor valley and at the mouth of the Zeya, its commercial advantages are good and its importance increases every year. It was founded in 1858 by General Mouravieff, but did not receive any population worthy of mention until after the treaty of Igoon in 1860. The government buildings are large and well constructed, logs being the material in almost universal use for making walls. A large unfinished house for the telegraph was pointed out to me, and several warehouses were in process of erection.

Late one afternoon the captain of the steamer Korsackoff invited me to visit Sakhalin-Oula-Hotun (city of the black river) on the opposite shore. Though called a city it cannot justly claim more than two thousand inhabitants. There was a crowd on the bank similar to the one at Igoon, most of the women and girls standing with their arms folded in their sleeves. Several were seated close to the water and met the same misfortune as those in similar positions at Igoon. The Korsackoff made a much greater swell than the Ingodah, and those who caught its effects were well moistened. We landed from the steamer's boat and ascended the bank to the village. Several fat old Manjours eyed us closely and answered with great brevity our various questions.

Sakhalin-Oula stretches more than a mile along the bank, but extends only a few rods back from the river. Practically it consists of a single street, which is quite narrow in several places. The houses are like those of Igoon, with frames of logs and coverings of boards, or with log walls plastered with mud. The windows of stores and dwellings are of lattice work covered with oiled paper, glass being rarely used.

The roofs of the buildings were covered with thatch of wheat straw several inches thick, that must offer excellent facilities for taking fire. Probably the character of this thatch accounts for the chimneys rising ten or fifteen feet from the buildings. I saw several men arranging one of these roofs. On a foundation of poles they laid bundles of straw, overlapping them as we overlap shingles, and cutting the boards to allow the straw to spread evenly. This kind of covering must be renewed every two or three years. Several thatches were very much decayed, and in one of them there was a fair growth of grass. The village was embowered in trees in contrast to the Russian shore where the only trees were those in the park. I endeavored to ascertain the cause of this difference, but could not. The Russians said there was often a variation of three or four degrees in the temperature of the two banks, the Chinese one being the milder. Timber for both Chinese and Russian use is cut in the forests up the Amoor and rafted down.

Sakhalin-Oula abounded in vegetable gardens, which supplied the market of Blagoveshchensk. The number of shops both there and at Igoon led me to consider the Manjours a population of shop-keepers. Dr. Snider said they brought him everything for ordinary table use, and would contract to furnish at less than the regular price, any article sold by the Russian merchants. In their enterprise and mode of dealing they were much like the Jews of Europe and America, which may account for their being called Manjours. Once a month during the full moon they come to Blagoveshchensk and open a fair, which continues seven days. They sell flour, buckwheat, beans, poultry, eggs, vegetables, and other edible articles. The Russians usually purchase a month's supply at these times, but when they wish anything out of the fair season the Manjours are ready to furnish it.

We walked along a narrow street, less muddy than the streets of Igoon, and passed several cattle yards enclosed with high fences, like California corrals. In one yard there were cattle and horses, so densely packed that they could not kick freely. Groups of natives stared at us while smoking their little pipes, and doubtless wondered why we came there. Several eyed me closely and asked my companions who and what I could be. The explanation that I was American conveyed no information, as very few of them ever heard of the land of the free and the former home of the slave.

One large building with a yard in front and an inscription over its gate was pointed out as a government office. Several employees of the Emperor of China were standing at the gateway, all smoking and enjoying the evening air. At a hitching post outside the gate there were three saddled horses of a breed not unlike the 'Canadian.' The saddles would be uncomfortable to an American cavalry officer, though not so to a Camanche Indian. According to my recollection of our equestrian savage I think his saddle is not much unlike the Mongolians'.

Beyond this establishment we entered a yard in front of a new and well-built house. Near the door was the traveling carriage of the governor of Igoon, who had arrived only an hour or two before. The carriage was a two-wheeled affair, not long enough to permit one to lie at full length nor high enough to sit bolt upright. It had no springs, the frame resting fairly on the axles. The top was rounded like that of a butcher's cart and the sides were curtained with blue cloth that had little windows or peep-holes. I looked behind the curtain and saw that the sides and bottom were cushioned to diminish the effect of jolting. Two or three small pillows, round and hard, evidently served to fill vacancies and wedge the occupant in his place.

MANJOUR TRAVELING CARRIAGE.

The shafts were like those of a common dray, and the driver's position was on a sort of shelf within ten inches of the horse's tail. There was room for a postillion on the shelf with the driver, the two sitting back to back and their legs hanging over the side. The wheel-tires were slightly cogged as if made for use in a machine, and altogether the vehicle did not impress me as a comfortable one. Being without springs it gives the occupant the benefit of all jolting, and as the Chinese roads are execrable, I imagine one might feel after a hundred miles in such a conveyance very much as if emerging from an encounter with a champion prize-fighter.

Sometimes the Chinese officials set the wheels of their carts very far aft so as to get a little spring from the long shafts. Even with this improvement the carriage is uncomfortable, and it is no wonder that the Chinese never travel when they can avoid it.

Entering a hall that led to a larger apartment, we reached the presence of the governor of Igoon. He was seated on a mat near the edge of a wide divan, his legs crossed like a tailor's at his work. He was in a suit of light-colored silk, with a conical hat bearing a crystal ball on the top. It is generally understood that the grade of a Chinese official may be known by the ball he wears on his hat. Thus there are red, blue, white, yellow, green, crystal, copper, brass, *et cetera*, according to the rank of the wearer. These balls take the place of the shoulder-strap and epaulettes of western civilization, and it must be admitted that they occupy the most conspicuous position one could select. As I am not versed in details of the orders of Chinese rank I will not attempt to give the military and civil status of my new acquaintance. I learned that he was a general in the army, had displayed skill and bravery in subduing the rebellion, and been personally decorated by the Emperor.

He was enjoying his pipe and a cup of tea, resting the latter on a little table at his side. He was an old man,—of how many years I dare not try to guess,—with a thin gray beard on his short chin, and a face that might have been worn by the Knight of the Sorrowful Countenance. I was introduced as an American who had come to see China, and especially the portion bordering on the Amoor. We shook hands and I was motioned to a seat at his side on the edge of the divan.

Tea and cigars opened the way to a slow fire of conversation. I spoke in French with Borasdine, who rendered my words in Russian to the governor's interpreter. The principal remarks were that we were mutually enchanted to see each other, and that I was delighted at my visit to Igoon and Sakhalin-Oula.

Several officials entered and bowed low before the governor, shaking their clenched hands at him during the obeisance. One wore a red and another a yellow ball, the first being in a black uniform and the second in a white one. The principal feature of each uniform was a long coat reaching below the knees, with a cape like the capes of our military cloaks. Both dresses were of silk, and the material was of excellent quality.

The floor of the room was of clay, beaten smooth and cleanly swept. The furniture consisted of the divan before mentioned, with two or three rolls of bedding upon it, a Chinese table, and two Chinese and three Russian chairs. The walls were covered with various devices produced from the oriental brain; and an American clock and a French mirror showed how the Celestials have become demoralized by commerce with outside barbarians. The odor from the kitchen filled the room, and as we thought the governor might be waiting for his supper, we bade him good evening and returned to the boat and the Russian shore.

During my stay at Blagoveshchensk I was invited to assist at a visit made by the governor of Igoon to Colonel Pedeshenk. The latter sent his carriage at the appointed hour to bring the Chinese dignitary and his chief of staff. A retinue of ten or twelve officers followed on foot, and on entering the audience hall they remained standing near the door. The greetings and hand-shakings were in the European style, and after they were ended the Chinese governor took a seat and received his pipe from his pipe-bearer. He wore a plain dress of grey silk and a doublet or cape of blue with embroidery along the front. He did not wear his decorations, the visit being unofficial.

In addition to the ball on his hat he wore a plume or feather that stood in a horizontal position. His chief of staff was the most elaborately dressed man of the party, his robes being more gaily decorated than the governor's. The members of the staff wore mandarin balls of different colors, and all had feathers in their hats. The governor's hair was carefully done up, and I suspect his queue was lengthened with black silk.

Conversation was carried on through the Colonel's interpreter, and ran upon various topics. General Bussy's death was mentioned in terms of regret, and then followed an interchange of compliments between the two governors who met for the first time. After this the Chinese governor spoke of my visit to Sakhalin-Oula, and said I was the first American he ever met in his province.

"How did I come from America," he asked, "and how far had I traveled to reach Blagoveshchensk?"

The interpreter named the distance and said I came to the Amoor in a ship connected with the telegraph service.

"When would the telegraph be finished?"

He was told that within two or three years they would probably be able to send messages direct to America.

Then he asked if the railway would not soon follow the telegraph. He had never seen either, but understood perfectly their manner of working. He expressed himself pleased at the progress of the telegraph enterprise, but did not intimate that China desired anything of the kind. The interview lasted about an hour, and ended with a leave-taking after the European manner.

There is much complaint among the Russians that the treaty of 1860 is not carried out by the Chinese. It is stipulated that trade shall be free along the entire boundary between the two empires, and that merchants can enter either country at will. The Chinese merchants are not free to leave their own territory and visit Russia, but are subject to various annoyances at the hands of their own officials. I was repeatedly informed at Blagoveshchensk that the restrictions upon commerce were very serious and in direct violation of the stipulations. One gentleman told me:

"Every Manjour trader that brings anything here pays a tax of twenty to fifty per cent. for permission to cross the river. We pay now a third more for what we purchase than when we first settled here. The merchants complain of the restriction, and sometimes, though rarely, manage to evade it. Occasionally a Manjour comes to me offering an article twenty or thirty per cent. below his usual price, explaining that he smuggled it and requesting me not to expose him."

I asked if the taxation was made by the Chinese government, and was answered in the negative.

"The police of Igoon and Sakhalin-Oula regulate the whole matter. It is purely a black-mail system, and the merchant who refuses to pay will be thrown into prison on some frivolous charge. The police master of Igoon has a small salary, but has grown very wealthy in a few years. The Russian and Chinese governors have considered the affair several times, but accomplish nothing. On such occasions the Chinese governor summons his police-master and asks him if there is any truth in the charges of the corruption of his subordinates. Of course he declares everything correct, and there the matter ends."

How history repeats itself! Compare this with the conduct of certain Treasury officials along the Mississippi during our late war. The cases were exactly parallel. The government scandalized, trade restricted, and merchants plundered, to fill the pockets of rapacious officers! I began to think the Mongol more like the Anglo-Saxon than ethnologists believe, and found an additional argument for the unity of the human race.

If I knew the Emperor of China I should counsel him to open his oblique eyes. If he does not he may find the conduct of the Igoon police a serious affair for his dominions. Russia, like Oliver Twist, desires more. When the opportunity comes she will quietly take possession of Manjouria and hold both banks of the Amoor. If the treaty of 1860 continues to be violated the Governor General of Eastern Siberia will have an excellent excuse for taking the district of Igoon and all it contains under his powerful protection.

On the day I reached Blagoveshchensk I saw an emigrant

camp near the town. The emigrants had just landed from the rafts with which they descended the Amoor. They came from Astrachan, near the mouth of the Volga, more than five thousand miles away, and had been two years on their travels. They came with wagons to the head waters of the Amoor, and there built rafts, on which they loaded everything, including wagons and teams, and floated to their destination. I did not find their wagons as convenient as our own, though doubtless they are better adapted to the road.

The Russian wagon had a semi-circular body, as if a long hogshead were divided lengthwise and the half of it mounted on wheels, with the open part uppermost. There was a covering of coarse cloth over a light framework, lower and less wide than our army wagons. Household goods fill the wagons, and the emigrants walk for the most part during all their land journey.

I spent a few minutes at the camp near the town, and found the picture much like what I saw years ago beyond the Mississippi. Men were busy with their cattle and securing them for the night; one boy was bringing water from the river, and another gathering fuel for the fire; a young woman was preparing supper, and an older one endeavored, under shelter of the wagon-cover, to put a crying child to sleep.

Westward our star of empire takes its way. Russian emigration presses eastward, and seeks the rising, as ours the setting sun.

CHAPTER XIX.

DURING my stay at Blagoveshchensk the governor invited me to assist at a gazelle hunt.

At nine o'clock on the day appointed we assembled at the house of the chief of staff. I breakfasted before going there, but it was necessary to discuss the coming hunt over a second breakfast. Six or eight ladies were of the party, and the affair had the general appearance of a picnic. The governor seated me in his carriage at the side of Madame Pedeshenk, and we led the company to the field of expected slaughter.

With four horses abreast,—two attached to a pole and two outside,—we dashed over an excellent road leading back from the town. There were three other carriages and two or three common wagons, in which the occupants rode on bundles of hay. There was a little vehicle on two wheels,—a sort of light gig with a seat for only one person,—driven by a lady. Five or six officers were on horseback, and we had a detachment of twenty mounted Cossacks to 'beat the bush.' Excluding the Cossacks and drivers, there were about thirty persons in the party. A mysterious wagon laden with boxes and kegs composed the baggage train. The governor explained that this wagon contained the ammunition for the hunters. No gazelle could have looked upon those kegs and boxes without trembling in his boots.

A range of low hills six miles from town was the spot selected for the hunt. There were nine armed men to be stationed across this range within shooting distance of each other. The Cossacks were to make a circuitous route and come upon the hills two or three miles away, where, forming a long line and making much noise, they would advance in our direction. Any game that happened in the way would be driven to us. We were to stand our ground with firmness and shoot any gazelle that attacked us. I determined to fight it out on that line.

The road from Blagoveshchensk led over a birch-covered plain to the bank of the Zeya, four miles away. We passed on the right a small mill, which was to be replaced in the following year by a steam flouring establishment, the first on the Amoor. On reaching the Zeya I found a village named Astrachanka, in honor of Astrachan at the mouth of the Volga. The settlers had lived there three or four years, and were succeeding well in agriculture. They were of the class known as German Mennonites, who settled on the steppes of Southern Russia at the commencement of the present century. They are members of the Lutheran church, and famed for their industry and their care in managing their flocks and fields. The governor praised them warmly, and expressed the kindest hopes for their prosperity.

THE AMMUNITION WAGON.

We left the road near the village and passed through a field in the direction of the hunting ground. Two men were at work with a yoke of oxen and a plough, whose beam rested on the axle of a pair of wheels. The yoke was like the one in use everywhere along the Amoor, and was made of two pieces of thick plank, one above and the other below the animals' necks, with wooden pins to join them and bear the strain. The plough was quite primitive and did not stir the soil like an American or English plough.

At the hunting ground we alighted and took our stations. The governor stood under a small oak, and the ladies rested on the grass near him. I went to the next post up the hollow, and the other hunters completed the line. Dr. Snider went to aid me in taking

> "a dear gazelle,
> To glad me with its soft black eye."

He was armed with a cigar, while I had a double-barreled gun, loaded at (not to) the muzzle.

The Cossacks went to rouse the game, but their first drive resulted in nothing beyond a prodigious noise. When they started for the second drive I followed the doctor in a temporary visit to the ladies. During this absence from duty a large gazelle passed within ten steps of my station. I ran toward my post, but was not as nimble as the frightened deer.

"*Tirez*," commanded the governor.

"Fire," shouted the doctor.

And I obeyed the double injunction. The distance was great and the animal not stationary. I fired, and the governor fired, but the only effect was to quicken the speed of our game. I never knew a gazelle to run faster. Three weeks later I saw a beast greatly resembling him running on a meadow a thousand miles from Blagoveshchensk. Whether it was the same or another I will not attempt to say.

A few minutes after this failure the horn of the hunter was heard on the hill, and two gazelles passed the line, but no game was secured. The governor proposed a change of base, and led us where the mysterious wagon had halted. The 'ammunition' was revealed. There were carpets and cloths on the grass, plates, knives and forks, edibles in variety, wine, ale, and other liquids, and the samovar steaming merrily at our side. I think we acquitted ourselves better at this part of the hunt than at any other. The picnic did not differ much from an American one, the most noticeable feature being the substantial character of solids and liquids. Most of us sat on the grass and stumps, the number of camp-stools not exceeding half a dozen.

Finishing the lunch we took a new hunting spot and managed to kill a gazelle and a large hare. A fourth drive brought no game, and we returned to enjoy another lunch and drink a Russian beverage called 'jonca.' In its preparation a pound or two of loaf sugar in a single lump is fixed on a wire frame above a copper pan. A bottle of cognac is poured over the sugar and set on fire. The sugar melts, and when the fire is almost extinguished a bottle of claret and one of champagne are added. The compound is taken hot, and has a sweet and very smooth taste. The Russians are fond of producing this beverage when they have foreign guests, and if taken freely it has a weakening tendency. The captain of the Variag told me he had placed several British officers under his table by employing this article, and there was a rumor that the Fox embassy to St. Petersburg was quite severely laid out by means of 'jonca.'

The lunch finished we discharged our guns and returned to town at a rapid pace. While descending the bank of a brook our horses turned suddenly and nearly overset the carriage. The doctor and I jumped out to lighten the lower side, and were just in season to keep the wheels on the ground. Madame Pedeshenk followed into the arms of the strong doctor, but the governor, true to the martial instinct, remained in his place and gave instructions to the driver. We did not re-enter the carriage until it was across the brook; the horses were exercised rather violently during the remainder of the journey.

I think the gazelle we killed was identical with the antelope of our western plains. He had a skin of the same color and a white tail, that retreating flag-of-truce so familiar to our overland emigrants. His feet, head, and body were shaped like the antelope's, and his eye had that liquid tenderness so often observed in the agile rover near the foot of the Rocky Mountains. Gazelles abound through the Amoor valley to within a hundred miles of the sea-coast. Many are killed every autumn and winter in the valley of the Zeya and along the middle Amoor. The flesh is eaten and the skin used for winter coats and similar articles.

The commerce of Blagoveshchensk is in the hands of half a dozen merchants, one French, one German, and the rest Russian. The Amoor company before its affairs were ended kept there one of its principal stores, which was bought, with stock and good will, by the company's clerk. The wants of the officers, soldiers, and civilians in the town and its vicinity are sufficient to create a good local trade. Prices are high, nearly double those of Nicolayevsk, and the stocks of goods on hand are neither large nor well selected. Officers complained to me of combinations among the merchants to maintain prices at an exorbitant scale.

I staid four days at Blagoveshchensk, and as the season was growing late was quite anxious to depart. The days were charming, corresponding to our Indian Summer, and the nights cool and frosty. The passenger on our steamer from Igoon said ice would be running in the river in twenty-five days unless the season should be unusually mild. Russians and Chinese were preparing for cold weather, and I wished to do the same farther westward. Borasdine contemplated a land journey in case we were delayed more than five days. The Korsackoff was the only steamer to ascend the river, and she was waiting for the Constantine to bring her a barge. On the evening of the 5th October the governor informed me the Korsackoff would start on the next day, barge or no barge. This was cheering, and I celebrated the occasion by boiling myself in a Russian bath.

I look upon the bath as one of the blessings of Russia. At the end of a journey, when one is sore and stiff in the joints, it is an effectual medicine. After it the patient sleeps soundly, and rises in the morning thoroughly invigorated. Too much bathing deadens the complexion and enfeebles the body, but a judicious amount is beneficial. It is the Russian custom, not always observed, to bathe once a week. The injury from the bath is in consequence of too high temperature of steam and water, causing a severe shock to the system. Taken properly the bath has no bad effects, and will cure rheumatism, some forms of neuralgia, and several other acute diseases.

The bath-house is a building of two, and generally three, rooms. In the outer room you undress, and your *chelavek*, or servant, does the same. If there is but another room you are led directly into it, and find a hot fire in a large stove. There is a cauldron of hot water and a barrel of cold water close at hand. The tools of the operator are a bucket, two or three basins, a bar of soap, a switch of birch boughs, and a bunch of matting. If there are three apartments the second is only an ante-room, not very warm and calculated to prepare you for the last and hottest of all.

The chelavek begins by throwing a bucket of warm water over you. He follows this with another, and then a third, fourth, and fifth, each a little warmer than its predecessor. On one side of the room is a series of benches like a terrace or flight of large steps. You are placed horizontally on a bench, and with warm water, soap, and bunch of matting the servant scrubs you from head to foot with a manipulation more thorough than gentle. The temperature of the room is usually about 110° Fahrenheit, but it may be more or less. It induces vigorous perspiration, and sets the blood glowing and tingling, but it never melts the flesh nor breaks the smallest blood vessel. The finishing touch is to ascend the platform near the ceiling and allow the servant to throw water upon hot stones from the furnace. There is always a cloud of steam filling the room and making objects indistinct. You easily become accustomed to the ordinary heat, but when water is dropped upon the stones there is a rush of blistering steam. It catches you on the platform and you think how unfortunate is a lobster when he goes to pot and exchanges his green for scarlet.

I declined this *coup de grace* after a single experience. To my view it is the objectionable feature of the Russian bath. I was always content after that to retire before the last course, and only went about half way up the terrace. The birchen switch is to whip the patient during the washing process, but is not applied with unpleasant force. To finish the bath you are drenched with several buckets of water descending from hot to cold, but not, as some declare, terminating with ice water. This little fiction is to amuse the credulous, and would be 'important if true.' Men have sometimes rushed from the bath into a snow bank, but the occurrence is unusual. Sometimes the peasants leave the bath for a swim in the river, but they only do so in mild weather. In all the cities there are public bath rooms, where men are steamed, polished, and washed in large numbers. In bathing the Russians are more gregarious than English or Americans. A Russian would think no more of bathing with several others than of dining at a hotel table. Nearly every private house has its bath room, and its frequent use can hardly fail to be noticed by travelers.

FINISHING TOUCH.

On the morning of the 6th the Constantine arrived, having left the Korsackoff's barge hard aground below Igoon. So we were to start unencumbered. I took my baggage to the Korsackoff, and was obliged to traverse two barges before I reached the boat. Twelve o'clock was the hour appointed for our departure, and at eleven the fires were burning in the furnaces. A hundred men were transferring freight from the Constantine to the Korsackoff, and made a busy scene. Four men carrying a box of muskets ran against me on a narrow plank, and had not my good friend the doctor seized me I should have plunged headlong into the river. The hey-day in my blood was tame; I had no desire to fall into *l'Amour* at that season.

At eleven there came an invitation to lunch with the governor at two. "How is this?" I said to the doctor; "start at twelve and lunch here two hours later!" Smiling the doctor replied:

"I see you have not yet learned our customs. The governor is the autocrat, and though the captain positively declares he will start at noon you need not be uneasy. He will not go till you are on board, and very likely you will meet him at lunch."

At two o'clock I was at the governor's, where I found the anxious captain. When our lunch was finished Madame Pedeshenk gave me some wild grapes of native production. They were about the size of peas, and quite acid in taste. With cultivation they might be larger and better flavored, just as many of our American grapes have improved in the past twenty years. Some of the hardier grapes might be successfully grown on the middle Amoor, but the cold is too long and severe for tender vines. Attached to his dwelling the governor has a hot-house that forms a pleasant retreat in winter. He hopes to introduce vines and raise hot-house grapes in Siberia within a few years.

I walked to the boat with Doctor and Madame Snider, our promenade being enlivened by a runaway horse that came near dragging a cart over us. The governor and his lady were there, with nearly all the officers, and after saying adieu I stepped on board, and we left the pier. We waved kerchiefs again and again as long as waves could be seen.

There was a cabin on the Korsackoff about eight feet square, with four small rooms opening out of it. Borasdine and I had two of these. My apartment had two bunks and no bedding, but the deficiency was atoned for by a large number of hungry and industrious fleas. Of my blankets and pillow I made my own bed, and slept in it as on the Ingodah. My only chair was a camp stool I carried from San Francisco with the design of giving it away on reaching the end of my water travel.

Going on board the steamer I met a drunken priest endeavoring to walk to the pier, and in the cabin I found another lying on a sofa, and, as I supposed, very ill. Borasdine observed my look of compassion, and indicated by signs the cause of the malady. The priest going ashore had been saying farewell to the one on board, and their partings were such as press the life from out young hearts and bottles. Our holy passenger did not feel himself again until the next day.

There are many good men among the priests of the Eastern church in Siberia, but it must also be admitted there are many bad ones. In a country where the clergy wields as great power as in Russia the authorities should take care that the representatives of the church set a good example. The intemperance so prevalent among the peasantry is partly due to the debaucheries of the priesthood. Where the people follow their religious leaders with blind faith and obey their commands in all the forms of worship, are they not in danger of following the example of drunkenness? Russian officers frequently spoke of the condition of the church in Eastern Siberia, and declared with emphasis that it needed reformation. "Our priests," said one, "have carried our religion wherever our armies have carried conquest, and their efforts to advance Christianity deserve all praise. But abuses exist and have grown up, and the whole system needs to be arranged anew."

We had much freight on board, consisting chiefly of muskets for the province of the Trans-Baikal. There were many passengers that lived literally on deck. They were aft of the engines and above our cabin. On deck we had the forward part of the boat as on the Ingodah. The deck passengers were soldiers, and Cossacks in their long grey coats, and peasants of all ages in garments of sheepskin. There were women with infants, and women without infants, the former being the more numerous. They were on deck day and night, unless when opportunity offered to go on shore. They did their cooking at the galley or at a stove near the stern of the boat. They never made any noise or disturbance, beyond the usual confusion where many persons are confined in a small space.

There were three horses tied just over my cabin with only a single plank between their heels and my head. Nearly every night their horse polkas and galops disturbed my sleep. Sometimes early in the morning, when the frost was biting, they would have kicking matches of twenty or thirty minutes, conducted with the greatest vigor. The temporary stable was close to the cabin skylight, so that we had the odors of a barn-yard without extra charge. This would have been objectionable under other circumstances, but the cabin was so dirty that one could not be fastidious about trifles.

The captain had a neat cabin of his own on the upper deck, and did not trouble himself much about the quarters of his passengers, as the regulations do not require him to look after their welfare. He was a careful commander and prompt in discharging his duties. By law steamboat captains cannot carry their wives on board. This officer had a little arrangement by which he was able to keep the word of promise to the ear and break it to the hope.

We were short of fuel at starting, and barely escaped trouble in consequence. The first pile visible contained only a cord or two; we took this and several posts that had been fixed in the ground to mark the locality. When this supply was burned we cut up our landing planks and all the spare bits of wood we could find. A court of inquiry was held over the horse-troughs, but they were considered too much water-soaked for our purpose. As a last resort I had a pound of candles and a flask of brandy, but we happily reached a wood-station without using my light baggage.

The Korsackoff was an iron boat of a hundred horse power, with hull and engines of English make. Her cabins were very small and as dirty as diminutive. There was no cabin steward, and I sincerely believe there had never been one.

We were warned of this before leaving Blagoveshchensk, and by way of precaution purchased enough bread, pickles, cheese, mustard, preserves, candles, etc., to stock a modest grocery. We bought eggs at the landings, and arranged for the samovar every morning. We engaged a Cossack passenger as our servant for the voyage, and when we wished our eggs boiled we sent him with them to the cook. Of course we had an arrangement with the latter functionary. Our next move was to make terms with the captain's steward for a dinner at the hour when he fed his chief. Our negociations required much diplomacy, but our existence depended upon it, and what will not man accomplish when he wants bread and meat?

We spread our table in one of our rooms. For breakfast we took tea and boiled eggs, and for dinner we had cabbage soup, roast beef or fowl, and cutlets. The cook succeeded very well, and as our appetites were pretty sharp we voted the dinners a success. We used our own bread, tea, pickles, and preserves, employing the latter as a concluding dish. Our Cossack was not very skillful at housework, and made many blunders in serving. Frequently he brought the soup tureen before arranging the table, and it took him some time to learn the disadvantage of this practice.

Leaving Blagoveshchensk the country continued level near the river, but the mountains gradually approached it and on the south bank they came to the water fifteen or twenty miles above Sakhalin-Oula. On the north the plain was wider, but it terminated about forty miles above Blagoveshchensk,—a series of low hills taking its place. The first day we ran twenty-five or thirty versts before sunset. The river was less than a mile wide, and the volume of water sensibly diminished above the Zeya. As the hills approached the river they assumed the form of bluffs or headlands, with plateaus extending back from their summits. The scenery reminded me of Lake Pepin and the region just above it. On the northern shore, between these bluffs and the river, there was an occasional strip of meadow that afforded clinging room to a

Russian village. At two or three settlements there was an abundance of hay and grain in stacks, and droves of well fed cattle, that indicated the favorable character of the country.

At most villages along the Amoor I found the crow and magpie abundant and very tame. At Blagoveshchensk several of these birds amused me in sharing the dinner of some hogs to the great disgust of the latter. When the meal was finished they lighted on the backs of the hogs and would not dismount until the latter rolled in the dirt. No one appears to think them worth shooting, and I presume they do no damage.

One day walking on shore I saw a flock of pigeons, and returned to the boat for Borasdine's gun. As I took it I remarked that I would shoot a few pigeons for dinner.

"Never think of it," said my friend.

"And why?"

"Because you will make the peasants your enemies. The news would spread that you had killed a pigeon, and every peasant would dislike you."

"For what reason?"

"The pigeon or dove is held sacred throughout Russia. He is the living symbol of the Holy Spirit in the faith of the Eastern church, and he brought the olive branch to The Ark when the flood had ceased. No Russian would harm one of these birds, and for you to do so would show disrespect to the religion of the country."

I went on shore again, but without a gun.

Every day we saw rafts moving with the stream or tied along the shore. They were of logs cut on the upper Amoor, and firmly fastened with poles and withes. An emigrant piles his wagon and household goods on a raft, and makes a pen at one side to hold his cattle. Two or three families, with as many wagons and a dozen or twenty animals, were frequently on one raft. A pile of earth was the fire place, and there was generally a tent or shelter of some kind. Cattle were fed with hay carried on board, or were turned ashore at night to graze.

Some rafts were entirely laden with cattle on their way to market or for government use at Nicolayevsk. This is the most economical mode of transportation, as the cattle feed themselves on shore at night, and the rafts float with the current by day. A great deal of heavy freight has been carried down the Amoor in this way, and losses are of rare occurrence. The system is quite analogous to the flat-boat navigation of the Mississippi before steamboats were established. We met a few Russian boats floating or propelled by oars, one of them having a crew of six Cossacks and making all haste in descending. We supposed it contained the mail due at Blagoveshchensk when we left. The government has not enough steamers to perform its service regularly, and frequently uses row boats. The last mail at Blagoveshchensk before my arrival came in a rowboat in fifteen days from Stratensk.

EMIGRANTS ON THE AMOOR.

Ascending the river we made slow progress even without a barge. Our machinery was out of order and we only carried half steam. We ran only by day, and unfortunately the nights had a majority of the time. We frequently took wood in the middle of the day, and on such occasions lost from one to three hours. Our average progress was about sixty miles a day. I could not help contrasting this with journeys I have made on the Mississippi at the rate of two hundred miles in twenty-four hours. A government boat has no occasion to hurry like a private one, and the pilot's imperfect knowledge of the Amoor operates against rapidity. In time I presume the Siberian boats will increase their speed.

The second day from Blagoveshchensk we were where the Amoor flows twenty-five versts around a peninsula only one verst wide. Just above this, at the village of Korsackoff, was the foot of another bend of twenty-eight versts with a width of three. Borasdine and I proposed walking and hunting across the last neck of land, but the lateness of the hour forbade the excursion, as we did not wish to pass the night on shore, and it was doubtful if the boat could double the point before dark. We should have crossed the first peninsula had it not been in Chinese territory. To prevent possible intrusion the Celestials have a guard-house at the bend.

At the guard-house we could see half a dozen soldiers with matchlocks and lances. There was a low house fifteen or twenty feet square and daubed with mud according to the Chinese custom. There was a quantity of rubbish on the ground, and a couple of horses were standing ready saddled near it. Fifty feet from the house was a building like a sentry-box, with two flag-staffs before it; it was the temple where the soldiers worshipped according to the ceremonies of their faith. I have been much with the army in my own country, but never saw a military post of two buildings where one structure was a chapel.

Above the village of Kazakavitch, at the upper extremity of the bend, there was some picturesque scenery. On one side there were precipitous cliffs two or three hundred feet high, and on the other a meadow or plateau with hills in the background. The villages on this part of the river are generally built twenty or thirty feet above high water mark. They have the same military precision that is observed below the Zeya, and each has a bath house set in the bank. Frequently we found these bath houses in operation, and on one occasion two boys came out clad in the elegant costume of the Greek Slave, without her fetters. They gazed at the boat with perfect *sang froid*, the thermometer being just above freezing point. The scene reminded me of the careless manners of the natives at Panama.

Opposite Komarskoi the cliffs on the Chinese shore are perpendicular, and continue so for several miles. At their base there is a strong current, where we met a raft descending nearly five miles an hour. In going against the stream our pilots did not seek the edge of the river like their brethren of the Mississippi, but faced the current in the center. Possibly they thought a middle course the safest, and remembered the fate of the celebrated youth who took a short route when he drove the sun.

Two miles above the settlement is Cape Komara, a perpendicular or slightly overhanging rock of dark granite three hundred feet high. Nothing but a worm or an insect could climb its face, and a fall from its top into the river would not be desirable. The Russians have erected a large cross upon the summit, visible for some distance up and down the river. Above this rock, which appears like a sentinel, the valley is wider and the stream flows among many islands.

We saw just below this rock a Manjour boat tied to the shore, the crew breakfasting near a fire and the captain smoking in apparent unconcern at a little distance. On the opposite bank there was a Chinese custom-house and military station. It had the same kind of house and temple and the same number of men and horses as the post farther down. Had it possessed a pile of rubbish and a barking dog the similarity would have been complete.

There is abundance of water in the Amoor except for drinking purposes. I was obliged to adopt the plan of towing a bottle out of the cabin window till it filled. The deck passengers used to look with wonder on my foreign invention, and doubtless supposed I was experimenting for scientific purposes. I have heard of a captain on the Ohio who forbade water to his passengers on account of the low stage of the river. Possibly the Russian captains are fearful that too much use of water may affect navigation in future years.

CHAPTER XX.

THERE is a sameness and yet a variety in the scenery of the Amoor two or three hundred miles above Komarskoi. The sameness is in the general outlines which can be described; the variety is in the many little details of distance, shadow, and coloring, which no pen can picture. In the general features there are cliffs, hills, ravines, islands, and occasional meadows, with forests of birch, pine, larch, and willow. The meadows are not abundant, and the attractions to settlers generally small. The hills are rugged and, though well timbered, not adapted to agriculture. The pine forests are dark and gloomy, and the leafless birches make the distant hills appear as if thinly snow-clad. The willows are generally upon the islands, and grow with great luxuriance. The large meadows are occupied by Russian settlers.

Many little streams enter the Amoor on both sides, but chiefly from the north. There is a famous cliff called Sa-ga-yan, where the river has washed and undermined the high bank so that portions fall away every few years. The current strikes this hill with great force, and where it is reflected the water is broken like the rapids above Niagara. It is a dangerous spot for small boats, and very difficult for them to ascend. When the expedition of 1854 descended the Amoor several barges were drawn into an eddy at this cliff and nearly swamped. Captain Fulyelm and Mr. Collins, in 1857, were in danger and trouble, especially where the current rebounds from the shore.

When our steamer struck this rapid it required all the strength of our engines to carry us through. I desired to examine the shore, but had no opportunity. Mr. Collins found the bank composed of amygdaloid sand, decomposed rock and sandstone, with many traces of iron. On the beach were chalcedony, cornelian, and agate. Two veins of coal have been traced in the cliff, and it is thought a large deposit

SA-GA-YAN CLIFF.

exists there. The natives have a story that the cliff smokes whenever a human being approaches it, but I saw no indications of smoke as I passed. They consider it the abode of evil spirits, and hold it in great dread.

The Russians told me that a few wreaths of smoke were visible in summer, caused probably by the decomposition of several coal seams on the upper side of the mountain.

Up to the present time no coal has been mined along the Amoor, though enough is known to exist. The cheapness and abundance of wood will render coal of little importance for many years to come. Nicolayevsk is supplied with coal from Sakhalin Island, where it is abundant and easily worked. Iron ore has been discovered on the upper Amoor and in the Buryea Mountains. Captain Anossoff proposes to erect a smelting establishment at Blagoveshchensk, supplying it with iron ore from the Buryea region and with coal from the Zeya. Copper and silver exist in several localities, but the veins have not been thoroughly examined. The mountains are like those in the Nerchinsk district that have yielded so richly in precious metals.

Captain Anossoff is the brother of my companion across the Pacific, and has seen ten years service in Eastern Siberia. Most of that time he has passed on the Amoor and its tributary streams. In many places he found rich deposits of gold, the last and best being on the Oldoi river, about a hundred miles north of Albazin. A ton of earth yielded six hundred dollars worth of gold. I saw the specimens which the captain took out in person. The gold was like the best gulch or scale gold in California, with nuggets up to four or five ounces in weight.

Gold has been found in other localities. On several tributaries of the Ousuree the Chinese have conducted washings for many years. The Russian settlers near Posyet find gold in the streams flowing into the sea. An engineer officer assured me the washings in that region could be made profitable.

The government has recently opened the Amoor and its tributaries to private enterprise and invited its citizens to search for gold where they please. This is a concession in the right way, and partially abandons the claim hitherto enforced that all mines belong to the Imperial family. Some of the surveys of Captain Anossoff have been for private parties at St. Petersburg, and the development of the mineral resources of the Amoor is confidently expected in a few years. At present the lack of laborers and machinery is a great drawback, but as the country grows older the mining facilities will increase. It is not impossible that a gold fever will sometime arise on the Amoor and extend to America.

Much of the country I saw along the Amoor resembles the gold-bearing regions on the Pacific coast. While we were taking wood at a village above Sa-ga-yan I walked on shore and stopped at a little brook flowing from the hills. Carelessly digging with a stick in the bottom of this brook I brought up some black sand, which I washed on a piece of bark. The washing left two or three shining particles that had every appearance of gold. I wrapped them in a leaf to carry on board the steamer, but as I afterward lost envelope and contents, the value of my discovery is to this day unknown.

The original inhabitants along this part of the Amoor are wandering Tungusians, in no great number and with little wealth. We saw their huts on both banks, principally the southern one. At a Russian village where we stopped there was a Managre hut or yourt of light poles covered with birch bark. The covering was wound around the framework in horizontal strips that overlapped at the edges like shingles on a house-roof. Entering the hut I found a varied assortment of deer skins, cooking and other utensils, dogs, dirt, and children. I gave a small coin to one of the latter, and was immediately surrounded by others who wished to be remembered. The mother of the infants sent one of them to me with a freshly killed goose, which I declined accepting.

The head of the establishment examined my watch attentively, but I think his curiosity was simulated, as he must have seen many watches among the Russians. Not to be outdone in curiosity, I admired the trappings attached to his belt. These were a knife, a pipe, pouches for bullets, tinder, powder, tobacco, and flints, a pointed iron for cleaning a pipe, and two or three articles whose use I could not ascertain. His dress was a deerskin frock and leggings, and his cap of Chinese felt cloth was in several thicknesses and fitted close to his head.

Outside the hut Borasdine gave the man a cigar, but the gift was not appreciated. The native preferred tobacco and was better satisfied when I gave him enough to fill his pipe. The Managres smoke the Manjourian tobacco, which is raised in large quantities along the middle Amoor and the Songaree. It is much like Connecticut leaf, but has a more pungent flavor, and lacks the delicacy of Havana tobacco. Men, women, and children are alike addicted to its use.

Our new acquaintance was a hunter, and allowed us, though with hesitation, to look at his rifle. It had a flint lock of curious construction, the hammer being drawn back to a horizontal position and held in place by a notched piece of bone. The breech-pin was gone, and a piece of stone fixed in the stock filled its place. The breech of the stock was but little larger than the other part, and seemed very awkwardly contrived. A forked stick is carried to form a rest, that ensures the accuracy of aim. Powder and lead are so expensive that great economy is shown in their use. I was told these natives were excellent marksmen and rarely missed a shot. When within proper distance of their game they place their supporting sticks very quickly and with such caution as to make no noise.

RIFLE SHOOTING.

One intoxicated aboriginal stood in the group of Cossacks on the bank and appeared quarrelsome, but found the Russians too good-natured for his purpose. A light shower scattered the crowd and left the inebriate addressing a horse and a wood-pile.

On the 11th of October the weather was like summer, the air still and clear and my thermometer standing at 71 degrees. During the night I found it necessary to take an extra blanket, and at noon of the 12th the thermometer was at 45°, with a cloudy sky and a breeze from the northeast. This change of twenty-six degrees was too much for comfort, but of little consequence compared to my subsequent experience. Instances have been known of a change of seventy degrees in twelve hours from a sudden shifting of the wind. On the morning of the 13th we had a light fall of snow, with the air at freezing point and the water at 40°.*

We passed a rock projecting far into the river, with precipitous sides and a sharp summit visible for some distance along the Amoor. Below it is a small harbor, where the Russian steamer Mala Nadeshda (Little Hope) passed the winter of 1855. She was on her way to Stratensk, carrying Admiral Puchachin on his return from a mission to Japan. Caught by ice the Nadeshda wintered under shelter of this rock, while the Admiral became a horse marine and mounted a saddle for a ride of four hundred miles. Since that time the rock has borne the name of the boat it protected.

In most of the villages there are schools for educating the boys of the Cossacks and peasants. Some pupils are admitted free, while from others a small fee is required. Occasionally I saw boys flocking to the schools at sound of the master's bell, or coming out at recess or dismissal. I had no opportunity to inspect one of these establishments, but presume my description of the one at Mihalofski will answer for all. The youths were as noisy as school-boys everywhere, and when out of restraint indulged in the same hilarity as if born on the banks of the Hudson or the Thames.

At noon on the 14th we stopped at Albazin to leave passengers and take wood. It was Sunday, and the population appeared in its best clothing, a few of the women sporting crinoline, and all wearing their best calicoes. Among the men there were Cossacks and soldiers in their grey coats or in plain cloth and sheepskin. I saw a few Yakuts with the narrow eyes of the Tunguze and their clothing of deerskin.

---

* I here enter a protest against the Fahrenheit thermometer, and think all who have used it to any extent will join me in preferring the Centigrade or Reaumer scales. Centigrade has the freezing point at zero and the boiling point at 100°. Reaumer freezes at zero and boils at 80°. Fahrenheit very clumsily freezes at 32° and boils at 212°. The difference in the graduation of the scale is of much less consequence than the awkwardness of beginning the reading at 32°. The Russians use Reaumer's method, and I always envied them their convenience of saying 'there are so many degrees of cold,' or 'so many of heat,' while I was forced to count from 32° to use my national scale.

A few Orochons stood apart from the Russians, but not less observant of the boat and those on board. Outside the village were three or four conical yourts belonging to the aboriginals. It is said this people formerly lived in the province of Yakutsk, whence they emigrated to the Amoor in 1825. One of their chiefs has a hunting knife with the initials of the Empress Catherine. It was presented to an ancestor of the present owner.

Albazin is finely situated on a plateau fifty feet high and extending some distance back to the mountains. Opposite is a small river abounding in fish, and in front an island several thousand acres in extent and very fertile. Though less than seven years old, Albazin had already begun to sell grain for transportation to Nerchinsk. A steamer laden with grain left for Stratensk three days before our arrival.

Albazin is of historical interest to the Russians. In the year 1669 a Polish adventurer named Chernigofsky built a fort at Albazin. That his men might not be without the comforts of religion he brought a priest, who founded a church at the new settlement. It is related that when organizing his expedition he forcibly seized this priest and kept him under guard during the journey to the Amoor. The Chinese twice besieged Albazin, once with eighteen thousand men, and afterward with nearly double that number. The Russians resisted a long time, and were only driven from the Amoor by the famous treaty of Nerchinsk in 1689.

When I landed at Albazin, Captain Porotof, superintendent of the Russian settlements between that point and Komarskoi, guided me through the ruins. The present village of Albazin is inside the line of Chinese works, and the church occupies the interior of the old fort. All the lines of intrenchment and siege can be easily seen, the fort being distinctly visible from the river. Its walls are about ten feet high, and the ditch is partially filled from the washing of earth during the many years since the evacuation. A drain that carries water from the church has cut a hole through the embankment. In it I could see the traces of the trees and brushwood used in making the fort.

In the fort and around it cannon shot, bullets, arrow heads, and pieces of pottery are frequently found. A few years ago a magazine of rye was discovered, the grains being perfect and little injured by time. Captain Porotof gave me two Chinese cannon shot recently found there and greatly roughened on the surface by the action of rust. The position and arrangement of their batteries and lines of circumvallation show that the Chinese were skilled in the art of war.

Albazin was valuable to the early adventurers on account of the fine sables taken in its vicinity. It is important now for the same reason. The Albazin sable is the best on the Amoor; that of the Buryea mountains is next, and that from Blagoveshchensk is third in grade. At several places I saw these furs, but found none of them equaling the furs of Kamchatka.

Some interesting stories about the siege of Albazin are told by the Russians. While the siege was progressing and the garrison was greatly distressed for want of food, Chernigofsky sent a pie weighing forty or fifty pounds to the Chinese commander to convince him that the fort was abundantly supplied. The latter was so delighted with the gift that he sent back for more, but his request was unheeded. He probably saw through the little game they were attempting to play on him and determined to beat them at it. History does not say whether the pie was pork, mutton, or anything else. Possibly the curs of Albazin may have entered into its composition.

CHAPTER XXI.

ABOVE Albazin the Amoor steadily narrows; the hills are more rugged; the trees less luxuriant; the meadows fewer, and the islands less extensive. On the morning of the 15th my thermometer was at +16°, and the trees on the shore were white with frost. The deck passengers shivered around the engines and endeavored to extract heat from them. The cabin passengers, excepting myself, were wrapped in their fur coats as if it were midwinter. I walked about in my ordinary clothing, finding the air bracing but not uncomfortable. I could not understand how the Russians felt the cold when it did not affect me, and was a little proud of my insensibility to frost. Conceit generally comes of ignorance, and as I learned wisdom I lost my vanity about resisting cold.

Nearly every day on the Korsackoff I was puzzled at finding laurel leaves in the soup, and did not understand it till I saw a barrel of beef opened. There were lots of laurel leaves packed with the meat, and I learned that they assist the preservative qualities of the salt and give an agreeable flavor. I can speak in favor of the latter theory, but know nothing about the former. The ancient Romans wore laurel crowns, but they did not prevent the decline and fall of their empire. Possibly the Russians may have better success in saving their beef by the use of the laurel.

During a fog on the river we grazed a rock, slid upon a sandbar, and then anchored, as we should have done at first. When in motion we employed all possible time, and, considering the state of our engines, made very good progress.

Borasdine learned from our Cossack the explanation of this haste.

"The pilots, firemen, and nearly all the crew," said the Cossack, "have their wives at Stratensk, and are anxious to winter with them. If the boat is frozen in below there they must remain till she thaws out again. Consequently their desire to finish the voyage before the ice is running."

At Ignatiena I met Colonel Shobeltsin, an officer identified with all the movements for the final occupation of the Amoor. In 1852 he made a journey from Irkutsk to Nicolayevsk, following a route up to that time untraveled. He accompanied Mouravieff's expedition in 1854, and was afterward intimately connected with colonization enterprises. A few years ago he retired from service and settled at this village. His face indicates his long and arduous service, and I presume he has seen enough hardship to enjoy comfort for the rest of his days.

His house was the best on the Amoor above Blagoveshchensk and very comfortably furnished. In the principal room there were portraits of many Russian notabilities, with lithographs and steel engravings from various parts of the world. Among them were two pictures of American country life, bearing the imprint of a New York publisher. I had frequently seen these lithographs in a window on Nassau street, little thinking I should find them on the other side of the world. One room was quite a museum and contained a variety of articles made by Manjours and Tunguze. There were heads of deer, sable, and birds, while a quantity of furs hung near the door.

With a spirit of hospitality the Colonel prepared us a breakfast during our brief stay, and invited us to join him in the beverage of the country. When we returned to the boat the steward was superintending the killing of a bullock at the bank. Half a dozen wolfish dogs were standing ready to breakfast as soon as the slaughtering was over. A Cossack officer in a picturesque costume stood on the bank near the boat. He wore an embroidered coat of sheepskin, the wool inside, a shaggy cap of coal-black wool, and a pair of fur-topped boots. All his garments were new and well fitting, and contrasted greatly with the greasy and long used coats of the Cossacks on the boat. Sheepskin garments can look more repulsive than cloth ones with equal wearing. Age can wither and custom stale their infinite variety.

Winding among the mountains and cliffs that enclose the valley we reached in the evening a village four miles below the head of the Amoor. I rose at daybreak on the 17th to make my adieus to the river. The morning was clear and frosty, and the stars were twinkling in the sky, save in the east where the blush of dawn was visible. The hills were faintly touched with a little snow that had fallen during the night. The trunks of the birches rose like ghosts among the pines and larches of the forest, while craggy rocks pushed out here and there like battlements of a fortress. The pawing steamer with her mane of stars breasted the current with her prow bearing directly toward the west.

"Just around that point," said the first officer of the Korsackoff as he directed his finger toward a headland on the Chinese shore, "you will see the mouth of the Argoon on the left and the Shilka on the right;—wait a moment, it is not quite time yet."

When we rounded the promontory dawn had grown to daylight, and the mountains on the south bank of the Argoon came into view. A few minutes later I saw the defile of the Shilka. Between the streams the mountains narrowed and came to a point a mile above the meeting of the waters. On the delta below the mountains is the Russian village and Cossack post of Oust-Strelka (Arrow Mouth,) situated in Latitude 53° 19′ 45″ North, and Longitude 121° 50′ 7″ East. It is on the Argoon side of the delta and contains but a few houses. I knew by the smoke that so gracefully curled in the cold atmosphere that the inhabitants were endeavoring to make themselves comfortable.

The Amoor is formed by the union of these rivers, just as the Ohio is formed by the Allegheny and Monongahela. Geographers generally admit that the parent stream of a river is the one whose source is farthest from the junction. The Argoon flows from the lake Koulon, which is filled by the river Kerolun, rising in the Kentei Khan mountains in Northern Mongolia. Together the Argoon and Kerolun have a development of more than a thousand miles. There are many Cossacks settled along the Argoon as a frontier guard. The river is not navigable, owing to numerous rocks and rapids.

Genghis Khan, who subdued China and began that wonderful career of Tartar conquest that extended to Middle Europe, was born on the banks of the Kerolun. Some of his early battles were fought in its valley.

The Shilka is formed by the Onon and Ingodah, that rise in the region north of the head waters of the Kerolun. From the sources of the Onon to Oust-Strelka is a distance of seven hundred and fifty miles. There are many gold mines along this river, and the whole mountain chain is known to be rich in minerals. Including its tributaries on both sides and at its formation, the Amoor as it flows into the Gulf of Tartary drains a territory of 766,000 square miles.

There is a little island just below the point of land extending between the two rivers. As we approached it the steamer turned to the right and proceeded up the Shilka, leaving the Amoor behind us. I may never see this great river again, but I shall never forget its magnificent valley and its waters washing the boundaries of two empires and bringing the civilization of the East and West in contact. I shall never forget its many islands, among which we wound our tortuous way; its green meadows, its steep cliffs, and its blue mountains, that formed an ever-changing and ever beautiful picture. I shall never forget its forests where the yellow hues of autumn contrasted with the evergreen pine and its kindred, and which nature has lavishly spread to shield the earth from the pitiless storm and give man wherewith to erect his habitation and light his hearthstone with generous fire.

Mountain, hill, forest, island, and river will rise to me hereafter in imagination as they rose then in reality. A voyage along the entire course of the Amoor is one that the longest lifetime cannot efface from the memory.

For a hundred and sixty years the little post of Oust-Strelka was the most easterly possession of Russia in the Amoor valley. In 1847 Lieutenant General Mouravieff, having been appointed Governor General of Eastern Siberia, determined to explore the river. In the following spring he sent an officer with four Cossacks to descend the Amoor as far as was prudent. The officer took a liberal supply of presents for the people along the banks, and was instructed to avoid all collisions with the natives and not to enter their towns. From the day of his departure to the present nothing has ever been heard of him or his men. Diligent inquiries have been made among the natives and the Chinese authorities, but no information gained. It is supposed the party were drowned by accident, or killed by hostile residents along the river.

In 1850 and the three following years the mouth of the Amoor was examined and settlements founded, as already described. The year 1854 is memorable for the first descent of the Amoor by a military expedition. The outbreak of the Crimean war rendered it necessary to supply the Russian fleet in the Pacific. The colonies on the Pacific needed provisions, and the Amoor offered the only feasible route to send them. General Mouravieff made his preparations, and obtained the consent of his government to the important step. He asked the permission of the Chinese, but those worthies were as dilatory as usual, and Mouravieff could not wait. He left Shilikinsk on the 27th of May, escorted by a thousand soldiers with several guns, and carrying an ample supply of provisions for the Pacific fleet.

The Chinese made no actual opposition, but satisfied themselves with counting the boats that passed. Mouravieff supplied the fleet at the mouth of the Amoor, and then returned by way of Ayan to Irkutsk. The troops were left to garrison the fortified points on or near the sea.

In 1855 three more expeditions left Shilikinsk with soldiers and colonists. General Mouravieff accompanied the first of these expeditions and went directly to Nicolayevsk. The allied fleet attempted to enter the Amoor but could not succeed. The general sent his compliments to the English Admiral and told him to come on if he could and he should be warmly received. In 1856 a few Cossack posts were established along the river, and in the next year nearly three thousand Cossacks were sent there. The Chinese made a formal protest against these movements, and there were fears of a hostile collision. The reverses that China suffered from the English and French prevented war with Russia, and in 1858 Mouravieff concluded a treaty at Igoon by which the Russian claim to the country north of the Amoor and east of the Ousuree was acknowledged. The Russians were thus firmly established, and the development of the country has progressed peacefully since that period.

As the Argoon from its mouth to Lake Kerolun forms the boundary between the empires I lost sight of China when we entered the Shilka. As I shivered on the steamer's bridge, my breath congealing on my beard, and the hills beyond the Amoor and Argoon white with the early snow of winter, I could not see why the Celestials call their land the 'Central Flowery Kingdom.'

The Shilka has a current flowing four or five miles an hour. The average speed of the Korsackoff in ascending was about four miles. The river wound among mountains that descended to the water without intervening plateaus, and only on rare occasions were meadows visible. The forests were pine and larch, with many birches. The lower part of the Shilka has very little agricultural land, and the only settlements are the stations kept by a few Cossacks, who cut wood for the steamers and supply horses to the post and travelers in winter.

The first night after leaving the Amoor there was a picturesque scene at our wooding station. The mountains were revealed by the setting moon, and their outline against the sky was sharply defined. We had a large fire of pine boughs burning on the shore, and its bright flames lighted both sides of the river. The boatmen in their sheepskin coats and hats walked slowly to and fro, and gave animation to the picture. While I wrote my journal the horses above me danced as though frolicking over a hornet's nest, and reduced sentimental thoughts to a minimum. To render the subject more interesting two officers and the priest grew noisy over a triple game of cards and a bottle of vodki. I wrote in my overcoat, as the thermometer was at 30° with no fire in the cabin.

We frequently met rafts with men and horses descending to supply the post stations, or bound on hunting excursions. I was told that the hunters float down the river on rafts and then make long circuits by land to their points of departure. The Siberian squirrel is very abundant in the mountains north of the Shilka, and his fur is an important article of commerce.

We stopped at Gorbitza, near the mouth of the Gorbitza river, that formerly separated Russia and China and was the boundary up to 1854.

Above this point the villages had an appearance of respectable age not perceptible in the settlements along the Amoor. Ten or twelve miles from our wooding place we met ice coming out of the Chorney river, but it gave us no inconvenience. The valley became wider and the hills less abrupt, while the villages had an air of irregularity more pleasing than the military precision on the Amoor. I saw many dwellings on which decay's effacing fingers were busy. The telegraph posts were fixed above Gorbitza, but the wires had not been strung.

There were many haystacks at the villages, and I could see droves of cattle and sheep on the cleared hills. At one landing I found a man preparing his house for winter by calking the seams with moss. Under the eaves of another house there were many birds that resembled American swallows. I could not say whether they were migratory or not, but if the former they were making their northern stay a late one.

Their twitterings reminded me of the time when I used to go at nightfall, 'when the swallows homeward fly,' and listen to the music without melody as the birds exchanged their greetings, told their loves, and gossipped of their adventures.

PREPARING FOR WINTER.

Just at sunset we reached Shilikinsk, a town stretching nearly two miles along the river, on a plateau thirty feet high. We stopped in the morning where there was abundance of wood, but only took enough to carry us to Shilikinsk. There was a lady in the case. Our first officer had a feminine acquaintance at the town, and accordingly wished to stop for wood, and, if possible, to pass the night there. His plan failed, as no wood could be discovered at Shilikinsk, though our loving mate scanned every part of the bank. We had enough fuel to take us a few miles farther, where we found wood and remained for the night. The disappointed swain pocketed his chagrin and solaced himself by playing the agreeable to a lady passenger.

I saw in the edge of the town a large building surrounded with a palisaded wall. "What is that?" I asked, pointing to the structure new to my eyes.

"It is a station for exiles," was my friend's reply, "when they pass through the town. They generally remain here over night, and sometimes a few days, and this is their lodging. You will see many such on your way through Siberia."

"Is it also the prison for those who are kept here permanently?"

"No; the prison is another affair. The former prison at Shilikinsk has been converted into a glass manufactory. Just behind it is a large tannery, heretofore celebrated throughout Eastern Siberia for its excellent leather."

As we proceeded the country became more open and less mountainous, and I saw wide fields on either side. A road was visible along the northern bank of the river, sometimes cut in the hillside where the slope was steep. On the southern bank there was no road beyond that for local use. The telegraph followed the northern side, but frequently left the road to take short cuts across the hills.

We struck a rock ten miles from our journey's end, and for several minutes I thought we should go gracefully to the bottom. We whirled twice around on the rock before we left it, and our captain feared we had sprung a leak. When once more afloat Borasdine and I packed our baggage and prepared for the shore. We ate the last of our preserves and gave sundry odds and ends to the Cossacks. As a last act we opened the remaining bottles of a case of champagne, and joined officers and fellow passengers in drinking everybody's health.

Late in the afternoon of the 20th October we were in sight of Stratensk. The summer barracks were first visible, and a moment later I could see the church dome. In nearly all Russian towns the churches are the first objects visible on arriving and the last on departing. The house of worship is no less prominent in the picture of a Russian village than the ceremonies of religion in the daily life of the people.

There was a large crowd on the bank to welcome us. Officers, soldiers, merchants, Cossacks, peasants, women, children, and dogs were in goodly numbers. Our own officers were in full uniform to make their calls on shore. The change of costume that came over several passengers was interesting in the extreme.

At last the steamer ceased her asthmatic wheeze and dropped her anchor at the landing. We gave our baggage to a Cossack to take to the hotel. Soon as the rush over the plank was ended I walked ashore from the Korsackoff for the last time.

So ended, for the present, my water journeying. I had zig-zagged from New York a distance, by my line of travel, not less than fifteen thousand miles. The only actual land route on my way had been forty-seven miles, between Aspinwall and Panama. I had traveled on two ocean passenger-steamers, one private steamer of miniature size, a Russian corvette, a gunboat of the Siberian fleet, and two river boats of the Amoor flotilla. Not a serious accident had occurred to mar the pleasure of the journey. There had been discomforts, privations, and little annoyances of sufficient frequency, but they only added interest to the way.

The proverb well says there is no rose without a thorn, and it might add that the rose would be less appreciable were there no thorn. Half our pleasures have their zest in the toil through which they are gained. In travel, the little hardships and vexations bring the novelties and comforts into stronger relief, and make the voyager's happiness more real. It is an excellent trait of human nature that the traveler can remember with increased vividness the pleasing features of his journey while he forgets their opposites. Privations and discomforts appeal directly to the body; their effect once passed the physical system courts oblivion. Pleasures reach our higher being, which experiences, enjoys, and remembers.

CHAPTER XXII.

STRATENSK is neither large nor handsome. The most I saw of it was near the hotel whither we went from the boat. The rooms we were shown into faced the river, and had high walls decorated with a few pictures. My apartment had a brick stove in one corner, a table, three or four chairs, and a wide sofa or cushioned bench without a back. This last article served as bed by night and seat by day. No bed clothing is furnished in a Siberian hotel, each traveler being expected to carry his own supply.

The government has a foundry and repair shop two miles above the town, where several steamers pass the winter and have their machinery repaired. Immediately on arrival we sent to request Mr. Lovett, the gentleman in charge of the works, to call upon us. He responded promptly, and came while we were at supper. Being English and with a slight tendency to *embonpoint*, he readily accepted several bottles of 'Bass & Co.' that remained from our small stores. He was accompanied by Captain Ivashinsoff, who spoke English easily and well. His knowledge of it was obtained rather romantically as the story was told me.

Two years earlier this officer happened in Hong Kong and during his stay an American vessel arrived. Her captain had been seriously ill for some weeks and totally incapable of duty. The first mate died on the voyage, and the second was not equal to the difficulties of navigation. The captain was accompanied by his daughter, who had been several years at sea and learned the mysteries of Bowditch more as a pastime than for anything else. In the dilemma she assumed control of the ship, making the daily observation and employing the mate as executive officer. When they reached Hong Kong the captain was just recovering. The young woman came on shore, saw and conquered the Russian. Neither spoke the other's language, and their conversation was conducted in French. After their marriage they began to study, and had made such progress that I found the captain speaking good English, and learned that the lady was equally fluent in Russian. She was living at Stratensk at the time of my visit, and I greatly regretted that our short stay prevented my seeing her. She was a native of Chelsea, Massachusetts, and was said to enjoy her home on the Amoor.

Three or four steamers were in winter quarters, and the Korsackoff was to join them immediately. Both at Stratensk and Nicolayevsk it is the custom to remove the machinery from steamers during winter. It is carefully housed to prevent its rusting, and I presume to lessen the loss in case of fire or damage from breaking ice.

We talked with our new friends till late in the evening, and then prepared to continue our journey. Lovett gave me his blessing and a feather pillow; the former to cover general accidents and the latter to prevent contusions from the jolting vehicle. Borasdine obtained a Cossack to accompany us on the road and ordered our baggage made ready. The Cossack piled it into a wagon and it was transported to the ferry landing and dumped upon the gravel. We followed and halted in front of the palisaded hotel of the exiles. The ferry boat was on the opposite shore, four or five hundred yards away. Borasdine called, but the boatmen did not rise.

"Dai sloopka!" (send a boat.)

After a moment's pause he repeated:

"Dai sloopka!"

He added the usually magic word "courier!" but it had no effect. He shouted repeatedly and grew hoarse. Then I lifted up my voice like a pelican in the wilderness, but with no better effect. When we had almost reached the pitch of despair a man appeared from behind a wood pile and tried his vocal organs in our behalf. At his second call a reply was given, and very soon a light twinkled at the ferry house.

The boat was a long time coming, and while we waited its arrival a drunken Bouriat made himself unpleasantly familiar. As often as I changed my position he would come to my side and endeavor to rest his dirty arm on my shoulder.

STRATENSK, EASTERN SIBERIA.

I finally walked through a pile of brushwood and crooked sticks, which was too much for the native with his weak knees and muddy brain. After struggling with a persistency that would have been commendable had the object to be attained been commensurate to the effort, he became inextricably tangled, and I left him in the loving embrace of a decayed tree-top.

The boat came with four shaggy ferrymen, who had some difficulty in reaching land. It was a kind of large skiff, high at both ends and having a platform, like that of a hay-scale, in the center. The platform projected a foot or more beyond the sides of the boat, and had no railing to prevent a frightened horse or drunken man going overboard. This is the general style of river ferry boats in Siberia. The boatmen do not appear very skillful in handling them, but I learned that serious accidents were very rare.

We piled our baggage and left the shore, running upon two rocks and colliding with a sandbar before getting fairly away. I fell asleep during the crossing, satisfied that the crew did not need my assistance. We landed where the road is cut into the rocky bank, and were obliged to lift the baggage over a pile of stony debris. The boatmen said it was impossible to go to the regular landing, but I suspect they wished an extra gratuity for handling our impedimenta. Before the work was finished they regretted their manœuvre.

As we touched the shore one man went to the station to bring horses and a vehicle. Borasdine and I scrambled over the rocks to the road fifteen feet above the water, and by the time the crew brought up our baggage the conveyance arrived. It was what the Russians call a *telyaga*, drawn by three horses.

This carriage is of Quaker simplicity. There are four wheels on wooden axles, with rough but strong 'reaches.' A body, shaped something like an old-fashioned baby-cart, rests upon the reaches or on poles fixed over them. The hood protects against wind and rain from behind, and the best of the vehicles have boots buttoned in front and attached to the hoods. The driver sits on the bow directly behind the shaft-horse, and one part of his duty is to keep from falling off. The traveler spreads his baggage inside as evenly as possible to form a bed or cushion. Angular pieces should be discarded, as the corners are disagreeable when jolted against one's sides. Two shafts are fixed in the forward axle, and a horse between them forms a sort of *point d'appui*. Any number from one to six can be tied on outside of him.

The fault of our baggage was that we, or rather I, had too

much. Worst of all, I had a wooden trunk that I proposed throwing away at Nicolayevsk, but had been told I could carry to Irkutsk without trouble. It could not ride inside, or if it did we could not. We placed the small articles in the interior of the vehicle, and tied the trunk and Borasdine's *chemadan* on the projecting poles behind. The *chemadan* is in universal use among Siberian travelers, and admirably adapted to the road. It is made of soft leather, fastens with a lacing of deer-skin thongs, and can be lashed nearly water tight. It will hold a great deal,—I never saw one completely filled,—and accommodates itself to the shape of its aggregate contents. It can be of any size up to three or four feet long, and its dimensions are proportioned to each other about like those of an ordinary pocket-book. A great advantage is the absence of sharp corners and the facility of packing closely.

We acted contrary to the custom of the country in tying our baggage behind. There are gentlemen of the road in Siberia as there are 'road agents' in California. The Siberian highwaymen rarely disturb the person of a traveler, but their chief amusement is to cut away outside packages. As a precaution we mounted our Cossack on the trunk, but before we went a mile he fell from his perch in spite of his utmost efforts to cling to the vehicle. After that event he rode by the driver's side.

On seeing Lovett at Stratensk my first question related to the condition of the road. "Horrid," said he. "The worst time to travel. There has been much rain and cold weather. You will find mud either soft or frozen most of the way to Chetah."

Before we started the driver brought an additional horse, and after a preliminary kick or two we took the road. For a few miles we went up and down hills along the edge of the river, where the route has been cut at much labor and expense. This was not especially bad, the worst places being at the hollows between the hills where the mud was half-congealed. When we left the river we found the mud that Lovett prophesied. Quality and quantity were alike disagreeable. All roads have length more or less; ours had length, breadth, depth, and thickness. The bottom was not regular like that of the Atlantic, but broken into inequalities that gave an uneasy motion to the telyaga.

To travel in Siberia one must have a *padaroshnia*, or road pass, from the government authorities, stating the number of horses to which he is entitled. There are three grades of padaroshnia; the first for high officials and couriers; the second for officers on ordinary business; and the third for civilian travelers. The first and second are issued free to those entitled to receive them, and the third is purchased at the rate of half a copeck a verst. These papers serve the double purpose of bringing revenue to government and preventing unauthorized persons traveling about the country. A traveler properly provided presents his papers at a post-station and receives horses in his turn according to the character of his documents.

A person with a courier's pass is never detained for want of animals; other travelers must take their chance. Of course the second class of passport precedes the third by an inflexible rule. Suppose A has a second class and B a third class padaroshnia. A reaches a station and finds B with a team ready to start. If there are no more horses the *smotretal* (station master) detaches the animals from B's vehicle and supplies them to A. B must wait until he can be served; it may be an hour, a day, or a week.

The stations are kept by contract. The government locates a station and its lessee is paid a stipulated sum each year. He agrees to keep the requisite horses and drivers, the numbers varying according to the importance of the route. He contracts to carry the post each way from his station to the next, the price for this service being included in the annual payment. He must keep one vehicle and three horses at all times ready for couriers. Couriers, officers, and travelers of every kind pay at each station the rate fixed by law.

In Kamchatka and North Eastern Siberia the post route is

equipped with dog-teams, just as it has horses in more southerly latitudes. In the northern part of Yakutsk the reindeer is used for postal or traveling service. A padaroshnia calls for a given number of horses, usually three, without regard to the number of persons traveling upon it. Generally the names of all who are to use it are written on the paper, but this is not absolutely necessary. Borasdine had a padaroshnia and so had I, but mine was not needed as long as we kept together.

The post carriages must be changed at every station. Constant changing is a great trouble, especially if one has much baggage. In a wet or cold night when you have settled comfortably into a warm nest, and possibly fallen asleep, it is an intolerable nuisance to turn out and transfer. To remedy this evil one can buy a *tarantass*, a vehicle on the general principle of the telyaga, but larger, stronger, and better in every way. When he buys there is a scarcity and the price is high, but when he has finished his journey and wishes to sell, it is astonishing how the market is glutted. At Stratensk I endeavored to purchase a tarantass, but only one could be had. This was too rheumatic for the journey, and very groggy in the springs, so at the advice of Lovett I adhered to the telyaga.

The Russians apply the term 'equipage' to any vehicle, whether on wheels or runners, and with or without its motive power. It is a generic definition, and can include anything drawn by horses, dogs, deer, or camels. The word sounds very well when applied to a fashionable turnout, but less so when speaking of a dirt-cart or wheelbarrow.

The same word, 'equipage,' is used in Russian as in French to denote a ship's crew. In this connection I heard an amusing story, vouched for as correct. A few years after the disappearance of Sir John Franklin the English Admiralty requested the Russian government to make inquiries for the lost navigator along the coast and islands of the Arctic Ocean. An order to that effect was sent to the Siberian authorities, and they in turn commanded all subordinates to inquire and report. A petty officer some where in Western Siberia was puzzled at the printed order to 'inquire concerning the English Captain, John Franklin, and his equipage.' In due time he reported:

"I have made the proper inquiries. I can learn nothing about Captain Franklin; but in one of my villages there is an old sleigh that no one claims, and it may be his equipage."

We carried one and sometimes two bells on the yoke of our shaft-horse to signify that we traveled by post. Every humbler vehicle was required to give us the entire road, at least such was the theory. Sometimes we obtained it, and sometimes the approaching drivers were asleep, and the horses kept their own way. When this occurred our driver generally took an opportunity to bring his whip lash upon the sleeper. It is a privilege he enjoys when driving a post carriage to strike his delinquent fellow man if in reach. I presume this is a partial consolation for the kicks and blows occasionally showered upon himself. Humanity in authority is pretty certain to give others the treatment itself has received. Only great natures will deal charity and kindness when remembering oppression and cruelty.

I was not consulted when our telyaga was built, else it would have been wider and longer. When our small parcels were arranged inside there was plenty of room for one but hardly enough for two. Borasdine and I were of equal height, and neither measured a hair's breadth less than six feet. When packed for riding I came in questionable shape, my body and limbs forming a geometric figure that Euclid never knew. Notwithstanding my cramped position I managed to doze a little, and contemplated an essay on a new mode of triangulation. We rattled our bones over the stones and frozen earth, and dragged and dripped through the mud to the first station. As we reached the establishment our Cossack and driver shouted "*courier!*" in tones that soon brought the smotretal and his attendants. They rubbed their half-open eyes and bestirred themselves to bring horses. The word 'courier' invigorates the attachés of a post route, as they well know that the bearer of a courier's pass must not be delayed. Ten minutes are allowed for changing a courier's horses, and the change is often made in six or eight minutes. The length of a journey depends considerably upon the time consumed at stations.

Here we found a tarantass, neither new nor elegant, but strong and capacious. We hired it to Nerchinsk, and our

A SIBERIAN TARANTASS.

Cossack transferred the baggage while four little rats of ponies were being harnessed. The harness used on this road was a combination of leather and hemp in about equal proportions. There were always traces of ropes more or less twisted. It is judicious to carry a quantity of rope in one's vehicle for use in case of accident. A Russian *yemshick* (driver) is quite skillful in repairing breakages if he can find enough rope for his purpose.

The horses, like many other terrestrial things, were better than they appeared, and notwithstanding the bad road they carried us at good speed. I was told that the horses between Stratensk and Lake Baikal were strangers to corn and oats, and not over familiar with hay. Those at the post stations must be fed in the stable, but nearly all others hunt their own food. In summer they can easily do this, but in winter they subsist on the dry grass standing on the hills and prairies. There is little snow in this region, but when it falls on the pastures the horses scrape it away to reach the grass. They are never blanketed in the coldest weather, and the only brushing they receive is when they run among bushes.

In the government of Yakutsk there are many horses that find their own living in winter as in summer. They eat grass, moss, fish, bushes, and sometimes the bark of trees. Captain Wrangell tells of the great endurance of these beasts, and says that like all other animals of that region they shed their coats in the middle of summer.

At the second station the smotretal sought our horses among the village peasants, as he had none of his own. He explained that a high official had passed and taken the horses usually kept for the courier. This did not satisfy Borasdine, who entered complaint in the regulation book, stating the circumstances of the affair. At every station there is a book sealed to a small table and open to public inspection. An aggrieved traveler is at liberty to record a statement of his trouble. At regular intervals an officer investigates the affairs of every station. Complaints are examined, and offences treated according to their character. This wholesome regulation keeps the station masters in proper restraint.

Day had fairly opened through a dense fog when our delay ended. While we descended a long hill one of our hinder wheels parted company and took a tangent to the road side. We were in full gallop at the time, but did not keep it up long. A pole from a neighboring fence, held by a Pole from Warsaw, lifted the axle so that the wheel could be replaced. I assisted by leaving the carriage and standing at the roadside till all was ready. We had some doubts about the vehicle holding together much longer, but it behaved very well. The tarantass is a marvel of endurance. To listen to the creaking of its joints, and observe its air of infirmity, lead to the belief that it will go to pieces within a few hours. It rattles and groans and threatens prompt analysis, but some how it continues cohesive and preserves its identity hundreds of miles over rough roads.

We were merciless to the horses as they were not ours and we were in a hurry. When the driver allowed them to lag, Borasdine ejaculated 'POSHOL!' with a great deal of emphasis and much effect. This word is like 'faster' in English, and is learned very early in a traveler's career in Russia. I acquired it before reaching the first station on my ride, and could use it very skillfully. In the same connection are the words '*droghi*' ('touch up,') '*skorey*' ('hurry,') and '*stupie*' ('go ahead.') All these commands have the accent upon the last syllable, and are very easy to the vocal organs. I learned them all and often used them, but to this day I do not know the Russian word for 'slower.' I never had occasion to employ it while in the empire, except once when thrown down an icy slope with a heap of broken granite at its base, and at another time when a couple of pretty girls were standing by the roadside and, as I presumed, wanted to look at me.

From Stratensk to Nerchinsk, a distance of sixty miles, our road led among hills, undulating ground, meadows, and strips of steppe, or prairie, sometimes close to the river, and again several miles away. The country is evidently well adapted to agriculture, the condition of the farms and villages indicating prosperity. I saw much grain in stacks or gathered in small barns. As it was Sunday no work was in progress, and there were but few teams in motion anywhere. The roads were such that no one would travel for pleasure, and the first day of the week is not used for business journeys.

From the top of a hill I looked into the wide and beautiful valley of the Nertcha, which enters the Shilka from the north. On its left bank and two or three miles from its mouth is the town of Nerchinsk with five or six thousand inhabitants. Its situation is charming, and to me the view was especially pleasing, as it was the first Russian town where I saw evidences of age and wealth. The domes of its churches glistened in the sunlight that had broken through the fog and warmed the tints of the whole picture. The public buildings and many private residences had an air of solidity. Some of the merchants' houses would be no discredit to New York or London. The approach from the east is down a hill sloping toward the banks of the Nertcha.

We entered the gateway of Nerchinsk, and after passing some of the chief buildings drove to the house of Mr. Kaporaki, where we were received with open arms. Borasdine and his acquaintance kissed affectionately, and after their greeting ended I was introduced. We unloaded from the tarantass, piled our baggage in the hallway, and dismissed the driver with the borrowed vehicle. Almost before we were out of our wrappings the samovar was steaming, and we sat down to a comforting breakfast, with abundance of tea. And didn't we enjoy it after riding eight or ten hours over a road that would have shaken skimmilk into butter? You bet we did.

CHAPTER XXIII.

THE heaviest fortunes at Nerchinsk have been made in commerce and gold mining, principally the latter. I met one man reputed to possess three million roubles, and two others who were each put down at over a million. Mr. Kaporaki, our host, was a successful gold miner, if I may judge by what I saw. His dwelling was an edifice somewhat resembling Arlington House, but without its signs of decay. The principal rooms I entered were his library, parlor, and dining-room; the first was neat and cozy, and the second elaborately fitted with furniture from St. Petersburg. Both were hung with pictures and paintings, the former bearing French imprints. His dining-room was in keeping with the rest of the establishment, and I could hardly realize that I was in Siberia, five thousand miles from the Russian capital and nearly half that distance from the Pacific Ocean. The realization was more difficult when our host named a variety of wines ready for our use. Would we take sherry, port, or madicra, or would we prefer Johannisberg, Hockheimer, or Verzenay? Would we try Veuve Cliquot, or Carte d'Or? A box of genuine Havanas stood upon his library table, and received our polite attention. We arrived about ten in the morning, and on consenting to remain till afternoon a half dozen merchants were invited to join us at dinner.

Mr. Kaporaki's gold mines were on the tributaries of the Nertcha, about a hundred miles away. From his satisfied air in showing specimens and figures I concluded his claims were profitable. The mining season had just closed, and he was footing up his gains and losses for the year. The gold he exhibited was in coarse scales, with occasional nuggets, and closely resembled the product I saw a few months earlier of some washings near Mariposa.

The gold on the Nertcha and its tributaries is found in the sand and earth that form the bed of the streams. Often it is many feet deep and requires much 'stripping.' I heard of one *priesk* (claim) where the pay-dirt commenced sixty-five feet from the surface. Notwithstanding the great expense of removing the superincumbent earth, the mine had been worked to a profit. Twenty or thirty feet of earth to take away is by no means uncommon. The pay-dirt is very rich, and the estimates of its yield are stated at so many *zolotniks* of gold for a hundred poods of earth. From one pood of dirt, of course unusually rich, Mr. Kaporaki obtained 24 zolotniks, or three ounces of gold. In another instance ten poods of dirt yielded 90 zolotniks of gold. The ordinary yield, as near as I could ascertain, was what a Californian would call five or six cents to the pan.

Each of these merchant-miners pays to the government fifteen per cent. of all gold he obtains, and is not allowed to sell the dust except to the proper officials. He delivers his gold and receives the money for it as soon as it is melted and assayed. It was hinted to me that much gold was smuggled across the frontier into China, and never saw the treasury of his Imperial Majesty, the Czar. The Cossacks of the Argoon keep a sharp watch for traffic of this kind. "They either," said my informant, "deliver a culprit over to justice or, what is the same thing, compel him to bribe them heavily to say nothing."

Nerchinsk formerly stood at the junction of the Nertcha and Shilka, on the banks of both rivers, but the repeated damage from floods caused its removal. Even on its present site it is not entirely safe from inundation, the lower part of the town having been twice under water and in danger of being washed away.

Many of the present inhabitants are exiles or the descendants of exiles, Nerchinsk having been a place of banishment for political and criminal offenders during the last hundred years. Those condemned to work in the mines were sent to Great Nerchinsk Zavod, about two hundred miles away. The town was the center of the military and mining district, and formerly had more importance than at present. Many participants in the insurrection of 1825 were sent there, among them the princes Trubetskoi and Volbonskoi. After laboring in the mines and on the roads of Nerchinsk, they were sent to Chetah, where they were employed in a polishing mill.

In many stories about Siberian exiles, published in England and America, Nerchinsk has occupied a prominent position. As far as I could observe it is not a place of perpetual frost and snow, its summers being warm though brief. In winter it has cold winds blowing occasionally from the Yablonoi mountains down the valley of the Nertcha. The region is very well adapted to agriculture, and the valley as I saw it had an attractive appearance.

The product of the Nerchinsk mines has been silver, gold, and lead. The search for silver and lead has diminished since the mines were opened to private enterprise. At one time 40,000 poods of lead were produced here annually, most of it being sent to the Altai mountains to be employed in reducing silver. In most places where explored the country is rich in gold, and I have little doubt that thorough prospecting would reveal many placers equaling the best of those in California.

Very few exiles are now sent to Nerchinsk in comparison with the numbers formerly banished there. Under the reign of Nicholas and his father Nerchinsk received its greatest accessions, the Polish revolutions and the revolt of 1825 contributing largely to its population. Places of exile have always been selected with relation to the offence and character of the prisoners. The worst offenders, either political or criminal, were generally sent to the mines of Nerchinsk, their terms of service varying from two to twenty years, or for life. I was told that the longest sentence now given is for twenty years. The condition of prisoners in former times was doubtless bad, and there are many stories of cruelty and extortion practiced by keepers and commandants. The dwellings of prisoners were frequently no better than the huts of savages; their food and clothing were poor and insufficient; they were compelled to labor in half frozen mud and water for twelve or fourteen hours daily, and beaten when they faltered.

The treatment of prisoners depended greatly upon the character of the commandant of the mines. Of the brutality of some officials and the kindness of others there can be little doubt. We have sufficient proof of the varied qualities of the human heart in the conduct of prison-keepers in America during our late war. There have been many exaggerations concerning the treatment of exiles. I do not say there has been no cruelty, but that less has occurred than some writers would have us believe. Before leaving America I read of the rigorous manner in which the sentence of the conspirators of 1825 was carried out. According to one authority the men were loaded with chains and compelled to the hardest labor in the mines under relentless overseers. They were badly lodged, fed with insufficient food, and when ill had little or no medical treatment.

Nearly all these unfortunates were of noble families and never performed manual labor before reaching the mines. They had been tenderly reared, and were mostly young and unused to the hardships of life outside the capitals. Thrust at once into the mines of Siberia they could hardly survive a lengthened period of the cruelty alleged. Most of them served out their sentences and retained their health. Some returned to Europe after more than thirty years exile, and a few were living in Siberia at the time of my visit, forty-one years after their banishment. I conclude they were either blessed with more than iron constitutions, or there is some mistake in the account of their suffering and privation.

Many attempts have been made to escape from these mines, but very few were completely successful. Some prisoners crossed into China after dodging the vigilant Cossacks on the frontier, but they generally perished in the deserts of Mongolia, either by starvation or at the hands of the natives. I have heard of two who reached the Gulf of Pecheli after many hardships, where they captured a Chinese fishing boat and put to sea. When almost dead of starvation they were picked up by an English barque and carried to Shanghae, where the foreign merchants supplied them with money to find their way to Paris.

A better route than this was by the Amoor, before it was open to Russian navigation. Many who escaped this way lost their lives, but others reached the seacoast where they were picked up by whalers or other transient ships. In 1844 three men started for the Ohotsk sea, traveling by way of the Yablonoi mountains. They had managed to obtain a rifle, and subsisted upon game they killed, and upon berries, roots, and the bark of trees. They escaped from the mines about midsummer, and hoped by rapid travel to reach the coast before winter overtook them.

One of the men was killed by falling from a rock during the first month of the journey. The others buried their dead companion as best they could, marking his grave with a cross, though with no expectation it would again be seen by human eyes. Traversing the mountains and reaching the tributaries of the Aldan river, they found their hardships commencing. The country was rough and game scarce, so that the fugitives were exhausted by fatigue and hunger. They traveled for a time with the wandering Tunguze of this region, and were caught by the early snows of winter when the coast was still two hundred miles away. They determined to wait until spring before crossing the mountains. Unluckily while with the Tunguze they were seen by a Russian merchant, who informed the authorities. Early in the spring they were captured and returned to their place of imprisonment.

The region around the Yablonoi mountains is so desolate that escape in that direction is almost impossible. By way of the post route to Lake Baikal it is equally difficult, as the road is carefully watched and there are few habitations away from the post villages and stations. No one can travel by post without a padaroshnia, and this can only be procured at the chief towns and is not issued to an unknown applicant.

I heard a story of a young Pole who attempted, some years ago, to escape from exile. He was teacher in a private family and passed his evenings in gambling. At one time he was very successful at cards, and gained in a single week three thousand roubles. With this capital he arranged a plan of escape.

By some means he procured a padaroshnia, not in his own name, and announced his intention to visit his friends a few miles away. As he did not return promptly search was made, and it was found that a person answering his description had started toward Lake Baikal. Pursuit naturally turned in that direction, exactly opposite to his real course of flight. He traveled by post with his padaroshnia and reached the vicinity of Omsk without difficulty. Very injudiciously he quarreled with the drivers at a post station about the payment of ten copecks, which he alleged was an overcharge. The padaroshnia was examined in consequence of the quarrel and found applicable to a Russian merchant of the third class, and not for a nobleman, which he claimed to be.

The station-master arrested the traveler and sent him to Omsk, when his real character was ascertained. On the third day of captivity he bribed his guards and escaped during the night. He remained free more than a month, but was finally recaptured and sent to Irkutsk.

At Nerchinsk I resumed my efforts to purchase a tarantass, but my investigations showed the Nerchinsk market 'out' of everything in the tarantass line and no promise of a new crop. Fortune and Kaporaki favored me, and found a suitable vehicle that I could borrow for the journey to Irkutsk. I was to answer for its safety and deliver it to a designated party on my arrival there.

The regulations did not permit, or at least encourage, Borasdine to invest in vehicles. A courier is expected, unless in winter, to travel by the post carriages. All breakages in that case are at the expense of government, with the possible exception of the courier's bones and head. If a carriage breaks down he takes another and leaves the wreck for the station men to pick up. If he should buy a tarantass and it gave out he would be forced to leave it till he came again, or sell it at any price offered. Nothing that relates to his personal comfort is allowed to detain a courier. He can stop only for change of team, hasty meals, and when leaving or taking despatches on his route. Sometimes a river gets high and refuses to respect his padaroshnia, or a severe and blinding storm stops all travel. A courier's pass is supposed to command everything short of the elements, and I have a suspicion that some Russians believe it powerful *with* the elements.

A courier ought to travel with only his baggage and servant, the former not exceeding 200 pounds. Borasdine had Cossack and baggage in proper quantity; adding me and my impedimenta, he was hardly in light moving order. I suggested that he drop me and I would trust to luck and my padaroshnia. I had confidence in the good nature of the Russians and my limited knowledge of the language. I could exhibit my papers, ask for horses, say I was hungry, and was perfectly confident I could pay out money as long as it lasted. But my companion replied that an extra day on the route would make no difference in his catching the boat to cross Lake Baikal, and we would remain together until new difficulties arose.

Having dined we visited the post-station and ordered horses sent to the house of our host. The servants filled our tarantass with baggage, while their master filled us with champagne. The vehicle displayed the best carrying capacity, as it had room for more when our hearts were too full for utterance, save in a half breathed sigh.

We rattled out of Kaporaki's yard and down to the Nertcha, where we had a ferry-boat like the one at Stratensk, though a little larger. The horses were detached and remained on the bank until the tarantass was safely on board.

There was not much room for them, but they managed to find standing places.

By the time we were over the river it was night, and the sentinel stars had set their watch in the sky. We found the road an unpleasant combination of snow, dirt, and water. We had four weak little horses, and the driver told us they had made one journey to the station and back again since morning.

In the Russian posting system the horses carry loads only one way. The driver takes your vehicle to the station, where he is allowed to rest himself and horses one hour and then starts on his return. In ordinary seasons when the traveling is good, each team of horses will make two round trips in twenty-four hours. This gives them from fifty to seventy miles daily travel, half of it without load and at a gentle pace.

After the third station the road improved, the snow and mud diminishing and leaving a comparatively dry track. The stations were generally so uncomfortably hot as to put me in a perspiration, and I was glad to get out of doors. The temperature was about 70° Fahrenheit, and the air at night contained odors from the breath and boots of dormant *moujiks*. The men sleep on the floor and benches, but the top of the stove is the favorite couch. The stove is of brick as already described, and its upper surface is frequently as wide as a common bed. Sometimes the caloric is a trifle abundant, but I have rarely known it complained of.

FAVORITE BED.

I could never clearly understand the readiness and ability of the Russians to endure contrasts of heat and cold with utter complacence and without apparent ill effect. I have seen a yemshick roused at midnight from the top of a stove where he was sleeping in a temperature of eighty-five or ninety degrees. He made his toilet by tightening his waist-belt and putting on his boots. When the horses were ready he donned his cap and extra coat, thrust his hands into mittens, and mounted the front of a sleigh. The cold would be anywhere from ten to fifty degrees below zero, but the man rarely appeared to suffer. In severe weather I hesitated to enter the stations on account of the different temperature of the house and the open air, but the Russians did not seem to mind the sudden changes.

All natives of Northern Siberia subject themselves without inconvenience to extremes of heat and cold. Major Abasa told me that when the cold was 40° below zero he had found the Koriaks in their yourts with a temperature 75° above. They passed from one to the other without a change of clothing and without perspiring. At night they ordinarily slept in their warm dwellings, but when traveling they rested in the snow under the open sky. In his exploration around Penjinsk Gulf the major saw a woman sleep night after night on the snow in the coldest weather with no covering but the clothing she wore in the day. She would have slept equally well if transferred to a hot room.

The Yakuts and Tunguze are equally hardy. Captain Wrangell gives examples of their endurance, especially of living in warm rooms or sleeping on the ice at a low temperature. Captain Cochrane, the English Pedestrian, had a wonderful experience with some natives that guided him from the Lena to the Kolyma. Though the Captain was an old traveler and could support much cold and fatigue, he was greatly outdone by his guides. He could never easily accommodate himself to wide extremes of heat and cold, and I believe this is the experience of nearly all persons not born and reared under a northern sky.

The road from Nerchinsk to Chetah is through an undulating country, the hills in many places being high enough to merit the name of mountains. Sometimes we followed the valley of the Ingodah, and again we left it to wind over the hills and far away where the bluffs prevented our keeping near the stream. When we looked upon the river from these mountains the scene was beautiful, and I shall long retain my impression of the loveliness of the Ingodah. Mr. Collins described this valley nine years before me, and with one exception I can confirm all he said of its charms. He had the good fortune to travel in spring when the flowers were in bloom, whereas my journey was late in autumn. My English friend at Stratensk spoke of this particular feature of the country, and described the thick carpet of blossoms that in some places almost hid the grass from view. To compensate for the long and dreary winter Nature spreads her floral beauties with lavish hand, and converts the once ice-bound region into a landscape of beautiful and fragrant flowers.

The valley is fertile and well cultivated, villages and farm houses being frequent. The road was excellent, wide, and well made; much labor had been expended upon it during the last two years. Its up and down-ishness was not to my liking, as the horses utterly refused to gallop in ascending hills a mile or two long. The descent was less difficult, but unfortunately we could not have it all descent. We had equal quantities of rising and falling, with the difference against us that we were ascending the valley. Fortunately the road was dry and in some places we found it dusty.

Late in the afternoon we halted for dinner, ordering the samovar almost before we stopped the tarantass. We ordered eggs and bread, and in hopes of something substantial Borasdine consulted the mistress of the house. He returned with disgust pictured on his countenance.

"Have they anything?" I asked.

"Nothing."

"Nothing at all?"

"No; nothing but mutton."

Nothing but mutton! *I* was entirely reconciled. When it came I made a fine dinner, but he took very little of it. There are great flocks of sheep belonging to the Bouriats in Eastern Siberia, and they form the chief support of that people. Curiously enough the Russians rarely eat mutton, though so abundant around them. Borasdine told me it seldom appeared on a Siberian table, and I observed that both nobles and peasants agreed in disliking it. While at dinner we caught sight of a pretty face and figure, more to my fellow traveler's taste than the *piece de resistance* of our meal.

After dinner we passed over a hill and entered a level region where we found plenty of mud. About midnight the yemshick exhibited his skill by driving into a mudhole where there was solid ground on both sides. We were hopelessly stuck, and all our cries and utterances were of no avail. The Cossack and the driver could accomplish nothing, and we were obliged to descend from the carriage. We required our subordinates to put their shoulders to the wheels, though the operation covered them with mud. While they lifted we shouted to the horses, Borasdine in Russian and I in French and English.

Twenty minutes of this toil accomplished nothing. Then we unloaded all our baggage down to the smallest articles. Another effort and we were still in our slough of despond. I retreated to a neighboring fence and returned with a stout pole. The Cossack brought another, and we arranged to lift the fore wheels to somewhere near the surface. It was my duty to urge the horses, and I flattered myself that I performed it.

I had the driver's whip to assist my utterance; the others lifted, while I struck and shouted. We had a long pull, a strong pull, and a pull all together, and pulled out of the depths. I attributed no small part of the success to the effect of American horse-vocabulary upon Russian quadrupeds. When we reloaded it was refreshing to observe the care with which the Cossack had placed our pillows on the wet ground and piled heavy baggage over them. Borasdine expressed his objection to this plan in such form that the Cossack was not likely to repeat the operation.

The motion of the tarantass, especially its jolting over the rough parts of the route, gave me a violent headache, the

CONCENTRATED ENERGIES.

worst I ever experienced. The journey commenced too abruptly for my system to be reconciled without complaint. Nearly four months I had been almost constantly on ships and steamboats, all my land riding in that time not amounting to thirty miles. I came ashore at Stratensk and began travel with a Russian courier over Siberian roads at the worst season of the year. It was like leaving the comforts of a Fifth Avenue parlor to engage in wood-sawing. At every bound of the vehicle my brain seemed ready to burst, and I certainly should have halted had we not intended delaying at Chetah.

A Russian yemshick centers his whole duty in driving his team. He gives no thought to the carriage or the persons inside; they must look out for their own interest. Let him come to a hill, rough or smooth, rocky or gravelly, provided there be no actual danger, he descends at his best speed. Sometimes the horses trot, and again they gallop down a long slope. Near the bottom they set out on a full run, as if pursued by a pack of hungry wolves. They dash down the hill, across the hollow, and part way up the opposite ascent without slacking speed. The carriage leaps, bumps, and rattles, and the contents, animate or inanimate, are tossed violently. If there is a log bridge in the hollow the effect is more than electric. The driver does not even turn his head to regard his passengers. If the carriage holds together and follows it is all that concerns him.

At first I was not altogether enamored of this practice. But as I never suffered actual injury and the carriages endured their rough treatment, I came in time to like it. As a class the Russian yemshicks are excellent drivers, and in riding behind more than three hundred of them I had abundant opportunity to observe their skill They are not always intelligent and quick to devise plans in emergencies, but they are faithful and know the duties of their profession. For speed and safety I would sooner place myself in their hands than behind professional drivers in New York. They know the rules of the road, the strength and speed of their horses, and are almost uniformly good natured.

We reached Chetah at five in the morning and roused the inmates of the only hotel. The sleepy *chelavek* showed us to a room containing two chairs, two tables, and a dirty sofa. The Cossack brought our baggage from the tarantass, and we endeavored to sleep. When we rose Borasdine went to call upon the governor while I ordered breakfast on my own account. Summoning the *chelavek* I began, "*Dai samovar, chi, saher e klehb*," (give the samovar, tea, bread, and sugar.) This accomplished, I procured beefsteaks and potatoes without difficulty. I spoke the language of the country in a fragmentary way, but am certain my Russian was not half as bad as the beefsteak.

CHAPTER XXIV.

CHETAH stands on the left bank of the Ingodah, nearly three hundred miles above Stratensk, and is the capital of the Trans-Baikal province. For many years it was a small town with a few hundred inhabitants, but the opening of the Amoor in 1854 changed its character. Below this point the Ingodah is navigable for boats and rafts, and during the early years of the Amoor occupation much material was floated down from Chetah. In 1866 its population, including the garrison, was about five thousand. Many houses were large and well fitted, and all were of wood. The officers lived comfortably, but complained of high rents.

The governor's mansion is the largest and best, and near it is the club-house where weekly soirees are held. I attended one of these and found a pleasant party. There was music and dancing, tea-drinking and card-playing, gossip and silence at varied and irregular intervals. Some of the officers read selections from Russian authors, and others recited pieces of prose and poetry. There were dialogues, evidently humorous to judge by the mirth they produced, and there was a paper containing original contributions. The association appeared prosperous, and I was told that its literary features were largely due to the efforts of the governor.

There is a *gastinni-dvor* or row of shops and a market-place surrounded with huckster's stalls, much like those near Fulton Ferry. Desiring to replace a broken watch-key I found a repair shop and endeavored to make my inquiries in Russian. "*Monsieur parle le Francais, je crois,*" was the response to my attempt, and greatly facilitated the transaction of business. Before I left New York an acquaintance showed me a photograph of a Siberian, who proved to be the watchmaker thus encountered.

Walking about the streets I saw many prisoners at work under guard, most of them wearing fetters. Though I became accustomed during my Siberian travels to the sight of chains on men, I could never hear their clanking without a shudder. The chains worn by a prisoner were attached at one end to bands enclosing his ankles and at the other to a belt around his waist. The sound of these chains as the men

PRISONERS AT CHETAH.

walked about was one of the most disagreeable I ever heard, and I was glad to observe that the Russians did not appear to admire it. The prisoners at Chetah were laboring on the streets, preparing logs for house-building, or erecting fences. Most of the working parties were under guard, but the overseers did not appear to push them severely. Some were taking it very leisurely and moved as if endeavoring to do as little as possible in their hours of work. I was told that they were employed on the eight hour system. Their dress was coarse and rough, like that of the peasants, but had no marks to show that its wearer was a prisoner.

There were between three and four thousand prisoners in the province of the Trans-Baikal. About one-sixth of them were at Chetah and in its vicinity. The prisoners were of two classes—political and criminal—and their punishment varied according to their offence. Some were sentenced to labor in chains, and others to labor without chains. Some could not go out without a guard, while others had more freedom. Some were sentenced to work in prison and others were imprisoned without labor. Some were exiled to Siberia but enjoyed the liberty of a province, a particular district, or a designated town or village. Some were allowed a certain amount of rations and others supported themselves. In fact there were all grades of prisoners, just as we have all grades in our penitentiaries.

The Polish revolution in 1863 sent many exiles to the country east of Lake Baikal. Among the prisoners at the time of my journey there was a Colonel Zyklinski confined in prison at a village north of Chetah. He had a prominent part in the Polish troubles, and was captured at the surrender of the armies. He served in America under M'Clellan during the Peninsular campaign, and was in regular receipt of a pension from our government.

The Trans-Baikal Province is governed by Major General Ditmar, to whom I brought letters of introduction. When Borasdine returned from his visit he brought invitation to transfer our quarters to the gubernatorial mansion, where we went and met the governor. I found him an agreeable gentleman, speaking French fluently, and regretting the absence of Madame Ditmar, in whose praise many persons had spoken. At dinner I met about twenty persons, of whom more than half spoke French and two or three English.

A military band occupied the gallery over the dining-room. When General Ditmar proposed "the United States of America," my ears were greeted with one of our national airs. It was well played, and when I said so they told me its history. On hearing of my arrival the governor summoned his chief musician and asked if he knew any American music. The reply was in the negative. The governor then sent the band-master to search his books. He soon returned, saying he had found the notes of "Hail Columbia."

"Is that the only American tune you have?" asked the general.

"Yes, sir."

"Have your band learn to play it by dinner time."

The order was obeyed, and the American music accompanied the first regular toast. It was repeated at the club-rooms and on two or three other occasions during my stay in Chetah, and though learned so hastily it was performed as well as by any ordinary band in our army.

The principal rooms in General Ditmar's house had a profusion of green plants in pots and tubs of different sizes. One apartment in particular seemed more like a greenhouse than a room where people dwelt. Whether so much vegetation in the houses affects the health of the people I am unable to say, but I could not ascertain that it did. The custom of cultivating plants in the dwellings prevails through Siberia, especially in the towns. I frequently found bushes like small trees growing in tubs, and I have in mind several houses where the plants formed a continuous line half around the walls of the principal rooms. The devotion to floriculture among the Siberians has its chief impulse in the long winters, when there is no out-door vegetation visible beyond that of the coniferous trees. I can testify that a dwelling which one enters on a cold day in midwinter appears doubly cheerful when the eye rests upon a luxuriance of verdure and flowers. Winter seems defeated in his effort to establish universal sway.

The winters in this region are long and cold, though very little snow falls. Around Chetah and in most of the Trans-Baikal province there is not snow enough for good sleighing, and the winter roads generally follow the frozen rivers. Horses, cattle, and sheep subsist on the dead and dry grass from October to April, but they do not fare sumptuously every day.

North and south of the head-waters of the Ingodah and

Onon there are mountain ranges, having a general direction east and west. Away to the north the Polar sea and the lakes and rivers near it supply the rain and snow-clouds. As they sweep toward the south these clouds hourly become less and their last drops are wrung from them as they strike the slopes of the mountains and settle about their crests. The winter clouds from the Indian Ocean and Caspian Sea rarely pass the desert of Gobi, and thus the country of the Trans-Baikal has a climate peculiar to itself.

During my stay at Chetah a party was organized to hunt gazelles. There were ten or fifteen officers and about twenty Cossacks, as at Blagoveshchinsk. Up to the day of the excursion the weather was delightful, but it suddenly changed to a cloudy sky, a high wind, and a freezing temperature. The scene of action was a range of hills five or six miles from town. We went there in carriages and wagons and on horseback, and as we shivered around a fire built by the Cossacks near an open work cabin, we had little appearance of a pleasure party.

ON THE HILLS NEAR CHETAH.

The first drive resulted in the death of two rabbits and the serious disability of a third. One halted within twenty steps of me and received the contents of my gun-barrel. I reloaded while he lay kicking, and just as I returned the ramrod to its place the beast rose and ran into the thick bushes. I hope he recovered and will live many years. He seemed gifted with a strong constitution, and I heard several stories of the tenacity of life displayed by his kindred.

The rabbit or hare (*lepus variabilis*) abounds in the valley of the Amoor and generally throughout Siberia. He is much larger than the New England rabbit I hunted in my boyhood, and smaller than the long-eared rabbit of the Rocky Mountains and California. He is grey or brown in summer and white in winter, his color changing as cold weather begins. No snow had fallen at Chetah, but the rabbits were white as chalk and easily seen if not easily killed. The peasants think the rabbit a species of cat and refuse to eat his flesh, but the upper classes have no such scruples. I found him excellent in a roast or stew and admirably adapted to destroying appetites. Our day's hunt brought us one gazelle, six rabbits, one lunch, several drinks, and one smashed wagon.

I saw at Chetah a chess board in a box ten inches square with a miniature tree six inches high on its cover. The figure of a man in chains leaning upon a spade near a wheelbarrow, stood under the tree. The expression of the face, the details of the clothing, the links of the chains, the limbs of the tree, and even the roughness of its bark, were carefully represented. It was the work of a Polish exile, who was then engaged upon something more elaborate. Chessmen, tree, barrow, chains, and all, were made from black bread! The man took part of his daily allowance, moistened it with water, and kneaded it between his fingers till it was soft like putty. In this condition he fashioned it to the desired shape.

When I called upon the watchmaker he told me of an American recently arrived from Kiachta. Two hours later while writing in my room I heard a rap at my door. On opening I found a man who asked in a bewildered air, "*Amerikansky doma?*"

"*Dah,*" I responded.

"*Parlez vous Francais?*" was his next question.

"*Oui, Monsieur, Francais ou Anglais.*"

"Then you are the man I want to find. How do you do?"

It was the American, who had come in search of me. He told me he was born in England and was once a naturalized citizen of the United States. He had lived in New York and Chicago, crossed the Plains in 1850, and passed through all the excitements of the Pacific coast, finishing and being finished at Frazer's River. After that he went to China and accompanied a French merchant from Shanghae across the Mongolian steppes to Kiachta. He arrived in Chetah a month before my visit, and was just opening a stock of goods to trade with the natives.

He was about to begin matrimonial life with a French lady whose acquaintance he made in Kiachta. He had sent for a Catholic priest to solemnize the marriage, as neither of the high contracting parties belonged to the Russian church. The priest was then among the exiles at Nerchinsk Zavod, three hundred miles away, and his arrival at Chetah was anxiously looked for by others than my new acquaintance. The Poles being Catholics have their own priests to attend them and minister to their spiritual wants. Some of these priests are exiles and others voluntary emigrants, who went to Siberia to do good. The exiled priests are generally permitted to go where they please, but I presume a sharp watch is kept over their actions. When there is a sufficient number of Poles they have churches of their own and use exclusively the Romish service.

The Germans settled in Russia, as well as Russians of German descent, usually adhere to the Lutheran faith. The Siberian peasants almost invariably speak of a Lutheran church as a 'German' one, and in like manner apply the name 'Polish' to Catholic churches. The government permits all religious denominations in Siberia to worship God in their own way, and makes no interference with spiritual leaders. Minor sects corresponding to Free Lovers, Shakers, and bodies of similar character, are not as liberally treated as the followers of any recognized Christian faith. Of course the influence of the government is for the Greek Church, but it allows no oppression of Catholics and Lutherans. So far as I could observe, the Greek Church in Siberia and the Established Church in England occupy nearly similar positions toward dissenting denominations.

Three days after my arrival General Ditmar started for Irkutsk, preceded a few hours by my late traveling companion. In the afternoon following the general's departure I witnessed an artillery parade and drill, the men being Cossacks of the Trans-Baikal province. The battery was a mounted one of six guns, and I was told the horses were brought the day before from their summer pastures. The affair was creditable to officers and men, the various evolutions being well and rapidly performed. The guns were whirled about the field, unlimbered, fired, dismounted, and passed through all the manipulations known to artillerists.

At the close of the review the commanding officer thanked his men and praised their skill. He received the response, simultaneously spoken, "We are happy to please you," or words of like meaning. At every parade, whether regular or Cossack, this little ceremony is observed. As the men marched from the field to their quarters they sang one of their native airs. These Cossacks meet at stated intervals for drill and discipline, and remain the balance of the time at their homes. The infantry and cavalry are subject to the same regulation, and the musters are so arranged that some part of the Cossack force is always under arms.

After the review I dined with a party of eighteen or twenty officers at the invitation of Captain Erifayeff of the governor's staff. The dinner was given in the house where my host and his friend, Captain Pantoukin, lived, *en garcon.* The Emperor of Russia and the President of the United States were duly remembered, and the toasts in their honor were greeted with appropriate music. In conversation after dinner, I found all the officers anxious to be informed concerning the United States. The organization of our army, the relations of our people after the war, our mode of life, manners, and customs, were subjects of repeated inquiry.

On the morning of the 26th October, Captain Molostoff, who was to be my companion, announced his readiness to depart. I made my farewell calls, and we packed our baggage into my tarantass, with the exception of the terrible trunk that adhered to me like a shadow. As we had no Cossack and traveled without a servant, there was room for the unwieldy article on the seat beside the driver. I earnestly advise every tourist in Siberia not to travel with a trunk. The Siberian ladies manage to transport all the articles for an elaborate toilet without employing a single 'dog house' or 'Saratoga.' If they can do without trunks, of what should not man be capable?

Our leave-taking consumed much time and champagne, and it was nearly sunset before we left Chetah. It is the general custom in Siberia to commence journeys in the afternoon or evening, the latter extending anywhere up to daybreak. As one expects to travel night and day until reaching his destination, his hour of starting is of no consequence. Just before leaving he is occupied in making farewell calls, and is generally 'seen off' by his friends. In the evening he has no warm bed to leave, no hasty toilet to make, and no disturbed household around him. With a vehicle properly arranged he can settle among his furs and pillows and is pretty likely to fall asleep before riding many miles. I was never reconciled to commencing a journey early in the morning, with broken sleep, clothing half arranged, and a 'picked-up' breakfast without time to swallow it leisurely.

On leaving Chetah we crossed a frozen stream tributary to the Ingodah, and proceeded rapidly over an excellent road. We met several carts, one-horse affairs on two wheels, laden with hay for the Chetah market. One man generally controlled three or four carts, the horses proceeding in single file. The country was more open than on the other side of Chetah, and the road had suffered little in the rains and succeeding cold.

For some distance we rode near two lines of telegraph; one was a temporary affair erected during the insurrection of 1866, while the other was the permanent line designed to connect America with Europe by way of Bering's Straits. The poles used for this telegraph are large and firmly set, and give the line an appearance of durability.

The Captain was fond of dogs and had an English pointer in his baggage. During the day the animal ran near the carriage, and at night slept at his master's feet. He was well inclined toward me after we were introduced, and before the journey ended he became my personal friend. He had an objectionable habit of entering the tarantass just before me and standing in the way until I was seated. Sometimes when left alone in the carriage he would not permit the yemshicks to attach the horses. On two or three occasions of this kind the Captain was obliged to suspend his tea-drinking and go to pacify his dog. Once as a yemshick was mounting the box of the tarantass, 'Boika' jumped at his face and very nearly secured an attachment to a large and ruddy nose. Spite of his eccentricities, he was a good dog and secured the admiration of those he did not attempt to bite.

We passed the Yablonoi mountains by a road far from difficult. Had I not been informed of the fact I could have hardly suspected we were in a mountain range. The Yablonoi chain forms the dividing ridge between the head streams of the Amoor and the rivers that flow to the Arctic Ocean.

On the south we left a little brook winding to reach the Ingodah, and two hours later crossed the Ouda, which joins the Selenga at Verchne Udinsk. The two streams flow in opposite directions. One threads its way to the eastward, where it assists in forming the Amoor; the other through the Selenga, Lake Baikal, and the Yenesei, is finally swallowed up among the icebergs and perpetual snows of the far north.

> "One to long darkness and the frozen tide;
> One to the Peaceful Sea."

CHAPTER XXV.

BEYOND the mountains the cold increased, the country was slightly covered with snow, and the lakes were frozen over. In the mountain region there is a forest of pines and birches, but farther along much of the country is flat and destitute of timber. Where the road was good our tarantass rolled along very well, and the cold, though considerable, was not uncomfortable. I found the chief inconvenience was, that the moisture in my breath congealed on my beard and the fur clothing near it. Two or three times beard and fur were frozen together, and it was not always easy to separate them.

From the Yablonoi mountains to Verkne Udinsk there are very few houses between the villages that form the posting stations. The principal inhabitants are Bouriats, a people of Mongol descent who were conquered by Genghis Khan in the thirteenth century and made a respectable fight against the Russians in the seventeenth. Since their subjugation they have led a peaceful life and appear to have forgotten all warlike propensities. Their features are essentially Mongolian, and their manners and customs no less so.

Some of them live in houses after the Russian manner, but the yourt is the favorite habitation. The Bouriats cling to the manners of their race, and even when settled in villages are unwilling to live in houses. At the first of their villages after we passed the mountains I took opportunity to visit a yourt. It was a tent with a light frame of trellis work covered with thick felt, and I estimated its diameter at fifteen or eighteen feet. In the center the frame work has no covering, in order to give the smoke free passage. A fire, sometimes of wood and sometimes of dried cow-dung, burns in the middle of the yourt during the day and is covered up at night. I think the tent was not more than five and a half feet high. There was no place inside where I could stand erect. The door is of several thicknesses of stitched and quilted felt, and hangs like a curtain over the entrance.

BOURIAT YOURTS.

The eyes of the Bouriats were nearly always red, a circumstance explainable by the smoke that fills their habitations and in which they appear to enjoy themselves. In sleeping they spread mats and skins on the ground and pack very closely. Two or three times at the stations in the middle of the night I approached their dwellings and listened to the nasal chorus within. The people are early risers, if I may judge by the hours when I used to find them out of doors.

As to furniture, they have mats and skins to sit upon by day and convert into beds at night. There are few or no tables, and little crockery or other household comforts. They have pots for boiling meat and heating water, and a few jugs, bottles, and basins for holding milk and other liquids. A wooden box contains the valuable clothing of the family, and there are two or three bags for miscellaneous use. In the first yourt I entered I found an altar that was doubtless hollow and utilized as a place of storage. A few small cups containing grain, oil, and other offerings were placed on this altar, and I was careful not to disturb them.

Their religion is Bhudistic, and they have their lamas, who possess a certain amount of sanctity frcm the Grand Lama of Thibet. The lamas are numerous and their sacred character does not relieve or deprive them of terrestrial labor and trouble. Many of the lamas engage in the same pursuits as their followers, and are only relieved from toil to exercise the duties of their positions. They perform the functions of priest, physician, detective officer, and judge, and are supposed to have control over souls and bodies, to direct the one and heal the other. Man, woman, child, or animal falling sick the lama is summoned. Thanks to the fears and superstitions of native thieves he can generally find and restore stolen articles, and has the power to inflict punishment.

The Russian priests have made very few converts among the Bouriats, though laboring zealously ever since the conquest of Siberia. In 1680 a monastery was founded at Troitsk for the especial purpose of converting the natives. The number who have been baptized is very small, and most of them are still pagans at heart. Two English missionaries lived a long time at Selenginsk, but though earnest and hard working I am told they never obtained a single proselyte.

It is a curious fact in the history of the Bouriats that Shamanism was almost universal among them two hundred years ago; practically it differed little from that of the natives on the Amoor. Toward the end of the seventeenth century a mission went from Siberia to Thibet, and its members returned as lamas and bringing the paraphernalia of the new religion which they at once declared to their people.

The Bhudistic faith was thus founded and spread over the country until Shamanism was gradually superseded. Traces of the old superstition are still visible in certain parts of the lama worship.

Most of their religious property, such as robes, idols, cups, bells, and other necessaries for the Bhudhist service come from Thibet. A Russian gentleman gave me a bell decorated with holy inscriptions and possessing a remarkably fine tone. Its handle was the bust and crown of a Bhudhist idol, and the bell was designed for use in religious services; it was to be touched only by a disciple of the true faith, and its possession prophesied good fortune. Since my return to America it occupied a temporary place on the dining-table of a New England clergyman.

A MONGOL BELL.

The Bouriats manufacture very few articles for their own use; they sell their sheep to the Russians, and buy whatever they desire. Their dress is partly Mongol and partly Russian, the inconvenient portions of the Chinese costume being generally rejected. Their caps were mostly conical in shape, made of quilted cloth and ornamented with a silken tassel attached to the apex. Their trowsers had a Chinese appearance, but their coats were generally of sheepskin, after the Russian model.

Their waist-belts were decorated with bits of steel or brass. They shave the head and wear the hair in a queue like the Chinese, but are not careful to keep it closely trimmed. A few are half Mongol and half Russian, caused no doubt by their owners being born and reared under Muscovite protection. I saw many pleasing and intelligent countenances, but few that were pretty according to Western notions. There is a famous Bouriat beauty of whose charms I heard much and was anxious to gaze upon. Unfortunately it was two o'clock in the morning when we reached the station where she lived. The unfashionable hour and a big dog combined to prevent my visiting her abode.

A MONGOL BELLE.

From the mountains to Verkne Udinsk most of our drivers were Bouriats. They were quite as skillful and daring as the Russian yemshicks, and took us at excellent speed where the road was good. The station-masters were Russian, but frequently all their employees were of Mongol blood. Some part of the carriage gave way on the road, and it was necessary to repair it at a station. A Bouriat man-of-all-work undertook the job and performed it very well. While waiting for the repairs I saw some good specimens of iron work from the hands of native blacksmiths.

The Bouriats engage in very little agriculture. Properly they are herdsmen, and keep large droves of cattle, horses, and sheep, the latter being most numerous. I saw many of their flocks near the road we traveled or feeding on distant parts of the plain. The country was open and slightly rolling, timber being scarce and the soil more or less stony. Each flock of sheep was tended by one or more herdsmen armed with poles like rake-handles, and attached to each pole was a short rope with a noose at the end. This implement is used in catching sheep, and the Bouriats are very skillful in handling it. I saw one select a sheep which became separated from the flock before he secured it. The animal while pursued attempted to double on his track. As he turned the man swung his pole and caught the head of the sheep in his noose. It reminded me of lasso throwing in Mexico and California.

CATCHING SHEEP.

In looking at these flocks I remembered a conundrum containing the inquiry, "Why do white sheep eat more hay than black ones?" The answer was, "Because there are more of them." In Siberia the question and its reply would be incorrect, as the white sheep are in the minority. In this the sheep of Siberia differ materially from those I ever saw in any other country. The flocks presented a great variety of colors, or rather, many combinations of white and black. Their appearance to an American eye was a very peculiar and novel one.

At one station a beggar crouched on the ground near the

door asked alms as we passed him. I threw him a small coin, which he acknowledged by thrice bowing his head and touching the earth. I trust this mode of acknowledging courtesy will never be introduced in my own country.

We frequently met or passed small trains of two-wheeled carts, some laden with merchandise and others carrying Bouriat or Russian families. Most of these carts were drawn by bullocks harnessed like horses between shafts. Occasionally I saw bullocks saddled and ridden as we ride horses, though not quite as rapidly. A few carts had roofs of birch bark to shield their occupants from the rain; from appearances I judged these carts belonged to emigrants on their way to the Amoor.

At the crossing of a small river we found the water full of floating ice that drifted in large cakes. There was much fixed ice at both edges and we waited an hour to have it cut away. When the smotretal announced that all was ready we proceeded to the river and found it anything but inviting. The Bouriat yemshick pronounced it safe, and as he was a responsible party we deferred to his judgment. While we waited a girl rode a horse through the stream without hesitation.

A COLD BATH.

We had four horses harnessed abreast and guided by the yemshick. Two others were temporarily attached ahead under control of a Bouriat. As we drove into the river the horses shrank from the cold water and ice that came against their sides. One slipped and fell, but was soon up again. The current drifted us with it and I thought for a moment we were badly caught. The drivers whipped and shouted so effectively that we reached the other side without accident.

On the second evening we had a drunken yemshick who lost the road several times and once drove us into a clump of bushes. As a partial excuse the night was so dark that one could not see ten feet ahead. About two o'clock in the morning we reached the station nearest to Verkne Udinsk. Here was a dilemma. Captain Molostoff had business at Verkne Udinsk which he could not transact before nine or ten in the morning. There was no decent hotel, and if we pushed forward we should arrive long before the Russian hour for rising. We debated the question over a steaming samovar and decided to remain at the station till morning. By starting after daylight we might hope to find the town awake.

The travelers' room at the station was clean and well furnished, but heated to a high temperature. The captain made his bed on a sofa, but I preferred the tarantass where the air was cool and pure. I arranged my furs, fastened the boot and hood of the carriage, and slept comfortably in a keen wind. At daylight the yemshicks attached horses and called the captain from the house. He complained that he slept little owing to the heat. Boika was in bad humor and opened the day by tearing the coat of one man and being kicked by another.

The ground was rougher and better wooded as we came near the junction of the Ouda and Selenga, and I could see evidences of a denser population. On reaching the town we drove to the house of Mr. Pantoukin, a brother of an officer I met at Chetah. The gentleman was not at home and we were received by his friend Captain Sideroff. After talking a moment in Russian with Captain Molostoff, our new acquaintance addressed me in excellent English and inquired after several persons at San Francisco. He had been there four times with the Russian fleet, and appeared to know the city very well.

Verkne Udinsk is at the junction of the Ouda and Selenga rivers, three hundred versts from Irkutsk and four hundred and fifty from Chetah. It presents a pretty appearance when approached from the east, when its largest and best buildings first catch the eye. It has a church nearly two hundred years old, built with immensely thick walls to resist occasional earthquakes. A large crack was visible in the wall of a newer church, and repairs were in progress.

In its earlier days the town had an important commerce, which has been taken away by Irkutsk and Kiachta. It has a few wealthy merchants, who have built fine houses on the principal street. I walked through the *gastinni-dvor* but found nothing I desired to purchase. There were many little articles of household use but none of great value. Coats of deerskin were abundant, and the market seemed freshly supplied with them. My costume was an object of curiosity to the hucksters and their customers, especially in the item of boots. The Russian boots are round-toed and narrow. I wore a pair in the American fashion of the previous year and quite different from the Muscovite style. There were frequent touches of elbows and deflections of eyes attracting attention to my feet.

A large building overlooking the town was designated as the jail, and said to be rapidly filling for winter. "There are many vagabonds in this part of the country," said my informant. "In summer they live by begging and stealing. At the approach of winter they come to the prisons to be housed and fed during the cold season. They are generally compelled to work, and this fact causes them to leave as early as possible in the spring. Had your journey been in midsummer you would have seen many of these fellows along the road."

While speaking of this subject my friend told me there was then in prison at Verkne Udinsk a man charged with robbery. When taken he made desperate resistance, and for a long time afterward was sullen and obstinate. Recently he confessed some of his crimes. He was a robber by profession and acknowledged to seventeen murders during the last three years! Once he killed four persons in a single family, leaving only a child too young to testify against him. The people he attacked were generally merchants with money in their possession. Robberies are not frequent in Siberia, though a traveler hears many stories designed to alarm the timorous. I was told of a party of three persons attacked in a lonely place at night. They were carrying gold from the mines to the smelting works, and though well armed were so set upon that the three were killed without injury to the robbers.

I was not solicitous about my safety as officers were seldom molested, and as I traveled with a member of the governor's staff I was pretty well guarded. Officers rarely carry more than enough money for their traveling expenses, and they are better skilled than merchants in handling fire arms and defending themselves. Besides, their molestation would be more certainly detected and punished than that of a merchant or chance traveler.

My tarantass had not been materially injured in the journey, but several screws were loose and there was an air of general debility about it. Like the deacon's one-horse shay in its eightieth year, the vehicle was not broken but had traces of age about it. As there was considerable rough road before me I thought it advisable to put everything in order, and therefore committed the carriage to a blacksmith. He labored all day and most of the night putting in bolts, nuts, screws, and bits of iron in different localities, and astonished me by demanding less than half I expected to pay, and still more by his guilty manner, as if ashamed at charging double.

The iron used in repairing my carriage came from Petrosky Zavod, about a hundred miles southeast of Verkne Udinsk. The iron works were established during the reign of Peter the Great, and until quite recently were mostly worked by convicts. There is plenty of mineral coal in the vicinity, but wood is so cheap and abundant that charcoal is principally used in smelting. I saw a specimen of the Petrosky ore, which appeared very good. The machine shops of these works are quite extensive and well supplied. The engines for the early steamers on the Amoor were built there by Russian workmen.

There are several private mining enterprises in the rigion around Verkne Udinsk. Most of them have gold as their object, and I heard of two or three lead mines.

During the night of my stay at this town Captain Sideroff insisted so earnestly upon giving up his bed that politeness compelled me to accept it. My blankets and furs on the floor would have been better suited to my traveling life especially as the captain's bed was shorter than his guest. I think travelers will agree with me in denouncing the use of beds and warm rooms while a journey is in progress. They weaken the system and unfit it for the roughness of the road While halting at night the floor or a hard sofa is preferable to a soft bed. The journey ended, the reign of luxuries can begin.

CHAPTER XXVI.

WHEN we left Verkne Udinsk we crossed the Selenga before passing the municipal limits. Our ferry-boat was like the one at Stratensk, and had barely room on its platform for our tarantass. A priest and an officer who were passengers on the steamer from Blagoveshchensk arrived while we were getting on board the ferry-boat. They had been greatly delayed on the way from Stratensk, and waited two days to cross the Nercha.

The Selenga was full of ice, some cakes being larger than the platform of our boat. The temperature of the air was far below freezing, and it was expected the river would close in a day or two. It might shut while we were crossing and confine us on the wretched flat-boat ten or twelve hours, until it would be safe to walk ashore. However, it was not my craft, and as there were six or eight Russians all in the same boat with me, I did not borrow trouble.

The ice-cakes ground unpleasantly against each other and had things pretty much their own way. One of them grated rather roughly upon our sides. I do not know there was any danger, but I certainly thought I had seen places of greater safety than that. When we were in the worst part of the stream two of the ferrymen rested their poles and began crossing themselves. I could have excused them had they postponed this service until we landed on the opposite bank or were stuck fast in the ice. The Russian peasants are more dependant on the powers above than were even the old Puritans. The former abandon efforts in critical moments and take to making the sign of the cross. The Puritans trusted in God, but were careful to keep their powder dry.

A wide sand bank where we landed was covered with smooth ice, and I picked my way over it much like a cat ex-

OUR FERRY BOAT.

ercising on a mirror. The tarantass was pushed ashore, and as soon as the horses were attached a rapid run took them up the bank to the station.

A temporary track led across a meadow that furnished a great deal of jolting to the mile. Eight versts from Verkne Udinsk the road divides, one branch going to Kiachta and the other to Lake Baikal and Irkutsk. A pleasing feature of the route was the well-built telegraph line, in working order to St. Petersburg. It seemed to shorten the distance between me and home when I knew that the electric current had a continuous way to America. Puck would put a girdle round the earth in forty minutes. From China to California, more than half the circuit of the globe, we can flash a signal in a second of time, and gain by the hands of the clock more than fourteen hours.

From the point of divergence the road to Kiachta ascends the valley of the Selenga, while that to Irkutsk descends the left bank of the stream. I found the Kiachta route rougher than any part of the way from Chetah to Verkne Udinsk, and as the yemshick took us at a rattling pace we were pretty thoroughly shaken up.

At the second station we had a dinner of *stchee*, or cabbage soup, with bread and the caviar of the Selenga. This caviar is of a golden color and made from the roe of a small fish that ascends from Lake Baikal. It is not as well liked as the caviar of the Volga and Amoor, the egg being less rich than that of the sturgeon, though about the same size. If I may judge from what I saw, there is less care taken in its preparation than in that of the Volga.

The road ascended the Selenga, but the valley was so wide and we kept so near its edge that the river was not often visible. The valley is well peopled and yields finely to the agriculturalist. Some of the farms appeared quite prosperous and their owners well-to-do in the world. The general appearance was not unlike that of some parts of the Wabash country, or perhaps better still, the region around Marysville, Kansas. Russian agriculture does not exhibit the care and economy of our states where land is expensive. There is such abundance of soil in Siberia that every farmer can have all he desires to cultivate. Many farms along the Selenga had a 'straggling' appearance, as if too large for their owners. *Per contra*, I saw many neat and well managed homesteads, with clean and comfortable dwellings.

With better implements of husbandry and a more thorough working of the soil, the peasants along the Selenga would find agriculture a sure road to wealth. Under the present system of cultivation the valley is pleasing to the eye of a traveler who views it with reference to its practical value. There were flocks of sheep, droves of cattle and horses, and stacks of hay and grain; everybody was apparently well fed and the houses were attractive. We had good horses, good drivers, and generally good roads for the first hundred versts. Sometimes we left the Selenga, but kept generally parallel to its course. The mountains beyond the valley were lofty and clearly defined. Frequently they presented striking and beautiful scenery, and had I been a skillful artist they would have tempted me to sketch them.

The night came upon us cold and with a strong wind blowing from the north. We wrapped ourselves closely and were quite comfortable, the dog actually lolling beneath our sheepskin coverlid. Approaching Selenginsk we found a few bits of bad road and met long caravans laden with tea for Irkutsk.

These caravans were made up of little two-wheeled carts, each drawn by a single horse. From six to ten chests of tea, according to the condition of the roads, are piled on each cart and firmly bound with cords. There is one driver to every four or five carts, and this driver has a dormitory on one of his loads. This is a rude frame two and a half by six feet, with sides about seven inches high. With a sheepskin coat and coverlid a man contrives to sleep in this box while his team moves slowly along the road or is feeding at a halting place.

All the freight between Kiachta and Lake Baikal is carried on carts in summer and on one-horse sleds in winter. From Kiachta westward tea is almost the only article of transport, the quantity sometimes amounting to a million chests per annum. The tea chests are covered with raw hide, which protects them from rain and snow and from the many thumps of their journey. The teams belong to peasants, who carry freight for a stipulated sum per pood. The charges are lower in winter than in summer, as the sledge is of easier draft than the cart.

The caravans travel sixteen hours of every twenty-four, and rarely proceed faster than a walk. The drivers are frequently asleep and allow the horses to take their own pace. The caravans are expected to give up the whole road on the approach of a post carriage, and when the drivers are awake they generally obey the regulation. Very often it happened that the foremost horses turned aside of their own accord as we approached. They heard the bells that denoted our character, and were aware of our yemshick's right to strike them if they neglected their duty. The sleeping drivers and delinquent horses frequently received touches of the lash. There was little trouble by day, but at night the caravan

EQUAL RIGHTS.

horses were less mindful of our comfort. Especially if the road was bad and narrow the post vehicles, contrary to regulation, were obliged to give way.

It was three or four hours before daylight when we reached Selenginsk, and the yemshick removed his horses preparatory to returning to his station. I believe Selenginsk is older than Verkne Udinsk, and very much the senior of Irkutsk. The ancient town is on the site of the original settlement, but frequent inundations caused its abandonment for the other bank of the river, five versts away. New Selenginsk, which has a great deal of antiquity in its appearance, is a small town with a few good houses, a well built church, and commodious barracks.

During the troubles between China and Russia concerning the early occupation of the Amoor and encroachments on the Celestial frontier, Selenginsk was an important spot. It was often threatened by the Chinese, and sustained a siege in 1687. A convention was held there in 1727, and some provisions of the treaty then concluded are still in force.

Mr. Bestoujeff, one of the exiles of 1825, was living at Selenginsk at the time of my visit. There were two brothers of this name concerned in the insurrection, and at the expiration of their sentences to labor they were settled at this place. Subsequently they were joined by three sisters, who sacrificed all their prospects in life to meet their brothers in Siberia. The family was permitted to return to Europe when the present emperor ascended the throne, but having been so long absent the permission was never accepted.

The river was full of floating ice and could not be crossed in the night, and we ordered horses so that we might reach the bank at dawn. Both banks of the river were crowded with carts, some laden and others empty. A government officer has preference over dead loads of merchandise, and so we were taken in charge without delay. To prevent accidents the horses were detached, and the carriage pushed on the ferry-boat by men. The tamed unfiery steeds followed us with some reluctance, and shivered in the breeze during the voyage. We remained in the tarantass through the whole transaction. The ice ran in the river as at Verkne Udinsk, but the cakes were not as large. Our chief ferryman was a Russian, and had a crew of six Bouriats who spoke Mongol among themselves and Russian with their commander.

From Selenginsk to Kiachta, a distance of ninety versts, the road is hilly and sandy. We toiled slowly up the ascents, and our downward progress was but little better. We met several caravans where the road was narrow and had but one beaten track. In such cases we generally found it better to turn aside ourselves than to insist upon our rights and compel the caravan to leave the road. The hills were sandy and desolate, and I could not see any special charm in the landscape. I employed much of the day in sleeping, which may possibly account for the lack of minute description of the road.

The only point where the cold touched me was at the tip of my nose, where I left my *dehar* open to obtain air. The Russian dehar is generally made of antelope or deer skin, and forms an admirable defence against cold. Mine reached to my heels, and touched the floor when I stood erect. When the collar was turned up and brought together in front my head was utterly invisible. The sleeves were four or five inches longer than my arms, and the width of the garment was enough for a man and a boy. I at first suspected I had bought by mistake a coat intended for a Russian giant then exhibiting in Moscow.

This article of apparel is comfortable only when one is seated or extended in his equipage. Walking is very difficult in a dehar, and its wearer feels about as free to move as if enclosed in a pork-barrel. It was a long time before I could turn my collar up or down without assistance, and frequently after several efforts to seize an outside object I found myself grasping the ends of my sleeves. The warmth of the garment atones for its cumbersome character, and its gigantic size is fully intentional. The length protects the feet and legs, the high collar warms the head, and the great width of the dehar allows it to be well wrapped about the body. The long sleeves cover the hands and preserve fingers from frost bites. Taken as a whole it is a mental discomfort but a physical good, and may be considered a necessary nuisance of winter travel in Siberia.

At Ust Kiachta, the last station before reaching our journey's end, we were waited upon by a young and tidy woman in a well-kept room. It was about nine in the evening when we reached Troitskosavsk, and entered town among the large buildings formerly occupied as a frontier custom house. As there was no hotel we drove to the house of the Police Master, the highest official of the place. I had letters to this gentleman, but did not find him at home. His brother took us in charge and sent a soldier to direct us to a house where we could obtain lodgings.

It is the custom in Siberian towns to hold a certain number of lodging places always ready for travelers. These are controlled by the Police Master, to whom strangers apply for quarters. Whether he will or no, a man who has registered lodging rooms with the police must open them to any guest assigned him, no matter what the hour. It was ten o'clock when we reached our destined abode. We made a great deal of noise that roused a servant to admit us to the yard. The head of the household came to the door in his shirt and rubbed his eyes as if only half awake. His legs trembled with the cold while he waited for our explanations, and it was not till we were admitted that he thought of his immodest exposure.

I would not wish it inferred that no one can find lodgings until provided by the police. On the contrary, it is rarely necessary to obtain them through this channel. Travelers are not numerous, and the few strangers visiting Siberia are most cordially welcomed. Officers are greeted and find homes with their fellow officers, while merchants enjoy the hospitalities of men of their class.

We ordered the samovar, and being within Parrott-gun range of China we had excellent tea. I passed the night on a sofa so narrow that I found it difficult to turn over, and fairly rolled to the floor while endeavoring to bestow myself properly. While finishing my morning toilet I received a visit from Major Boroslofski, Master of Police, who came to acknowledge General Ditmar's letter of introduction. He tendered the hospitalities of the place, and desired me to command his services while I remained.

We had two rooms with a bedstead and sofa, besides lots of chairs, mirrors, tables, and flower pots. Then we had an apartment nearly thirty feet square, that contained more chairs, tables, and flower pots. In one corner there was a huge barrel-organ that enabled me to develop my musical abilities. I spent half an hour the morning after our arrival in turning out the national airs of Russia. Molostoff amused himself by circulating his cap before an invisible audience and collecting imperceptible coin. While dancing to one of my liveliest airs he upset a flower pot, and the crash that followed brought our concert to a close. Two sides of the large room were entirely bordered with horticultural productions, some of them six or eight feet high.

AMATEUR CONCERT IN SIBERIA.

Troitskosavsk and Kiachta have a sort of husband and wife singleness and duality. They are about two miles apart, the former having five or six thousand inhabitants and the latter about twelve hundred. In government, business, and interest the two places are one, the Master of Police having jurisdiction over both, and the merchants living indifferently in one or the other. Many persons familiar with the name of Kiachta never heard of the other town. It may surprise London merchants who send Shanghai telegrams "via Kiachta" to learn that the wires terminate at Troitskosavsk, and do not reach Kiachta at all.

The treaty which established trade between Russia and China at Kiachta provided that no one should reside there except merchants engaged in traffic. No officer could live there, nor could any person whatever beyond merchants and their employees and families remain over night. No stone buildings except a church could be erected, and visits of strangers were to be discouraged. Kiachta was thus restricted to the business of a trading post, and the town of Troitskosavsk, two miles away, was founded for the residence of the officials, outside traders, and laborers. Most of the restrictions above mentioned exist no longer, but the towns have not quite lost their old relations. There is an excellent road from one to the other, and the carriages, carts, and pedestrians constantly thronging it present a lively scene.

The police master tendered his equipage and offered to escort me in making calls upon those I wished to know. Etiquette is no less rigid in Siberian towns and cities than in Moscow and St. Petersburg. One must make ceremonial visits as soon as possible after his arrival, officials being first called upon in the order of rank and civilians afterward. Officers making visits don their uniforms, with epaulettes and side arms, and with all their decorations blazing on their breasts. Civilians go in evening dress arranged with fastidious care. The hours for calling are between eleven A. M. and three P. M. A responsive call may be expected within two days, and must be made with the utmost precision of costume.

Arrayed for the occasion I made eight or ten visits in Kiachta and Troitskosavsk. The air was cold and the frost nipped rather severely through my thin boots as we drove back from Kiachta. After an early dinner we went to Maimaichin to visit the *sargootchay*, or Chinese governor. We passed under a gateway surmounted with the double-headed eagle, and were saluted by the Cossack guard as we left the borders of the Russian empire. Outside the gateway we traversed the neutral ground, two hundred yards wide, driving toward a screen or short wall of brick work, on which a red globe was represented. We crossed a narrow ditch and, passing behind the screen, entered a gateway into Maimaichin, the most northern city of China.

CHAPTER XXVII.

FROM 1727 to 1860 nearly all the trade between Russia and China was transacted at Kiachta and Maimaichin. The Russians built the one and the Chinese the other, exclusively for commercial purposes. To this day no Chinese women are allowed at Maimaichin. The merchants consider themselves only sojourners, though the majority spend the best part of their lives there. Contact with Russians has evidently improved the Celestials, as this little frontier city is the best arranged and cleanest in all China.

After passing the gateway, the street we entered was narrow compared to our own, and had but a single carriage track. On the sidewalks were many Chinese, who stopped to look at us, or rather at me. We drove about two hundred yards and turned into an enclosure, where we alighted. Near at hand were two masts like flag-staffs, gaily ornamented at the top but bearing no banners. Our halting place was near the Temple of Justice, where instruments of punishment were piled up. There were rattans and bamboos for flogging purposes by the side of yokes, collars, and fetters, carefully designed for subduing the refractory. There was a double set of stocks like those now obsolete in America, and their appearance indicated frequent use. To be cornered in these would be as unpleasant as in Harlem or Erie.

From this temple we passed through a covered colonnade and entered an ante-room, where several officers and servants were in attendance. Here we left our overcoats and were shown to another apartment where we met the sargootchay. His Excellency shook hands with me after the European manner. His son, a youth of sixteen, was then presented, and made the acquaintance of Major Boroslofski. The sargootchay had a pleasing and interesting face of the true Chinese type, with no beard beyond a slight mustache, and a complexion rather paler than most of his countrymen. He

A CHINESE MANDARIN.

wore the dress of a Mandarin, with the universal long robe and a silk jacket with wide sleeves.

After the ceremony of introduction was ended the sargootchay signed for us to be seated. He took his own place on a divan, and gave the 'illustrious stranger' the post of honor near him. Tea and cigars were brought, and we had a few moments of smoky silence. The room was rather bare of furniture, and the decorations on the walls were Russian and Chinese in about equal proportion. I noticed a Russian stove in one corner and a samovar in the adjoining room. The sargootchay had been newly appointed, and arrived only a week before. I presume his housekeeping was not well under way.

The interview was as interesting as one could expect where neither party had anything important to say to the other. We attempted conversation which expressed our delight at meeting and the good-will of our respective countries toward each other. The talk was rather slow, as it went through many translations in passing between me and my host. Tea and smoke were of immense service in filling up the chinks.

When I wished to say anything to the sargootchay I spoke in French to Major Boroslofski, who sat near me.

The major then addressed his Bouriat interpreter in Russian.

This interpreter turned to a Mongol-Chinese official at his side and spoke to him in Mongol.

The latter translated into Chinese for the understanding of his chief.

The replies of the sargootchay returned by the same route. I have a suspicion that very little of what we really said ever reached its destination. His reply to one remark of mine had no reference to what I said, and the whole conversation was a curious medley of compliments. Our words were doubtless polarized more than once in transmission.

We had tea and sweetmeats, the latter in great variety. The manner of preparing tea did not please me as well as the Russian one. The Chinese boil their tea and give it a bitter flavor that the Russians are careful to avoid. They drink it quite strong and hot, using no milk or sugar. Out of deference to foreign tastes they brought sugar for us to use at our liking. After the tea and sweetmeats the sargootchay ordered champagne, in which we drank each other's health. At the close of the interview I received invitation to dine with His Excellency two days later and witness a theatrical performance.

Our adieus were made in the European manner, and after leaving the sargootchay we visited a temple in the northern part of the town. We passed through a large yard and wound among so many courts and colonnades that I should have been sorely puzzled to find my way out alone. The public buildings of Maimaichin are not far from each other, but the routes between them are difficult for one whose ideas of streets were formed in American cities. On passing the theatre we were shown two groups larger than life in rooms on opposite sides of a covered colonnade. They were cut in sand-stone, one representing a rearing horse which two grooms were struggling to hold. The other was the same horse walking quietly under control of one man.

The figures evidently came from Greek history, and I had little doubt that they were intended to tell of Alexander and Bucephalus. I learned that the words 'Philip of Macedon' were the literal translation of the Chinese title of the groups. How or when the Celestials heard the story of Alexander, and why they should represent it in stone, I cannot imagine. No one could tell the age and origin of these works of art.

On the walls of buildings near the temple there were paintings from Chinese artists, some of them showing a creditable knowledge of perspective. 'John' can paint very well when he chooses, and any one conversant with his skill will testify that he understands perspective. Why he does not make more use of it is a mystery that demands explanation.

When we entered the temple it was sunset, and the gathering shadows rendered objects indistinct. From the character of the windows and the colonnades outside I suppose a 'dim religious light' prevails there at all times. The temple contains several idols or representations of Chinese deities in figures larger than life, dressed with great skill and literally gotten up regardless of expense. Their garments were of the finest silk, and profusely ornamented with gold, silver, and precious stones.

There were the gods of justice, peace, war, agriculture, mechanics, love, and prosperity. The god of love had a most hideous countenance, quite in contrast to that of the gentle Cupid with whom the majority of my readers are doubtless familiar. The god of war brandished a huge sword, and reminded me of the leading tragedian of the Bowery Theatre ten years ago. The temple was crowded with idols, vases, censers, pillars, and other objects, and it was not easy for our party to move about. In the middle of the apartment there were tables supporting offerings of cooked fowls and other edibles. These articles are eaten by the attendants at the temple, but whether the worshippers know this fact or believe their gods descend to satisfy their appetites, I cannot say.

To judge from what I saw the Chinese are accustomed to decorate their houses of worship at great cost. There were rich curtains and a thousand and one articles of more or less value filling the greater part of the temple. Lanterns and chandeliers displayed the skill and patience of the Chinese in manipulating metals. There were imitations of butterflies and other insects, and of delicate leaves and flowers in metal, painted or burnished in the color of the objects represented. The aggregate time consumed in the manufacture of these decorations must be thousands of years. In a suspended vase I saw one boquet which was a clever imitation of nature, with the single exception of odor. The Chinese make artificial roses containing little cups which they fill with rose-water.

On our return we found the gate closed, and were obliged to wait until the ponderous key was brought to open it. The officer controlling the gate made no haste, and we were delayed in a crowd of Chinese men and dogs for nearly fifteen minutes. It was a peculiar sensation to be shut in a Chinese town and fairly locked in. It is the custom to close the gates of Kiachta and Maimaichin and shut off all communication between sunset and sunrise. The rule is less rigidly enforced than formerly.

INTERIOR OF CHINESE TEMPLE

After this introduction I visited Maimaichin almost every day until leaving for Irkutsk. Maimaichin means 'place of trade,' and the name was given by the officer who selected the site. The town is occupied by merchants, laborers, and government employees, all dwelling without families. The sargootchay is changed every three years, and it was hinted that his short term of office sufficed to give him a fortune.

The houses were only one story high and plastered with black mud or cement. The streets cross at right angles, but are not very long, as the town does not measure more than half a mile in any direction. At the intersection of the principal streets there are towers two or three stories high, overlooking the town, and probably intended for use of the police. Few houses are entered directly from the street, most of them having court yards with gateways just wide enough for a single cart or carriage. The dwelling rooms and magazines open upon the court yards, which are provided with folding gates heavily barred at night.

Apart from the public buildings the houses were pretty much alike. Every court yard was liberally garnished with dogs of the short-nosed and wide-faced breed peculiar to China. They were generally chained and invariably made an unpleasant tumult. The dwelling rooms, kitchens, and magazines had their windows and doors upon the yards, the former being long and low with small panes of glass, talc, or oiled paper. In the magazines there were generally two apartments, one containing most of the goods, while the other was more private and only entered by strangers upon invitation. At the end of each room there was a divan, where the inmates slept at night or sat by day. Near the edge of the divan was a small furnace, where a charcoal fire burned constantly. The rooms were warmed by furnaces with pipes passing beneath the divans or by Russian stoves.

In every place I visited there were many employees, and I did not understand how all could be kept busy. Everything was neat and well arranged, and the Chinese appeared very particular on the subject of dust. I attempted to buy a few souvenirs of my visit, but very little was to be purchased. Few strangers come to Maimaichin, and the merchants have no inducement to keep articles rarely called for.

I found they were determined to make me pay liberally. "How much?" I asked on picking up an article in one of their shops. "*Chetira ruble*," (four roubles) was the reply. My Russian companion whispered me not to buy, and after a few moments chaffering we departed. In a neighboring shop I purchased something precisely similar for one rouble, and went away rejoicing. On exhibiting my prize at Kiachta I learned that I paid twice its real value.

The Chinese merchants are frequently called scoundrels from their habit of overreaching when opportunity occurs. In some respects they are worse and in others better than the same class of men in Western nations. The practice of asking much more than they expect to receive prevails throughout their empire, and official peculation confined in certain limits is considered entirely consistent with honesty. Their cheating, if it can be called by that name, is conducted on certain established principles. A Chinese will 'beat about the bush,' and try every plan to circumvent the man with whom he deals, but when he once makes a bargain he adheres to it unflinchingly. Among the merchants I was told that a word is as good as a bond. Their slipperiness is confined to preliminaries.

China contains good and bad like other countries, but in some things its merchants rank higher than outside barbarians. When the English were at war with the Viceroy of Canton, the foreigners were driven out and compelled to leave much property with Chinese merchants. These Chinese never thought of repudiation, but on the contrary made their way to Hong Kong during the blockade of the Canton river for the purpose of settling with the foreigners.

Old John Bell of Antermony, who traveled to Pekin in the reign of Peter the Great, in the suite of a Russian Ambassador, makes the following observations on the Chinese:

"They are honest, and observe the strictest honor and justice in their dealings. It must, however, be acknowledged that not a few of them are much addicted to knavery and well skilled in the art of cheating. They have, indeed, found many Europeans as great proficients in that art as themselves."

In the shops at Maimaichin there is no display of goods, articles being kept in closets, drawers, show-cases, and on shelves, whence they are taken when called for. This arrangement suggests the propriety of the New York notice: "If you don't see what you want, ask for it." Many things are kept in warerooms in other parts of the building, and brought when demanded or the merchant thinks he can effect a sale. In this way they showed me Thibet sheep skins, intended for lining dressing-gowns, and of the most luxurious softness. There were silks and other goods in the piece, but the asking prices were very high. I bought a few small articles, but was disappointed when I sought a respectable assortment of knick-knacks.

One of the merchants admired my watch and asked through my Russian friend how much it cost. I was about to say in Russian, 'two hundred roubles,' when my friend checked me.

"*Dites un enorme prix ; deux mille roubles au moins.*"

Accordingly I fixed the price at two thousand roubles. Probably the Chinaman learned the real value of the watch from this exaggerated figure better than if I had spoken as I first intended.

The merchants were courteous and appeared to have plenty of time at command. They brought sweetmeats, confectionery, and tea, in fact the latter article was always ready. They gave us crystalized sugar, resembling rock candy, for sweetening purposes, but themselves drank tea without sugar or milk. They offered us pipes for smoking, and in a few instances Russian cigarettes. I found the Chinese tobacco very feeble and the pipes of limited capacity. It is doubtless owing to the weakness of their tobacco that they can smoke so continuously. The pipe is in almost constant requisition, the operator swallowing the smoke and emitting it in a double stream through his nostrils. They rarely offered us Chinese wine, as that article is repugnant to any but Celestials. Sometimes they brought sherry and occasionally champagne.

I was interested in studying the decorations on window screens and fans, and the various devices on the walls. The Chinese mind runs to the hideous in nearly everything fanciful, and most of its works of art abound in griffins and dragons. Even the portrait of a tiger or other wild beast is made to look worse than the most savage of his tribe. If there ever was a dog with a mouth such as the Chinese artists represent on their canines, he could walk down his own throat with very little difficulty.

THROUGH ORDINARY EYES.

THROUGH CHINESE EYES

The language spoken in the intercourse of Russians and Chinese at Kiachta is a mongrel tongue in which Russian predominates. It is a 'pigeon-Russian' exactly analagous to the 'pigeon-English' of Shanghai, Hong Kong, and San Francisco. The Chinese at Maimaichin can reckon in Russian and understand the rudiments of that language very well. I observed at Maimaichin, as at San Francisco, the tendency to add an 'e' sound to monosyllabic consonant words. A Chinese merchant grew familiar during one of my visits, and we exchanged lingual lessons and cards. He held up a tea-spoon and asked me its name. I tried him repeatedly with 'spoon,' but he would pronounce it 'spoonee' in spite of my instructions. When I gave him a card and called it such, he pronounced it 'cardee.' His name was Chy-Ping-Tong, or something of the kind, but I was no more able to speak it correctly than was he to say 'spoon.' He wrote his name in my note-book and I wrote mine in his. Beyond the knowledge of possessing chirographic specimens of another language, neither party is wiser.

Whoever has visited St. Petersburg or Moscow has doubtless seen the *abacus*, or calculating machine used in Russian shops. It is found throughout the empire from the German frontier to Bering's Straits, not only in the hands of merchants but in many private houses. It consists of a wooden frame ordinarily a foot long and six inches wide. There are ten metal wires strung across this frame, and ten balls of wood on each wire. The Russian currency is a decimal one, and by means of this machine computations are carried on with wonderful rapidity. I have seen numbers added by a boy and a machine faster than a New York bank teller could make the same reckoning. It requires long practice to become expert in its use, but when once learned it is preferred by all merchants, whether native or foreign.

I saw the same machine at Maimaichin, and learned that it was invented by the Chinese. The Celestials of San Francisco employ it in precisely the same manner as their countrymen in Mongolia.

Beside the Chinese dwellers in Maimaichin there are many Mongol natives of the surrounding region, most of them engaged in transporting merchandise to and from the city. I saw several trains of their little two-wheeled carts bringing tea from the southward or departing with Russian merchandise; and in one visit I encountered a drove of camels on the neutral ground.

CHAPTER XXVIII.

I HAVE already mentioned the prevalence of feast-days, both national and personal. During my stay in Kiachta there were several of these happy occasions, and I was told they would last the entire winter. One man opened his house on his name's day, and another on that of his wife. A third received friends on the anniversary of his daughter's birth, and a fourth had a regular house-warming. Each kept open mansion in the forenoon and greeted all who came. There was a grand dinner in the afternoon, followed by a *soiree dansante* and a supper at a late hour. In a population like that of Kiachta there is a weekly average of at least three feast days for the entire year. During my stay Major Boroslofski had a morning reception on the anniversary of the death of a child, but there was naturally neither dinner nor dance after it.

The dinner and dancing parties were much alike, the same company being present at all. Even the servants were the same, there being a regular organization to conduct household festivities. At the first dinner I attended there were about forty persons at table, all of the sterner sex. According to the custom among Russian merchants the ladies were by themselves in another room. Between their apartment and ours there was a large room, corresponding, as I thought, to the neutral ground between Kiachta and Maimaichin. Doors were open, and though nobody occupied the *terre neutrale* during dinner, both parties retired to it at the end of the meal.

The dinner would have been a success in St. Petersburg or

Paris; how much more was it a triumph on the boundary between China and Siberia. Elegant and richly furnished apartments, expensive table ware, and a profusion of all procurable luxuries, were the attractions of the occasion. We had apples from European Russia, three thousand miles westward, and grapes from Pekin, a thousand miles to the south. There were liberal quantities of dried and preserved fruits, and the wines were abundant and excellent. Of the local productions we had many substantials, till all appetites were satisfied.

According to Russian custom the host does not partake of the dinner, but is supposed to look after the welfare of his guests. At Kiachta I found this branch of etiquette carefully observed. Two or three times during the dinner the host passed around the entire table and filled each person's glass with wine. Where he found an unemptied cup he urged its drainage.

After we left the table tea was served, and I was fain to pronounce it the best I ever tasted. The evening entertainments for those who did not dance consisted of cards and conversation, principally the former. Tea was frequently passed around, and at regular intervals the servants brought glasses of iced champagne.

The houses of the Kiachta merchants are large and well built, their construction and adornment requiring much outlay. Nearly all the buildings are of two stories and situated in large court yards. There is a public garden, evidently quite gay and pretty in summer. The church is said to be the finest edifice of the kind in Eastern Siberia. The double doors in front of the altar are of solid silver, and said to weigh two thousand pounds avoirdupois. Besides these doors I think I saw nearly a ton of silver in the various paraphernalia of the church. There were several fine paintings executed in Europe at heavy cost, and the floors, walls, and roof of the entire structure were of appropriate splendor. The church was built at the expense of the Kiachta merchants.

Troilskosavsk contains some good houses, but they are not equal in luxury to those at Kiachta. Many dwellings in the former town are of unpainted logs, and each town has its gastinni-dvor, spacious and well arranged. I visited the market place every morning and saw curious groups of Russians, Bouriats, Mongols, and Chinese, engaged in that little commerce which makes the picturesque life of border towns.

From 1727 to 1860 the Kiachta merchants enjoyed almost a monopoly of Chinese trade. Fortunes there are estimated at enormous figures, and one must be a four or five-millionaire to hold respectable rank. Possibly many of these worldly possessions are exaggerated, as they generally are everywhere. The Chinese merchants of Maimaichin are also reputed wealthy, and it is quite likely that the trade was equally profitable on both sides of the neutral ground. Money and flesh have affinities. These Russian and Chinese Astors were almost invariably possessed of fair, round belly, with good capon lined. They have the spirit of genuine hospitality, and practice it toward friends and strangers alike.

The treaty of 1860, which opened Chinese ports to Russian ships, was a severe blow to Kiachta and Maimaichin. Up to that time only a single cargo of tea was carried annually into Russia by water; all the rest of the herb used in the empire came by land. Unfortunately the treaty was made just after the Russian and Chinese merchants had concluded contracts in the tea districts; these contracts caused great losses when the treaty went into effect, and for a time paralized commerce. Kiachta still retains the tea trade of Siberia and sends large consignments to Nijne Novgorod and Moscow. There is now a good percentage of profit, but the competition by way of Canton and the Baltic has destroyed the best of it. Under the old monopoly the merchants arranged high prices and did not oppose each other with quick and low sales.

The Kiachta teas are far superior to those from Canton and Shanghae. They come from the best districts of China and are picked and cured with great care. There is a popular notion, which the Russians encourage, that a sea voyage injures tea, and this is cited as the reason for the character of the herb brought to England and America. I think the notion incorrect, and believe that we get no first class teas in America because none are sent there. I bought a small package of the best tea at Kiachta and brought it to New York. When I opened it I could not perceive it had changed at all in flavor. I have not been able to find its like in American tea stores.

Previous to 1850 all trade at Kiachta was in barter, tea being exchanged for Russian goods. The Russian government prohibited the export of gold and silver money, and various subterfuges were adopted to evade the law. Candlesticks, knives, idols, and other articles were made of pure gold and sold by weight. Of course the goods were "of Russian manufacture."

Before 1860 the importation of tea at Kiachta was about one million chests annually, and all of good quality and not including brick tea. The "brick tea" of Mongolia and Northern China is made from stalks, large leaves, and refuse matter generally. This is moistened with sheep's or bullock's blood and pressed into brick-shaped cakes. When dried it is ready for transportation, and largely used by the Mongols, Bouriats, Tartars, and the Siberian peasantry. In some parts of Chinese Tartary it is the principal circulating medium of the people. Large quantities are brought into Siberia, but "brick-tea" never enters into the computation of Kiachta trade.

LEGAL TENDER.

Since 1860 the quantity of fine teas purchased at Kiachta has greatly fallen off. The importation of brick-tea is undiminished, and some authorities say it has increased.

None of the merchants speak any language but Russian, and most of them are firmly fixed at Kiachta. They make now and then journeys to Irkutsk, and regard such a feat about as a countryman on the Penobscot would regard a visit to Boston. The few who have been to Moscow and St. Petersburg have a reputation somewhat analogous to that of Marco Polo or John Ledyard. Walking is rarely practiced, and the numbers of smart turnouts, compared to the population, is pretty large. There is no theatre, concert-room, or newspaper office at Kiachta, and the citizens rely upon cards, wine, and gossip for amusement. They play much and win or lose large sums with perfect nonchalance. Visitors are rare, and the advent of a stranger of ordinary consequence is a great sensation.

Kiachta and Maimaichin stand on the edge of a Mongolian steppe seven or eight miles wide. Very little snow falls there and that little does not long remain. Wheeled carriages are in use the entire year. The elevation is about twenty-five hundred feet above sea level.

There was formerly a custom house at Troitskosavsk, where the duties on tea were collected. After the occupation of the Amoor the government opened all the country east of Lake Baikal to free trade. The custom house was removed to Irkutsk, where all duties are now arranged.

There were two Englishmen and one Frenchman residing at Kiachta. The latter, Mr. Garnier, was a merchant, and was about to marry a young and pretty Russian whose mother had a large fortune and thirteen dogs. The old lady appeared perfectly clear headed on every subject outside of dogs. A fortnight before my visit she owned fifteen, but the police killed two on a charge of biting somebody. She was inconsolable at their loss, took her bed from grief, and seriously contemplated going into mourning. I asked Garnier what would be the result if every dog of the thirteen should have his day. "Ah!" he replied, with a sigh, "the poor lady could never sustain it. I fear it would cause her death."

One Englishman, Mr. Bishop, had a telegraph scheme which he had vainly endeavored for two years to persuade the stubborn Chinese to look upon with favor. The Chinese have a superstitious dread of the electric telegraph, and the government is unwilling to do anything not in accordance with the will of the people.

RUSSIAN PETS.

A few years ago some Americans at Shanghae thought it a good speculation to construct a telegraph line between that city and the mouth of the river. The distance was about fifteen miles, and the line when finished operated satisfactorily. The Chinese made no interference, either officially or otherwise, with its construction. They did not understand its working, but supposed the foreigners employed agile and invisible devils to run along the wires and convey intelligence. All went well for a month or two. One night a Chinese happened to die suddenly in a house that stood near a telegraph pole. A knowing Celestial suggested that one of the foreign devils had descended from the wire and killed the unfortunate native. A mob very soon destroyed the dangerous innovation.

The other Englishman, Mr. Grant, was the projector and manager of a Pony Express from Kiachta to Pekin. He forwarded telegrams between London and Shanghae merchants, or any others who chose to employ him. He claimed that his Mongol couriers made the journey to Pekin in twelve days, and that he could outstrip the Suez and Ceylon telegraph and steamers. He seemed a permanent fixture of Kiachta, as he had married a Russian lady, the daughter of a former governor. All these foreigners placed me under obligations for various favors, and the two Britons were certainly more kind to me than to each other.

PONY EXPRESS.

I spent an evening at the club-rooms, where there was some heavy card-playing. One man lost nine hundred roubles in half an hour, and they told me that such an occurrence was not uncommon. In all card playing I ever witnessed in Russia there was 'something to make it interesting.' Money is invariably staked, and the Russians were surprised when I said, in answer to questions, that people in America generally indulged in cards for amusement alone. Ladies had no hesitation in gambling, and many of them followed it passionately. '*Chaque pays a sa habitude*,' remarked a lady one evening when I answered her query about card playing in America. It was the Russian fashion to gamble, and no one dreamed of making the slightest concealment of it. Though I saw it repeatedly I could never rid myself of a desire to turn away when a lady was reckoning her gains and losses, and keeping her accounts on the table cover. Russian card tables are covered with green cloth and provided with chalk pencils and brushes for players' use. Cards are a government monopoly.

On the day fixed for my dinner with the sargoochay I accompanied the Police Master and Captain Molostoff to Maimaichin. As we entered the court yard of the government house several officers came to receive us. In passing the temple of Justice I saw an unfortunate wretch undergoing punishment in a corner of the yard. He was wearing a collar about three feet in diameter and made of four inch plank. It was locked about his neck, and the man was unable to bring his hand to his head. A crowd was gazing at the culprit, but he seemed quite unconcerned and intent upon viewing the strangers. The Chinese have a system of yokes and stocks that seem a refinement of cruelty. They have a cheerful way of confining a man in a sort of cage about three feet square, the top and bottom being of plank and the sides of square sticks. His head passes through the top, which forms a collar precisely like the one described above, while the sides are just long enough to force him to stand upon the tip of his toes or hang suspended by his head. In some in-

CHINESE COLLAR.

SUSPENDED FREEDOM.

stances a prisoner's head is passed through a hole in the bottom of a heavy cask. He cannot stand erect without lifting the whole weight, and the cask is too long to allow him to sit

PUNISHMENT FOR BURGLARY.

down. He must remain on his knees in a torturing position, and cannot bring his hands to his head. He relies on his friends to feed him, and if he has no friends he must starve. The jailers think it a good joke when a man loses the number of his mess in this way.

The sargoochay met us in the apartment where our reception took place. He seated us around a table in much the same manner as before. While we waited dinner I exhibited a few photographs of the Big Trees of California, which I took with me at Molostoff's suggestion. I think the representative of His Celestial Majesty was fairly astonished on viewing these curiosities. The interpreter told him that all trees in America were like those in the pictures, and that we had many cataracts four or five miles high.

To handle our food we had forks and chopsticks, and each

guest had a small saucer of *soy*, or vinegar, at his right hand. The food was roast pig and roast duck, cut into bits the size of one's thumb nail, and each piece was to be dipped in the vinegar before going into the mouth. Then there were dishes of hashed meat or stew, followed by minced pies in miniature. I was a little suspicious of the last articles and preferred to stick to the pig.

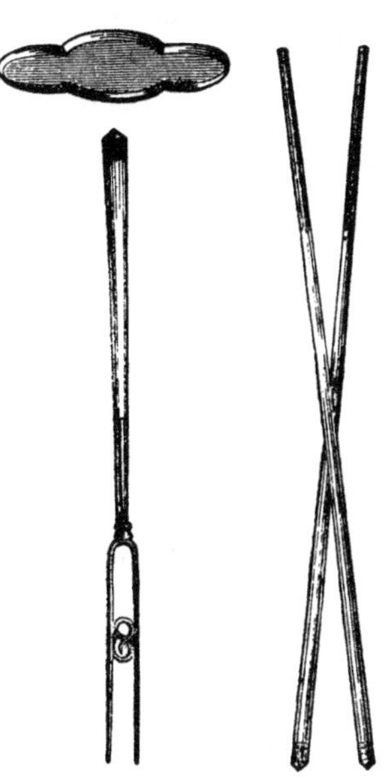
CHOPSTICKS, FORK, & SAUCER.

We had good claret and bad sherry, followed by Chinese wine. Champagne was brought when we began drinking toasts. Chinese wine, *sam-shoo*, is drank hot, from cups holding about a thimblefull. It is very strong, one cup being quite sufficient. The historic Bowery boy drinking a glass of Chinese wine might think he had swallowed a pyrotechnic display on Fourth of July night.

We conversed as before, going through English, French, Russian, Mongol, and Chinese, and after dinner smoked our pipes and cigars. The sargoochay had a pipe with a slender bowl that could be taken out for reloading, like the shell of a Remington rifle. A single whiff served to exhaust it, and the smoke passing through water became purified. An attendant stood near to manage the pipe of His Excellency whenever his services were needed. We endeavored to smoke each others' pipes and were quite satisfied after a minute's experience. His tobacco was very feeble, and I presume mine was too strong for his taste.

The sargoochay had ordered a theatrical display in my honor, though it was not 'the season,' and the affair was hastily gotten up. When all was ready he led the way to the theatre; the pipe-bearer came respectfully in our rear, and behind him was the staff and son of the sargoochay. The stage of the theatre faced an open court yard, and was provided with screens and curtains, but had no scenery that

CHINESE THEATRE.

could be shifted. About thirty feet in front of the stage was a pavilion of blue cloth, open in front and rear. We were seated around a table under this pavilion, and drank tea and smoked while the performance was in progress. There was a crowd of two or three hundred Chinese between the pavilion and the stage. The Mongol soldiers kept an open passage five or six feet wide in front of us so that we had an unobstructed view.

A comedy came first, and I had little difficulty in following the story by the pantomime alone. Female characters were represented by men, Chinese law forbidding women to act on the stage. Certain parts of the play were open to objections on account of immodesty, but when no ladies are present I presume a Chinese audience is not fastidious. The comedy was followed by something serious, of which I was unable to learn the name. I supposed it represented the superiority of the deities over the living things of earth.

First, there came representations of different animals. There were the tiger, bear, leopard, and wolf, with two or three beasts whose genera and species I could not determine. There was an ostrich and an enormous goose, both holding their heads high, while a crocodile, or something like it, brought up the rear. Each beast and bird was made of painted cloth over light framework, with a man inside to furnish action. While the tiger was making himself savage the mask fell off, and revealed the head of a Chinese. A rent in the skin of the ostrich disclosed the arm of the performer inside. The animals were not very well made, and the accident to the tiger's head reminded me of the Bowery elephant whose hind legs became very drunk and fell among the orchestra, leaving the fore legs to finish the play.

CHINESE TIGER.

Each animal made a circuit of the stage, bowed to the sargoochay, and retired. Then came half a dozen performers, only one being visible at a time. They were dressed, as I conjectured, to represent Chinese divinities, and as each appeared upon the stage he made a short recitation in a bombastic tone. The costumes of these actors were brilliantly decorated with metal ornaments, and there was a luxuriance of beard on most of the performer's faces, quite in contrast to the scanty growth which nature gave them. When the deities were assembled the animals returned and prostrated themselves in submission. A second speech from each actor closed the theatrical display. During all the time we sat under the pavilion the crowd looked at me far more intently than at the stage. An American was a great curiosity in the city limits of Maimaichin.

The performance began about two o'clock and lasted less than an hour. At its close we thanked the sargoochay for his courtesy, and returned to Kiachta. One of my Russian acquaintances had invited me to dine with him; "you can dine with the sargoochay at one o'clock," he said, "and will be entirely able to enjoy my dinner two hours later." I found the dinner at Maimaichin more pleasing to the eye than the stomach, and returned with a good appetite.

Some years ago the Russian government abolished the office of Governor of Kiachta and placed its military and kindred affairs in the hands of the Chief of Police. Diplomatic matters were entrusted to a 'Commissary of the Frontier,' who resided at Kiachta, while the Chief of Police dwelt at Troitskosavsk. When I arrived there, Mr. Pfaffius, the Commissary of the Frontier, was absent, though hourly expected from Irkutsk.

Mr. Pfaffius arrived on the third day of my visit, and invited me to a dinner at his house on the afternoon of my departure for Irkutsk. As the first toast of the occasion he proposed the President of the United States, and regretted deeply the misfortune that prevented his drinking the health of Mr. Lincoln. In a few happy remarks he touched upon the cordial feeling between the two nations, and his utterance of good-will toward the United States was warmly applauded by all the Russians present. In proposing the health of the Emperor I made the best return in my power for the courtesy of my Muscovite friends.

CHAPTER XXIX.

IN the year 1786 a vessel of three hundred and fifty tons burden sailed from an American port for Canton. She was the first to carry the flag of the United States to the shores of Cathay, and to begin a commerce that has since assumed enormous proportions. European nations had carried on a limited trade with the Chinese before that time, but they were restricted to a single port, and their jealousy of each other prevented their adopting those measures of co-operation that have recently proved so advantageous. China was averse to opening her territory to foreign merchants, and regarded with suspicion all their attempts to gain a foothold upon her soil. On the north, since 1727, the Russians had a single point of commercial exchange. In the south Canton was the only port open to those who came to China by sea, while along the coast-line, facing to the eastward, the ports were sealed against foreign intrusion. Commerce between China and the outer world was hampered by many restrictions, and only its great profits kept it alive. But once fairly established, the barbarian merchants taught the slow-learning Chinese that the trade brought advantage to all engaged in it. Step by step they pressed forward, to open new ports and extend commercial relations, which were not likely to be discontinued, if only a little time were allowed to show their value.

As years rolled on, trade with China increased. For a long time the foreigners trading with China had no direct intercourse with the General Government, but dealt only with the local and provincial authorities. It was not until after the famous "Opium War" that diplomatic relations were opened with the court at Pekin, and a common policy adopted for all parts of the empire, in its dealings with the outer world. Considering the extremely conservative character of the Chinese, their adherence to old forms and customs, their general unwillingness to do differently from their ancestors, and the not over-amiable character of the majority of the foreigners that went there to trade, it is not surprising that many years were required for commercial relations to grow up and become permanent. The wars between China and the Western powers did more than centuries of peace could have done to open the Oriental eyes. Austria's defeat on the field of Sadowa advanced and enlightened her more than a hundred years of peace and victory could have done, at her old rate of progress. The victories of the allied forces in China, culminating in the capture of Pekin and dictation of terms by the foreign leaders, opened the way for a free intercourse between the East and West, and the immense advantages that an unrestricted commerce is sure to bring to an industrious, energetic, and economical people.

With a river-system unsurpassed by that of any other nation of the world, China relied upon navigation by junks, which crept slowly against the current when urged by strong winds, and lay idle or were towed or poled by men when calms or head-breezes prevailed. Of steam applied to propulsion, she had no knowledge, until steamboats of foreign construction appeared in her waters and roused the wonder of the oblique-eyed natives by their mysterious powers. The first steamboat to ascend a Chinese river created a greater sensation than did the Clermont on her initial voyage along the Hudson or her Western prototype, several years later, among the Indians of the upper Missouri.* In 1839 the first

* A gentleman once described to me the sensation produced by the first steam vessel that ascended one of the Chinese rivers. "It was," said he, "a screw steamer, and we were burning anthracite coal that made no smoke. The current was about two miles an hour, and with wind and water unfavorable, the Chinese boats bound upward were slowly dragged by men pulling at long tow-lines. We steamed up the middle of the stream, going as rapidly as we dared

steam venture was made in China. An English house placed a boat on the route between Canton and Macao, and advertised it to carry freight and passengers on stated days. For the first six months the passengers averaged about a dozen to each trip—half of them Europeans, and the rest natives. The second half-year the number of native patrons increased, and by the end of the second year the boat, on nearly every trip, was filled with Chinese. The trade became so lucrative that another boat was brought from England and placed on the route, which continued to be a source of profit until the business was overdone by opposition lines. As soon as the treaties permitted, steamers were introduced into the coasting-trade of China, and subsequently upon the rivers and other inland waters. The Chinese merchants perceived the importance of rapid and certain transportation for their goods in place of the slow and unreliable service of their junks, and the advance in rates was overbalanced by the increased facilities and the opportunities of the merchants to make six times as many ventures annually as by the old system.

Probably there is no people in the world that can be called a nation of shop-keepers more justly than the Chinese; thousands upon thousands of them are engaged in petty trade, and the competition is very keen. Of course, where there is an active traffic the profits are small, and any thing that can assist the prompt delivery of merchandise and the speedy transmission of intelligence, money, credits, or the merchant himself, is certain to be brought into full use. No accurate statistics are at hand of the number of foreign steamers now in China, but well-informed parties estimate the burden of

---

with our imperfect knowledge, and the necessity of constant sounding. Our propeller was quite beneath the water, and so far as outward appearance went there was no visible power to move us. Chinamen are generally slow to manifest astonishment, and not easily frightened, but their excitement on that occasion was hardly within bounds. Men, women, and children ran to see the monster, and after gazing a few moments a fair proportion of them took to their heels for safety. Dogs barked and yelped on all the notes of the chromatic scale, occasional boats' crews jumped to the shore, and those who stuck to their oars did their best to get out of our way."

American coasting and river-vessels at upward of thirty thousand tons, while that of other nationalities is much larger. Steamboats, with a burden of more than ten thousand tons, are owned by Chinese merchants, and about half that quantity is the joint property of Chinese and foreigners. In managing their boats and watching the current expenses, the Chinese are quite equal to the English and Americans, and are sometimes able to carry freight upon terms ruinous to foreign competitors.

Foreign systems of banking and insurance have been adopted, and work successfully. The Chinese had a mode of banking long before the European nations possessed much knowledge of financial matters; and it is claimed that the first circulating-notes and bills-of-credit ever issued had their origin during a monetary pressure at Pekin. But they were so unprogressive that, when intercourse was opened with the Western World, they found their own system defective, and were forced to adopt the foreign innovation. Insurance companies were first owned and managed by foreigners at the open ports, and as soon as the plan of securing themselves against loss by casualties was understood by the Chinese merchants, they began to form companies on their own account, and carry their operations to the interior of the empire. All the intricacies of the insurance business—even to the formation of fraudulent companies, with imaginary officers, and an explosion at a propitious moment—are fully understood and practised by the Chinese.

By the facilities which the advent of foreigners has introduced to the Chinese, the native trade along the rivers and with the open ports has rapidly increased. On the rivers and along the coast the steamers and native boats are actively engaged, and the population of the open ports has largely increased in consequence of the attractions offered to the people of all grades and professions. The greatest extension has been in the foreign trade, which, from small beginnings, now amounts to more than nine hundred millions of dollars annually. Where formerly a dozen or more vessels crept into

CHINESE PUNISHMENT

Canton yearly, there are now hundreds of ships and steamers traversing the ocean to and from the accessible points of the coast of the great Eastern Empire. America has a large share of this commerce with China, and from the little beginning, in 1786, she has increased her maritime service, until she now has a fleet of sailing ships second to none in the world, and a line of magnificent steamers plying regularly across the Pacific, and bringing the East in closer alliance with the West than ever before.

Railways will naturally follow the steamboat, and an English company is now arranging to supply the Chinese with a railway-system to connect the principal cities, and especially to tap the interior districts, where the water communications are limited. There is no regular system of mail-communication in China; the Government transmits intelligence by means of couriers, and when merchants have occasion to communicate with persons at a distance they use private expresses. Foreign and native merchants, doing an extensive business, keep swift steamers, which they use as despatch-boats, and sometimes send them at heavy expense to transmit single messages. It has happened that, on a sudden change of markets, two or more houses in Hong Kong or Shanghae have despatched boats at the same moment; and some interesting and exciting races are recorded in the local histories.

The barriers of Chinese exclusion were broken down when the treaties of the past ten years opened the empire to foreigners, and placed the name of China on the list of diplomatic and treaty powers. The last stone of the wall that shut the nation from the outer world was overthrown when the court at Pekin sent an embassy, headed by a distinguished American, to visit the capitals of the Western nations, and cement the bonds of friendship between the West and the East. It was eminently fitting that an American should be selected as the head of this embassy, and eminently fitting, too, that the ambassador of the oldest nation should first visit the youngest of all the great powers of the world. America, just emerged from the garments of childhood, and with full pride and consciousness of its youthful strength, presents to ruddy England, smiling France, and the other members of the family of nations, graybeard and dignified China, who expresses joy at the introduction, and hopes for a better acquaintance in the years that are to come.

During his residence at Pekin, Mr. Burlingame interested himself in endeavoring to introduce the telegraph into China, and though meeting with opposition on account of certain superstitions of the Chinese, he was ultimately successful. The Chinese do not understand the working of the telegraph —at least the great majority of them do not—and like many other people elsewhere, with regard to any thing incomprehensible, they are inclined to ascribe it to a satanic origin. In California, the Chinese residents make a liberal use of the telegraph; though they do not trouble themselves with an investigation of its workings, they fully appreciate its importance. John, in California, is at liberty to send his messages in "pigeon-English," and very funny work he makes of it occasionally. Chin Lung, in Sacramento, telegraphs to Ming Yup, in San Francisco, "You me send one piecee me trunk," which means, in plain language, "Send me my trunk." Mr. Yup complies with the request, and responds by telegraph, "Me you trunkee you sendee." The inventor of pigeon-English is unknown, and it is well for his name that it has not been handed down; he deserves the execration of all who are compelled to use the legacy he has left. It is just as difficult for a Chinese to learn pigeon-English as it would be to learn pure and honest English, and it is about as intelligible as Greek or Sanscrit to a newly-arrived foreigner. In Shanghae or Hong Kong, say to your Chinese *ma-foo*, who claims to speak English, "Bring me a glass of water," and he will not understand you. Repeat your order in those words, and he stands dumb and uncomprehending, as though you had spoken the dialect of the moon. But if you say, "You go me catchee bring one piecee glass water; savey," and his tawny face beams intelligence as he obeys the order.

In the phrase, "pigeon-English," the word pigeon means

"business," and the expression would be more intelligible if it were "business-English." Many foreigners living in China have formed the habit of using this and other words in their Chinese sense, and sometimes one hears an affair of business called "a pigeon." A gentleman whom I met in China used to tell, with a great deal of humor, his early experiences with the language.

"When I went to Shanghae," said he, "I had an introduction to a prominent merchant, who received me very kindly, and urged me to call often at his office. A day or two later I called, and inquired for him. 'Won't be back for a week or two,' said the clerk; 'he has gone into the country, about two hundred miles, after a little pigeon.' I asked no questions, but as I bowed myself out, I thought, 'He must be a fool, indeed. Go two hundred miles into the country after a pigeon, and a little one at that! He has lost his senses, if he ever possessed any.'"

Nearly all the trade with China is carried on at the Southern and Eastern ports, and comparatively few of the foreign merchants in China have ever been at Pekin, which was opened only a few years ago. But the war with the allied powers, the humiliation of the government, the successes of the rebels, and the threatened extinction of the ruling dynasty, led to important changes of policy. The treaty of Tientsin, in 1860, opened the empire as it had never been open before. Foreigners could travel in China where they wished, for business or pleasure, and the navigable rivers were declared free to foreign boats. Pekin was opened to travelers but not to foreign merchants; but it is probable that commerce will be carried to that city before long. There is an extensive trade at Tientsin, ninety miles south of the capital, and when it becomes necessary to carry it to the doors of the palace of the Celestial ruler, the diplomats will not be slow to find a sufficient pretext for it.

CHAPTER XXX.

THE great cities of China are very much alike in their general features. None of them have wide streets, except in the foreign quarters, and none of them are clean; in their abundance of dirt they can even excel New York, and it would be worth the while for the rulers of the American metropolis to visit China and see how filthy a city can be made without half trying. The most interesting city in China is Pekin, for the reason that it has long been the capital, and contains many monuments of the past greatness and the glorious history of the Celestial empire. Its temples are massive, and show that the Chinese, hundreds of years ago, were no mean architects; its walls could resist any of the ordinary appliances of war before the invention of artillery, and even the tombs of its rulers are monuments of skill and patience that awaken the admiration of every beholder. Throughout China Pekin is reverentially regarded, and in many localities the man who has visited it is regarded as a hero. Though the capital, it is the most northern city of large population in the whole empire.

Pekin is divided into the Chinese city and the Tartar one; the division was made at the time of the Tartar conquest, and for many years the two people refused to associate freely. A wall separates the cities; the gates through it are closed at night, and only opened when sufficient reason is given. If the party who desires to pass the gate can give no verbal excuse he has only to drop some money in the hands of the gate-keeper, and the pecuniary apology is considered entirely satisfactory. Time has softened the asperities of Tartar and

Chinese association, so that the two people mingle freely, and it is impossible for a stranger to distinguish one from the other. Many Chinese live in the Tartar town and transact business, and I fancy that they would not always find it easy to explain their pedigree, or, at all events, that of some of their children. The foreign legations are in the Tartar city, for the reason that the government offices are there, and also for the reason that it is the most pleasant, (or the least unpleasant,) part of Pekin to reside in. All the embassies have spacious quarters, with the exception of the Russian one, which is the oldest; when it was established there it was a great favor to be allowed any residence whatever.

From the center gate between the Chinese and Tartar cities there is a street two or three miles long, and having

PROVISION DEALER.

the advantages of being wide, straight, and dirty. It is blocked up with all sorts of huckster's stalls and shops, and is kept noisy with the shouts of the people who have innumerable articles for sale. Especially in summer is there a liberal assemblage of peddlers, jugglers, beggars, donkey drivers, merchants, idlers, and all the other professions and non-professions that go to make up a population. The peddlers have fruit and other edibles, not omitting an occasional string of rats suspended from bamboo poles, and attached to cards on which the prices, and sometimes the excellent qualities of the rodents, are set forth. It is proper to remark that the Chinese are greatly slandered on the rat question. As a people they are not given to eating these little animals; it is only among the poorer classes that they are tolerated, and then only because they are the cheapest food that can be obtained. I was always suspicious when the Chinese urged me to partake of little meat pies and dumplings, whose components I could only guess at, and when the things were forced upon me I proclaimed a great fondness for stewed duck and chicken, which were manifestly all right. But I frankly admit that I do not believe they would have inveigled me into swallowing articles to which the European mind is prejudiced, and my aversion arose from a general repugnance to hash in all forms—a repugnance which had its origin in American hotels and restaurants.

The jugglers are worth a little notice, more I believe than they obtain from their countrymen. They attract good audiences along the great street of Pekin, but after swallowing enough stone to load a pack-mule, throwing up large bricks and allowing them to break themselves on his head, and otherwise amusing the crowd for half an hour or so, the poor necromancer cannot get cash enough to buy himself a dinner. Those who feel disposed to give are not very liberal, and their donations are thrown into the ring very much as one would toss a bone to a bull-dog. Sometimes a man will stand with a white painted board, slightly covered with thick ink, and while talking with his auditors he will throw off, by means of his thumb and fingers, excellent pictures of birds and fishes, with every feather, fin, and scale done with accuracy. Such genius ought to be rewarded, but it rarely receives pecuniary recognition enough to enable its possessor to dress decently. Other slight-of-hand performances abound; the Chinese are very skillful at little games of thimble-rig and the like, and when a stranger chooses to make a bet on their operations they are sure to take in his money. In sword-swallowing and knife-throwing, the natives of the Flowery Kingdom are without rivals, and the uninitiated spectator can never understand how a man can make a breakfast of Asiatic cutlery without incurring the risk of dyspepsia.

China is the paradise of beggars—I except Italy from the mendicant list—so far as numbers are concerned, though they

CHINESE MENDICANTS.

do not appear to flourish and live in comfort. There are many dwarfs, and it is currently reported at Pekin that they are produced and cultivated for the special purpose of asking alms. One can be very liberal in China at small expense, as the smallest coin is worth only one-fifteenth of a cent, and a shilling's worth of "cash" can be made to go a great way if the giver is judicious. Many of the beggars are blind, and they sometimes walk in single file under the direction of a chief; they are nearly all musicians, and make the most hideous noises, which they call melody. Anybody with a sensitive ear will pay them to move on where they will annoy somebody beside himself. Many of the beggars are almost naked, and they attract attention by striking their hands against their hips and shouting at the top of their voices. One day the wife of the French minister at Pekin gave some garments to those who were the most shabbily dressed; the next morning they returned as near naked as ever, and some of them entirely so.

Outside of the Tartar city there is a beggar's lodging house, which bears the name of "the House of the Hen's Feathers." It is a hall, with a floor of solid earth and a roof of thin laths caulked and plastered with mud. The floor is covered with a thick bed of feathers, which have been gathered in the markets and restaurants of Pekin, without much regard to their cleanliness. There is an immense quilt of thick felt the exact size of the hall, and raised and lowered by means of mechanism. When the curfew tolls the knell of parting day, the beggars flock to this house, and are admitted on payment of a small fee. They take whatever places they like, and at an appointed time the quilt is lowered. Each lodger is at liberty to lie coiled up in the feathers, or if he has a prejudice in favor of fresh air, he can stick his head through one of the numerous holes that the coverlid contains.

A view of this quilt when the heads are protruding is suggestive of an apartment where dozens of dilapidated Chinese have been decapitated. All night long the lodgers keep up a frightful noise; the proprietor, like the individual in the same business in New York, will tell you, "I sells the place to sleep, but begar, I no sells the sleep with it." The couch is a lively one, as the feathers are a convenient warren for a miscellaneous lot of living things not often mentioned in polite society.

In the southern cities of China one sees fewer women in the street than in the north. Those that appear in public are always of the poorer classes, and it is rare indeed that one can get a view of the famous small-footed women. The odious custom of compressing the feet is much less common at Pekin than in the southern provinces. The Manjour emperors of China opposed it ever since their dynasty ascended the throne, and on several occasions they issued severe edicts against it. The Tartar and Chinese ladies that compose the court of the empresses have their feet of the natural size, and the same is the case with the wives of many of the officials. But such is the power of fashion that many of these ladies have adopted the theatrical slipper, which is very difficult to walk with. No one can tell where the custom of compressing the feet originated, but it is said that one of the empresses was born with deformed feet, and set the fashion, which soon spread through the empire. The jealousy of the men and the idleness and vanity of the women have served to continue the custom. Every Chinese who can afford it will have at least one small-footed wife, and she is maintained in the most perfect indolence. For a woman to have a small foot is to show that she is of high birth and rich family, and she would consider herself dishonored if her parents failed to compress her feet.

THE FAVORITE.

When remonstrated with about the practice, the Chinese retort by calling attention to the compression of the waist as practiced in Europe and America. "It is all a matter of taste," said a Chinese merchant one day when addressed on the subject. "We like women with small feet and you like them with small waists. What is the difference?"

And what *is* the difference?

The compression is begun when a girl is six years old, and is accomplished with strong bandages. The great toe is pressed beneath the others, and these are bent under, so that the foot takes the shape of a closed fist. The bandages are drawn tighter every month, and in a couple of years the foot has assumed the desired shape and ceased to grow.

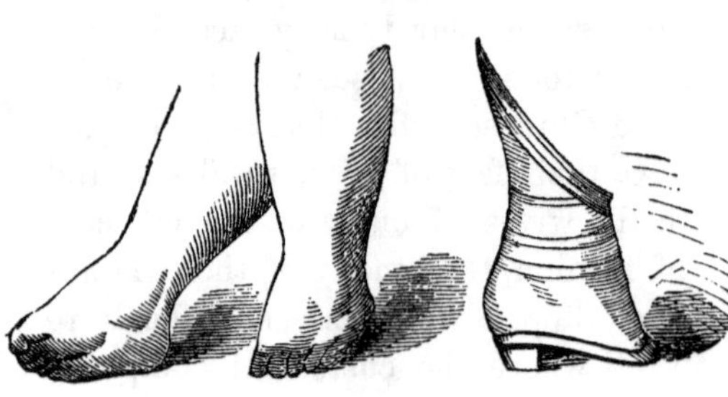

FEMALE FEET AND SHOE.

Very often this compression creates diseases that are difficult to heal; it is always impossible for the small-footed woman to walk easily, and sometimes she cannot move without support. To have the finger-nails very long is also a mark of aristocracy; sometimes the ladies enclose their nails in silver cases, which are very convenient for cleansing the ears of their owner or tearing out the eyes of somebody else.

Walking along the great street of Pekin, one is sure to see a fair number of gamblers and gambling houses. Gambling is a passion with the Chinese, and they indulge it to a greater extent than any other people in the world. It is a scourge in China, and the cause of a great deal of the poverty and degradation that one sees there. There are various games, like throwing dice, and drawing sticks from a pile, and there is hardly a poor wretch of a laborer who will not risk the chance of paying double for his dinner on the remote possibility of getting it for nothing. The rich are addicted to the vice quite as much as the poor, and sometimes they will lose their money, then their houses, their lands, their wives, their children, and so on up to themselves, when they have nothing else that their adversaries will accept. The winter is severe at Pekin, and it sometimes happens that men who have lost

A LOTTERY PRIZE.

everything, down to their last garments, are thrust naked into the open air, where they perish of cold. Sometimes a man will bet his fingers on a game, and if he loses he must submit to have them chopped off and turned over to the winner.

There is a tradition that one of the Chinese emperors used to get up lotteries, in which the ladies of the court were the prizes. He obtained quite a revenue from the business, which was popular with both the players and the prizes, as the latter were enabled to obtain husbands without the trouble of negotiation.

The lottery has a place in the Chinese courts of justice. There is one mode of capital punishment in which a dozen or twenty knives are placed in a covered basket, and each knife is marked for a particular part of the body. The executioner puts his hand under the cover and draws at random. If the knife is for the toes, they are cut off one after another; if for the feet, they are severed, and so on until a knife for the heart or neck is reached. Usually the friends of the victim bribe the executioner to draw early in the game a knife whose wound will be fatal, and he generally does as he agrees. The bystanders amuse themselves by betting as to how long the culprit will stand it. Facetious dogs, those Chinese.

To enumerate all the ways of inflicting punishment in China would be to fill a volume. Punishment is one of the fine arts, and a man who can skin another elegantly is entitled to rank as an artist. The bastinado and floggings are common, and then they have huge shears, like those used in tin shops, for snipping off feet and arms, very much as a gardener would cut off the stem of a rose.

Some years ago the environs of Tien-tsin were infested by bands of robbers who were suspected of living in villages a few miles away. The governor was ordered by the imperial authority to suppress these robberies, and in order to get the right persons he sent out his soldiers and arrested everybody, old and young, in the suspected villages. Of course there were innocent persons among the captives, but that made no difference; some of them were blind, and others crippled, but the police had orders to bring in everybody. The prisoners were summarily tried; some of them had their heads cut off, others were imprisoned, and others were whipped. Nobody escaped without some punishment; the result was that the robber bands were broken up and the robberies ceased.

It is not easy to go about Pekin. It is a city of magnificent distances, and the sights which one wants to see are far apart. The streets are bad, being dusty in dry weather and muddy when it rains, and the carriage way is cut up with deep ruts that make riding very uncomfortable. The cabs of Pekin are little carts, just large enough for two persons of medium size. They are without springs, and not very neatly arranged inside. If one does not like them he can walk or take a palanquin —there are plenty of palanquins in the city, and they do not cost an exorbitant sum. They are not very commodious, but infinitely preferable to the carts.

A CHINESE PALANQUIN.

The comforts of travel are very few in China. A Chinese never travels for pleasure, and he does not understand the spirit that leads tourists from one end of the world to the other in search of adventure. When he has nothing to do he sits down, smokes his pipe, and thinks about his ancestors. He never rides,

A PEKIN CAB.

walks, dances, or takes the least exercise for pleasure alone. It is business and nothing else that controls his movements.

When an English ship touched at Hong Kong some years ago, the captain gave a ball to the foreign residents, and invited several Chinese merchants to attend the festivities. One heavy old merchant who had never before seen anything of the kind, looked on patiently, and when the dance was concluded he beckoned the captain to his side and asked if he could not get his servants to do that work and save him the trouble.

PRIEST IN TEMPLE OF CONFUCIUS.

One of the great curiosities of Pekin is the temple of Confucius, where once a year the Emperor worships the great sage without the intervention of paintings or images. In the central shrine there is a small piece of wood, a few inches long, standing upright and bearing the name of Confucius in Chinese characters. The temple contains several stone tablets, on which are engraved the records of honor conferred on literary men, and it is the height of a Chinese scholar's ambition to win a place here. There are several fine trees in the spacious court yard, and they are said to have been planted by the Mongol dynasty more than five hundred years ago. The building is a magnificent one, and contains many curious relics of the various dynasties, some of them a thousand years old. The ceiling is especially gorgeous, and the tops of the interior walls are ornamented with wooden boards bearing the names of the successive emperors in raised gilt characters. As soon as an emperor ascends the throne he at once adds his name to the list.

The Temple of Heaven and the Temple of Earth are also among the curiosities of Pekin. The former stands in an enclosed space a mile square, and has a great central pavilion, with a blue roof, and a gilt top that shines in the afternoon sun like the dome of St. Isaac's church at St. Petersburg. The enclosed space includes a park, beautifully laid out with avenues of trees and with regular, well paved walks. In the park are some small buildings where the priests live, that is to say, they are small compared with the main structure, though they are really fine edifices. The great pavilion is on a high causeway, and has flights of steps leading up to it from different directions. The pavilion is three stories high, the eaves of each story projecting very far and covered with blue enameled tiles. An enormous gilt ball crowns the whole, and around the building there is a bewildering array of arches and columns, with promenades and steps of white marble, evincing great skill and care in their construction. Unfortunately, the government is not taking good care of the temple, and the grass is growing in many places in the crevices of the pavements.

The Temple of Earth is where the emperor goes annually to witness the ceremony of opening the planting season, and to inaugurate it by ploughing the first furrow. The ceremony is an imposing one, and never fails to draw a large assemblage.

One of the most interesting objects in the vicinity of Pekin previous to 1860 was "Yuen-ming Yuen," or the summer palace of the emperor, Kien Loong. It was about eight miles northwest of the city, and bore the relation to Pekin that Versailles does to Paris. I say *was*, because it was ravaged by the English and French forces in their advance upon the Chinese capital, and all the largest and best of the buildings were burned. The country was hilly, and advantage was taken of this fact, so that the park presented every variety of hill, dale, woodland, lawn, garden, and meadow, interspersed with canals, pools, rivulets, and lakes, with their banks in imitation of nature. The park contained about twelve square miles, and there were nearly forty houses for the residence of the emperor's ministers, each of them surrounded with buildings for large retinues of servants. The summer palace, or central hall of reception, was an elaborate structure, and when it was occupied by the French army thousands of yards of the finest silk and crape were found there. These articles were so abundant that the soldiers used them for bed clothes and to wrap around other plunder. The cost of this palace amounted to millions of dollars, and the blow was severely felt by the Chinese government. The park is still worth a visit, but less so than before the destruction of the palace.

In the country around Pekin there are many private burying grounds belonging to families; the Chinese do not, like ourselves, bury their dead in common cemeteries, but each family has a plot of its own. Sometimes a few families combine and own a place together; they generally select a spot in a grove of trees, and make it as attractive as possible. The Chinese are more careful of their resting places after death than before it; a wealthy man will live in a miserable hovel, but he looks forward to a commodious tomb beneath pretty shade trees. The tender regard for the dead is an admirable trait in the Chinese character, and springs, no doubt, from that filial piety which is so deeply engraved on the Oriental mind.

In Europe and America it is the custom not to mention

coffins in polite society, and the contemplation of one is always mournful. But in China a coffin is a thing to be made a show of, like a piano. In many houses there is a room set apart for the coffins of the members of the family, and the owners point them out with pride. They practice economy to lay themselves out better than their rivals, and sometimes a man who has made a good thing by swindling or robbing somebody, will use the profits in buying a coffin, just as an American would treat himself to a gold watch or diamond pin. The most elegant gift that a child can make to his sick father is a coffin that he has paid for out of his own labor; it is not considered a hint to the old gentleman to hand in his checks and get out of the way, but rather as a mark of devotion which all good boys should imitate. The coffins are finely ornamented, according to the circumstances of the owner, and I have heard that sometimes a thief will steal a fine one and commit suicide—first arranging with his friends to bury him

COMFORTS AND CONVENIENCES.

FILIAL ATTENTION.

in it before his theft is discovered. If he is not found out he thinks he has made a good thing of it.

Whenever the Chinese sell ground for building purposes they always stipulate for the removal of the bones of their ancestors for many generations. The bones are carefully dug up and put in earthen jars, when they are sealed up, labeled, and put away in a comfortable room, as if they were so many pots of pickles and fruits. Every respectable family in China has a liberal supply of potted ancestors on hand, but would not part with them at any price.

Nothing can surpass the calm resignation with which the Chinese part with life. They die without groans, and have no mental terror at the approach of death. Abbe Huc says that when they came for him to administer the last sacraments to a dying convert, their formula of saying that the danger was imminent, was in the words, "The sick man does not smoke his pipe."

When a Chinese wishes to revenge himself upon another he furtively places a corpse upon the property of his enemy. This subjects the man on whose premises the body is found to many vexatious visits from the officials, and also to claims on the part of the relations of the dead man. The height of a joke of this kind is to commit suicide on another man's property in such a way as to appear to have been murdered there. This will subject the unfortunate object of revenge to all sorts of legal vexations, and not unfrequently to execution. Suicide for revenge would be absurd in America, but is far from unknown at the antipodes.

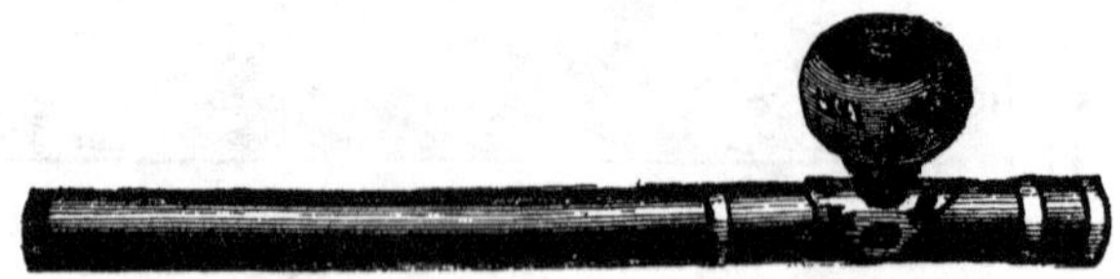

CHAPTER XXXI.

IT was my original intention to make a journey from Kiachta to Pekin and back again, but the lateness of the season prevented me. I did not wish to be caught in the desert of Gobi in winter. I talked with several persons who had traversed Mongolia, and among them a gentleman who had just arrived from the Chinese capital. I made many notes from his recital which I found exceedingly interesting.

For a time the Chinese refused passports to foreigners wishing to cross Mongolia; but on finding their action was likely to cause trouble, they gave the desired permission, though accompanying it with an intimation that the privilege might be suspended at any time. The bonds that unite Mongolia to the great empire are not very strong, the natives being somewhat indifferent to their rulers and ready at any decent provocation to throw off their yoke. Though engaged in the peaceful pursuits of sheep-tending, and transporting freight between Russia and China, they possess a warlike spirit and are capable of being roused into violent action. They are proud of tracing their ancestry to the soldiers that marched with Genghis Khan, and carried his victorious banners into Central Europe; around their fires at night no stories are more eagerly heard than those of war, and he who can relate the most wonderful traditions of daring deeds may be certain of admiration and applause.

The first "outside barbarian," other than Russians, who attempted this overland journey, was a young French Count, who traveled in search of adventure. Proceeding eastward from St. Petersburg. he reached Kiachta in 1859. After some hesitation, the governor-general of Eastern Siberia appointed him secretary to a Russian courier *en route* for Pekin. He made the journey without serious hindrance, but on reaching the Chinese capital his nationality was discovered, and he was forced to return to Siberia.

From Pekin the traveller destined for Siberia passes through the northern gate amid clouds of dust or pools of mud, according as the day of his exit is fair or stormy. He meets long strings of carts drawn by mules, oxen, or ponies, carrying country produce of different kinds to be digested in the great maw of the Imperial city. Animals with pack-saddles, swaying under heavy burdens, swell the caravans, and numerous equestrians, either bestriding their steeds, or sitting sidewise in apparent carelessness, are constantly encountered. Now and then an unruly mule causes a commotion in the crowd by a vigorous use of his heels, and a watchful observer may see an unfortunate native sprawling on the ground in consequence of approaching too near one of the hybrid beasts. Chinese mules *will* kick as readily as their American cousins; and I can say from experience, that their hoofs are neither soft nor delicate. They can bray, too, in tones terribly discordant and utterly destructive of sleep. The natives have a habit of suppressing their music when it becomes positively unbearable, and the means they employ may be worth notice. A Chinaman says a mule cannot bray without elevating his tail to a certain height; so to silence the beast he ties a stone to that ornamental appendage, and depends upon the weight to shut off the sound. Out of compassion to the mule, he attaches the stone so that it rests upon the ground and makes no strain as long as the animal behaves himself.

A MUSICAL STOP.

A Chinese pack-mule will carry about four hundred pounds of dead weight, if properly adjusted. The loads are not lashed on the animals' backs, but simply balanced; consequently, they must be very nicely divided and arranged on each side of the saddles.

On the road from Pekin the track is so wretched, and the carts so roughly made, that journeying with wheeled vehicles is next to an impossibility. Travelers go on horseback—if their circumstances allow—and by way of comfort, especially if there be ladies in the party, they generally provide themselves with mule-litters. The mule-litter is a goodly-sized palanquin, not quite long enough for lying at full length, but high enough to allow the passenger to sit erect. There is a box or false flooring in the bottom, to accommodate baggage in small parcels that can be easily stowed. A good litter has the sides stuffed to save the occupant from bruises; and with plenty of straw and a couple of pillows, he generally finds himself quite comfortable. The body is fastened to two strong and flexible poles that extend fore and aft far enough to serve as shafts for a couple of mules. At the ends of the shafts their points are connected by stout bands of leather that pass over the saddles of the respective mules; each band is kept in place by an iron pin fixed in the top of the saddle, and passing through a hole in the leather. As the shafts are long enough to afford the animals plenty of walking room, there is a good deal of spring to the concern, and the motion is by no means disagreeable. Sometimes the bands slip from the shafts, and in such case the machine comes to the ground with disagreeable thump; if the traveler happens to be asleep at the time he can easily imagine he is being shot from a catapult.

Just outside of Pekin there is a sandy plain, and beyond it a fine stretch of country under careful cultivation, the principal cereal being millet, that often stands ten or twelve feet high. Some cotton is grown, but the region is too far north to render its culture profitable.

About twenty miles from Pekin is the village of Sha-ho,

near two old stone bridges that span a river now nearly dried away. The village is a sort of half-way halting place between Pekin and the Nankow pass, a rocky defile twelve or fifteen miles long. The huge boulders and angular fragments of stone have been somewhat worn down and smoothed by constant use, though they are still capable of using up a good many mule-hoofs annually. With an eye to business, a few traveling farriers hang about this pass, and find occasional employment in setting shoes. Chinese shoeing, considered as a fine art, is very much in its infancy. Animals are only shod when the nature of the service requires it; the farriers do not attempt to make shoes to order, but they keep a stock of iron plates on hand, and select the nearest size they can find. They hammer the plate a little to fit it to the hoof and then fasten it on; an American blacksmith would be astonished at the rapidity with which his Chinese brother performs his work.

The pass of Nankow contains the remains of several old forts, which were maintained in former times to protect China from Mongol incursions. The natural position is a strong one, and a small force could easily keep at bay a whole army. Just outside the northern entrance of the pass there is a branch of one of the "Great Walls" of China. It was built some time before *the* Great Wall. Foreigners visiting Pekin and desiring to see the Great Wall are usually taken to Nankow, and gravely told they have attained the object they seek. Perhaps it is just as well for them to believe so, since they avoid a journey of fifty miles farther over a rough road to reach the real Great Wall; besides, the Chinese who have contracted to take them on the excursion are able to make a nice thing of it, since they charge as much for one place as for the other.

The country for a considerable distance is dotted with old forts and ruins, and the remains of extensive earthworks. Many battles were fought here between the Chinese and the Mongols when Genghis Khan made his conquest. For a long time the assailants were kept at bay, but one fortress after

NANKOW PASS.

another fell into their hands, and finally the capture of the Nankow pass by Che-pee, one of Genghis Khan's generals, laid Pekin at their mercy.

There is a tradition that the loss of the first line of northern forts was due to a woman. Intelligence was transmitted in those days by means of beacon fires, and the signals were so arranged as to be rapidly flashed through the empire. Once a lady induced the Emperor to give the signal and summon his armies to the capital. The Mandarins assembled with their forces, but on finding they had been simply employed at the caprice of a woman, they returned angrily to their homes. By-and-by the enemy came; the beacon fires were again lighted; but this time the Mandarins did not heed the call for assistance.

The Great Wall—the real one—crosses the road at Chan-kia-kow, a large and scattered town lying in a broad valley, pretty well enclosed by mountains. The Russians call the town Kalgan (gate), but the natives never use any other than the Chinese name. In maps made from Russian authorities, Kalgan appears, while in those taken from the Chinese, the other appellation is used. Kalgan (I stick to the Russian term, as more easily pronounced, though less correct) is the centre of the transit trade from Pekin to Kiachta, and great quantities of tea and other goods pass through it annually. Several Russians are established there, and the town contains a population of Chinese from various provinces of the empire, mingled with Mongols and Thibetans in fair proportion. The religion is varied, and embraces adherents to all the branches of Chinese theology, together with Mongol lamas and a considerable sprinkling of Mahommedans. There are temples, lamissaries, and mosques, according to the needs of the faithful; and the Russian inhabitants have a chapel of their own, and are thus able to worship according to their own faith. The mingling of different tribes and kinds of people in a region where manners and morals are not severely strict, has produced a result calculated to puzzle the present or future ethnologist. Many of the merchants have grown wealthy, and take life as comfortably as possible; they furnish their houses in the height of Chinese style, and some of them have even sent to Russia for the wherewith to astonish their neighbors.

The Great Wall runs along the ridge of hills in a direction nearly east and west; where it crosses the town it is kept in good repair, but elsewhere it is very much in ruins, and could offer little resistance to an enemy. Many of the towers remain, and some of them are but little broken. They seem to have been better constructed than the main portions of the wall, and, though useless against modern weapons, were, no doubt, of importance in the days of their erection. The Chinese must have held the Mongol hordes in great dread, to judge by the labor expended to guard against incursions.

As Kalgan is the frontier town between China and Mongolia, many Mongols go there for all purposes, from trading down to loafing. They bring their camels to engage in transporting goods across the desert, and indulge in a great deal of traffic on their own account. They drive cattle, sheep, and horses from their pastures farther north, and sell them for local use, or for the market at Pekin. Mutton is the staple article of food, and nearly always cheap and abundant. The hillsides are covered with flocks, which often graze where nothing else can live. In the autumn, immense numbers of sheep are driven to Pekin, and sometimes the road is fairly blocked with them.

Every morning there is a horse-fair on an open space just beyond the Great Wall, and on its northern side. The modes of buying and selling horses are very curious, and many of the tricks would be no discredit to American jockeys. The horses are tied or held wherever their owners can keep them, and in the centre of the fair grounds there is a space where the beasts are shown off. They trot or gallop up and down the course, their riders yelling as if possessed of devils, and holding their whips high in air. These riders are generally Mongols; their garments flutter like the decorations of a scarecrow in a morning breeze, and their pig-tails, if not carefully triced up, stand out at right angles like ships' pennants in a north-east gale. Notwithstanding all the confusion, it rarely happens that anybody is run over, though there are many narrow escapes.

RACING AT THEKALGAN FAIR.

The fair is attended by two classes of people—those who want to trade in horses, and those who don't; between them they manage to assemble a large crowd. There are always plenty of curbstone brokers, or intermediaries, who hang around the fair to negotiate purchases and sales. They have a way of conducting trades by drawing their long sleeves over their hands, and making or receiving bids by means of the concealed fingers. This mode of telegraphing is quite convenient when secrecy is desired, and prevails in many parts of Asia. Tavernier and other travelers say the diamond merchants conduct their transactions in this manner, even when no one is present to observe them.

STREET IN KALGAN.

Unless arrangements have been made beforehand, it will be necessary to spend three or four days at Kalgan in preparing for the journey over the desert. Camels must be hired, carts purchased, baggage packed in convenient parcels, and numerous odds and ends provided against contingencies. Of course, there is generally something forgotten, even after careful attention to present and prospective wants.

But we are off at last. The start consumes the greater part of a day, as it is best to have nothing done carelessly at the outset. The heavy baggage is loaded upon the camels, the animals lying down and patiently waiting while their cargoes are stowed. Pieces of felt cloth are packed between and around their humps, to prevent injury from the cords that sustain the bundles. The drivers display much ingenuity in arranging the loads so that they shall be easily balanced, and the sides of the beasts as little injured as possible. Spite of precautions, the camels get ugly sores in their sides and backs, which grow steadily worse by use. Occasionally their hoofs crack and fill with sand, and when this occurs, their owner has no alternative but to rest them a month or two, or risk losing their services altogether. The principal travel over the desert is in the cold season. In the autumn, the camels are fat, and their humps appear round and hard. They are then steadily worked until spring, and very often get very little to eat. As the camel grows thin, his humps fall to one side, and the animal assumes a woe-begone appearance. In the spring, his hair falls off; his naked skin wrinkles like a wet glove, and he becomes anything but an attractive object.

IN GOOD CONDITION.

As a beast of burden, the camel is better than for purposes of draft. He can carry from six hundred to eight hundred pounds, if the load be properly placed on his back ; but when he draws a cart the weight must be greatly diminished. In crossing Mongolia, heavy baggage is carried on camels, but every traveler takes a cart for riding purposes, and alternates between it and his saddle horse. The cart is a sort of dog-house on two wheels; its frame is of wood, and has a covering of felt cloth, thick enough to ward off a light fall of rain, and embarrass a heavy one. It is barely high enough to allow a man to sit erect, but not sufficiently long to enable him to lie at full length. The body rests directly upon the axle, so that the passenger gets the full benefit of every jolt. The camel walks between the shafts, and his great body is the chief feature of the scenery when one looks ahead. The harness gives way occasionally, and allows the shafts to fall to the ground; when this happens, the occupant runs the risk of being dumped among the ungainly feet that propel his vehicle. One experience of this kind is more than satisfactory.

After passing a range of low mountains north of Kalgan, the road enters the table-land of Mongolia, elevated about five thousand feet above the sea. The country opens into a series of plains and gentle swells, not unlike the rolling prairies of Kansas and Nebraska, with here and there a stretch of hills. Very often not a single tree is visible, and the only stationary objects that break the monotony of the scene are occasional yourts, or tents of the natives. All the way along the road there are numerous trains of ox-carts, and sometimes they form a continuous line of a mile or more. Those going southward are principally laden with logs of wood from the valley of the Tolla, about two hundred miles from the Siberian frontier. The logs are about six or seven feet long, and their principal use is to be cut into Chinese coffins. Many a gentleman of Pekin has been stowed in a coffin whose wood grew in the middle of Mongolia; and possibly when our relations with the empire become more intimate, we shall supply the Chinese coffin market from the fine forests of our Pacific coast.

CHAPTER XXXII.

NORTH of Kalgan the native habitations are scattered irregularly over the country wherever good water and grass abound. The Mongols are generally nomadic, and consult the interest of their flocks and herds in their movements. In summer they resort to the table-land, and stay wherever fancy or convenience dictates; in winter they prefer the valleys where they are partially sheltered from the sharp winds, and find forage for their stock.

The desert is not altogether a desert; it has a great deal of sand and general desolation to the day's ride, but is far from being a forsaken region where a wolf could not make a living. Antelopes abound, and are often seen in large droves as upon our Western plains; grouse will afford frequent breakfasts to the traveler if he takes the trouble to shoot them; there are wild geese, ducks, and curlew in the ponds and marshes; and taken for all in all, the country might be much worse than it is—which is bad enough.

The flat or undulating country is, of course, monotonous. Sunset and sunrise are not altogether unlike those events on the ocean, and if a traveler wishes to feel himself quite at sea, he has only to wander off and lose his camp or caravan. The natives make nothing of straying out of sight, and seem to possess the instincts which have been often noted in the American Indian. Without landmarks or other objects to guide them, they rarely mistake their position, even at night, and can estimate the extent of a day's journey with surprising accuracy. Where a stranger can see no difference between one square mile of desert and a thousand others, the

Mongol can distinguish it from all the rest, though he may not be able to explain why. Perception is closely allied to instinct, and as fast as we are developed and educated the more we trust to acquired knowledge and the less to the unaided senses.

Of course it is quite easy for a stranger to be lost in the Mongolian desert beyond all hope of finding his way again, unless some one comes to his aid. A Russian gentleman told me his experience in getting lost there several years ago. "I used," said he, "to have a fondness for pursuing game whenever we sighted any, which was pretty often, and as I had a couple of hardy ponies, I did a great deal of chasing. One afternoon I saw a fine drove of antelopes, and set out in pursuit of them. The chase led me further than I expected: the game was shy, and I could not get near enough for a good shot; after a long pursuit I gave up, and concluded to return to the road. Just as I abandoned the chase the sun was setting. My notion of the direction I ought to go was not entirely clear, as I had followed a very tortuous course in pursuing the antelopes.

"I was not altogether certain which way I turned when I left the road. It was my impression that I went to the eastward and had been moving away from the sun; so I turned my pony's head in a westerly direction and followed the ridges, which ran from east to west. Hour after hour passed away, the stars came out clear and distinct in the sky, and marked off the progress of the night as they slowly moved from east to west. I grew hungry and thirsty, and longed most earnestly to reach the caravan. My pony shared my uneasiness, and moved impatiently, now endeavoring to go in one direction and now in another. Thinking it possible that he might know the proper route better than I, I gave him free rein, but soon found he was as much at fault as myself. Then I fully realized I was lost in the desert.

"Without compass or landmark to guide me, there was no use in further attempts to find the caravan. Following the Mongol custom, I carried a long rope attached to my saddle-bow, and with this I managed to picket the pony where he could graze and satisfy his hunger. How I envied his ability to eat the grass, which, though scanty, was quite sufficient. I tried to sleep, but sleeping was no easy matter. First, I had the consciousness of being lost. Then I was suffering from hunger and thirst, and the night, like all the nights in Mongolia, even in midsummer, was decidedly chilly, and as I had only my ordinary clothing, the cold caused me to shiver violently. The few snatches of sleep I caught were troubled with many dreams, none of them pleasant. All sorts of horrible fancies passed through my brain, and I verily believe that though I did not sleep half an hour in the whole night, the incidents of my dreams were enough for a thousand years.

LOST IN THE DESERT OF GOBI.

"Thoughts of being devoured by wild beasts haunted me, though in truth I had little of this fate to fear. The only carnivorous beasts on the desert are wolves, but as game is abundant, and can be caught with ordinary exertion, they have no occasion to feed upon men. About midnight my fears were roused by my pony taking alarm at the approach of some wild beast. He snorted and pulled at his rope, and had it not been for my efforts to soothe him, he would have broken away and fled. I saw nothing and heard nothing, though I fancied I could discover half a dozen dark forms on the horizon, and hear a subdued howl from an animal I supposed to be a wolf.

"Morning came. I was suffering from hunger, and more from thirst. My throat was parched, my tongue was swollen, and there was a choking sensation as if I were undergoing strangulation. How I longed for water! Mounting my horse, I rode slowly along the ridge toward the west, and after proceeding several miles, discovered a small lake to my right. My horse scented it earlier than I, and needed no urging to reach it. Dismounting, I bent over and drank from the edge, which was marked with the tracks of antelopes, and of numerous aquatic birds. The water was brackish and bitter, but I drank it with eagerness. My thirst was satisfied, but the water gave me a severe pain in my stomach, that soon became almost as unendurable as the previous dryness. I stood for some minutes on the shore of the lake, and preparing to remount my horse, the bridle slipped from my hand. Mongol ponies are generally treacherous, and mine proved no exception to the rule. Finding himself free, he darted off and trotted back the way we had come.

"I knew that search would be made for me, and my hope now lay in some one coming to the lake. It did not require long deliberation to determine me to remain in the vicinity of the water. As long as I was near it I could not perish of thirst; and moreover, the Mongols, who probably knew of the lake, might be attracted here for water, and, if looking for me, would be likely to take the lake in the way. Tying my kerchief to my ramrod, which I fixed in the ground, I lay down on the grass and slept, as near as I could estimate, for more than two hours.

"Seeing some water-fowl a short distance away, I walked in their direction, and luckily found a nest among the reeds, close to the water's edge. The six or eight eggs it contained were valuable prizes; one I swallowed raw, and the others I carried to where I left my gun. Gathering some of the dry grass and reeds, I built a fire and roasted the eggs, which gave me a hearty meal. The worst of my hardships seemed over. I had found water—bad water, it is true—but still it was possible to drink it; by searching among the reeds I could find an abundance of eggs; my gun could procure me game, and the reeds made a passable sort of fuel. I should be discovered in a few days at furthest, and I renewed my determination to remain near the lake.

"The day passed without any incident to vary the monotony. Refreshed by my meal and by a draught from a small pool of comparatively pure water, I was able to sleep most of the afternoon, so as to keep awake during the night, when exercise was necessary to warmth. About sunset a drove of antelopes came near me, and by shooting one I added venison to my bill of fare. In the night I amused myself with keeping my fire alive, and listening to the noise of the birds that the unusual sight threw into a state of alarm. On the following morning, as I lay on my bed of reeds, a dozen antelopes, attracted by my kerchief fluttering in the wind, stood watching me, and every few minutes approaching a few steps. They were within easy shooting distance, but I had no occasion to kill them. So I lay perfectly still, watching their motions and admiring their beauty.

"All at once, though I had not moved a muscle, they turned and ran away. While I was wondering what could have disturbed them I heard the shout of two Mongol horsemen, who were riding toward me, and leading my pony they had caught a dozen miles away. A score of men from the caravan had been in search of me since the morning after my disappearance, and had ridden many a mile over the desert."

The Mongols are a strong, hardy, and generally good-natured race, possessing the spirit of perseverance quite as much as the Chinese. They have the free manners of all nomadic people, and are noted for unvarying hospitality to visitors. Every stranger is welcome, and has the best the host can give; the more he swallows of what is offered him, the better will be pleased the household. As the native habits are not especially cleanly, a fastidiously inclined guest has a trying time of it. The staple dish of a Mongol yourt is boiled mutton, but it is unaccompanied with capers or any other kind of sauce or seasoning. A sheep goes to pot immediately on being killed, and the quantity that each man will consume is something surprising. When the meat is cooked it is lifted out of the hot water and handed, all dripping and steamy, to the guests. Each man takes a large lump on his lap, or any convenient support, and then cuts off little chunks which he tosses into his mouth as if it were a mill-hopper. The best piece is reserved for the guest of honor, who is expected to divide it with the rest; after the meat is devoured they drink the broth, and this concludes the meal. Knives and cups are the only aids to eating, and as every man carries his own "outfit," the Mongol dinner service is speedily arranged. The entire work consists in seating the party around a pot of cooked meat.

MONGOL DINNER TABLE.

The desert is crossed by various ridges and small mountain chains, that increase in frequency and make the country more broken as one approaches the Tolla, the largest stream between Pekin and Kiachta. The road, after traversing the last of these chains, suddenly reveals a wide valley which bears evidence of fertility in its dense forests, and the straggling fields which receive less attention than they deserve.

The Tolla has an ugly habit of rising suddenly and falling deliberately. When at its height, the stream has a current of about seven miles an hour, and at the fording place the water is over the back of an ordinary pony. The bottom of the river consists of large boulders of all sizes from an egg up to a cotton bale, and the footing for both horses and camels is not specially secure. The camels need a good deal of persuasion with clubs before they will enter the water; they have an instinctive dread of that liquid and avoid it when-

CROSSING THE TOLLA

ever they can. Horses are less timorous, and the best way to get a camel through the ford is to lead him behind a horse and pound him vigorously at the same time. When the river is at all dangerous there is always a swarm of natives around the ford ready to lend a hand if suitably compensated. They all talk very much and in loud tones; their voices mingle with the neighing of horses, the screams of camels, the roaring of the river, and the laughter of the idlers when any mishap occurs. The confused noises are in harmony with the scene on either bank, where baggage is piled promiscuously, and the natives are grouped together in various picturesque attitudes. Men with their lower garments rolled as high as possible, or altogether discarded, walk about in perfect nonchalance; their queues hanging down their backs seem designed as rudders to steer the wearers across the stream.

About two miles from the ford of the Tolla there is a Chinese settlement, which forms a sort of suburb to the Mongol town of Urga. The Mongols have no great friendship for the Chinese inhabitants, who are principally engaged in traffic and the various occupations connected with the transport of goods. Between this suburb and the main town the Russians have a large house, which is the residence of a consul and some twenty or thirty retainers. The policy of maintaining a consulate there can only be explained on the supposition that Russia expects and intends to appropriate a large slice of Mongolia whenever opportunity offers. She has long insisted that the chain of mountains south of Urga was the "natural boundary," and her establishment of an expensive post at that city enables her to have things ready whenever a change occurs. In the spirit of annexation and extension of territory the Russians can fairly claim equal rank with ourselves. I forget their phrase for "manifest destiny," and possibly they may not be willing that I should give it.

Urga is not laid out in streets like most of the Chinese towns; its by-ways and high-ways are narrow and crooked, and form a network very puzzling to a stranger. The Chinese and Russian settlers live in houses, and there are temples and other permanent buildings, but the Mongols live generally in yourts, which they prefer to more extensive structures. Most of the Mongol traffic is conducted in a large esplanade, where you can purchase anything the country affords, and at very fair prices.

The principal feature of Urga is the lamissary or convent where a great many lamas or holy men reside. I have heard the number estimated at fifteen thousand, but cannot say if it be more or less. The religion of the Mongols came originally from Thibet, by direct authority of the Grand Lama, but a train of circumstances which I have not space to explain, has made it virtually independent. The Chinese government maintains shrewd emissaries among these lamas, and thus manages to control the Mongols and prevent their setting up for themselves. As a further precaution it has a lamissary at Pekin, where it keeps two thousand Mongol lamas at its own expense. In this way it is able to influence the nomads of the desert, and in case of trouble it would possess a fair number of hostages for an emergency.

About the year 1205 the great battle between Timoujin and the sovereign then occupying the Mongol throne was fought a short distance from Urga. The victory was decisive for the former, who thus became Genghis Khan and commenced that career of conquest which made his name famous.

Great numbers of devotees from all parts of Mongolia visit Urga every year, the journey there having something of the sacred character which a Mahommedan attaches to a pilgrimage to Mecca. The people living at Urga build fences around their dwellings to protect their property from the thieves who are in large proportion among the pious travelers.

From Urga to the Siberian frontier the distance is less than two hundred miles; the Russian couriers accomplish it in fifty or sixty hours when not delayed by accidents, but the caravans require from four to eight days. There is a system of relays arranged by the Chinese so that one can travel very speedily if he has proper authority. Couriers have passed from Kiachta to Pekin in ten or twelve days; but the rough road and abominable carts make them feel at their journey's end about as if rolled through a patent clothes-wringer. A mail is carried twice a month each way by the Russians. Several schemes have been proposed for a trans-Mongolian telegraph, but thus far the Chinese government has refused to permit its construction.

The desert proper is finished before one reaches the mountains bordering the Tolla; after crossing that stream and leaving Urga the road passes through a hilly country, sprinkled, it is true, with a good many patches of sand, but having plenty of forest and frequently showing fertile valleys. These valleys are the favorite resorts of the Mongol shepherds and herdsmen, some of whom count their wealth by many thousand animals. In general, Mongolia is not agricultural, both from the character of the country and the disposition of the people. A few tribes in the west live by tilling the soil in connection with stock raising, but I do not suppose they take kindly to the former occupation. The Mongols engaged in the caravan service pass a large part of their lives on the road, and are merry as larks over their employment. They seem quite analogous to the teamsters and miscellaneous "plainsmen" who used to play an important part on our overland route.

A large proportion of the men engaged in this transit service are lamas, their sacred character not excusing them, as many suppose, from all kinds of employment. Many lamas are indolent and manage in some way to make a living without work, but this is by no means the universal character of the holy men. About one-fifth of the male population belong to the religious order, so that there are comparatively few families which do not have a member or a relative in the pale of the church. If not domiciled in a convent or blessed by fortune in some way, the lama turns his hand to labor, though he is able at the same time to pick up occasional presents for professional service. Many of them act as teachers or schoolmasters. Theoretically he cannot marry any more than a

Romish priest, but his vows of celibacy are not always strictly kept. One inconvenience under which he labors is in never daring to kill anything through fear that what he slaughters may contain the soul of a relative, and possibly that of the divine Bhudda. A lama will purchase a sheep on which he expects to dine, and though fully accessory before and after the fact, he does not feel authorized to use the knife with his own hand. Even should he be annoyed by fleas or similar creeping things

THE SCHOOLMASTER.

(if it were a township or city the lama's body could return a flattering census,) he must bear the infliction until patience is thoroughly exhausted. At such times he may call an unsanctified friend and subject himself and garments to a thorough examination.

Every lama carries with him a quantity of written prayers,

which he reads or recites, and the oftener they are repeated the greater is their supposed efficacy. Quantity is more important than quality, and to facilitate matters they frequently have a machine, which consists of a wheel containing a lot of prayers. Sometimes it is turned by hand and sometimes attached to a wind-mill; the latter mode being preferred.

Abbe Huc and others have remarked a striking similarity between the Bhuddist and Roman Catholic forms of worship and the origin of the two religions. Huc infers that Bhuddism was borrowed from Christianity; on the other hand, many lamas declare that the reverse is the case. The question has caused a great deal of discussion first and last, but neither party appears disposed to yield.

The final stretch of road toward the Siberian frontier is across a sandy plain, six or eight miles wide. On emerging from the hills at its southern edge the dome of the church in Kiachta appears in sight, and announces the end of Mongolian travel. No lighthouse is more welcome to a mariner than is the view of this Russian town to a traveler who has suffered the hardships of a journey from Pekin.

CHAPTER XXXIII.

THE week I remained at Kiachta was a time of festivity from beginning to end. I endeavored to write up my journal but was able to make little more than rough notes. The good people would have been excusable had they not compelled me to drink so much excellent champagne. The amiable merchants of Kiachta are blessed with such capacities for food and drink that they do not think a guest satisfied until he has swallowed enough to float a steamboat.

I found an excellent *compagnon du voyage*, and our departure was fixed for the evening after the dinner with Mr Pfaffins. A change from dinner dress to traveling costume was speedily made, and I was '*gotovey*' when my friend arrived with several officers to see us off. About eight o'clock we took places in my tarantass, and drove out of the northern gate of Troitskosavsk.

My traveling companion was Mr. Richard Maack, Superintendent of Public Instruction in Eastern Siberia. He was just finishing a tour among the schools in the Trans-Baikal province, and during fourteen years of Siberian life, he had seen a variety of service. He accompanied General Mouravieff on the first expedition down the Amoor, and wrote a detailed account of his journey. Subsequently he explored the Ousurce in the interest of the Russian Geographical Society. He said that his most arduous service was in a winter journey to the valley of the Lena, and along the shores of the Arctic Ocean. The temperature averaged lower than in Dr. Kane's hibernation on the coast of Greenland, and once remained at – 60° for nearly three weeks. Of five persons comprising the party, Maack is the only survivor. One of his companions fell dead in General Mouravieff's parlor while giving his account of the exploration.

We determined to be comfortable on the way to Irkutsk. We put our baggage in a telyaga with Maack's servant and took the tarantass to ourselves. The road was the same I traveled from Verkne Udinsk to Kiachta, crossing the Selenga at Selenginsk. We slept most of the first night, and timed our arrival at Selenginsk so as to find the school in session. During a brief halt while the smotretal prepared our breakfast, Maack visited the school-master at his post of duty.

Over the hills behind a lake about a day's ride from Selenginsk there is a Bouriat village of a sacred character. It is the seat of a large temple or lamisary whence all the Bouriats in Siberia receive their religious teachings. A grand lama specially commissioned by the great chief of the Bhuddist faith at Thibet, presides over the lamisary. He is supposed to partake of the immortal essence of Bhudda, and when his body dies, his spirit enters a younger person who becomes the lama after passing a certain ordeal.

The village is wholly devoted to religious purposes, and occupied exclusively by Bouriats. I was anxious to visit it, but circumstances did not favor my desires.

We made both crossings of the Selenga on the ice without difficulty. It was only a single day from the time the ferry ceased running until the ice was safe for teams. We reached Verkne Udinsk late in the evening, and drove to a house where my companion had friends. The good lady brought some excellent nalifka of her own preparation, and the more we praised it the more she urged us to drink. What with tea, nalifka, and a variety of solid food, we were pretty well filled during a halt of two hours.

It was toward midnight when we emerged from the house to continue our journey. Maack found his tarantass at Verkne Udinsk, and as it was larger and better than mine we assigned the latter to Evan and the baggage, and took the best to ourselves. Evan was a Yakut whom my friend brought from the Lena country. He was intelligent and active, and assisted greatly to soften the asperities of the route. With my few words of Russian, and his quick comprehension, we understood each other very well.

During the first few hours from Verkne Udinsk the sky was obscured and the air warm. My furs were designed for cold weather, and their weight in the temperature then prevailing threw me into perspiration. In my dehar I was unpleasantly warm, and without it I shivered. I kept alternately opening and closing the garment, and obtained very little sleep up to our arrival at the first station. While we were changing horses the clouds blew away and the temperature fell several degrees. Under the influence of the cold I fell into a sound sleep, and did not heed the rough, grater-like surface of the recently frozen road.

From Verkne Udinsk to Lake Baikal, the road follows the Selenga valley, which gradually widens as one descends it. The land appears fertile and well adapted to farming purposes but only a small portion is under cultivation. The inhabitants are pretty well rewarded for their labor if I may judge by the appearance of their farms and villages. Until reaching Ilyensk, I found the cliffs and mountains extending quite near the river. In some places the road is cut into the rocks in such a way as to afford excitement to a nervous traveler.

The villages were numerous and had an air of prosperity. Here and there new houses were going up, and made quite a contrast to the old and decaying habitations near them. My attention was drawn to the well-sweeps exactly resembling those in the rural districts of New England. From the size of the sweeps, I concluded the wells were deep. The soil in the fields had a loose, friable appearance that reminded me of the farming lands around Cleveland, Ohio.

One of the villages where we changed horses is called Kabansk from the Russian word '*Kaban*' (wild boar). This animal abounds in the vicinity and is occasionally hunted for sport. The chase of the wild boar is said to be nearly as dangerous as that of the bear, the brute frequently turning upon his pursuer and making a determined fight. We passed the Monastery of Troitska founded in 1681 for the conversion of the Bouriats. It is an imposing edifice built like a Russian church in the middle of a large area surrounded by a high wall. Though it must have impressed the natives by its architectural effects it was powerless to change their faith.

WILD BOAR HUNT.

As it approaches Lake Baikal the Selenga divides into several branches, and encloses a large and very fertile delta. The afternoon following our departure from Verkne Udinsk, we came in sight of the lake, and looked over the blue surface of the largest body of fresh water in Northern Asia. The mountains on the western shore appeared about eight or ten miles away, though they were really more than thirty. We skirted the shore of the lake, turning our horses' heads to the southward. The clear water reminded me of Lake Michigan as one sees it on approaching Chicago by railway from the East. Its waves broke gently on a pebbly beach, where the cold of commencing winter had changed much of the spray to ice.

There was no steamer waiting at Posolsky, but we were told that one was hourly expected. Maack was radiant at finding a letter from his wife awaiting him at the station. I enquired for letters but did not obtain any. Unlike my companion I had no wife at Irkutsk.

A WIFE AT IRKUTSK.

The steamboat landing is nine versts below the town, and as the post route ended at Posolsky, we were obliged to engage horses at a high rate, to take us to the port. The alternate freezing and thawing of the road—its last act was to freeze—had rendered it something like the rough way in a Son-of-Malta Lodge. The agent assured us the steamer would arrive during the night. Was there ever a steamboat agent who did not promise more than his employers performed?

NO WIFE AT IRKUTSK.

According to the tourist's phrase the port of Posolsky can be 'done' in about five minutes. The entire settlement comprised two buildings, one a hotel, and the other a storehouse and stable. A large quantity of merchandise was piled in the open air, and awaited removal.

It included tea from Kiachta, and vodki or native whiskey from Irkutsk. There are several distilleries in the Trans-Baikal province, but they are unable to meet the demand in the country east of the lake. From what I saw *in transitu* the consumption must be enormous. The government has a tax on vodki equal to about fifty cents a gallon, which is paid by the manufacturers. The law is very strict, and the penalties are so great that I was told no one dared attempt an evasion of the excise duties, except by bribing the collector.

The hotel was full of people waiting for the boat, and the accommodations were quite limited. We thought the tarantass preferable to the hotel, and retired early to sleep in our carriage. A teamster tied his horses to our wheels, and as the brutes fell to kicking during the night, and attempted to break away, they disturbed our slumbers. I rose at daybreak and watched the yemshiks making their toilet. The whole operation was performed by tightening the girdle and rubbing the half-opened eyes.

Morning brought no boat. There was nothing very interesting after we had breakfasted, and as we might be detained there a whole week, the prospect was not charming. We organized a hunting excursion, Maack with his gun and I with my revolver. I assaulted the magpies which were numerous and impertinent, and succeeded in frightening them. Gulls were flying over the lake; Maack desired one for his cabinet at Irkutsk, but couldn't get him. He brought down an enormous crow, and an imprudent hawk that pursued a small bird in our vicinity. His last exploit was in shooting a partridge which alighted, strange to say, on the roof of the hotel within twenty feet of a noisy crowd of yemshiks. The bird was of a snowy whiteness, the Siberian partridge changing from brown to white at the beginning of winter, and from white to brown again as the snow disappears.

A "soudna" or sailing barge was anchored at the entrance of a little bay, and was being filled with tea to be transported to Irkutsk. The soudna is a bluff-bowed, broad sterned craft, a sort of cross between Noah's Ark and a Chinese junk. It is strong but not elegant, and might sail backward or sidewise nearly as well as ahead. Its carrying capacity is great in proportion to its length, as it is very wide and its sides rise very high above the water. Every soudna I saw had but one mast which carried a square sail. These vessels can only sail with the wind, and then not very rapidly. An American pilot boat could pass a thousand of them without half trying.

A SOUDNA.

About noon we saw a thin wreath of smoke betokening the approach of the steamer. In joy at this welcome sight we dined and bought tickets for the passage, ours of the first class being printed in gold, while Evan's billet for the deck was in Democratic black. It cost fifteen roubles for the transport of each tarantass, but our baggage was taken free, and we were not even required to unload it.

There is no wharf at Posolsky and no harbor, the steamers anchoring in the open water half a mile from shore. Passengers, mails, and baggage are taken to the steamer in large row boats, while heavy freight is carried in soudnas. The boat that took us brought a convoy of exiles before we embarked. They formed a double line at the edge of the lake where they were closely watched by their guards. When we reached the steamer we found another party of prisoners waiting to go on shore. All were clad in sheepskin pelisses and some carried extra garments. Several women and children accompanied the party, and I observed two or three old men who appeared little able to make a long journey. One sick man too feeble to walk, was supported by his guards and his fellow prisoners.

Though there was little wind, and that little blew from shore, the boat danced uneasily on the waves. Our carriages came off on the last trip of the boat, and were hoisted by means of a running tackle on one of the steamer's yards.

While our embarkation was progressing a crew of Russians and Bouriats towed the now laden soudna to a position near our stern. When all was ready, we took her hawser, hoisted our anchor and steamed away. For some time I watched the low eastern shore of the lake until it disappeared in the distance. Posolsky has a monastery built on the spot where a Russian embassador with his suite was murdered by Bouriats about the year 1680. The last objects I saw behind me were the walls, domes, and turrets of this monastery glistening in the afternoon sunlight. They rose clear and distinct on the horizon, an outwork of Christianity against the paganism of Eastern Asia.

The steamer was the *Ignatienif*, a side wheel boat of about 300 tons. Her model was that of an ocean or coasting craft, she had two masts, and could spread a little sail if desired. Her engines were built at Ekaterineburg in the Ural Mountains, and hauled overland 2500 miles. She and her sister boat, the *General Korsackoff*, are very profitable to their owners during the months of summer. They carry passengers, mails, and light freight, and nearly always have one or two soudnas in tow. Their great disadvantage at present is the absence of a port on the eastern shore.

The navigation of Lake Baikal is very difficult. Storms arise with little warning, and are often severe. At times the boats are obliged to remain for days in the middle of the lake as they cannot always make the land while a gale continues. There was very little breeze when we crossed, but the steamer was tossed quite roughly. The winds blowing from the mountains along the lake, frequently sweep with great violence and drive unlucky soudnas upon the rocks.

The water of the lake is so clear that one can see to a very great depth. The lake is nearly four hundred miles long by about thirty or thirty-five in width ; itis twelve hundred feet above the sea level, and receives nearly two hundred tributaries great and small. Its outlet, the Angara, is near the southwestern end, and is said to carry off not more than a tenth of the water that enters the lake. What becomes of the surplus is a problem no one has been able to solve. The natives believe there is an underground passage to the sea, and some geologists favor this opinion. Soundings of 2000 feet have been made without finding bottom.

On the western shore the mountains rise abruptly from the water, and in some places no bottom has been found at 400 feet depth, within pistol shot of the bank. This fact renders navigation dangerous, as a boat might be driven on shore in even a light breeze before her anchors found holding ground.

The natives have many superstitions concerning Lake Baikal. In their language it is the "Holy Sea," and it would be sacrilege to term it a lake. Certainly it has several marine peculiarities. Gulls and other ocean birds frequent its shores, and it is the only body of fresh water on the globe where the seal abounds. Banks of coral like those in tropical seas exist in its depths.

AFTER THE EARTHQUAKE.

The mountains on the western shore are evidently of volcanic origin, and earthquakes are not unfrequent. A few

LAKE BAIKAL IN WINTER

years ago the village of Stepnoi, about twenty miles from the mouth of the Selenga, was destroyed by an earthquake. Part of the village disappeared beneath the water while another part after sinking was lifted twenty or thirty feet above its original level. Irkutsk has been frequently shaken at the foundations, and on one occasion the walls of its churches were somewhat damaged. Around Lake Baikal there are several hot springs, some of which attract fashionable visitors from Irkutsk during the season.

The natives say nobody was ever lost in Lake Baikal. When a person is drowned there the waves invariably throw his body on shore.

The lake does not freeze until the middle of December, and sometimes later. Its temperature remains pretty nearly the same at all seasons, about 48° Fahrenheit. In winter it is crossed on the ice, the passage ordinarily occupying about five hours. The lake generally freezes when the air is perfectly still so that the surface is of glossy smoothness until covered with snow. A gentleman in Irkutsk described to me his feelings when he crossed Lake Baikal in winter for the first time. The ice was six feet thick, but so perfectly transparent that he seemed driving over the surface of the water. The illusion was complete, and not wholly dispelled when he alighted. "Starting from the western side, the opposite coast was not visible, and I experienced" said my friend, "the sensation of setting out in a sleigh to cross the Atlantic from Liverpool to New York."

In summer and in winter communication is pretty regular, but there is a suspension of travel when the ice is forming, and another when it breaks up. This causes serious inconvenience, and has led the government to build a road around the southern extremity of the lake. The mountains are lofty and precipitous, and the work is done at vast expense. The road winds over cliffs and crags sometimes near the lake and again two thousand feet above it. Large numbers of peasants, Bouriats, and prisoners have been employed there for several years, but the route was not open for wheeled vehicles at the time I crossed the lake.

One mode of cutting the road through the mountains was to build large bonfires in winter when the temperature was very low. The heat caused the rock to crack so that large masses could be removed, but the operation was necessarily slow. The insurrection of June, 1866, occurred on this road.

Formerly a winter station was kept on the ice half-way across the lake. By a sudden thaw at the close of one winter the men and horses of a station were swallowed up, and nothing was known of them until weeks afterward, when their bodies were washed ashore. Since this catastrophe the entire passage of the lake, about forty miles, is made without change of horses.

We left Posolsky and enjoyed a sunset on the lake. The mountains rise abruptly on the western and southeastern shores, and many of their snow covered peaks were beautifully tinged by the fading sunlight. The illusion regarding distances was difficult to overcome, and could only be realized by observing how very slowly we neared the mountains we were approaching. The atmosphere was of remarkable purity, and its powers of refraction reminded me of past experience in the Rocky Mountains. We had sunset and moonrise at once. 'Adam had no more in Eden save the head of Eve upon his shoulder.'

The boat went directly across and then followed the edge of the lake to Listvenichna, our point of debarkation. There was no table on board. We ordered the samovar, made our own tea, and supped from the last of our commissary stores. Our fellow passengers in the cabin were two officers traveling to Irkutsk, and a St. Petersburg merchant who had just finished the Amoor Company's affairs. We talked, ate, drank, smoked, and slept during the twelve hours' journey.

Congratulate us on our quick passage! On her very next voyage the steamer was eight days on the lake, the wind blowing so that she could not come to either shore. To be cooped on this dirty and ill-provided boat long enough to cross the Atlantic is a fate I hope never to experience.

There is a little harbor at Listvenichna and we came alongside a wharf. Maack departed with our papers to procure horses, and left me to look at the vanishing crowd. Take the passengers from the steerage of a lake or river steamer in America, dress them in sheepskin coats and caps, let them talk a language you cannot understand, and walk them into a cloud of steam as if going overboard in a fog, and you have a passable reproduction of the scene. A bright fire should be burning on shore to throw its contrast of light and shadow over the surroundings and heighten the picturesque effect.

Just as the deck hands were rolling our carriages on shore my companion returned, and announced our horses ready. We sought a little office near the head of the wharf where the chief of the '*tamojna*' (custom house) held his court. This official was known to Mr. Maack, and on our declaring that we had no dutiable effects we were passed without search.

As before remarked all the country east of Lake Baikal is open to free trade. This result has been secured by the efforts of the present governor general of Eastern Siberia. Under his liberal and enlightened policy he has done much to break down the old restrictions and develop the resources of a country over which he holds almost autocratic power. It was about three in the morning when we started over the frozen earth. Two miles from the landing we reached the custom house barrier where a pole painted with the government colors stretched across the road. Presenting our papers from the chief officer we were not detained. On the steamer when we were nearing harbor our conversation turned upon the custom house. It was positively asserted that the officials were open to pecuniary compliments, much, I presume like those in other lands. The gentleman from the Amoor had considerable baggage, and prepared a five rouble note to facilitate his business. Evidently he gave too little or did not bribe the right man, as I left him vainly imploring to be let alone in the centre of a pile of open baggage, like Marius in the ruins of Carthage.

The road follows the right bank of the Angara from the point where it leaves the lake. The current here is very strong, and the river rushes and breaks like the rapids of the St. Lawrence. For several miles from its source it never freezes even in the coldest winters. During the season of ice this open space is the resort of many waterfowl, and is generally enveloped in a cloud of mist. At the head of the river rises a mass of rock known as *Shaman Kamen* (spirit's rock). It is held in great veneration by the natives, and is believed to be the abode of a spirit who constantly overlooks the lake. When shamanism prevailed in this region many human sacrifices were made at the sacred rock. The most popular method was by tying the hands of the victim and tossing him into the 'hell of waters' below.

Many varieties of fish abound in the lake, and ascend its tributary rivers. The fishery forms quite a business for the inhabitants of the region, who find a good market at Irkutsk. The principal fish taken are two or three varieties of sturgeon, the herring, pike, carp, the *askina*, and a white fish called *tymain*. There is a remarkable fish consisting of a mass of fat that burns like a candle and melts away in the heat of the sun or a fire. It is found dead on the shores of the lake after violent storms. A live one has never been seen.

A SPECIMEN.

The distance to Irkutsk from our landing was about forty miles, and we hoped to arrive in time for breakfast. A snow storm began about daylight, so that I did not see much of the wooded valley of the river. We met a train of sixty or seventy carts, each carrying a cask of vodki. This liquid misery was on its way to the Trans-Baikal, and the soudna which brought a load of tea would carry vodki as a return cargo.

The clouds thinned and broke, the snow ceased falling, and the valley became distinct. While I admired its beauty, we reached the summit of a hill and I saw before me a cluster of glittering domes and turrets, rising from a wide bend in the Angara. At first I could discern only churches, but very soon I began to distinguish the streets, avenues, blocks, and houses of a city. We entered Irkutsk through its eastern gate, and drove rapidly along a wide street, the busiest I had yet seen in Asiatic Russia.

Just as the sun burst in full splendor through the departing clouds, I alighted in the capital of Oriental Siberia, half around the world from my own home.

CHAPTER XXXIV.

AS we entered the city a Cossack delivered a letter announcing that I was to be handed over to the police, who had a lodging ready for me. On learning of my presence at Kiachta the Governor General kindly requested an officer of his staff to share his rooms with me. Captain Paul, with whom I was quartered, occupied pleasant apartments overlooking the *gastinnidvor*. He was leading a bachelor life in a suite of six rooms, and had plenty of space at my disposal. That I might lose no time, the Chief of Police stationed the Cossack with a letter telling me where to drive.

I removed the dust and costume of travel as soon as possible, and prepared to pay my respects to the Governor General. My presentation was postponed to the following day, and as the Russian etiquette forbade my calling on other officials before I had seen the chief, there was little to be done in the matter of visiting.

The next morning I called upon General Korsackoff, delivered my letters of introduction, and was most cordially welcomed to Irkutsk. The Governor General of Eastern Siberia controls a territory larger than all European Russia, and much of it is not yet out of its developing stage. He has a heavy responsibility upon his shoulders in leading his subjects in the way best for their interests and those of the crown. Much has been done under the energetic administration of General Korsackoff and his predecessor, and there is room to accomplish much more. The general has ably withstood the cares and hardships of his Siberian life. He is forty-five years of age, active and vigorous, and capable of doing much before his way of life is fallen into the sere and yellow leaf. Like Madame De Stael, he possesses the power of putting visitors entirely at their ease. To my single countrywomen I will whisper that General Korsackoff is of about medium height, has a fair complexion, blue eyes, and Saxon hair, and a face which the most crabbed misanthrope could not refuse to call handsome. He is unmarried, and if rumor tells the truth, not under engagement.

GOV. GEN'L KORSACKOFF.

The Governor General lives in a spacious and elegant house on the bank of the Angara, built by a merchant who amassed an immense fortune in the Chinese trade. On retiring from business he devoted his time and energies to constructing the finest mansion in Eastern Siberia. It is a stone building of three stories, and its halls and parlors are of liberal extent. Furniture was brought from St. Petersburg at enormous cost, and the whole establishment was completed without regard to expense. At the death of its builder the house was purchased by government, and underwent a few changes to adapt it to its official occupants. On the opposite bank of the river there is a country seat, the private property of General Korsackoff, and his dwelling place in the hot months.

It was my good fortune that Mr. Maack was obliged by etiquette to visit his friends on returning from his journey. I arranged to accompany him, and during that day and the next we called upon many persons of official and social position. These included the Governor and Vice Governor of Irkutsk, the chief of staff and heads of departments, the mayor of the city, and the leading merchants. Succeeding days were occupied in receiving return visits, and when these were ended I was fairly a member of the society of the Siberian capital.

The evening after my arrival I returned early to my lodgings to indulge in a Russian bath. Captain Paul was absent, but his servant managed to inform me by words and pantomime that all was ready On the captain's return the man said he had told me in German that the bath was waiting.

"How did you speak German?" asked the captain, aware that his man knew nothing but Russian.

"Oh," said the servant, "I rubbed my hands over my face and arms and pointed toward the bath-room."

On the morning after my arrival the proprietor of the house asked for my passport; when it returned it bore the visa of the chief of police. There is a regulation throughout Russia that every hotel keeper or other householder shall register his patrons with the police. By this means the authorities can trace the movements of '*suspects*,' and prevent unlicensed travel. In Siberia the plan is particularly valuable in keeping exiles on the spots assigned them.

At St. Petersburg and Moscow the police keep a directory and hold it open to the public. When I reached the capital and wished to find some friends who arrived a few days before me, I obtained their address from this directory. Those who sought my whereabouts found me in the same way.

The weather was steadily cold—about zero Fahrenheit—and was called mild for the season by the residents of Irkutsk. I brought from New York a heavy overcoat that braved the storms of Broadway the winter before my departure. My Russian friends pronounced it *nechevo* (nothing,) and advised me to procure a '*shooba*,' or cloak lined with fur. The shooba reaches nearly to one's feet, and is better adapted to riding than walking. It can be lined according to the means and liberality of the wearer. Sable is most expensive, and sheep-skin the least. Both accomplish the same end, as they contain about equal quantities of heat.

The streets of Irkutsk are of good width and generally intersect at right angles. Most of the buildings are of wood, and usually large and well built. The best houses are of stone, or of brick covered with plaster to resemble stone. Very few dwellings are entered directly from the street, the outer doors opening into yards according to the Russian custom. To visit a person you pass into an enclosure through a strong gateway, generally open by day but closed at night. A '*dvornik*' (doorkeeper) has the control of this gate, and is responsible for everything within it. Storehouses and all other buildings of the establishment open upon the enclosure, and frequently two or more houses have one gate in common.

The stores or magazines are numerous, and well supplied with European goods. Some of the stocks are very large, and must require heavy capital or excellent credit to manage them. Tailors and milliners are abundant, and bring their modes from Paris. Occasionally they paint their signs in French, and display the latest novelties from the center of fashion. Bakers are numerous and well patronized. '*Frantsooski kleb*,' (French bread,) which is simply white bread made into rolls, is popular and largely sold in Irkutsk.

One of my daily exercises in Russian was to spell the signs upon the stores. In riding I could rarely get more than half through a word before I was whisked out of sight. I never before knew how convenient are symbolic signs to a man who cannot read. A picture of a hat, a glove, or a loaf of bread was far more expressive to my eye than the word *shapka*, *perchatki*, or *kleb*, printed in Russian letters.

The Russians smoke a great deal of tobacco in paper cigarettes or '*papiros*.' Everywhere east of Lake Baikal the papiros of Irkutsk is in demand, and the manufacture there is quite extensive. In Irkutsk and to the westward the brand of Moscow is preferred. The consumption of tobacco in this form throughout the empire must be something enormous.

I have known a party of half a dozen persons to smoke a hundred cigarettes in an afternoon and evening. Many ladies indulge in smoking, but the practice is not universal. I do not remember any unmarried lady addicted to it.

Irkutsk was founded in 1680, and has at present a population of twenty-eight or thirty thousand. About four thousand gold miners spend the winter and their money in the city. Geographically it is in Latitude 52° 40′ north, and Longitude 104° 20′ east from Greenwich. Little wind blows there, and storms are less frequent than at Moscow or St. Petersburg. The snows are not abundant, the quantity that falls being

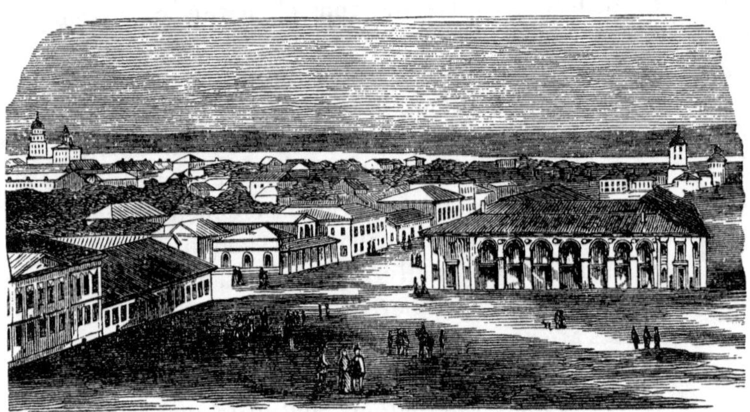

VIEW IN IRKUTSK.

smaller than in Boston and very much less than in Montreal or Quebec. In summer or winter the panorama of Irkutsk and its surroundings is one of great beauty.

There are twenty or more churches, of which nearly all are large and finely placed. Several of them were planned and constructed by two Swedish engineer officers captured at Pultawa and exiled to Siberia. They are excellent monuments of architectural skill, and would be ornamental to any European city.

The Angara at Irkutsk is about six hundred yards wide, and flows with a current of six miles an hour. It varies in height not more than ten or twelve inches during the entire year. It does not freeze until the middle of January, and opens early in May. There are two swinging ferries for crossing the river. A stout cable is anchored in mid-stream, and the ferry-boat attached to its unanchored end. The slack of the cable is buoyed by several small boats, over which it passes at regular intervals. The ferry swings like a horizontal pendulum, and is propelled by turning its sides at an angle against the current. I crossed on this ferry in four minutes from bank to bank.

There are many public carriages in the streets, to be hired at thirty copecks the hour; but the drivers, like their profession everywhere, are inclined to overcharge. Every one who thinks he can afford it, keeps a team of his own, the horses being generally of European stock. A few horses have been brought from St. Petersburg; the journey occupies a full year, and the animals, when safely arrived, are very costly. Private turnouts are neat and showy, and on a fine afternoon the principal drives of the city are quite gay. General Korsackoff has a light wagon from New York for his personal driving in summer.

I found here a curious regulation. Sleighs are prohibited by municipal law from carrying bells in the limits of the city. Reason: in a great deal of noise pedestrians might be run over. In American cities the law requires bells to be worn. Reason: unless there is a noise pedestrians might be run over.

"You pays your money and you takes your choice."

Cossack policemen watch the town during the day, and at night there are mounted and foot patrols carrying muskets with fixed bayonets. Every block and sometimes every house has its private watchman, and at regular intervals during the night you may hear these guardians thumping their long staves on the pavement to assure themselves and others that they are awake. The fire department belongs to the police, and its apparatus consists of hand engines, water carts, and hook and ladder wagons. There are several watch towers, from which a semaphore telegraph signals the existence of fire. An electric apparatus was being arranged during my stay.

During my visit there was an alarm of fire, and I embraced the opportunity to see how the Russians 'run with the machine.' When I reached the street the engines and water carts were dashing in the direction of the fire. The water carts were simply large casks mounted horizontally on four wheels; a square hole in the top served to admit a bucket or a suction hose. These carts bring water from the nearest point of supply, which may be the river or an artificial reservoir, according to the locality of the fire. Engines and carts are drawn by horses, which appear well selected for strength and activity. All the firemen wore brass helmets.

The burning house was small and quite disengaged from others, and as there was no wind there was no danger of a serious conflagration. The Chief of Police directed the movements of his men. The latter worked their engines vigorously, but though the carts kept in active motion the supply of water was not equal to the demand. For some time it seemed doubtful which would triumph, the flames or the police. Fortune favored the brave. The building was saved, though in a condition of incipient charcoalism.

The Chief of Police wore his full uniform and decorations as the law requires of him when on duty. During the affair he was thoroughly spattered with water and covered with dirt and cinders. When he emerged he presented an appearance somewhat like that of a butterfly after passing through a sausage machine. A detachment of soldiers came to the spot but did not form a cordon around it. Every spectator went as near the fire as he thought prudent, but was careful not to get in the way. Two or three thousand officers, soldiers, merchants, exiles, moujiks, women, boys, and beggars gathered in the street to look at the display.

The Russian fire engines and water carts with their complement of men, and each drawn by three horses abreast, present a picturesque appearance as they dash through the streets. The engines at Irkutsk are low-powered squirts, worked by hand, less effective than the hand engines used in America twenty or thirty years ago, and far behind our steamers of the present day. In Moscow and St. Petersburg the fire department has been greatly improved during the past ten years, and is now quite efficient.

The markets of Irkutsk are well supplied with necessaries of life. Beef is abundant and good, at an average retail price of seven copecks a pound. Fish and game are plentiful, and sell at low figures. The *rebchik*, or wood-hen, is found throughout Siberia, and is much cheaper in the market than any kind of domestic fowl. Pork, veal, and mutton are no more expensive than beef, and all vegetables of the country are at corresponding rates. In fact if one will eschew European luxuries he can live very cheaply at Irkutsk. Everything that comes from beyond the Urals is expensive, on account of the long land carriage.

Champagne costs five or six roubles a bottle, and a great quantity of it is drank. Sherry is from two to seven roubles according to quality, and the same is the case with white and red wines. The lowest price of sugar is thirty copecks the pound, and it is oftener forty-five or fifty. Porter and ale cost two or three roubles a bottle, and none but the best English brands are drank. The wines are almost invariably excellent, and any merchant selling even a few cases of bad wine would very likely lose his trade. Clothes and all articles of personal wear cost about as much as in St. Louis or New Orleans. Labor is neither abundant nor scarce. A good man-servant receives ten to fifteen roubles a month with board.

Wood comes in soudnas from the shores of Lake Baikal and is very cheap. These vessels descend the river by the force of the current, but in going against it are towed by horses. The principal market place is surrounded with shops where a varied and miscellaneous lot of merchandise is sold. I found ready-made clothing, crockery, boots, whisky, hats, furniture, flour, tobacco, and so on through a long list of saleable and unsaleable articles. How such a mass could find customers was a puzzle. Nearly all the shops are small and plain, and there are many stalls or stands which require but a small capital to manage. A great deal of haggling takes place in transactions at these little establishments, and I occasionally witnessed some amusing scenes.

The best time to view the market is on Sunday morning, when the largest crowd is gathered. My first visit was made one Sunday when the thermometer stood at —15° Fahrenheit. The market houses and the open square were full of people, and the square abounded in horses and sleds from the country. A great deal of traffic was conducted on these sleds or upon the solid snow-packed earth. The crowd comprised men, women, and children of all ages and all conditions in life. Peasants from the country and laborers from the city, officers, tradesmen, heads of families, and families without heads, busy men, and idlers, were mingled as at a popular gathering in City Hall Park. Everybody was in warm garments, the lower classes wearing coats and pelisses of sheepskin, while the others were in furs more or less expensive. Occasionally a drunken man was visible, but there were no indications of a tendency to fight. The intoxicated American, eight times out of ten, endeavors to quarrel with somebody, but our Muscovite neighbor is of a different temperament. When drunk he falls to caressing and gives kisses in place of blows.

A COLD ATTACHMENT.

The most novel sight that day in the market at Irkutsk

was the embrace of two drunken peasants. They kissed each other so tenderly and so long that the intense cold congealed their breath and froze their beards together. I left them as they were endeavoring to arrange a separation.

A few beggars circulated in the crowd and gathered here and there a copeck.

The frost whitened the beards of the men and reddened the cheeks of the women. Where hands were bared to the breeze they were of a corned-beefy hue, and there were many persons stamping on the ground or swinging their arms to keep up a circulation. The little horses, standing, were white with frost, but none of them covered with blankets. The Siberian horses are not blanketed in winter, but I was told they did not suffer from cold. Their coats are thick and warm and frequently appear more like fur than hair.

Everything that could be frozen had succumbed to the frost. There were frozen chickens, partridges, and other game, thrown in heaps like bricks or stove wood. Beef, pork, and mutton were alike solid, and some of the vendors had placed their animals in fantastic positions before freezing them. In one place I saw a calf standing as if ready to walk away. His skin remained, and at first sight I thought him alive, but was undeceived when a man overturned the unresisting beast. Frozen fish were piled carelessly in various places, and milk was offered for sale in cakes or bricks. A stick or string was generally frozen into a corner of the mass to facilitate carrying. One could swing a quart of milk at his side or wrap it in his kerchief at discretion.

There were many peripatetic dealers in cakes and tea, the latter carrying small kettles of the hot beverage, which they served in tumblers. Occasionally there was a man with a whole litter of sucking pigs frozen solid and slung over his shoulder or festooned into a necklace. The diminutive size of these pigs awakened reflections upon the brevity of swinish life.

CHAPTER XXXV.

CUSTOM is the same at Irkutsk as in all fashionable society of the empire. Visits of ceremony are made in full dress—uniform for an officer and evening costume for a civilian. Ceremonious calls are pretty short, depending of course upon the position and intimacy of the parties. The Russians are very punctilious in making and receiving visits. So many circumstances are to be considered that I was always in dread of making a mistake of etiquette somewhere.

Nearly all my acquaintances in Irkutsk spoke French or English, though comparatively few conversed with me in the latter tongue. The facility with which the Russians acquire language has been often remarked. Almost all Russians who possess any education, are familiar with at least one language beside their own. Very often I found a person conversant with two foreign languages, and it was no unusual thing to find one speaking three. I knew a young officer at Irkutsk who spoke German, French, English, and Swedish, and had a very fair smattering of Chinese, Manjour, and Japanese. A young lady there conversed well and charmingly in English, French, and German and knew something of Italian. It was more the exception than the rule that I met an officer with whom I could not converse in French. French is the society language of the Russian capital, and one of the first requisites in education.

Children are instructed almost from infancy. Governesses are generally French or English, and conversation with their charges is rarely conducted in Russian. Tutors are generally Germans familiar with French. There is no other country in the world where those who can afford it are so attentive to the education of their children. This attention added to the peculiar temperament of the Russians makes them the best linguists in the world.

An English gentleman and lady, the latter speaking Russian fluently, lived in Siberia several years. During their sojourn a son was born to them. It was a long time before he began talking, so long in fact, that his parents feared he would be dumb. When he commenced he was very soon fluent in both English and Russian. His long hesitation was doubtless caused by the confusion of two languages.

The present emperor is an accomplished linguist, but no exception in this particular to the Imperial family in general. The Queen of Greece, a niece of the Emperor of Russia, is said to be very prompt to learn a new language whenever it comes in her way, and when she was selected for that royal position she conquered the greek language in a very short time. French is the leading foreign language among the Russians, and the second rank is held by the German. Of late years English has become very popular, and is being rapidly acquired. The present *entente cordiale* between Russia and the United States is exerting an influence for the increased study of our language. Why should we not return the compliment and bestow a little attention upon the Slavonic tongue?

QUEEN OF GREECE.

Most persons in society at Irkutsk were from European

Russia or had spent some time in Moscow at St. Petersburg. Of the native born Siberians there were few who had not made a journey beyond the Ural Mountains. Among the officials, St. Petersburg was usually the authority in the matter of life and habit, while the civilians turned their eyes toward Moscow. Society in Irkutsk was not less polished than in the capitals, and it possessed the advantage of being somewhat more open and less rigid than under the shadow of the Imperial palace. Etiquette is etiquette in any part of the empire, and its forms must everywhere be observed. But after the social forms were complied with there was less stiffness than in European Russia.

Some travelers declare that they found Siberian society more polished than that of Old Russia. On this point I cannot speak personally, as my stay in the western part of the empire was too brief to afford much insight into its life. There may be some truth in the statement. Siberia has received a great many individuals of high culture in the persons of its political exiles. Men of liberal education, active intellects, and refined manners have been in large proportion among the banished Poles, and the exiles of 1825 included many of Russia's ablest minds. The influence of these exiles upon the intelligence, habits, and manners of the Siberians, has left an indelible mark. As a new civilization is more plastic than an old one, so the society of Northern Asia may have become more polished than that of Ancient Russia.

I could learn of only six of my countrymen who had been at Irkutsk before me. Of these all but two passed through the city with little delay, and were seen by very few persons. I happened to reach Siberia when our iron-clad fleet was at Cronstadt, and its officers were being feasted at St. Petersburg and elsewhere. The Siberians regretted that Mr. Fox and his companions could not visit them, and experience their hospitality. So they determined to expend their enthusiasm on the first American that appeared, and rather unexpectedly I became the recipient of the will of the Siberians toward the United States.

Two days after my arrival I was visited by Mr. Hamenof, one of the wealthiest merchants of Irkutsk. As he spoke only Russian, he was accompanied by my late fellow-traveler who came to interpret between us, and open the conversation with—

"Mr. Hamenof presents his compliments, and wishes you to dine with him day after to-morrow."

I accepted the invitation, and the merchant departed. Maack informed me that the dinner would be a ceremonious one, attended by the Governor General and leading officials.

About forty persons were present, and seated according to rank. The tables were set on three sides of a square apartment, the post of honor being in the central position facing the middle of the room. The dinner was served in the French manner, and but for the language and uniforms around me, and a few articles in the bill of fare, I could have thought myself in a private parlor of the *Trois Freres* or the *Cafe Anglais*.

Madame Ditmar, the wife of the governor of the Trans-Baikal, was the only lady present. When the champagne appeared, Mr. Hamenof proposed "The United States of America," and prefaced his toast with a little speech to his Russian guests. I proposed the health of the Emperor, and then the toasts became irregular and applied to the Governor General, the master of the house, the ladies of Siberia, the Russo-American Telegraph, and various other persons, objects, and enterprises.

From the dinner table we adjourned to the parlors where tea and coffee were brought, and most of the guests were very soon busy at the card tables. On reaching my room late at night, I found a Russian document awaiting me, and with effort and a dictionary, I translated it into an invitation to an official dinner with General Korsackoff. Five minutes before the appointed hour I accompanied a friend to the Governor General's house. As we entered, servants in military garb took our shoobas, and we were ushered into a large parlor. General Korsackoff and many of the invited guests were assembled in the parlor, and within two minutes the entire party had gathered. As the clock struck five the doors were thrown open, and the general led the way to the dining hall.

I found at Irkutsk a great precision respecting appointments. When dinners were to come off at a fixed hour all the guests assembled from three to ten minutes before the time specified. I never knew any one to come late, and all were equally careful not to come early. No one could be more punctual than General Korsackoff, and his example was no doubt carefully watched and followed. It is a rule throughout official circles in Russia, if I am correctly informed, that tardiness implies disrespect. Americans might take a few lessons of the Russians on the subject of punctuality.

The table was liberally decorated with flowers and plants, and the whole surroundings were calculated to make one forget that he was in cold and desolate Siberia. A band of music was stationed in the adjoining parlor, and furnished us with Russian and American airs. At the first toast General Korsackoff made a speech in Russian, recounting the amity existing between the two nations and the visit of our special embassy to congratulate the Emperor on his escape from assassination. He thought the Siberians felt no less grateful at this mark of sympathy than did the people of European Russia, and closed by proposing, "The President, Congress, and People of the United States."

EMPEROR OF RUSSIA.

The toast was received with enthusiasm, the band playing Yankee Doodle as an accompaniment to the cheering.

The speech was translated to me by Captain Linden, the private Secretary of the Governor General, who spoke French and English fluently. Etiquette required me to follow with a toast to the emperor in my little speech. I spoke slowly to facilitate the hearing of those who understood English. The Captain then translated it into Russian.

General Korsackoff spoke about four minutes, and I think my response was of the same length. Both speeches were considered quite elaborate by the Siberians, and one officer declared it was the longest dinner-table address the general ever made. Two days later at another dinner I asked a friend to translate my remarks when I came to speak. He asked how long I proposed talking.

"About three minutes," was my reply.

"Oh," said he, "you had better make it one or two minutes. You made a long speech at the Governor General's, and when you dine with a person of less importance he will not expect you to speak as much."

I had not taken this view of the matter, as the American custom tends to brevity on the ascending rather than on the descending scale.

Ten years earlier Major Collins dined with General Mouravieff in the same hall where I was entertained. After dinner I heard a story at the expense of my enterprising predecessor. It is well known that the Major is quite a speech maker at home, and when he is awakened on a favorite subject he has no lack either of ideas or words.

On the occasion just mentioned, General Mouravieff gave the toast, "Russia and America," Major Collins rose to reply and after speaking six or eight minutes came to a pause. Captain Martinoff, who understood English, was seated near the Major. As the latter stopped, General Mouravieff turned to the Captain and asked:

"Will you be kind enough to translate what has been said?"

"*Blagodariete*," (he thanks you) said the captain.

The Major proceeded six or eight minutes more and paused again.

"Translate," was the renewed command of the Governor General.

"He thanks you very much."

Again another period of speech and the address was finished.

"Translate if you please," the general suggested once more to his aid.

"He thanks you very much indeed."

The Major was puzzled, and turning to Captain Martinoff remarked that the Russian language must be very comprehensive when a speech of twenty minutes could be translated in three or four words.

On days when I was disengaged I dined at the *Amoorski Gastinitza* or Amoor Hotel. The hotel comprised two buildings, one containing the rooms of lodgers, and the other devoted to restaurant, dining and billiard rooms. In the dining department there were several rooms, a large one for a restaurant and table d'hote, and the rest for private parties. Considering the general character of Russian hotels the one at Irkutsk was quite creditable. In its management, cookery, and service it would compare favorably with the establishments on Courtlandt Street or Park Row.

In the billiard room there were two tables on which I sometimes complied with a request to 'show the American game.' The tables had six pockets each, and as the cues had no leather tips, there was an unpleasant clicking whenever they were used. The Russian game of billiards is played with five balls, and the science consists in pocketing the balls. The carom does not count.

The first time I dined at the hotel the two candles burned dimly, and we called for a third. When it was brought the servant drew a small table near us and placed the extra candle upon it. I asked the reason for his doing so, and it was thus explained.

There is a superstition in Russia that if three lighted candles are placed upon a table some one in the room will die within a year. Everybody endeavors to avoid such a calamity. If you have two candles and order another, the servant will place the third on a side table or he will bring a fourth and make your number an even one.

There was formerly a theatre at Irkutsk, but it was burned a few years ago, and has not been rebuilt. During my stay there was a musical concert in the large hall of the officers' club, and a theatrical display was prepared but not concluded before my departure. At the concert a young officer, Captain Lowbry, executed on the piano several pieces of his own composition, and was heartily applauded by the listeners. Once a week there was a social party at the club house where dancing, cards, billiards, and small talk continued till after midnight.

Nearly every one in society kept 'open house' daily. In most of the families where I was acquainted tea was taken at 8 P. M., and any friend could call at that hour without ceremony. The samovar was placed on the table, and one of the ladies presided over the tea. Those who wished it could sit at table, but there was no formal spreading of the cloth. Tea was handed about the room and each one took it at his liking. I have seen in these social circles a most pleasing irregularity in tea drinking. Some were seated on sofas and chairs, holding cups and saucers in their hands or resting them upon tables; other stood in groups of two, three, or more; others were at cards, and sipped their tea at intervals of the games; and a few were gathered around the hostess at the samovar. The time passed in whatever amusements were attainable. There were cards for some and conversation for others, with piano music, little dances and general sports of considerable variety. Those evenings at Irkutsk were delightful, and I shall always remember them with pleasure.

What with visits, dinners, balls, suppers, social evenings, and sleigh rides, I had little time to myself, and though I economized every minute I did not succeed in finishing my letters and journal until the very day before my departure. The evening parties lasted pretty late. They generally closed with a supper toward the wee small hours, and the good nights were not spoken until about two in the morning.

There is a peculiarity about a Russian party,—whether a quiet social assemblage or a stately ball,—that the whole house is thrown open. In America guests are confined to the parlors and the dancing and supper apartments, from the time they leave the cloaking rooms till they prepare for departure. In Russia they can wander pretty nearly where they please, literally "up stairs, down stairs, or in my lady's chamber." Of course all the rooms are prepared for visitors, but I used at first to feel a shrinking sensation when I sauntered into the private study and work room of my official host, or found myself among the scent bottles and other toilet treasures of a lady acquaintance. This literal keeping of 'open house' materially assists to break the stiffness of an assemblage though it can hardly be entirely convenient to the hosts.

Immediately after my entertainment with General Korsackoff, the mayor of Irkutsk invited me to an official dinner at his house. This was followed a few days later by a similar courtesy on the part of Mr. Trepaznikoff, the son of a wealthy merchant who died a few years ago. Private dinners followed in rapid succession until I was qualified to speak with practical knowledge of the Irkutsk cuisine. No stranger in a strange land was ever more kindly taken in, and no hospitality was ever bestowed with less ostentation. I can join in the general testimony of travelers that the Russians excel in the ability to entertain visitors.

Mr. Kartesheftsoff, the Mayor, or *Golovah* as he is called, resided in a large house that formerly belonged to Prince Trubetskoi, one of the exiles of 1825. My host was an extensive owner of gold mines, and had been very successful in working them. He was greatly interested in the means employed in California for separating gold from earth, and especially in the 'hydraulic' process. On my first visit Madame

Karteshcftsoff spoke very little French. She must have submitted her studies to a thorough revision as I found her a week later able to conduct a conversation with ease. There were other instances of a vigorous overhauling of disused French and English that furnished additional proof of the Russian adaptability to foreign tongues.

To reach the golovah's house we crossed the Ouska-kofka, a small river running through the northern part of Irkutsk; it had been recently frozen, and several rosy-cheeked boys were skating on the ice. The view from the bridge is quite picturesque, and the little valley forms a favorite resort in certain seasons of the year. The water of the Ouska-kofka is said to be denser than that of the Angara, and on that account is preferred for culinary purposes.

CHAPTER XXXVI.

I HAVE made occasional mention of the exiles of 1825, and it may be well to explain how they went to Siberia. In the early part of the present century Russia was not altogether happy. The Emperor Paul, called to the throne by the death of Catherine II., did not display marked ability, but, 'on the contrary, quite the reverse.' What his mother had done for the improvement of the country he was inclined to undo. Under his reign great numbers were banished to Siberia upon absurd charges or mere caprice. The emperor issued manifestoes of a whimsical character, one of which was directed against round hats, and another against shoe strings. The glaring colors now used upon bridges, distance posts, watch boxes, and other imperial property, were of his selection, and so numerous were his eccentricities that he was declared of unsound mind. In March, 1801, he was smothered in his palace, which he had just completed. It is said that within an hour after the fact of his death was known round hats appeared on the street in great numbers.

Alexander I. endeavored to repair some of the evils of his father's reign. He recalled many exiles from Siberia, suppressed the secret inquisition, and restored many rights of which the people had been deprived. His greatest abilities were displayed during the wars with France. After the general peace he devoted himself to inspecting and developing the resources of the country, and was the first, and thus far the only, emperor of Russia to cross the Ural Mountains and visit the mines of that region. His death occurred during a tour through the southern provinces of the empire. Some of his reforms were based upon the principles of other European governments, which he endeavored to study. On his return from England he told his council that the best thing he saw there was the opposition in Parliament. He thought it a part of the government machinery, and regretted it could not be introduced in Russia.

Constantine, the eldest brother of Alexander I., had relinquished his right to the crown, thus breaking the regular succession. From the time of Paul a revolutionary party had existed, and once at least it plotted the assassination of Alexander. There was an interregnum of three weeks between the death of Alexander and the assumption of power by his second brother, Nicholas. The change of succession strengthened the revolutionists, and they employed the interregnum to organize a conspiracy for seizing the government.

The conspiracy was wide spread, and included many of the ablest men of the day. The army was seriously implicated. The revolutionists desired a constitutional government, and their rallying cry of "CONSTITUTIA!" was explained to the soldiers as the name of Constantine's wife. The real design of the movement was not confided to the rank and file, who supposed they were fighting for Constantine and the regular succession of the throne.

Nicholas learned of the conspiracy the day before his ascension; the Imperial guard of the palace was in the plot, and expected to seize the emperor's person. The guard was removed during the night and a battalion from Finland substituted. It is said that on receiving intelligence of the assembling of the insurgents, the emperor called his wife to the chapel of the palace, where he spent a few moments in prayer. Then taking his son, the present emperor, he led him to the soldiers of the new guard, confided him to their protection, and departed for St. Isaac's Square to suppress the revolt. The soldiers kept the boy until the emperor's return, and would not even surrender him to his tutor.

The plot was so wide-spread that the conspirators had good promise of success, but whole regiments backed out at the last moment and left only a forlorn hope to begin the struggle. Nicholas rode with his officers to St. Isaac's square, and twice commanded the assembled insurgents to surrender. They refused, and were then saluted with "the last argument of kings." A storm of grape shot, followed by a charge of cavalry, put in flight all who were not killed, and ended the insurrection.

A long and searching investigation followed, disclosing all the ramifications of the plot. The conspirators declared they were led to what they undertook by the unfortunate condition of the country and the hope of improving it. Nicholas, concealed behind a screen, heard most of the testimony and confessions, and learned therefrom a wholesome lesson. The end of the affair was the execution of five principal conspirators and the banishment of many others to Siberia. The five that suffered capital punishment were hanged in front of the Admiralty buildings in St. Petersburg. One rope was broken, and the victim, falling to the ground, suffered such agony that the officer in charge of the execution sent to the emperor asking what to do. "Take a new rope and finish your duty," was the unpitying answer of Nicholas.

The accession of Nicholas and the attempted revolt occurred on the 14th December, (O. S.) 1825. Within six months from that date the most of the conspirators reached Siberia. They were sent to different districts, some to labor in the mines for specified periods, and others to become colonists. They included some of the ablest men in Russia, and were nearly all young and enterprising. Many of them were married, and were followed into exile by their wives, though the latter were only permitted to go to Siberia on condition of never returning. Each of the exiles was deprived of all civil or political rights, and declared legally dead. His property was confiscated to the crown, and his wife considered a widow and could marry again if she chose. To the credit of the Russian women, not one availed herself of this privilege. I was told that nearly every married exile's family followed him, and some of the unmarried ones were followed by their sisters and mothers.

I have previously spoken of the effect of the unfortunates of the 14th December upon the society and manners of Siberia. These men enjoyed good social positions, and their political faults did not prevent their being well received. Their sentence to labor in the mines was not rigorously enforced, and lasted but two or three

HOME OF TWO EXILES.

years at farthest. They were subsequently employed at in-door work, and, as time wore on and passion subsided, were allowed to select residences in villages. Very soon they were permitted to go to the larger towns, and once there, those whose wives possessed property in their own right built themselves elegant houses and took the position to which their abilities entitled them.

General Korsackoff told me that when he first went to serve in Siberia there was a ball one evening at the Governor General's. Noticing one man who danced the Mazurka splendidly, he whispered to General Mouravieff and asked his name.

"That," said Mouravieff, "is a revolutionist of 1825. He is one of the best men of society in Irkutsk."

After their first few years of exile, the Decembrists had little to complain of except the prohibition to return to Europe. To men whose youth was passed in brilliant society and amid the gayeties of the capital, this life in Siberia was no doubt irksome. Year after year went by, and on the twenty-fifth anniversary of their banishment they looked for pardon. Little else was talked of among them for some weeks, but they were doomed to disappointment. Nicholas had no forgiving disposition, and those who plotted his overthrow were little likely to obtain favor, even though a quarter of a century had elapsed since their crime.

But the death of Nicholas and the coronation of Alexander II. wrought a change for the exiles. Nicholas began his reign with an act of severity; Alexander followed his ascension with one of clemency. By imperial ukase he pardoned the exiles of 1825, restored them to their civil and political rights, and permitted their return to Europe. As the fathers were legally dead when sent into exile, the children born to them in Siberia were illegitimate in the eye of the law and could not even bear their own family name. Properly they belonged to the government, and inherited their father's exile in not being permitted to go to Europe. The ukase removed all these disabilities and gave the children full authority to succeed to their father's hereditary titles and social and political rights.

These exiles lived in different parts of Siberia, but chiefly in the governments of Irkutsk and Yeneseisk. But the thirty years of the reign of Nicholas were not uneventful. Death removed some of the unfortunates. Others had dwelt so long in Siberia that they did not wish to return to a society where they would be strangers. Some who were unmarried at the time of their exile had acquired families in Siberia, and thus fastened themselves to the country. Not more than half of those living at the time of Alexander's coronation availed themselves of his permission to return to Russia.

The princes Trubetskoi and Volbonskoi hesitated for some time, but finally concluded to return. Both died in Europe quite recently. Their departure was regretted by many persons in Irkutsk, as their absence was quite a loss to society. I heard some curious reminiscences concerning the Prince Volbonskoi. It was said that his wife and children, with the servants, were the occupants of the large and elegant house, the prince living in a small building in the court yard. He had a farm near the town and sold the various crops to his wife. Both the princes paid great attention to educating their children and fitting them for ultimate social position in Europe.

While in Irkutsk I saw one of the Decembrists who had grown quite wealthy as a wine merchant. Another of these exiles was mentioned, but I did not meet him. Another resided at Selenginsk, a third near Verkne Udinsk, and a fourth near Lake Baikal. There are several at other points, but I believe the whole number of the Decembrists now in Siberia is less than a dozen. Forty-two years have brought them to the brink of the grave, and very soon the active spirits of that unhappy revolt will have passed away.

The other political exiles in Siberia are almost entirely Poles. Every insurrection in Poland adds to the population of Asiatic Russia, and accomplishes very little else. The revolt of 1831 was prolific in this particular, and so was that of 1863. Revolutions in Poland have been utterly hopeless of success since the downfall and division of the kingdom, but the Poles remain undaunted.

I do not propose entering into a discussion of the Polish question, as it would occupy too much space and be foreign to the object of my book; but I will briefly touch a few points. The Russians and Poles were not inclined to amiability when both had separate governments. Europe has never been converted to Republican principles, and however much the Western powers may sympathize with Poland, they would be unwilling to adopt for themselves the policy they desire for Russia. England holds India and Ireland, regardless of the will of Indians and Irish. France has her African territory which did not ask to be taken under the tri-color, and we are all aware of the relations once held by her emperor toward Mexico. It is much easier to look for generosity and forbearance in others than in ourselves.

Those who are disposed to shed tears over the fate of Poland, should remember that the unhappy country has only suffered the fortune of war. When Russia and Poland began to measure swords the latter was the more powerful, and for a time overran a goodly portion of the Muscovite soil. We all know there has been a partition of Poland, but are we equally aware that the Russia of Rurik and Ivan IV. was partitioned in 1612 by the Swedes (at Novgorod) and the Poles (at Moscow?) In 1612 the Poles held Moscow. The Russians rose against them in that year, just as the Poles have since risen against the Russians, but with a different result.

The Polish exiles of 1831 and previous years were pardoned by the same ukase that liberated the Russian exiles of 1825. Just before the insurrection of 1863 there were not many Poles in Siberia, except those who remained of their own free will. The last insurrection caused a fresh deportation, twenty-four thousand being banished beyond the Ural Mountains. Ten thousand of these were sent to Eastern Siberia, the balance being distributed in the governments west of the Yenesei. The decree of June, 1867, allowed many of these prisoners to return to Poland.

The government has always endeavored to scatter the exiles and prevent their congregating in such numbers as to cause inconvenience. The prime object of deportation to Siberia is to people the country and develop its natural wealth. Though Russia occupies nearly an eighth of the land on the face of the globe, her population numbers but about seventy millions. It is her policy to people her territory, and she bends her energies to this end. She does not allow the emigration of her subjects to any appreciable extent, and she punishes but few crimes with death. Notwithstanding her general tolerance on religious matters, she punishes with severity a certain sect that discourages propagation. There are other facts I might mention as illustrations were it not for the fastidiousness of the present age. Siberia is much more in need of population than European Russia, and exiles are sent thither to become inhabitants.

So far as the matter of sentence goes there is little difference between political and criminal exiles. The sentence is in accordance with the offence to be punished, and may be light or severe. Some exiles are simply banished to Siberia, and can do almost anything except go away. They may travel as they choose, engage in business, and even hold official position. It is no bar to their progress that they emigrated involuntarily. If they forget their evil ways and are good citizens, others will be equally oblivious and encourage them. They have special inducements to become colonists and till the soil or develop its mineral wealth. With honesty and industry they have at least a fair chance in life.

Some exiles are confined to certain districts, governments, towns, or villages, and must report at stated intervals to the Chief of Police. These intervals are not the same in all cases, but vary from one day to a month, or even more. Some are not allowed to go beyond specified limits without express permission from the authorities, while others may absent themselves as they choose during the intervals of reporting to the police. Some can engage in whatever business they find advantageous, while others are prohibited certain employments but not restricted as to others.

If a man is sentenced to become a colonist, the government gives him a house or means to build it, a plot of ground, and the necessary tools. He is not allowed to be anything else than a colonist. Criminals of a certain grade cannot engage in commerce, and the same restriction applies to 'politiques.' No criminal can be a teacher, either in a public or private school, and no politique can teach in a public school. While I was in Siberia an order was issued prohibiting the latter class engaging in any kind of educational work except music, drawing, and painting.

Many criminal and political offenders are 'drafted in the army' in much the same manner that our prisons sent their able-bodied men into military service during our late war. Their terms of enlistment are various, but generally not less than fifteen years. The men receive the pay and rations of soldiers, and have the possibility of promotion before them. They are sent to regiments stationed at distant posts in order to diminish the chances of desertion. The Siberian and Caucasian regiments receive the greater portion of these recruits. Many members of the peculiar religious sect mentioned elsewhere are sent to the Caucasian frontier. They are said to be very tractable and obedient, but not reliable for aggressive military operations.

An exile may receive from his friends money to an amount not exceeding twenty-five roubles a month. If his wife has property of her own she may enjoy a separate income. Those confined in prisons or kept at labor may receive money to the same extent, but it must pass through the hands of the officials. Of course the occupants of prisons are fed by government, and so are those under sentence of hard labor. The men restricted to villages and debarred from profitable employment receive monthly allowances in money and flour, barely enough for their subsistence. There are complaints that dishonest officials steal a part of these allowances, but the practice is not as frequent as formerly. A prisoner's comfort in any part of the world depends in a great measure upon the character of the officer in charge of him. Siberia offers no exception to this rule.

Formerly the Polish exiles enjoyed more social freedom than at present. The cause of the change was thus explained to me:

Five or six years ago a Polish noble who had been exiled lived at Irkutsk and enjoyed the friendship of several officers. The Amoor had been recently opened, and this man asked and obtained the privilege of visiting it, giving his parole not to leave Siberia. At Nicolayevsk he embraced the opportunity to escape, and advised others to do the same. This breach of confidence led to greater circumspection, and the distrust was increased by the conduct of other exiles. Since that time the Poles have been under greater restraint.

Many books on Russia contain interesting stories of the brutality toward exiles, both on the road and after they have reached their destination. Undoubtedly there have been instances of cruelty, just as in every country in Christendom, but I do not believe the Russians are worse in this respect than other people. I saw a great many exiles during my journey through Siberia. Frequently when on the winter road I met convoys of them, and never observed any evidence of needless severity. Five-sixths of the exiles I met on the road were in sleighs like those used by Russian merchants when traveling. There were generally three persons in a sleigh, and I thought them comfortably clad. I could see no difference between them and their guards, except that the latter carried muskets and sabres. Any women among them received special attention, particularly when they were young and pretty. I saw two old ladies who were handled tenderly by the soldiers and treated with apparent distinction. When exiles were on foot, their guards marched with them and the women of the party rode in sleighs.

The object of deportation is to people Siberia; if the government permitted cruelties that caused half of the exiles to die on the road, as some accounts aver, it would be inconsistent with its policy. As before mentioned, the ripe age to which most of the Decembrists lived, is a proof that they were not subjected to physical torture. In the eyes of the government these men were the very worst offenders, and if they did not suffer hardships and cruelties it is not probable that all others would be generally ill-used. I do not for a moment suppose exile is either attractive or desirable, but, so far as I know, it does not possess the horrors attributed to it. The worst part of exile is to be sent to hard labor, but the unpleasant features of such punishment are not confined to Siberia. Plenty of testimony on this point can be obtained at Sing Sing and Pentonville.

It is unpleasant to leave one's home and become an involuntary emigrant to a far country. The Siberian road is one I would never travel out of pure pleasure, and I can well understand that it must be many times disagreeable when one journeys unwillingly. But, once in Siberia, the worldly circumstances of many exiles are better than they were at home. If a man can forget that he is deprived of liberty, and I presume this is the most difficult thing of all, he is not, under ordinary circumstances, very badly off in Siberia. Certainly many exiles choose to remain when their term of banishment is ended. A laboring man is better paid for his services and is more certain of employment than in European Russia. He leads a more independent life and has better prospects of advancement than in the older civilization. Many Poles say they were drawn unwillingly into the acts that led to their exile, and if they return home they may be involved in like trouble again. In Poland they are at the partial mercy of malcontents who have nothing to lose and can never remain at ease. In Siberia there are no such disturbing influences.

About ten thousand exiles are sent to Siberia every year. Except in times of political disturbance in Poland or elsewhere, nearly all the exiles are offenders against society or property. The notion that they are generally 'politiques,' is very far from correct. As well might one suppose the majority of the convicts at Sing Sing were from the upper classes of New York. The regular stream of exiles is composed almost entirely of criminal offenders; occasional floods of revolutionists follow the attempts at independence.

I made frequent inquiries concerning the condition of the exiles, and so far as I could learn they were generally well off. I say 'generally,' because I heard of some cases of poverty and hardship, and doubtless there were others that I never heard of. A large part of the Siberian population is made up of exiles and their descendants. A gentleman frequently sent me his carriage during my stay at Irkutsk. It was managed by an intelligent driver who pleased me with his skill and dash. One evening, when he was a little intoxicated, my friend and myself commented in French on his condition, and were a little surprised to find that he understood us. He was an exile from St. Petersburg, where he had been coachman to a French merchant.

The clerk of the hotel was an exile, and so was one of the waiters. *Isvoshchiks*, or hackmen, counted many exiles in their ranks, and so did laborers of other professions. Occasionally clerks in stores, market men, boot makers, and tailors ascribed their exile to some discrepancy between their conduct and the laws. I met a Polish gentleman in charge of the museum of the geographical society of Eastern Siberia, and was told that the establishment rapidly improved in his hands. Two physicians of Irkutsk were 'unfortunates' from Warsaw, and one of them had distanced all competitors in the extent and success of his practice. Then there were makers of cigarettes, dealers in various commodities, and professors of divers arts. Some of the educated Siberians I met told me they had been taught almost entirely by exiles.

Before the abolition of serfdom a proprietor could send his human property into exile. He was not required to give any reason, the record accompanying the order of banishment stating only that the serf was exiled "by the will of his master." This privilege was open to enormous abuse, but happily the ukase of liberty has removed it. The design of the system was no doubt to enable proprietors to rid themselves of serfs who were idle, dissolute, or quarrelsome, but had not committed any act the law could touch.

A proprietor exiling a serf was required to pay his traveling expenses of twenty-five roubles, and to furnish him an outfit of summer and winter clothing. A wife was allowed to follow her husband, with all their children not matured, and all their expenses were to be paid. The abuse of the system consisted in the power to banish a man who had committed no offence at all. The loss of services and the expense of exiling a serf may have been a slight guarantee against this, but if the proprietor were an unprincipled tyrant or a sensualist, (and he might be both,) there was no protection for his subjects. It has happened that the best man on an estate incurred the displeasure of his owner and went to Siberia in consequence. Exile is a severe punishment to the Russian peasant, who clings with enduring tenacity to the place where his youthful days were passed.

Every serf exiled for a minor offense or at the will of his master was appointed on his arrival in Siberia to live in a specified district. If he could produce a certificate of good behavior at the end of three years, he was authorized to clear and cultivate as much land as he wished. If single he could marry, but he was not compelled to do so. He was exempt from taxes for twelve years, and after that only paid a trifle. He had no master and could act for himself in all things except in returning to Russia. He was under the disadvantage of having no legal existence, and though the land he worked was his own and no one could disturb him, he did not hold it under written title. The criminal who served at labor in the mines was placed, at the expiration of his sentence, in the same category as the exile for minor offences. Both cultivated land in like manner and on equal terms. Some became wealthy and were able to secure the privileges of citizenship.

CHAPTER XXXVII.

THE descendants of exiles are in much greater number than the exiles themselves. Eastern Siberia is mainly peopled by them, and Western Siberia very largely so. They are all free peasants and enjoy a condition far superior to that of the serf under the system prevalent before 1859. Many of them have become wealthy through gold mining, commerce, and agriculture, and occupy positions they never could have obtained had they lived in European Russia. I know a merchant whose fortune is counted by millions, and who is famous through Siberia for his enterprise and generosity. He is the son of an exiled serf and has risen by his own ability. Since I left Siberia I learn with pleasure that the emperor has honored him with a decoration. Many of the prominent merchants and proprietary miners were mentioned to me as examples of the prosperity of the second and third generation from banished men. I was told particularly of a wealthy gold miner whose evening of life is cheered by an ample fortune and two well educated children. Forty years ago his master capriciously sent him to Siberia. The man found his banishment 'the best thing that could happen.'

The system of serfdom never had any practical hold in Siberia. There was but one Siberian proprietor of serfs in existence at the time of the emancipation. This was Mr. Rodinkoff of Krasnoyarsk, whose grandfather received a grant of serfs and a patent of nobility from the empress Catherine. None of the family, with a single exception, ever attempted more than nominal exercise of authority over the peasants, and this one paid for his imprudence with his life.

He attempted to put in force his full proprietary rights, and the result was his death by violence during a visit to one of his estates.

The difference between the conditions of the Russian and Siberian peasantry was that between slavery and freedom. The owner of serfs had rarely any common interest with his people, and his chief business was to make the most out of his human property. Serfdom was degrading to master and serf, just as slavery degraded owner and slave. The moujik bore the stamp of servility as the negro slave bore it, and it will take as much time to wear it away in the one as the other. Centuries of oppression in Russia could not fail to open a wide gulf between the nobility and those who obeyed them. Thanks to Alexander the work of filling this gulf has begun, but it will require many years and much toil to complete it.

The comparative freedom enjoyed in Siberia was not without visible result. The peasants were more prosperous than in Russia, they lived in better houses and enjoyed more real comforts of life. The absence of masters and the liberty to act for themselves begat an air of independence in the peasant class that contrasted agreeably with the cringing servility of the serf. Wealth was open to all who sought it, and the barriers between the different ranks of society were partially broken down. The peasants that acquired wealth began to cultivate refined tastes. They paid more attention to the education of their children than was shown by the same class in Russia, and the desire for education rapidly increased. The emancipation of the serfs in Russia was probably brought about by the marked superiority of the Siberian population in prosperity and intelligence.

In coming ages the Russians will revere the name of Alexander not less than that of Peter the Great. To the latter is justly due the credit of raising the nation from barbarism; the former has the immortal honor of removing the stain of serfdom. The difficulties in the way were great and the emperor had few supporters, but he steadily pursued his object and at length earned the eternal gratitude of his people. Russia is yet in her developing stage. The shock of the change was severe and not unattended with danger, but the critical period is passed, and the nation has commenced a career of freedom. The serf has been awakened to a new life, and his education is just commencing. Already there is increased prosperity in some parts of the empire, showing that the free man understands his new condition. The proprietors who were able to appreciate and prepare for the change have been positively benefited, while others who continued obstinate were ruined. On the whole the derangement by the transition has been less than many friends of the measure expected, and by no means equal to that prophesied by its opponents. But the grandest results in the nation's progress are yet to come, and it is from future generations that Alexander will receive his warmest praise.

The working of mines on government account has greatly diminished in the past few years, and the number of hard labor convicts in Siberia more than equals the capacity of the mines. When the political exiles, after the revolution of 1863, arrived at Irkutsk, the mines were already filled with convicts. The 'politiques' sentenced to hard labor were employed in building roads, most of them being sent to the southern end of Lake Baikal. In June, 1866, seven hundred and twenty prisoners were sent to this labor, and divided into eight or ten parties to work on as many sections of the road. Before the end of the month a revolt occurred. Various accounts have been given and different motives assigned for it. I was told by several Poles that the prisoners were half starved, and the little food they received was bad. Hunger and a desire to escape were the motives to the insurrection. On the other hand the Russians told me the prisoners were properly fed, and the revolt must be attributed entirely to the hope of escaping from Siberia.

I obtained from an officer, who sat on the court-martial which investigated the affair, the following particulars:

On the 24th of June, (O. S.,) the working party at Koultoukskoi, the western end of the road, disarmed its guard by a sudden and bloodless attack. The insurgents then moved eastward along the line of the road, and on their way overpowered successively the guards of the other parties. Many of the prisoners refused to take part in the affair and remained at their work. A Polish officer named Sharamovitch assumed command of the insurgents, who directed their march toward Posolsky.

TARTAR CAVALRY.

As soon as news of the affair reached Irkutsk, the Governor General ordered a battalion of soldiers by steamer to Posolsky. On the 28th of June a fight occurred at the river Bestriya. The insurgents were defeated with a loss of twenty-five or thirty men, while the force sent against them lost five men and one officer. The Polish leader was among the killed. After the defeat the insurgents separated in small bands and fled into the mountains. They were pursued by Tartar cavalry, who scoured the country thoroughly and retook all the fugitives. The insurrection caused much alarm at its outbreak, as it was supposed all prisoners in Siberia were in the conspiracy. Exaggerated reports were spread, and all possible precautions taken, but they proved unnecessary. The conspiracy extended no farther than the working parties on the Baikal road.

The prisoners were brought to Irkutsk, where a court-martial investigated the affair. A Russian court-martial does not differ materially from any other in the manner of its proceedings. It requires positive evidence for or against a person accused, and, like other courts, gives him the benefit of doubts. My informant told me that the court in this case listened to all evidence that had any possible bearing on the question. The sitting continued several weeks, and after much deliberation the court rendered a finding and sentence.

In the finding the prisoners were divided into five grades, and their sentences accorded with the letter of the law. The first grade comprised seven persons, known to have been leaders in the revolt. These were sentenced to be shot. In the second grade there were a hundred and ninety-seven, who knew the design to revolt and joined in the insurrection. One-tenth of these were to suffer death, the choice being made by lot; the remainder were sentenced to twenty years labor. The third grade comprised a hundred and twenty-two, ignorant of the conspiracy before the revolt, but who joined the insurgents. These received an addition of two or three years to their original sentences to labor. The fourth grade included ninety-four men, who knew the design to revolt but refused to join the insurgents. These were sentenced "to remain under suspicion." In the fifth and last grade there were two hundred and sixty, who were ignorant of the conspiracy and remained at their posts. Their innocence was fully established, and, of course, relieved them from all charge.

It was found that the design of the insurgents was to escape into Mongolia and make their way to Pekin. This would have been next to impossible, for two reasons: the character of the country, and the treaty between China and Russia. The region to be traversed from the Siberian frontier toward Pekin is the Mongolian steppe or desert. The only food obtainable on the steppe is mutton from the flocks of the nomad inhabitants. These are principally along the road from Kiachta, and even there are by no means numerous. The escaping exiles in avoiding the road to ensure safety would have run great risk of starvation. The treaty between China and Russia requires that fugitives from one empire to the other shall be given up. Had the exiles succeeded in crossing Mongolia and reaching the populous parts of China, they would have been once more in captivity and returned to Russian hands.

The finding of the court-martial was submitted to General Korsackoff for approval or revision. The general commuted the sentence of three men in the first grade to twenty years labor. Those in the second grade sentenced to death were relieved from this punishment and placed on the same footing as their companions. In the third grade the original sentence (at the time of banishment) was increased by one or two years labor. Other penalties were not changed.

During my stay in Irkutsk the four prisoners condemned to death suffered the extreme penalty, the execution occurring in the forest near the town. A firing party of forty-eight men was divided into four squads. According to the custom at all military executions one musket in each squad was charged with a blank cartridge. The four prisoners were shot simultaneously, and all died instantly. Two of them were much dejected; the others met their deaths firmly and shouted "*Vive la Pologne*" as they heard the order to fire.

I was told that the crowd of people, though large, was very

quiet, and moved away in silence when the execution was over. Very few officers and soldiers were present beyond those whose duty required them to witness or take part in the affair.

One of the most remarkable escapes from Siberia was that of Rufin Piotrowski, a Polish emigrant who left Paris in 1844 to return to his native country, with impossible plans and crude ideas for her relief. The end of his journey was Kaminietz, in Podolia, where he gave himself out as a Frenchman who had come to give private lessons in foreign languages, and received the usual permit from the authorities without exciting any suspicion. He was soon introduced into the best society; and the better to shield his connections, he chose the houses of Russian employés. His security rested upon his not being supposed to understand the Polish language; and, during the nine months that he remained, he obtained such command over himself, that the police had not the slightest suspicion of his being a Pole. The warning voice came from St. Petersburg, through the spies in Paris.

Early one winter's morning he was roughly shaken out of slumber by the director of police, and carried before the governor of the province, who had come specially on this errand. His position was represented to him as one of the greatest danger, and he was recommended to make a full confession. This for many days he refused to do, until a large number of those who were his accomplices were brought before him; and their weary, anxious faces induced him to exclaim loudly, and in his native tongue—"Yes, I am a Pole, and have returned because I could not bear exile from my native land any longer. Here I wished to live inoffensive and quiet, confiding my secret to a few countrymen; and I have nothing more to say." An immediate order was made out for the culprit's departure to Kiev. According to the story he has published his sufferings were frightful, and were not lessened when they stopped at a hut, where some rusty chains were brought out, the rings of which were thrust over his ankles: they proved much too small, and the rust prevented the bars from turning in the sockets, so that the pain was insupportable. He was rudely carried and thrown into the carriage, and thus arrived in an almost insensible condition at the fortress of Kiev.

After many months' detention in this prison, being closely watched and badly treated, he was sentenced to hard labor in Siberia for life, degraded from his rank as a noble, and ordered to make the journey in chains. As soon as this was read to him, he was taken to a kibitka, with three horses, irons were put on, and he was placed between two armed soldiers; the gates of the fortress were shut, and the road to Siberia was before him. An employee came up to M. Piotrowski, and timidly offered him a small packet, saying—"Accept this from my saint." The convict not understanding, he added, "You are a Pole, and do not know our customs. It is my fête-day, when it is above all a duty to assist the unfortunate. Pray, accept it, then, in the name of my saint, after whom I am called." The packet contained bread, salt, and money.

Night and day the journey continued, with the utmost rapidity, for about a month, when, in the middle of the night, they stopped at the fortress of Omsk, where he was placed for a few hours with a young officer who had committed some breach of discipline. They talked on incessantly until the morning, so great was the pleasure of meeting with an educated person. A map of Siberia was in the room, which Piotrowski examined with feverish interest. "Ah!" said his companion, "are you meditating flight? Pray, do not think of it: many of your fellow-countrymen have tried it, and never succeeded."

At midday he was brought before Prince Gortchakoff, and the critical moment of his fate arrived: he might either be sent to some of the government factories in the neighborhood, or to the mines underground. An hour passed in cruel suspense while this was debated. At length one of the council announced to him that he was to be sent to the distillery of Ekaterinski, three hundred miles to the north of Omsk.

The clerks around congratulated him on his destination, and his departure was immediate.

On a wintry morning he reached a vast plain near the river Irtish, on which a village of about two hundred wooden huts was built around a factory. When introduced into the clerks' office, a young man who was writing jumped up and threw himself into his arms: he also was a Pole from Cracow, a well-known poet, and sent away for life as "a measure of precaution." Soon they were joined by another political criminal: these spoke rapidly and with extreme emotion, entreating their new friend to bear everything in the most submissive and patient manner, as the only means of escaping from menial employment, and being promoted to the clerks' office. Not long was he permitted to rest. A convict came and ordered him to take a broom and sweep away a mass of dirt that some masons had left; a murderer was his companion; and thus he went on until nightfall, when his two friends were permitted to visit him, in the presence of the soldiers and convicts, most of the latter of whom had been guilty of frightful crimes.

Thus day after day passed on, in sweeping, carrying wood and water, amid snow and frost. His good conduct brought him, in a year and a half, to the office, where he received ten francs a month and his rations, and the work was light. During this time he saw and conversed with many farmers and travelers from a distance, and gained every information about the roads, rivers, etc., with a view to the escape he was ever meditating. Some of the natives unite with the soldiers in exercising an incessant supervision over the convicts, and a common saying among the Tartars is: "In killing a squirrel you get but one skin, whilst a convict has three—his coat, his shirt, and his skin."

Slowly and painfully he collected the materials for his journey. First of all, a passport was an essential. A convict who had been sentenced for making false money, still possessed an excellent stamp of the royal arms; this Piotrowski bought for a few francs. The sheet of paper was easily obtained in the office, and the passport forged. After long waiting, he procured a Siberian wig—that is, a sheepskin with the wool turned in, to preserve the head from the cold—three shirts, a sheepskin bournouse, and a red velvet cap bordered with fur—the dress of a well-to-do peasant. On a sharp frosty night he quitted Ekaterinski for Tara, having determined to try the road to the north for Archangel, as the least frequented. A large fair was shortly to be held at Irbit, at the foot of the Urals, and he hoped to hide himself in the vast crowd of people that frequented it. Soon after he had crossed the river a sledge was heard behind him. He trembled for his safety—his pursuers were perhaps coming.

"Where are you going?" shouted the peasant who drove it.

"To Tara."

"Give me ten sous, and I will take you."

"No; it is too much. I will give eight."

"Well, so let it be. Jump in quickly."

He was set down in the street; and knocking at a house, inquired in the Russian fashion—"Have you horses to hire?"

"Yes—a pair. Where to?"

"To Irbit. I am a commercial traveler, and going to meet my master. I am behind my time, and wish to go as quickly as possible."

No sooner had they set off than a snow-storm came on, and the driver lost his way. They wandered about all night in the forest, and it was impossible to describe the anguish and suffering Piotrowski endured.

"Return to Tara," said he, as the day broke; "I will engage another sledge; and you need not expect any money from me, after the folly you have shown in losing your way."

They turned, but had hardly gone a mile before the driver jumped up, looked around, and cried—"This is our road." Then making up for lost time, he set him down at a friend's house, where he procured some tea and fresh horses. On he went in safety, renewing his horses at small expense, until late at night, when he suffered from a most unfortunate robbery. He had not money at hand to pay the conductor. They turned into a public-house, where a crowd of drunken people were celebrating the carnival. He drew out some paper-money to get change, when the crowd coming round, some one seized his papers, among which were several rouble notes, his invaluable passport, and a note in which he had minutely inscribed all the towns and villages he must pass through on the road to Archangel. He was in despair. The very first day, a quarter of his money was gone, and the only thing by which he hoped to evade suspicion, his passport. He dare not appeal to the police, and was obliged to submit.

Regret and hesitation were not to be thought of. He soon found himself on the high-road to Irbit, crowded with an innumerable mass of sledges, going or returning to the fair. It is the season of gain and good humor, and the people show it by unbounded gaiety. Piotrowski took courage, returned the salutations of the passers-by—for how could he be distinguished in such a crowd? The gates of Irbit were reached on the third day. "Halt, and shew your passport," cried an official; but added in a whisper—"Give me twenty copecks, and pass quickly." The demand was willingly gratified, and with some difficulty he procured a night's lodging, lying on the floor amidst a crowd of peasants, who had previously supped on radish-soup, dried fish, oatmeal gruel, with oil and pickled cabbage.

Up at daybreak, he took care to make the orthodox salutations, and passing rapidly through the crowded town, he walked out of the opposite gate, for, henceforwards, his scanty funds demanded that the journey should be made on foot. In the midst of a heavily falling snow, he managed to keep the track, avoiding the villages, and, when hungry, drawing a piece of frozen bread from his bag. At nightfall, he buried himself in the forest, hollowed a deep hole in the snow, and found a hard but warm bed, where he gained the repose he so greatly needed. Another hard day, with a dry cutting wind, forced him to ask for shelter at night in a cottage, which was granted without hesitation. He described himself as a workman, going to the iron-foundries at Bohotole, on the Ural Mountains. Whilst the supper was preparing, he dried his clothes, and stretched himself on a bench with inexpressible satisfaction. He fancied he had neglected no precautions; his prayers and salutations had been made; and yet suspicion was awakened, as it appeared, by the sight of his three shirts, which no peasant possesses. Three men entered, and roughly shook him from sleep, demanding his passport.

"By what right do you ask for it? Are you police?"

"No; but we are inhabitants of the village."

"And can you enter houses, and ask for passports! Who can say whether you do not mean to rob me of my papers? But my answer is ready. I am Lavrenti Kouzmine, going to Bohotole; and it is not the first time I have passed through the country."

He then entered into details of the road and the fair at Irbit, ending by showing his permission to pass, which, as it bore a stamp, satisfied these ignorant men.

"Forgive us," said they. "We thought you were an escaped convict; some of them pass this way."

Henceforward, he dared not seek the shelter of a house. From the middle of February to the beginning of April, in the midst of one of the severest winters ever known, his couch was in the snow. Frozen bread was his food for days together, and the absence of warm aliments brought him face to face with the terrible spectres of cold and hunger. The Urals were reached, and he began to climb their wooded heights. On passing through a little village at nightfall, a voice cried: "Who is there?"

"A traveler."

"Well, would you like to come and sleep here?"

"May God recompense you, yes; if it will not inconvenience you."

An aged couple lived there—good people, who prepared a meagre repast, which seemed a feast to Piotrowski: the greatest comfort of all being that he could take off his clothes.

SIBERIAN EXILES.

They gave him his breakfast, and would not accept any remuneration but his warm and cordial thanks.

One evening Piotrowski's life was nearly extinct. The way was lost, the hail pierced his skin, his supply of bread was exhausted, and after vainly dragging his weary limbs, he fell into a kind of torpor. A loud voice roused him—"What are you doing here?"

"I am making a pilgrimage to the monastery of Solovetsk, but the storm prevented my seeing the track, and I have not eaten for several days."

"It is not surprising. We who live on the spot often wander away. There, drink that."

The speaker gave him a bottle containing some brandy, which burned him so fearfully, that in his pain he danced about.

"Now try to calm yourself," said the good Samaritan, giving him some bread and dried fish, which Piotrowski ate ravenously, saying—"I thank you with all my heart. May God bless you for your goodness."

"Ah, well, do not say so much; we are both Christians. Now, try to walk a little."

He was a trapper; and led him into the right path, pointing out a village inn where he could get rest and refreshment. Piotrowski managed to crawl to the place, and then fainted away. When he recovered himself, he asked for radish-soup, but could not swallow it; and toward noon he fell asleep on the bench, never awaking until the same time on the next day, when the host roused him. Sleep, rest, and warmth restored him, and he again started on his long pilgrimage.

The town of Veliki-Ustiug was reached, where he determined to change his character and become a pilgrim, going to pray to the holy images of Solovetsk, on the White Sea. There are four of these holy places to which pious Russians resort, and everywhere the wayfarers are well received, hospitality and alms being freely dispensed to those who are going to pray for the peace of the donor. Passports are not rigorously exacted, and he hoped to join himself to a company, trusting to be less marked than if alone. As he was standing irresolute in the market-place, a young man accosted him, and finding that they were bound to the same place, invited him to join their party. There were about twenty; but no less than two thousand were in the city on their way, waiting until the thaw should have opened the Dwina for the rafts and boats which would transport them to Archangel, and then to Solovetsk. It was a scene for Chaucer: the half-idiot, who sought to be a saint; the knave who played upon the charity of others; and the astute hypocrite. The rafts are loaded with corn, and the pilgrims receive a free passage; or a small sum of money is given them if they consent to row; from forty to sixty sailors being required for each, the oars consisting of a thin fir-tree. Piotrowski was only too happy to increase his small store of money by working. At the break of day, before starting, the captain cried —"Seat yourselves, and pray to God." Every one squatted down like a Mussulman for a moment, then rose and made a number of salutations and crossings; and next, down to the poorest, each threw a small piece of money into the river to secure a propitious voyage.

Fifteen days passed, during which Piotrowski learned to be an expert oarsman. Then the golden spires of Archangel rose before them; a cry of joy was uttered by all; and the rowers broke off the lower parts of their oars with a frightful crash, according to the universal custom. It was a heartfelt prayer of gratitude that Piotrowski raised to God for having brought him thus far in safety. How pleasant was the sight of the ships, with their flags of a thousand colors, after the snow and eternal forests of the Urals! But there was again disappointment. He wandered along the piers, but could not find a single vessel bound for France or Germany, and not daring to enter the cafés, where perhaps the captains might have been, he left Archangel in sadness, determined to skirt the coast towards Onega. He would thus pass the celebrated monastery without the necessity of stopping, and pretend that he was proceeding to Novgorod and Moscow on the same pious pilgrimage.

Through marshes and blighted fir-plantations the weary wayfarer sped, the White Sea rising frequently into storms of the utmost grandeur; but the season was lovely, and the sun warm, so that camping out offered less hardship. The wolves howled around him, but happily he never saw them. Many soldiers, who were Poles, were established at different points to take charge of the canals.

Having reached Vytegra, he was accosted on the shore by a peasant, who asked where he was going. On hearing his story, he said—"You are the man I want. I am going to St. Petersburg. My boat is small, and you can assist me to row."

The crafty fellow evidently intended to profit by the pilgrim's arms without wages; but, after long debate, he agreed to supply Piotrowski with food during the transport. It seemed strange, indeed, to go to the capital—like running into the jaws of the lion—but he seized every occasion to pass on, lest his papers should be asked for. As they coasted down through Lake Ladoga and the Neva, they took in some women as passengers, who were servants, and had been home to see their parents. One of them, an aged washerwoman, was so teased by the others, that Piotrowski took her part, and in return she offered him some very useful assistance.

"My daughter," she said, "will come to meet me, and she will find you a suitable lodging."

It will be guessed with what joy he accepted the proposal; and during all the time spent in the boat, no one came to ask for passports. The house she took him to was sufficiently miserable; as the Russians say, "It was the bare ground, with the wrist for a pillow." He asked his hostess if he must see the police to arrange the business of his passport.

"No," she said. "If you only stay a few days, it is useless. They have become so exacting, that they would require me to accompany you, and my time is too precious."

As he passed along the quays, looking for a ship, his eyes

rested on one to sail for Riga on the following morning. He could scarcely master his emotion. The pilot on board called out—"If you want a place to Riga, come here."

"I certainly want one; but I am too poor to sail in a steamer. It would cost too much."

He named a very small sum, and said—"Come; why do you hesitate?"

"I only arrived yesterday, and the police have not *visé* my passport."

"That will occupy three days. Go without a visé. Be here at seven o'clock, and wait for me."

Both were to their time. The sailor said, "Give me some money," and handed him a yellow paper; the clock struck; the barrier was opened, and, like a dream, he was safely on the ocean.

From Riga he went through Courland and Lithuania. The difficulty of crossing the Russian frontier into Prussia was still to be managed. He chose the daytime; and when sentinels had each turned their backs, he jumped over the wall of the first of the three glacis. No noise was heard. The second was tried, and the firing of pistols showed that he was perceived. He rushed on to the third, and, breathless and exhausted, gained a little wood, where for many hours he remained concealed. He was in Prussia. Wandering on through Memel, Tilsit, and Konigsberg, he decided at the last place to take a ship the next morning to Elbing, where he would be near to Posen, and among his compatriots. Sitting down on a heap of stones, he intended taking refuge for the night in a corn-field; but sleep overcame him, and he was rudely awakened in the darkness by a policeman. His stammering and confused replies awakened suspicion, and to his shame and grief, he was carried off to prison. He announced himself as a French cotton-spinner, but returning from Russia, and without a passport. Not a word he said was believed. At length, after a month's detention, weary of being considered a concealed malefactor, he asked to speak to M. Fleury, a French advocate, who assisted at his trial.

To him he confessed the whole truth. Nothing could equal his advocate's consternation and astonishment.

"What a misfortune!" he said. "We must give you up to the Russians; they have just sent many of your countrymen across the frontier. There is but one way. Write to Count Eulenberg; tell your story, and trust to his mercy."

After ten days he received a vague reply, desiring him to have patience. The affair got wind in the town, and a gentleman came to him, asking if he would accept him ás bail. Efforts had been made in his favor, and the police were ready to set him free. M. Kamke, his kind friend, took him home, and entertained him for a week; but an order came from Berlin to send the prisoner back to Russia, and he received warning in time to escape. Letters to various friends on the way were given him, to facilitate his journey; and just four years after he had left Paris he reached it in safety again, after having crossed the Urals, slept for months in the snow, jumped over the Russian frontier in the midst of balls, and passed through so many sufferings and privations.

CHAPTER XXXVIII.

I REMAINED in Irkutsk until snow fell, and the winter roads were suitable for travel. One day the moving portion of the city was on wheels: the next saw it gliding on runners. The little sleighs of the *isvoshchiks* are exactly like those of St. Petersburg and Moscow,—miniature affairs where you sit with your face within six inches of the driver's back, and cannot take a friend at your side without much crowding. They move rapidly, and it is a fortunate provision that they are cheap. In all large cities and towns of Russia many *isvoshchiks* go to spend the winter. With a horse and little sleigh and a cash capital sufficient to buy a license, one of these enterprising fellows will set up in business. Nobody thinks of walking in Moscow or St. Petersburg, unless his journey or his purse is very short. It is said there are thirty thousand sleighs for public hire in St. Petersburg alone, during the winter months, and two-thirds that number in Moscow. The interior towns are equally well supplied in proportion to their population.

One may naturally suppose that accidents are frequent where there are many vehicles and fast driving is the fashion. Accidents are rare from the fact that drivers are under severe penalties if they run over any one. Furthermore the horses are quick and intelligent, and being driven without blinkers, can use their eyes freely. To my mind this plan is better than ours, and most foreigners living in Russia are inclined to adopt it. Considered as an ornament a blinker decorates a horse about as much as an eye shade does a man.

With the first fall of snow, I began preparations for departure. I summoned a tailor and gave orders for a variety of articles in fur and sheep-skin for the road. He measured me for a coat, a cap, a pair of stockings, and a sleigh robe, all in sheep-skin. He then took the size of my ears for a pair of lappets, and proposed fur socks to be worn under the stockings. When the accumulated result of his labors was piled upon the floor of my room, I was alarmed at its size, and wondered if it could ever be packed in a single sleigh. Out of a bit of sable skin a lady acquaintance constructed a mitten for my nose, to be worn when the temperature was lowest. It was not an improvement to one's personal appearance though very conducive to comfort.

To travel by *peraclodnoi* (changing the vehicle at every station) is bad enough in summer but ten times bad in winter. To turn out every two or three hours with the thermometer any distance below zero, and shift baggage and furs from one sleigh to another is an absolute nuisance. Very few persons travel by *peraclodnoi* in winter, and one does not find many sleighs at the post stations from the fact that they are seldom demanded. Nearly all travelers buy their sleighs before starting, and sell them when their journeys are ended.

I surveyed the Irkutsk market and found several sleighs 'up' for sale. Throughout Siberia a sleigh manufactured at Kazan is preferred, it being better made and more commodious than its rivals. My attention was called to several vehicles of local manufacture but my friends advised me not to try them. I sought a *Kazanski kibitka* and with the aid of an intelligent *isvoshchik* succeeded in finding one. Its purchase was accomplished in a manner peculiarly Russian.

The seller was a *mischanin* or Russian merchant of the peasant class. Accompanied by a friend I called at his house and our negotiation began over a lunch and a bottle of nalifka. We said nothing on the subject nearest my heart and his, for at least a half hour, but conversed on general topics. My friend at length dropped a hint that I thought of taking up my residence at Irkutsk. This was received with delight, and a glass of nalifka, supplementary to at least half a dozen glasses I had already swallowed.

"Why don't you come to sleighs at once, and settle the matter?" I asked. "He probably knows what we want, and if we keep on at this rate I shall need a sleigh to go home in."

"Don't be impatient," said my friend; "you don't understand these people; you must angle them gently. When you want to make a trade, begin a long way from it. If you want to buy a horse, pretend that you want to sell a cow, but don't mention the horse at first. If you do you will never succeed."

We hedged very carefully and finally reached *the* subject. This was so overpowering that we took a drink while the merchant ordered the sleigh dragged into the court yard. We had another glass before we adjourned for the inspection, a later one when we returned to the house, and another as soon as we were seated. After this our negotiations proceeded at a fair pace, but there were many vacuums of language that required liquid filling. After endeavoring to lower his price, I closed with him and we clenched the bargain with a drink. Sleighs were in great demand, as many persons were setting out for Russia, and I made sure of my purchase by paying on the spot and taking a glass of nalifka. As a finale to the transaction, he urged me to drink again, begged my photograph, and promised to put an extra something to the sleigh.

The Siberian peasant classes are much like the Chinese in their manner of bargaining. Neither begins at the business itself, but at something entirely different. A great deal of time, tea, and tobacco is consumed before the antagonists are fairly met. When the main subject is reached they gradually approach and conclude the bargain about where both expected and intended. An American would come straight to the point, and dealing with either of the above races his bluntness would endanger the whole affair. In many matters this patient angling is advantageous, and nowhere more so than in diplomacy. Every one will doubtless acknowledge the Russians unsurpassed in diplomatic skill. They possess the faculty of touching gently, and playing with their opponents, to a higher degree than any nation of Western Europe. Other things being equal, this ability will bring success.

There are several descriptions of sleigh for Siberian travel. At the head, stands the *vashok*, a box-like affair with a general resemblance to an American coach on runners. It has a door at each side and glass windows and is long enough for one to lie at full length. Three persons with limited baggage can find plenty of room in a vashok. A *kibitka* is shaped much like a tarantass, or like a New England chaise stretched to about seven feet long by four in width. There is a sort of apron that can be let down from the hood and fastened with straps and buckles to the boot. The boot can be buttoned to the sides of the vehicle and completely encloses the occupants. The vashok is used by families or ladies, but the kibitka is generally preferred by men on account of the ability to open it in fine weather, and close it at night or in storms.

A VASHOK.

A sleigh much like this but less comfortable is called a *povoska*. In either of them the driver sits on the forward part with his feet hanging over the side. His perch is not very secure, and on a rough road he must exercise care to prevent falling off. "Why don't you have a better seat for your driver?" I asked of my friend, when negotiating for a sleigh. "Oh," said he, "this is the best way as he cannot go to sleep. If he had a better place he would sleep and lose time by slow traveling."

A sleigh much used by Russian merchants is shaped like an elongated mill-hopper. It has enormous carrying capacity, and in bad weather can be covered with matting to exclude cold and snow. It is large, heavy, and cumbersome, and adapted to slow travel, and when much luggage is to be carried. All these concerns are on runners about thirty inches apart, and generally shod with iron. On each side there is a fender or outrigger which serves the double purpose of diminishing injury from collisions and preventing the overturn of the sleigh. It is a stout pole attached to the forward end of the sleigh, and sloping downward and outward toward the rear where it is two feet from the runner, and held by strong braces. On a level surface it does not touch the snow, but should the sleigh tilt from any cause the outrigger will generally prevent an overturn. In collision with other sleighs, the fender plays an important part. I have been occasionally dashed against sleds and sleighs when the chances of a smash-up appeared brilliant. The fenders met like a pair of fencing foils, and there was no damage beyond the shock of our meeting.

A KIBITKA.

The horses are harnessed in the Russian manner, one being under a yoke in the shafts, and the others, up to five or six, attached outside. There is no seat in the interior of the sleigh. Travelers arrange their baggage and furs to as good a level as possible and fill the crevices with hay or straw. They sit, recline, or lie at their option. Pillows are a necessity of winter travel.

I exchanged my trunk for a chemidan of enormous capacity, and long enough to extend across the bottom of my sleigh. For the first thousand versts, to Krasnoyarsk, I arranged to travel with a young officer of engineers whose baggage consisted of two or three hundred pounds of geological specimens. For provisions we ordered beef, cabbage soup, little cakes like 'mince turnovers,' and a few other articles. Tea and sugar were indispensable, and had a prominent place. Our soups, meat, pies, *et cetera* were frozen and only needed thawing at the stations to be ready for use.

The day before my departure was the peculiar property of Saint Inakentief, the only saint who belongs especially to Siberia. Everybody kept the occasion in full earnest, the services commencing the previous evening when nearly everybody got drunk. I had a variety of preparations in the shape of mending, making bags, tying up bundles and the like, but though I offered liberal compensation neither man-servant nor maid-servant would lend assistance. Labor was not to be had on any terms, and I was obliged to do my own packing. There are certain saints' days in the year when a Russian peasant will no more work than would a Puritan on Sunday. All who could do so on the day above mentioned visited the church four miles from Irkutsk, where Saint Inakentief lies buried.

I occupied the fashionable hours of the two days before my departure in making farewell visits according to Russian etiquette. Not satisfied with their previous courtesy my friends arranged a dinner at the club rooms for the last evening of my stay at Irkutsk. The other public dinners were of a masculine character, but the farewell entertainment possessed the charm of the presence of fifteen or twenty ladies. General Shelashnikoff, Governor of Irkutsk, and acting Governor General during the absence of General Korsackoff, presided at the table. We dined directly before the portraits of the last and present emperors of Russia, and as I looked at the likeness of Nicholas I thought I had never seen it half as amiable.

After the dinner the tables disappeared with magical rapidity and a dance began. While I was talking in a corner behind a table, a large album containing views of Irkutsk was presented to me as a souvenir of my visit. The *golovah* was prominent in the presentation, and when it was ended he urged me to be his *vis a vis* in a quadrille. Had he asked me to walk a tight rope or interpret a passage of Sanscrit, I should have been about as able to comply. My education in 'the light fantastic' has been extremely limited, and my acquaintances will testify that nature has not adapted me to achievements in the Terpsichorean art.

I resisted all entreaties to join the dance up to that evening. I urged that I never attempted it a dozen times in my life, and not at all within ten years. The golovah declared he had not danced in twenty-five years, and knew as little of the art as I did. There was no more to be said. I resigned myself to the pleasures awaiting me, and ventured on the floor very much as an elephant goes on a newly frozen mill-pond. Personal diffidence and a regard for truth forbid a laudatory account of my success. I did walk through a quadrille, but when it came to the Mazurka I was as much out of place as a blind man in a picture gallery.

My arrangement to travel with the geologic officer and his heavy baggage fell through an hour before our starting time. A new plan was organized and included my taking Captain Paul in my sleigh to Krasnoyarsk. Two ladies of our acquaintance were going thither, and I gladly waited a few hours for the pleasure of their company. When my preparations were completed, I drove to the house of Madame Rodstvenny whence we were to set out. The madame and her daughter were to travel in a large kibitka, and had bestowed two servants with much baggage and provisions in a vashok. With our three vehicles we made a dignified procession.

We dined at three o'clock, and were ready to start an hour later. Just before leaving the house all were seated around the principal room, and for a minute there was perfect silence. On rising all who professed the religion of the Greek Church bowed to the holy picture and made the sign of the cross. This custom prevails throughout Russia, and is never omitted when a journey is to be commenced.

There was a gay party to conduct us to the first station,

conveniently situated only eight miles away. At the ferry we found the largest assemblage I saw in Irkutsk, not excepting the crowd at the fire. The ferry boat was on the other side of the river, and as I glanced across I saw something that caused me to look more intently. It was a little past sunset, and the gathering night showed somewhat indistinctly the American and Russian flags floating side by side on the boat. My national colors were in the majority.

The scene was rendered more picturesque by a profusion of Chinese lanterns lighting every part of the boat. The golovah stood at my side to enjoy my astonishment. It was to his kindness and attention that this farewell courtesy was due. He had the honor of unfurling the first American flag that ever floated over the Angara—and his little surprise raised a goodly sized lump in the throat of his guest.

FAREWELL TO IRKUTSK.

Our party was so large that the boat made two journeys to ferry us over the water. I remained till the last, and on the bank of the river bade adieu to Irkutsk and its hospitable citizens. I may not visit them again, but I can never forget the open hearted kindness I enjoyed. The Siberians have a climate of great severity, but its frosts and snows have not been able to chill the spirit of genuine courtesy, as every traveler in that region can testify. Hospitality is a custom of the country, and all the more pleasing because heartily and cheerfully bestowed.

The shades of night were falling fast as I climbed the river bank, and began my sleigh ride toward the west. The arched gateway at Irkutsk close by the ferry landing, is called the Moscow entrance, and is said to face directly toward the ancient capital. As I reached the road, I shouted "*poshol*," to the yemshick, and we dashed off in fine style. At the church or monastery six versts away, I overtook our party. The ladies were in the chapel offering their prayers for a prosperous journey. When they emerged we were ready to go forward over a road not remarkable for its smoothness.

At the first station our friends joined us in taking tea. Cups, glasses, cakes, champagne bottles, cakes and cold meats, crept somehow from mysterious corners in our vehicles. The station master was evidently accustomed to visits like this, as his rooms were ready for our reception. We were two hours in making our adieus, and consuming the various articles provided for the occasion. There was a general kissing all around at the last moment.

We packed the ladies in their sleigh, and then entered our own. As we left the station our friends joined their voices in a farewell song that rang in our ears till lost in the distance, and drowned by nearer sounds. Our bells jingled merrily in the frosty air as our horses sped rapidly along the road. We closed the front of our sleigh, and settled among our furs and pillows. The night was cold, but in my thick wrappings I enjoyed a tropical warmth and did not heed the low state of the thermometer.

Our road for seventy versts lay along the bank of the Angara. A thick fog filled the valley and seemed to hug close to the river. In the morning every part of our sleigh except at the points of friction, was white with frost. Each little fibre projecting from our cover of canvas and matting became a miniature stalactite, and the head of every nail, bolt, and screw, buried itself beneath a mass like oxydised silver. Everything had seized upon and congealed some of the moisture floating in the atmosphere. Our horses were of the color, or no color, of rabbits in January; it was only by brushing away the frost that the natural tint of their hair could be discovered, and sometimes there was a great deal of frost adhering to them.

During my stay at Irkutsk I noticed the prevalence of this fog or frost cloud. It usually formed during the night and was thickest near the river. In the morning it enveloped the whole city, but when the sun was an hour or two in the heavens, the mist began to melt away. It remained longest over the river, and I was occasionally in a thick cloud on the bank of the Angara when the atmosphere a hundred yards away was perfectly clear. The moisture congealed on every stationary object. Houses and fences were cased in ice, its thickness varying with the condition of the weather. Trees and bushes became masses of crystals, and glistened in the sunlight as if formed of diamonds. I could never wholly rid myself of the impression that some of the trees were fountains caught and frozen when in full action. The frost played curious tricks of artistic skill, and its delineations were sometimes marvels of beauty.

Any one who has visited St. Petersburg in winter remembers the effect of a fog from the Gulf of Finland after a period of severe cold. The red granite columns of St. Isaac's church are apparently transformed into spotless marble by the congelation of moisture on their surface. In the same manner I have seen a gray wall at Irkutsk changed in a night and morning to a dazzling whiteness. The crystalline formation of the frost had all the varieties of the kaleidoscope without its colors.

I slept well during the night, awaking occasionally at the stations or when the sleigh experienced an unusually heavy thump. In the morning I learned we had traveled a hundred and sixty versts from Irkutsk. The road was magnificent after leaving the valley of the Angara, and the sleigh glided easily and with very little jolting.

> "No cloud above, no earth below;
> A universe of sky and snow."

I woke to daylight and found a monotonous country destitute of mountains and possessing few hills. It was generally wooded, and where under cultivation near the villages there was an appearance of fertility. There were long distances between the clusters of houses, and I was continually reminded of the abundant room for increase of population.

We stopped for breakfast soon after sunrise. The samovar was ordered, and our servants brought a creditable supply of toothsome little cakes and pies. These with half a dozen cups of tea to each person prepared us for a ride of several hours. We dined a little before sunset, and for one I can testify that full justice was done to the dinner.

Very little can be had at the stations on this road, so that experienced travelers carry their own provisions. One can always obtain hot water, and generally bread, and eggs, but nothing else is certain. In winter, provisions can be easily carried as the frost preserves them alike from decaying or crushing. Soup, meats, bread, and other edibles can be carried on long routes with perfect facility. There is a favorite preparation for Russian travel under the name of *pilmania.* It is a little ball of minced meat covered with dough, the whole being no larger than a robin's egg. In a frozen state a bag full of pilmania is like the same quantity of walnuts or marbles, and can be tossed about with impunity. When a traveler wishes to dine upon this article he orders a pot of boiling water and tosses a double handful of pilmania into it. After five minutes boiling the mass is ready to be eaten in the form of soup. Salt, pepper, and vinegar can be used with it to one's liking.

Our *diner du voyage* consisted of pilmania, roast beef, and partridge with bread, cakes, tea, and quass. Our table furniture was somewhat limited, and the room was littered with garments temporarily discarded. The ladies were crinoline-less, and their coiffures were decidedly not Parisian. My costume was a cross between a shooting outfit and the every-day dress of a stevedore, while my hair appeared as if recently dressed with a currant bush. Captain Paul was equally unpresentable in fastidious parlors, but whatever our apparel it did not diminish the keenness of our appetites. The dinner was good, and the diners were hungry and happy. Fashion is wholly rejected on the Siberian road, and each one makes his toilet without regard to French principles and tastes.

According to Russian custom somebody was to be thanked for the meal. As the dinner came from the provisions in the servants' sleigh we presented our acknowledgments to Madame Rodstvenny. With the forethought of an experienced traveler the lady had carefully provided her edibles and so abundant was her store that my supply was rarely drawn upon. We were more like a pic-nic party than a company of travelers on a long journey in a Siberian winter. Mademoiselle was fluent in French, and charming in its use. The only drawback to general conversation was my inability to talk long with Madame except by interpretation. In our halts we managed to pass the time in tea-drinking, conversation, and sometimes with music of an impromptu character. I remember favoring an appreciative audience with a solo on a trunk key, followed by mademoiselle and the captain in a duett on a tin cup and a horn comb covered with letter paper.

There was very little scenery worthy of note. The villages generally lay in single streets each containing from ten to a hundred houses. Between these clusters of dwellings there was little to be seen beyond a succession of wooded ridges with stretches of open ground. The continued snow-scape offered no great variety on the first day's travel, and before night I began to think it monotonous. The villages were from ten to twenty miles apart, and very much the same in general characteristics. The stations had a family likeness. Each had a travelers' room more or less comfortable, and a few apartments for the smotretal and his attendants.

The travelers' room had some rough chairs, one or two hard sofas or benches, and the same number of tables. While the horses were being changed we had our option to enter the station or stay out of doors. I generally preferred the latter alternative on account of the high temperature of the waiting rooms, which necessitated casting off one's outer garment on entering. During our halts I was fain to refresh myself with a little leg stretching and found it a great relief.

The first movement at a station is to present the padaroshnia and demand horses. Marco Polo says, that the great Khan of Tartary had posting stations twenty-five miles apart on the principal roads of his empire. A messenger or traveler carried a paper authorizing him to procure horses, and was always promptly supplied. The padaroshnia is of ancient date, if Marco be trustworthy. It is not less important to a Russian traveler at present than to a Tartar one in earlier times. Our documents were efficacious, and usually brought horses with little delay. The size of our party was a disadvantage as we occasionally found one or two sets of horses ready but were obliged to wait a short time for a third. Paul had a permit to impress horses in the villages while I carried a special passport requesting the authorities to 'lend me all needed assistance.' This was generally construed into despatching me promptly, and we rarely failed with a little persuasion and money, to secure horses for the third sleigh.

When we entered the stations for any purpose the sleighs and their contents remained unguarded in the streets, but we never lost anything by theft. With recollections of my experience at stage stations in America, I never felt quite at ease at leaving our property to care for itself. My companions assured me that thefts from posting vehicles seldom occur although the country numbers many convicts among its inhabitants. The native Siberians have a reputation for honesty, and the majority of the exiles for minor offences lead correct lives. I presume that wickedly inclined persons in villages are deterred from stealing on account of the probability of detection and punishment. So far as my experience goes the inhabitants of Siberia are more honest that those of European Russia. In Siberia our sleighs required no watching when we left them. After passing the Ural mountains it was necessary to hire a man to look after our property when we breakfasted and dined.

The horses being the property of the station we paid for them at every change. On no account was the *navodku* or drink-money to the driver forgotten, and it varied according to the service rendered. If the driver did well but made no special exertion we gave him eight or ten copecks, and increased the amount as we thought he deserved. On the other hand if he was obstinate and unaccommodating he obtained nothing. If he argued that the regulations required only a certain speed we retorted that the regulations said nothing about drink-money. In general we found the yemshicks obliging and fully entitled to their gratuities. We went at breakneck pace where the roads permitted, and frequently where they did not. A travelers' speed depends considerably on the drink-money he is reported to have given on the previous stage. If illiberal to a good driver or liberal to a bad one he cannot expect rapid progress.

The regulations require a speed of ten versts (6 2-3 miles) per hour for vehicles not on government service. If the roads are bad the driver can lessen his pace, but he must make all proper exertion to keep up to the schedule. When they are good and the driver is thirsty (as he generally is), the regulations are not heeded. We arranged for my sleigh to lead, and that of the servants to bring up the rear. Whatever speed we went the others were morally certain to follow, and our progress was frequently exciting. Money was potent, and we employed it. Fifteen copecks was a liberal gratuity, and twenty bordered on the munificent. When we increased our offer to twenty-five or thirty it was pretty certain to awaken enthusiasm. Sometimes the pecuniary argument failed, and obliged us to proceed at the legal rate. In such cases we generally turned aside and placed the ladies in advance.

We made twelve, fourteen, or sixteen versts per hour, and

on one occasion I held my watch, and found that we traveled a trifle less than twenty-two versts or about fourteen and a half miles in sixty minutes. I do not think I ever rode in America at such a pace (without steam) except once when a horse ran away with me. Ordinarily we traveled faster than the rate prescribed by regulation, and only when the roads were bad did we fall below it. We studied the matter of drink-money till it became an exact science.

About noon on the first day from Irkutsk we took a yemshick who proved sullen in the highest degree. The country was gently undulating, and the road superb but our promises of navodku were of no avail. We offered and entreated in vain. As a last resort we shouted in French to the ladies and suggested that they take the lead. Our yemshick ordered his comrade to keep his place, and refused to turn aside to allow him to pass. He even slackened his speed and drew his horses to a walk. Our stout-armed *garcon* took a position on our sleigh, and by a fistic argument succeeded in turning us aside. We made only fair progress, and were glad when the drive was ended.

When we began our rapid traveling, I had fears that the sleigh would go to pieces in consequence, but was soon convinced that everything was lovely. The sport was exciting, and greatly relieved the monotony of travel. We were so protected by furs, pillows, blankets, and hay, that our jolting and bounding had no serious result. The ladies enjoyed it as much as ourselves, and were not at all inconvenienced by any ordinary shaking. Once at the end of a furious ride of twenty versts, I found the madame asleep and learned that she had been so since leaving the last station.

I have ridden much in American stage coaches, and witnessed some fine driving in the west and in California. But for rapidity and dash, commend me always to the Siberian yemshicks.

CHAPTER XXXIX.

ON the second morning we stopped at Tulemsk to deliver several boxes that encumbered the sleighs. The servants have a way of putting small articles, and sometimes large ones, in the forward end of the vehicle. They are no special annoyance to a person of short stature, but in my own case I was not reconciled to the practice. A Russian sleigh is shaped somewhat like a laundry smoothing-iron, much narrower forward than aft, so that a traveler does not usually find the space beneath the driver a world too wide for his shrunk shanks.

We thawed out over a steaming samovar with plenty of hot tea. The lady of the house brought a bottle of nalifka of such curious though agreeable flavor that I asked of what fruit it was made. "Nothing but orange peel," was the reply. Every Siberian housewife considers it her duty to prepare a goodly supply of nalifka during the autumn. A glass jar holding two or three gallons is filled to the neck with any kind of fruit or berries, currants and gooseberries being oftenest used. The jar is then filled with native whisky, and placed in a southern window where it is exposed to the sunlight and the heat of the room for ten days. The whisky is then poured off, mixed with an equal quantity of water, placed in a kettle with a pound of sugar to each gallon, and boiled for a few minutes. When cooled and strained it is bottled and goes to the cellar. Many Siberians prefer nalifka to foreign wines, and a former governor-general attempted to make it fashionable. He eschewed imported wine and substituted nalifka, but his example was not imitated to the extent he desired.

Our halt consumed three or four hours. After we started an unfortunate pig was found entangled in the framework of my sleigh, and before we could let him out he was pretty well bruised and skaken up. How he came there we were puzzled to know, but I do not believe he ever willingly troubled a sleigh again.

We encountered many caravans of sleds laden with merchandise. They were made up much like the trains I described between Kiachta and Lake Baikal, there being four or five sleds to each man. The horses generally guided themselves, and followed their leaders with great fidelity. While we were stopping to make some repairs near the foot of a hill, I was interested in the display of equine intelligence. As a caravan reached the top of the hill each horse stopped till the one preceding him had descended. Holding back as if restrained by reins he walked half down the descent, and then finished the hill and crossed the hollow below it at a trot. One after another passed in this manner without guidance, exactly as if controlled by a driver.

I noticed that the horses were quite skillful in selecting the best parts of the road. I have occasionally seen a horse pause when there were three or four tracks through the snow, and make his choice with apparent deliberation. I recollect a school boy composition that declared in its first sentence, 'the horse is a noble animal,' but I never knew until I traveled in Siberia how much he is entitled to a patent of nobility.

In the daytime we had little trouble with these caravans, as they generally gave us the road on hearing our bells. If the way was wide the horses usually turned aside of their own accord; where it was narrow they were unwilling to step in the snow, and did not until directed by their drivers. If the latter were dilatory our yemshicks turned aside and revenged themselves by lashing some of the sled horses and all the drivers they could reach. In the night we found more difficulty as the caravan horses desired to keep the road, and their drivers were generally asleep. We were bumped against innumerable sleds in the hours of darkness. The outriggers alone prevented our sleighs going to pieces. The trains going eastward carried assorted cargoes of merchandise for Siberia and China. Those traveling westward were generally loaded with tea in chests, covered with cowhide. The amount of traffic over the principal road through Siberia is very large.

When we halted for dinner I brought a bottle of champagne from my sleigh. It was the best of the 'Cliquot' brand and frozen as solid as a block of ice. It stood half an hour in a warm room before thawing enough to drip slowly into our glasses and was the most perfect *champagne frappé* I ever saw. A bottle of cognac was a great deal colder than ordinary ice, and when we brought it into the station the moisture in the warm room congealed upon it to the thickness of card-board. After this display I doubted the existance of latent heat in alcohol.

Just as we finished dinner the post with five vehicles was announced. We hastened to put on our furs and sprang into the sleighs with the least possible delay. There was no fear that we should lose the first and second set of horses, but the last one might be taken for the post as the ladies had only a third-class padaroshnia. The yemshicks were as anxious to escape as ourselves, as the business of carrying the mail does not produce návodka. The post between Irkutsk and Krasnoyarsk passes twice a week each way, and we frequently encountered it. Where it had just passed a station there was occasionally a scarcity of horses that delayed us till village teams were brought.

A postillion accompanies each convoy, and is responsible for its security. Travelers sometimes purchase tickets and have their vehicles accompany the post, but in so doing their patience is pretty severely taxed. The postillion is a soldier or other government employé, and must be armed to repel robbers. One of these conductors was a boy of fourteen who appeared under heavy responsibility. I watched him loading a pistol at a station and was amused at his ostentatious manner. When the operation was completed he fixed the weapon in his belt and swaggered out with the air of the heavy tragedian at the Old Bowery. Another postillion stuck around with pistols and knives looked like a military museum on its travels.

THE CONDUCTOR.

From our dining station we left the main road, and traveled several versts along the frozen surface of the Birusa river. The snow lay in ridges, and as we drove rapidly over them we were tossed like a yawl in a hopping sea. It was a foretaste of what was in store for me at later periods of my journey. The Birusa is rich in gold deposits, and the government formerly maintained extensive mining establishments in its valley.

About nine o'clock in the evening we voted to take tea. On entering the station I found the floor covered with a dormant mass, exhaling an odor not altogether spicy. I bumped my head against a sort of wide shelf suspended eighteen or twenty inches from the ceiling, and sustaining several sleepers.

"Here" said Paul, "is another *chambre á coucher*" as he attempted to pull aside a curtain at the top of the brick stove. A female head and shoulders were exposed for an instant, until a stout hand grasped and retained the curtain. The suspended shelf or false ceiling is quite common in the peasant houses, and especially at the stations. The yemshicks and other attaches of the concern are lodged here and on the floor, beds being a luxury they rarely obtain. Frequently a small house would be as densely packed as the steerage of a passenger ship, and I never desired to linger in these crowded apartments. A Russian house has little or no ventilation, and the effect of a score of sleepers on the air of a room is 'better imagined than described.'

On the road west of Irkutsk the rules require each smotretal to keep ten teams or thirty horses, ready for use. Many of them have more than that number, and the villages can supply any ordinary demand after the regular force is exhausted. Fourteen yemshicks are kept at every station, and always ready for service. They are boarded at the expense of the smotretal, and receive about five roubles each per month, with as much drink-money as they can obtain. Frequently they make two journeys a day to the next station, returning without loads. They appeared on the most amiable terms with each other, and I saw no quarreling over their work.

On our first and second nights from Irkutsk the weather was cold, the thermometer standing at fifteen or twenty degrees below zero. On the third day the temperature rose quite rapidly, and by noon it was just below the freezing point. Our furs designed for cold weather became uncomfortably warm, and I threw off my outer garments and rode in my sheepskin coat. In the evening we experienced a feeling of suffocation on closing the sleigh, and were glad to open it again. We rode all night with the wind beating pleasantly against our faces, and from time to time lost our consciousness in sleep. For nearly two days the warm weather continued, and subjected us to inconveniences. We did not travel as rapidly as in the colder days, the road being less favorable, and the horses diminishing their energy with the increased warmth. Some of our provisions were in danger of spoiling as they were designed for transportation only in a frozen state.

Between Nijne Udinsk and Kansk the snow was scanty, and the road occasionally bad. The country preserved its slightly undulating character, and presented no features of interest. Where we found sufficient snow we proceeded rapidly, sometimes leaving the summer road and taking to the open ground, and forests on either side. We pitched into a great many *oukhabas*, analagous to American "hog wallows" or "cradle holes." To dash into one of these at full speed gives a shock like a boat's thumping on the shore. It is only

JUMPING CRADLE HOLES.

with pillows, furs, and hay that a traveler can escape contusions. In mild doses *oukhabas* are an excellent tonic, but the traveler who takes them in excess may easily imagine himself enjoying a field-day at Donnybrook Fair.

An hour before reaching Kansk one of our horses fell dead and brought us to a sudden halt. The yemshick tried various expedients to discover signs of life but to no purpose. Paul and I formed a board of survey, and sat upon the beast; the other sleighs passed us during our consultation, and were very soon out of sight. When satisfied that the animal, as a horse, was of no further use, the yemshick pulled him to the roadside, stripped off his harness, and proceeded with our reduced team. I asked who was responsible for the loss, and was told it was no affair of ours. The government pays for horses killed in the service of couriers, as these gentlemen compel very high speed. On a second or third rate padaroshnian the death of a horse is the loss of its owner. Horses are not expensive in this region, an ordinary roadster being worth from fifteen to twenty roubles.

Within a mile of Kansk the road was bare of snow, and as we had but two horses to our sleigh I proposed walking into town. We passed a long train of sleds on their way to market with loads of wood and hay. Tea was ready for us when we arrived at the station, and we were equally ready for it. After my fifth cup I walked through the public square as it was market day, and the people were in the midst of traffic. Fish, meat, hay, wood, and a great quantity of miscellaneous articles were offered for sale. In general terms the market was a sort of pocket edition of the one at Irkutsk. I practiced my knowledge of Russian in purchasing a quantity of rope to use in case of accidents. Foreigners were not often seen there if I may judge of the curiosity with which I was regarded.

Kansk is a town of about three thousand inhabitants, and stands on the Kan, a tributary of the Yenesei. We were told there was little snow to the first station, and were advised to take five horses to each sleigh. We found the road a combination of thin snow and bare ground, the latter predominating. We proceeded very well, the yemshicks maintaining sublime indifference to the character of the track. They plied their whips vigorously in the probable expectation of drink-money. The one on my sleigh regaled us with an account of the perfectly awful condition of the road to Krasnoyarsk.

About sunset we changed horses, thirty versts from Kansk, and found no cheering prospect ahead. We drowned our sorrows in the flowing tea-cup, and fortified ourselves with a large amount of heat. Tea was the sovereign remedy for all our ills, and we used it most liberally. We set out with misgivings and promised liberal rewards to the yemshicks, if they took us well and safely. The road was undeniably bad, with here and there a redeeming streak of goodness. Notwithstanding the jolts I slept pretty well during the night. In the morning we took tea fifty versts from Krasnoyarsk, and learned there was absolutely no snow for the last thirty versts before reaching the city. There was fortunately a good snow road to the intervening village where we must change to wheels. Curiously enough the snow extended up to the very door of the last station, and utterly disappeared three feet beyond. Looking one way we saw bare earth, while in the other direction there was a good road for sleighing.

At this point we arranged our programme over the inevitable cakes and tea. The ladies were to leave their vashok until their return to Irkutsk ten or twelve days later. The remaining sleighs were unladen and mounted upon wheels. We piled our baggage into telyagas with the exception of a few articles that remained in the sleighs. The ladies with their maid took one wagon, while Paul and myself rode in another, the man servant conveying the sleighs. The whole arrangement was promptly effected; the villagers scented a job on our arrival, and were ready for proposals. My sleigh was lifted and fastened into a wagon about as quickly as a hackman would arrange a trunk. *Place aux dames toujours.* We sent away the ladies half an hour in advance of the rest of the party.

Our telyaga was a rickety affair, not half so roomy as the sleigh, but as the ride was short the discomfort was of little consequence. We had four ill conditioned steeds, but before we had gone twenty rods one of the brutes persistently faced about and attempted to come inside the vehicle, though he did not succeed. After vain efforts to set him right, the yemshick turned him loose, and he bolted homeward contentedly.

We climbed and descended a long hill near the village, and then found a level country quite free from snow, and furnishing a fine road. I was told that very little snow falls within twenty miles of Krasnoyarsk, and that it is generally necessary to use wheels there in the winter months. The reason was not explained to me, but probably the general configuration of the country is much like that near Chetah. Krasnoyarsk lies on the Yenesei which has a northerly course into the Arctic Ocean. The mountains bounding the valley are not lofty, but sufficiently high to wring the moisture from the snow clouds. Both above and below Krasnoyarsk, there is but little snow even in severe seasons.

Our animals were superbly atrocious, and made good speed only on descending grades. We were four hours going thirty versts, and for three-fourths that distance our route was equal to the Bloomingdale Road. Occasionally we saw farm houses with a dejected appearance as if the winter had come upon them unawares. From the quantity of ground enclosed by fences I judged the land was fertile, and well cultivated.

Toward sunset we saw the domes of Krasnoyarsk rising beyond the frozen Yenesei. We crossed the river on the ice, and passed near several women engaged in rinsing clothes.

A laundress does her washing at the house, but rinses her linen at the river. In summer this may be well enough, but it seemed to me that the winter exercise of standing in a keen wind with the thermometer below zero, and rinsing clothes in a hole cut through the ice was anything but agreeable. It was a cold day, and I was well wrapped in furs, but these women were in ordinary clothing, and some had bare legs. They stood at the edges of circular holes in the ice, and after 'swashing' the linen a short time in the water, wrung it with their purple hands. How they escaped frost bites I cannot imagine

The Yenesei is a magnificent river, one of the largest in Siberia. It is difficult to estimate with accuracy any distance upon ice, and I may be far from correct in considering the Yenesei a thousand yards wide at Krasnoyarsk. The telegraph wires are supported on tall masts as at the crossing of the Missouri near Kansas City. In summer there are two steamboats navigating the river from Yeneseiek to the Arctic Ocean. Rapids and shoals below Krasnoyarsk prevent their ascending to the latter town. The tributaries of the Yenesei are quite rich in gold deposits, and support a mining business of considerable extent.

Krasnoyarsk derives its name from the red hills in its vicinity, and the color of the soil where it stands. It is on the left bank of the Yenesei, and has about ten thousand inhabitants.

It was nearly night when we climbed the sloping road in the hillside, and reached the level of the plateau. The ladies insisted that we should occupy their house during our stay, and utterly forbade our going to the hotel. While walking up the hill the captain hailed a washerwoman, and asked for the residence of Madame Rodstvenny. Her reply was so voluminous, and so rapidly given that my friend was utterly bewildered, and comprehended nothing. To his astonishment I told him that I understood the direction.

"*C'est impossible*," he declared.

"By no means," I replied. "The madame lives in a stone house to the left of the gastinni dvor. The washerwoman said so."

Following my advice we found the house. As we entered the courtyard, the captain begged to know by what possibility I understood in his own language what he could not.

I explained that while the woman spoke so glibly I caught the words "*doma, kamen, na leva, gastinni dvor.*" I understood only the essential part of her instruction, and was not confused by the rest.

I was somewhat reluctant to convert a private house into a hotel as I expected to remain four or five days. But Siberian hospitality does not stop at trifles, and my objections were promptly overruled. After toilet and dinner, Paul and I were parboiled in the bath house of the establishment. An able-bodied moujik scrubbed me so thoroughly as to suggest the possibility of removing the cuticle.

In the morning I went to the bank to change some large bills into one-rouble notes for use on the road. Horses must be paid for at every station, and it is therefore desirable to carry the smallest notes with abundance of silver and copper to make change. The bank was much like institutions of its class elsewhere, and transacted my business promptly. The banks in Siberia are branches of the Imperial Bank at St. Petersburg. They receive deposits, and negotiate exchanges and remittances just like private banks, but do not undertake risky business. The officers are servants of the government, and receive their instructions from the parent bank.

My finances arranged, I went to the telegraph office to send a message to a friend. My despatch was written in Russian, and I paid for message and response. A receipt was given me stating the day, hour, and minute of filing the despatch, its destination, address, length, and amount paid. When I received the response I found a statement of the exact time it was filed for transmission, and also of its reception at Krasnoyarsk. This is the ordinary routine of the Russian telegraph system. I commend it to the notice of interested persons in America.

There is no free telegraphing on the government lines, every despatch over the wires being paid for by somebody. If on government business the sender pays the regular tariff and is reimbursed from the treasury. I was told that the officers of the telegraph paid for their own family messages, but had the privilege of conversing on the lines free of charge. High position does not confer immunity. When the Czarevitch was married, General Korsackoff sent his congratulations by telegraph, and received a response from the Emperor. Both messages were paid for by the sender without reduction or trust.

I found the general features of Krasnoyarsk much like those of Irkutsk. Official and civilian inhabitants dressed, lived, walked, breathed, drank, and gambled like their kindred nearer the east. It happened to be market day, and the public square was densely crowded. I was interested in observing the character and abundance of the fish offered for sale. Among those with a familiar appearance were the sturgeon, perch, and pike, and a small fish resembling our alewife. There was a fish unknown to me, with a long snout like a duck's bill, and a body on the extreme clipper model. All these fish are from the Yenesei, some dwelling there permanently while others ascend annually from the Arctic Ocean. All in the market were frozen solid, and the larger ones were piled up like cord-wood.

From the bank overlooking the river there is a fine view of the valley of the Yenesei. There are several islands in the vicinity, and I was told that in the season of floods the stream has a very swift current. It is no easy work to ferry across it, and the boats generally descend a mile or two while paddling over. A few years ago a resident of Krasnoyarsk made a remarkable voyage on this river. He had been attending a wedding several miles away on the other bank, and started to return late at night so as to reach the ferry about daybreak. His equipage was a wooden telyaga drawn by two powerful horses. Having partaken of the cup that inebriates, the man fell asleep and allowed his horses to take their own course. Knowing the way perfectly they came without accident to the ferry landing, their owner still wrapped in his drunken slumber.

VALLEY OF THE YENESEI.

The boat was on the other side, and the horses, no doubt hungry and impatient, plunged in to swim across. The telyaga filled with water, but had sufficient buoyancy not to sink. The cold bath waked and sobered the involuntary voyager when about half way over the river. He had the good sense, aided by fright, to remain perfectly still, and was landed in safety. Those who saw him coming in the early dawn were struck with astonishment, and one, at least, imagined that he beheld Neptune in his marine chariot breasting the waters of the Yenesei.

My informant vouched for the correctness of the story, and gave it as an illustration of the courage and endurance of Siberian horses. According to the statement of the condition of the river, the beasts could have as easily crossed the Mississippi at Memphis in an ordinary stage of water.

Wolves are abundant in the valley of the Yenesei, though they are not generally dangerous to men. An officer whom I met there told me they were less troublesome than in Poland, and he related his experience with them in the latter country while on a visit to the family of a young lady to whom he was betrothed. I give his story as nearly as possible in his own words.

"One day my friend Rasloff proposed a wolf hunt. We selected the best horses from his stable; fine, quick, sure-footed beasts, with a driver who was unsurpassed in all that region for his skill and dash. The sleigh was a large one, and we fitted it with a good supply of robes and straw, and put a healthy young pig in it to serve as a decoy. We each had a gun, and carried a couple of spare guns, with plenty of ammunition, so that we could kill as many wolves as presented themselves.

"Just as we were preparing to start, Christina asked to accompany us. I suggested the coldness of the night, and Rasloff hinted that the sleigh was too small for three. But Christina protested that the air, though sharp, was clear and still, and she could wrap herself warmly; a ride of a few hours would do her more good than harm. The sleigh, she insisted, was a large one, and afforded ample room. 'Besides,' she added, 'I will sit directly behind the driver, and out of your way, and I want to see a wolf-hunt very much indeed.'

"So we consented. Christina arrayed herself in a few moments, and we started on our excursion.

"The servants were instructed to hang out a light in front of the entrance to the courtyard. It was about sunset when we left the chateau and drove out upon the plain, covered here and there with patches of forest. The road we followed was well trodden by the many peasants on their way to the fair at the town, twenty-five miles away. We traveled slowly, not wishing to tire our horses, and, as we left the half dozen villages that clustered around the chateau, we had the road entirely to ourselves. The moon rose soon after sunset, and as it was at the full, it lighted up the plain very clearly, and seemed to stand out quite distinct from the deep blue sky and the bright stars that sparkled everywhere above the horizon. We chatted gayly as we rode along. The time passed so rapidly that I was half surprised when Rasloff told me to get ready to hunt wolves.

"The pig had been lying very comfortably in the bottom of the sleigh, and protested quite loudly as we brought him out. The rope had been made ready before we started from home, and so the most we had to do was to turn the horses around, get our guns ready, and throw the pig upon the ground. He set up a piercing shriek as the rope dragged him along, and completely drowned our voices. Paul had hard work to keep the horses from breaking into a run, but he succeeded, and we maintained a very slow trot. Christina nestled in the place she had agreed to occupy, and Rasloff and I prepared to shoot the wolves.

"We drove thus for fifteen or twenty minutes. The pig gradually became exhausted, and reduced his scream to a sort of moan that was very painful to hear. I began to think we should see no wolves, and return to the chateau without firing our guns, when suddenly a howl came faintly along the air, and in a moment, another and another.

"'There,' said Rasloff; 'there comes our game, and we shall have work enough before long.'

"A few moments later I saw a half dozen dusky forms emerging from the forest to the right and behind us. They seemed like moving spots on the snow, and had it not been for their howling I should have failed to notice them as early as I did. They grew more and more numerous, and, as they gathered behind us, formed a waving line across the road that gradually took the shape of a crescent, with the horns pointing toward our right and left. At first they were timid, and kept a hundred yards or more behind us, but as the hog renewed his scream, they took courage, and approached nearer.

"By the time they were within fifty yards there were two or three hundred of them—possibly half a thousand. I could see every moment that their numbers were increasing, and it was somewhat impatiently that I waited Rasloff's signal to fire. At last he told me to begin, and I fired at the center of the pack. The wolf I struck gave a howl of pain, and his companions, roused by the smell of blood, fell upon and tore him to pieces in a moment. Rasloff fired an instant after me, and then we kept up our firing as fast as possible. As the wolves fell, the others sprung upon them, but the pack was so large that they were not materially detained by stopping to eat up their brethren. They continued the pursuit, and what alarmed me, they came nearer, and showed very little fear of our guns.

"We had taken a large quantity of ammunition—more by half than we thought would possibly be needed—but its quantity diminished so rapidly as to suggest the probability of exhaustion. The pack steadily came nearer. We cut away the pig, but it stopped the pursuit only for a moment. Directly behind us the wolves were not ten yards away; on each side they were no further from the horses, who were snorting with fear, and requiring all the efforts of the driver to hold them. We shot down the beasts as fast as possible, and as I saw our danger I whispered my thoughts to Rasloff.

"He replied to me in Spanish, which Christina did not understand, that the situation was really dangerous, and we must prepare to get out of it. 'I would stay longer,' he suggested, 'though there is a good deal of risk in it; but we must think of the girl, and not let her suspect anything wrong, and, above all, must not risk her safety.'

"Turning to the driver, he said, in a cheery tone:

"'Paul, we have shot till we are tired out. You may let the horses go, but keep them well in control.'

"While he spoke a huge wolf sprang from the pack and dashed toward one of the horses. Another followed him, and in twenty seconds the line was broken and they were upon us. One wolf jumped at the rear of the sleigh and caught his paws upon it. Rasloff struck him with the butt of his gun, and at the same instant he delivered the blow, Paul let the horses have their way. Rasloff fell upon the edge of the vehicle and over its side. Luckily, his foot caught in one of the robes and held him for an instant—long enough to enable me to seize and draw him back. It was the work of a moment, but what a moment!

"Christina had remained silent, suspecting, but not fully comprehending our danger. As her brother fell she screamed and dropped senseless to the bottom of the sleigh. I confess that I exerted all my strength in that effort to save the brother of my affianced, and as I accomplished it, I sank powerless, though still conscious, at the side of the girl I loved. Rasloff's right arm was dislocated by the fall, and one of the pursuing wolves had struck his teeth into his scalp as he was dragging over the side, and torn it so that it bled profusely. How narrow had been his escape!

"'Faster, faster, Paul!' he shouted; 'drive for your life and for ours.'

"Paul gave the horses free rein, and they needed no urging. They dashed along the road as horses rarely ever dashed before. In a few minutes I gained strength enough to raise my head, and saw, to my unspeakable delight, that the distance between us and the pack was increasing. We were safe if no accident occurred and the horses could maintain their pace.

"One horse fell, but, as if knowing his danger, made a tremendous effort and gained his feet. By-and-by we saw the light at the chateau, and in a moment dashed into the courtyard, and were safe."

A WOLF HUNT.

CHAPTER XL.

I FOUND at Krasnoyarsk more beggars than in Irkutsk, in proportion to the population. Like beggars in all parts of the empire, they made the sign of the cross on receiving donations. A few were young, but the great majority were old, tattered, and decrepid, who shivered in the frosty air, and turned purple visages upon their benefactors. The peasantry in Russia are liberal to the poor, and in many localities they have abundant opportunities to practice charity.

With its abundance of beggars Krasnoyarsk can also boast a great many wealthy citizens. The day before my departure one of these Siberian Croesuses died, and another was expected to follow his example before long. A church near the market place was built at the sole expense of this deceased individual. Its cost exceeded seven hundred thousand roubles, and its interior was said to be finely decorated. Among the middle classes in Siberia the erection of churches is, or has been, the fashionable mode of public benefaction. The endowment of schools, libraries, and scientific associations has commenced, but is not yet fully popular.

The wealth of Krasnoyarsk is chiefly derived from gold digging. The city may be considered the center of mining enterprises in the government of Yeneseisk. Two or three thousand laborers in the gold mines spend the winter at Krasnoyarsk, and add to the volume of local commerce. The town of Yeneseisk, three hundred versts further north, hibernates an equal number, and many hundreds are scattered through the villages in the vicinity. The mining season begins in May and ends in September. In March and April the clerks and superintendents engage their laborers, paying a part of their wages in advance. The wages are not high, and only those in straitened circumstances, the dissolute, and profligate, who have no homes of their own, are inclined to let themselves to labor in gold mines.

Many works are extensive, and employ a thousand or more laborers each. The government grants mining privileges to individuals on certain conditions. The land granted must be worked at least one year out of every three, else the title reverts to the government, and can be allotted again. The grantee must be either a hereditary nobleman or pay the tax of a merchant of the second guild, or he should be able to command the necessary capital for the enterprise he undertakes. His title holds good until his claim is worked out or abandoned, and no one can disturb him on any pretext. He receives a patent for a strip of land seven versts long and a hundred fathoms wide, on the banks of a stream suitable for mining purposes. The claim extends on both sides of the stream, and includes its bed, so that the water may be utilized at the will of the miner.

Sometimes the grantee desires a width of more than a hundred fathoms, but in such case the length of his claim is shortened in proportion.

It requires a large capital to open a claim after the grant is obtained. The location is often far from any city or large town, where supplies are purchased. Transportation is a heavy item, as the roads are difficult to travel. Sometimes a hundred thousand roubles will be expended in supplies, transportation, buildings, and machinery, before the work begins. Then men must be hired, taken to the mines, clothed, and furnished with proper quarters. The proprietor must have at hand a sufficient amount of provisions, medical stores, clothing, and miscellaneous goods to supply his men during the summer. Everything desired by the laborer is sold to him at a lower price than he could buy elsewhere, at least such is the theory. I was told that the mining proprietors make no profits from their workmen, but simply add the cost of transportation to the wholesale price of the merchandise. The men are allowed to anticipate their wages by purchase, and it often happens that there is very little due them at the end of the season.

Government regulations and the interest of proprietors require that the laborers should be well fed and housed and tended during sickness. Every mining establishment maintains a physician either on its own account or jointly with a neighbor. The national dish of Russia, *schee*, is served daily, with at least a pound of beef. Sometimes the treatment of the men lapses into negligence toward the close of the season, especially if the enterprise is unfortunate; but this is not the case in the early months. The mining proprietors understand the importance of keeping their laborers in good health, and to secure this end there is nothing better than proper food and lodging. Vodki is dealt out in quantities sufficiently small to prevent intoxication, except on certain feast-days, when all can get drunk to their liking. No drinking shops can be kept on the premises until the season's work is over and the men are preparing to depart.

Every laborer is paid for extra work, and if industrious and prudent his wages will equal thirty-five or forty roubles a month beside his board. While in debt he is required by law to work every day, not even resting on Saints' days or Sundays. The working season lasting only about four months, early and late hours are a necessity. When the year's operations are ended the most of the men find their way to the larger towns, where they generally waste their substance in riotous living till the return of spring. As in mining communities everywhere, the prudent and economical are a minority.

The mines in the government of Yeneseisk are generally on the tributaries of the Yenesei river. The valley of the Pit is rich in gold deposits, and has yielded large fortunes to lucky operators during the past twenty years. Usually the pay-dirt begins twenty or thirty feet below the surface, and I heard of a mine that yielded handsome profits though the gold-bearing earth was under seventy feet of soil. Prospecting is conducted with great care, and no mining enterprise is commenced without a thorough survey of the region to be developed. Wells or pits are dug at regular intervals, the exact depth and the character of the upper earth being noted. This often involves a large expenditure of money and labor, and many fortunes have been wasted, by parties whose lucky star was not in the ascendant, in their persistent yet unsuccessful search for paying mines.

Solid rock is sometimes struck sooner or later after commencing work, which renders the expense of digging vastly greater. In such cases, unless great certainty exists of striking a rich vein of gold beneath, the labor is suspended, the spot vacated, and another selected with perhaps like results. Occasionally some sanguine operator will push his well down through fifty feet of solid rock at a great outlay, and with vast labor, to find himself possessed of the means for a large fortune, while another will find himself ruined by his failure to strike the expected gold.

When the pay-dirt is reached, its depth and the number of zolotniks of gold in every pood taken out are ascertained. With the results before him a practical miner can readily decide whether a place will pay for working. Of course he must take many contingent facts into consideration, such as the extent of the placer, the resources of the region, the roads or the expense of making them, provisions, lumber, transportation, horses, tools, men, and so on through a long list.

The earth over the pay-dirt is broken up and carted off; its great depth causes immense wear of horseflesh. A small mine employs three or four hundred workmen, and larger ones in proportion. I heard of one that kept more than three thousand men at work. The usual estimate for horses is one to every two men, but the proportion varies according to the character of the mine.

The pay-dirt is hauled to the bank of the river, where it is washed in machines turned by water power. Various machines have been devised for gold-washing, and the Russians are anxious to find the best invention of the kind. The one in most general use and the easiest to construct is a long cylinder of sheet iron open at both ends and perforated with many small holes. This revolves in a slightly inclined position, and receives the dirt and a stream of water at the upper end. The stones pass through the cylinder and fall from the opposite end, where they are examined to prevent the loss of 'nuggets.' Fine dirt, sand, gold, and water pass through the perforations, and are caught in suitable troughs, where the lighter substance washes away and leaves the black sand and gold.

Great care is exercised to prevent thefts, but it does not always succeed. The laborers manage to purloin small quantities, which they sell to contraband dealers in the larger towns. The government forbids private traffic in gold dust, and punishes offences with severity; but the profits are large and tempting. Every gold miner must send the product of his diggings to the government establishment at Barnaool, where it is smelted and assayed. The owner receives its money value, minus the Imperial tax of fifteen per cent.

The whole valley of the Yenesei, as far as explored, is auriferous. Were it not for the extreme rigor of its climate and the disadvantages of location, it would become immensely productive. Some mines have been worked at a profit where the earth is solidly frozen and must be thawed by artificial means. One way of accomplishing this is by piling wood to a height of three or four feet and then setting it on fire. The earth thawed by the heat is scraped off, and fresh fires are made. Sometimes the frozen earth is dug up and soaked in water. Either process is costly, and the yield of gold must be great to repay the outlay. A gentleman in Irkutsk told me he had a gold mine of this frozen character, and intimated that he found it profitable. The richest gold mines thus far worked in Siberia are in the government of Yeneseisk, but it is thought that some of the newly opened placers in the Trans-Baikal province and along the Amoor will rival them in productiveness.

In Irkutsk I met a Russian who had spent some months in California, and proposed introducing hydraulic mining to the Siberians. No quartz mines have been worked in Eastern

HYDRAULIC MINING.

Siberia, but several rich leads are known to exist, and I presume a thorough exploration would reveal many more. I saw excellent specimens of gold-bearing quartz from the governments of Irkutsk and Yeneseisk. One specimen in particular, if in the hands of certain New York operators, would be sufficient basis for a company with a capital of half a million. In the Altai and Ural mountains quartz mills have been in use for many years.

The Siberian gold deposits were made available long before Russia explored and conquered Northern Asia. There are many evidences in the Ural mountains of extensive mining operations hundreds of years ago. Large areas have been dug over by a people of whom the present inhabitants can give no account. It is generally supposed that the Tartars discovered and opened these gold mines shortly after the time of Genghis Khan.

The native population of the valley of the Yenesei comprises several distinct tribes, belonging in common to the great Mongolian race. In the extreme north, in the region bordering the Arctic Ocean, are the Samoyedes, who are of the same blood as the Turks. The valley of the Lena is peopled by Yakuts, whose development far exceeds that of the Samoyedes, though both are of common origin. The latter are devoted entirely to the chase and the rearing of reindeer, and show no fondness for steady labor. The Yakuts employ the horse as a beast of burden, and are industrious, ingenious, and patient. As much as the character of the country permits they till the soil, and are not inclined to nomadic life. They are hardy and reliable laborers, and live on the most amicable terms with the Russians.

Before the opening of the Amoor the carrying trade from Yakutsk to Ohotsk was in their hands. As many as forty thousand horses used to pass annually between the two points, nearly all of them owned and driven by Yakuts.

Most of these natives have been converted to Christianity, but they still adhere to some of their ancient practices. On the road, for example, they pluck hairs from their horse's tails and hang them upon trees to appease evil spirits. Some of the Russians have imbibed native superstitions, and there is a story of a priest who applied to a shaman to practice his arts and ward off evil in a journey he was about to make. Examples to the natives are not always of the best, and it would not be surprising if they raised doubts as to the superiority of Christian faith. A traveler who had a mixed party of Cossacks and natives, relates that the former were accustomed to say their prayers three or four times on evenings when they had plenty of leisure and omit them altogether when they were fatigued. At Nijne Kolymsk Captain Wrangell found the priests holding service three times on one Sunday and then absenting themselves for two weeks.

South of Krasnoyarsk are the natives belonging to the somewhat indefinite family known as Tartars. They came originally from Central Asia, and preserve many Mongol habits added to some created by present circumstances. Some of them dwell in houses, while others adhere to yourts of the same form and material as those of the Bouriats and Mongols. They are agriculturists in a small way, but only adopt tilling the soil as a last resort. Their wealth consists in sheep, cattle, and horses, and when one of them has large possessions he changes his habitation two or three times a year, on account of pasturage. A gentleman told me that he once found a Tartar, whose flocks and herds were worth more than a million roubles, living in a tent of ordinary dimensions and with very little of what a European would call comfort. These natives harmonize perfectly with the Russians, of whom they have a respectful fear.

Like their kindred in Central Asia, these Tartars are excellent horsemen, and show themselves literally at home in the saddle. Dismounted, they step clumsily, and are unable to walk any distance of importance. On horseback they have an easy and graceful carriage, and are capable of great endurance. They show intense love for their horses, caressing them constantly and treating their favorite riding animals as household pets. In all their songs and traditions the horse occupies a prominent place.

One of the most popular Tartar songs, said to be of great antiquity, relates the adventures of "Swan's Wing," a beautiful daughter of a native chief. Her brother had been overpowered by a magician and carried to the spirit land. According to the tradition the horse he rode came to Swan's Wing and told her what had occurred. The young girl begged him to lead her by the road the magician had taken, and thus guided, she reached the country of the shades. Assisted by the horse she was able to rescue her brother from the prison where he was confined. On her return she narrated to her people the incidents of her journey, which are chanted at the present time. The song tells how one of the supernatural guardians was attracted by her beauty and became her *valet de place* during her visit.

Near the entrance of the grounds she saw a fat horse in a sandy field, and a lean one in a meadow. A thin and apparently powerless man was wading against a torrent, while a large and muscular one could not stop a small brook.

"The first horse," said her guide, "shows that a careful master can keep his herds in good condition with scanty pasturage, and the second shows how easily one may fail to prosper in the midst of plenty. The man stemming the torrent shows how much one can accomplish by the force of will, even though the body be weak. The strong man is overpowered by the little stream, because he lacks intelligence and resolution."

She was next led through several apartments of a large building. In the first apartment several women were spinning incessantly, while others attempted to swallow balls of hemp. Next she saw women holding heavy stones in their hands and unable to put them down. Then there were parties playing without cessation upon musical instruments, and others busy over games of chance. In one room were men and dogs enraged and biting each other. In a dormitory were many couples with quilts of large dimensions, but in each couple there was an active struggle, and its quilt was frequently pulled aside. In the last hall of the establishment there were smiling couples, at peace with all the world and 'the rest of mankind.' The song closes with the guide's explanation of what Swan's Wing had seen.

"The women who spin now are punished because in their

lives they continued to spin after sunset, when they should be at rest.

Those who swallow balls of hemp were guilty of stealing thread by making their cloth too thin.

Those condemned to hold heavy stones were guilty of putting stones in their butter to make it heavy.

The parties who make music and gamble did nothing else in their life time, and must continue that employment perpetually.

The men with the dogs are suffering the penalty of having created quarrels on earth.

The couples who freeze under ample covering are punished for their selfishness when mortals, and the couples in the next apartment are an example to teach the certainty of happiness to those who develop kindly disposition."

The region of the Lower Yenesei contains many exiles whom the government desired to remove far from the centers of population. These include political and criminal prisoners, whose offences are of a high grade, together with the members of a certain religious order, known as "The Skoptsi." The latter class is particularly obnoxious on account of its practice of mutilation. Whenever an adherent of this sect is discovered he is banished to the remotest regions, either in the north of Siberia or among the mountains of Circassia. It is the only religious body relentlessly persecuted by the Russian government, and the persecution is based upon the sparseness of population. Some of these men have been incorporated into regiments on the frontier, where they prove obedient and tractable. Those who become colonists in Siberia are praised for their industry and perseverance, and invariably win the esteem of their neighbors. They are banished to distant localities through fear of their influence upon those around them. Most of the money-changers of Moscow are reputed to believe in this peculiar faith.

Many prominent individuals were exiled to the Lower Yenesei and regions farther eastward, under former sovereigns. Count Golofkin, one of the ministers of Catherine II., was banished to Nijne Kolymsk, where he died. It is said that he used to put himself, his servants, and house in deep mourning on every anniversary of Catherine's birthday. Two officers of the court of the emperor Paul were exiled to a small town on the Yenesei, where they lived until recalled by Alexander I.

The settlers on the Angara are freed from liability to conscription, on condition that they furnish rowers and pilots to boats navigating that stream. The settlers on the Lena enjoy the same privilege under similar terms. On account of the character of the country and the drawbacks to prosperity, the taxes are much lighter than in more favored regions. In the more northern districts there is a considerable trade in furs and ivory. The latter comes in the shape of walrus tusks, and the tusks and teeth of the mammoth, which are gathered on the shores of the Arctic Ocean and the islands scattered through it. This trade is less extensive than it was forty or fifty years ago.

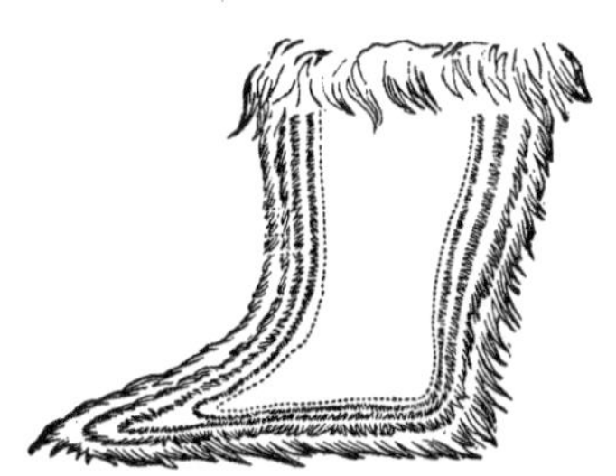

CHAPTER XLI.

I SPENT three days in Krasnoyarsk, chiefly employed upon my letters and journal. My recent companions were going no farther in my direction, and knowing this beforehand, I arranged with a gentleman at Irkutsk to travel with him from Krasnoyarsk. He arrived two days behind me, and after sending away a portion of his heavy baggage, was ready to depart. There was no snow to the first station, and so we sent our sleighs on wheels and used the post carriages over the bare ground. A peasant who lived near the station sought me out and offered to transport my sleigh for three roubles and a little drink-money. As I demurred, he proposed to repair, without extra charge, one of my fenders which had come to grief, and we made a bargain on this proposition.

My companion, Dr. Schmidt, had recently returned from a mammoth-hunting expedition within the Arctic circle. He had not secured a perfect specimen of this extinct beast, but contented himself with some parts of the stupendous whole, and a miscellaneous collection of birds, bugs, and reptiles. He despatched a portion of his treasures by post; the balance, with his assistant, formed a sufficient load for one sleigh. The doctor was to ride in my sleigh, while his assistant in another vehicle kept company with the relicts. The kegs, boxes, and bundles of Arctic zoology did not form a comfortable couch, and I never envied their conductor.

On the day fixed for our departure we sent our papers to the station in the forenoon, and were told we could be supplied at sunset or a little later. This was not to our liking, as we desired to reach the first station before nightfall. A friend suggested an appeal to the Master of the post, and together we proceeded to that functionary's office. An amiable, quiet man he was, and listened to our complaint with perfect composure. After hearing it he summoned the smotretal with his book of records, and an animated discussion followed. I expected to see somebody grow indignant, but the whole affair abounded in good nature.

The conversation was conducted with the decorum of a school dialogue on exhibition day. In half an hour by the clock I was told I could have a troika at once, in consideration of my special passport. "Wait a little," whispered my friend in French, "and we will have the other troika for Schmidt."

So I waited, kicking my heels about the room, studying the posters on the walls, eyeing a bad portrait of the emperor, and a worse one of the empress, and now and then drawing near the scene of action. The clerks looked at me in furtive glances. At every pronunciation of my name, coupled with the word "Amerikansky," there was a general stare all around. I am confident those attaches of the post office at Krasnoyarsk had a perfect knowledge of my features.

In exactly another half hour our point and the horses were gained. When we entered the office it was positively declared there were no horses to be had, and it was a little odd that two troikas and six horses, could be produced out of nothing, and each of them at the end of a long talk. I asked an explanation of the mystery, but was told it was a Russian peculiarity that no American could understand.

The horses came very promptly, one troika to Schmidt's lodgings and the other to mine. The servants packed my baggage into the little telyaga that was to carry me to the first station. Joining Schmidt with the other team, we rattled out of town on an excellent road, and left the red hills of Krasnoyarsk. The last object I saw denoting the location of the town was a church or chapel on a high cliff overlooking the Yenesei valley.

The road lay over an undulating region, where there were few streams and very little timber. The snow lay in little patches here and there on the swells least exposed to the sun, but it did not cover a twentieth part of the ground. In several hollows the mud had frozen and presented a rough surface to our wheels. Our telyaga had no springs, and when we went at a rapid trot over the worst places the bones of my spinal column seemed engaged in a struggle for independence. A thousand miles of such riding would have been too much for me. A dog belonging to Madame Radstvenny's house-keeper followed me from Krasnoyarsk, but did not show himself till we were six or eight versts away. Etiquette, to say nothing of morality, does not sanction stealing the dog of your host, and so I arranged for the brute's return. In consideration of fifty copecks the yemshick agreed to take the dog on his homeward trip and deliver him in good order and condition at Krasnoyarsk.

Just before reaching the first station we passed through a village nearly four miles long, but only a single street in width. The station was at the extreme end of the village; our sleighs were waiting for us, and so were the men who brought them from Krasnoyarsk. There was no snow for the next twenty versts, and consequently the sleighs needed further transportation. Schmidt's sleigh was dragged empty over the bare ground, but mine, being heavier, was mounted upon wheels.

Other difficulties awaited us. There was but one troika to spare and only one telyaga. We required two vehicles for ourselves and baggage, but the smotretal could not accommodate us. We ordered the samovar, and debated over our tea. I urged my friend to try the effect of my special passport, which had always been successful in Paul's hands. He did so after our tea-drinking, but the document was powerless, the smotretal doubtless arguing that if the paper were of consequence we should have shown it on our arrival. We sent it to the *starost*, or head man of the village, but that worthy declined to honor it, and we were left to shift for ourselves. Evidently the power of the Governor General's passport was on the wane.

The document was a request, not an order, and therefore had no real force. Paul always displayed it as if it were an Imperial ukase. His manner of spreading the double page and exhibiting seal and signature carried authority and produced horses. The amiable naturalist had none of the quality called 'cheek,' and the adoption of an authoritative air did not accord with his character. He subsequently presented the passport as if he thought it all-powerful, and on such occasions it generally proved so. A man who wishes to pass a doorkeeper at a caucus, enter a ladies' car on a railway, or obtain a reserved seat in a court room, is much more certain of success if he advances with a confident air than if he hesitates and appears fearful of ejection. Humanity is the same the world over, and there is more than a shadow of truth in the saying that society values a man pretty much as he appears to value himself. I can testify that the smotretals in Siberia generally regarded our papers according to our manner of showing them.

We took tea a second time, parlayed with the yemshicks and their friends, and closed by chartering a team at double the regular rates. Just before reaching the snow we passed the sleighs, and halted for them to come up. My sleigh was very soon ready, and we rejoiced at our transfer of baggage. During the change a bottle of cognac disappeared mysteriously, and I presume we shall never see it again. The other and more cumbersome articles preserved their numbers faithfully. Our party halting in the moonlight and busy about the vehicles, presented a curiously picturesque appearance. Schmidt was in his Arctic costume, while I wore my winter dress, minus the dehar. The yemshicks were wrapped in their inevitable sheepskins, and bustled about with unwavering good humor.

In the sleigh we were at home, and had a roof to cover us; we made very good speed to the station, where we found no horses. The floor of the travelers' room was covered with dormant figures, and after bumping my head over the doorway, I waded in a pond of bodies, heads, and legs. The moon was the only light, and its beams were not sufficient to prevent my stepping on several sleepers, and extracting Russian oaths for my carelessness.

"Now for it," I whispered to the good-natured doctor, as we waked the smotretal. "Make him think our papers are important."

The official rubbed his eyes over the passport, and then hastened to arouse the starost. The latter ordered horses from the village without delay.

It had been a fete-day in honor of the Emperor, and most of the villagers were drunk, so that it required some time to assemble the requisite yemshicks and horses. A group of men and women from an evening party passed the station, and amused us with native songs. An inebriated moujik, riding on a small sled, turned from the road to enter the station yard. One side of the sled passed over a log, and as the man had not secured his balance, he rolled out of sight in a snow drift. I watched him as he emerged, much as Neptune might appear from the crest of a foamy wave.

The Siberians keep all the Imperial fete-days with scrupulous exactness, and their loyalty to the emperor is much akin to religious awe. The whole Imperial family is the object of great respect, and whatever is commanded in the name of the emperor meets the most cheerful acquiescence. One finds the portrait of Alexander in almost every house, and I never heard the name of that excellent ruler mentioned disrespectfully. If His Majesty would request that his subjects abstain from vodki drinking on Imperial fete-days, he would do much toward their prosperity. It would be an easy beginning in the cause of temperance, as no one could consider it out of place for the emperor to prescribe the manner of celebrating his own festivals. The work once begun in this way, would be likely to lead to good results. Drunkenness is the great vice of the Russian peasant, and will never be suppressed without the active endeavors of the government.

When we started from the station we ran against the gate post, and were nearly overturned in consequence. My head came against the side of the sleigh with a heavy thump that affected me more than it did the vehicle. We descended a long hill at a full run, and as our yemshick was far from sober I had a lively expectation of a general smash at the bottom. About half way down the descent we met a sleigh and dashed our fenders against it. The strong poles rubbed across each other like fencing foils, and withstood the shock finely.

DOWN HILL.

At sunset there were indications of a snow storm in the gradual ascent of the thermometer. An hour past midnight the temperature was above freezing point, and the sleigh runners lost that peculiar ringing sound that indicates cold weather. I threw off my furs and endeavored to sleep, but accomplished little in that direction. My clothing was too thick or too thin. Without my furs I shivered, and with them I perspired. My sleigh robe was too much for comfort, and the absence of it left something to be desired. Warm weather is a great inconvenience in a Siberian winter journey. The best temperature for travel is from five to fifteen degrees below the freezing point.

The road was abominable, though it might have been worse. It was full of drifts, bare spots, and *oukhabas*, and our motion was as varied as a politician's career. Sometimes it was up, then down, then sidewise, and then all ways at once. We pitched and rolled like a canoe descending the Lachine rapids, or a whale-boat towed by a hundred-barrel "bow-head." In many places the snow was blown from the regular road, and the winter track wound through fields and forests wherever snow could be found. There was an abundance of rocks, stumps, and other inequalities to relieve the monotony of this mode of travel. We went much out of our way to find snow, and I think we sometimes increased, by a third or a half, the distance between stations. The road was both horizontally and vertically tortuous.

My companion took every occurrence with the utmost coolness, and taught me some things in patience I had not known before. He was long accustomed to Siberian travel, having made several scientific journeys through Northern Asia. In 1859 the Russian Geographical Society sent him to visit the Amoor valley and explore the island of Sakhalin. His journey thither was accomplished in winter, and when he returned he brought many valuable data touching the geology and the vegetable and animal life of the island. He told me he spoke the American language, having learned it among my countrymen at Nicolayevsk, but had never studied English. His journey to the Arctic Circle was made on behalf of the Russian Academy of Science, of which he was an active member.

In 1865 the captain of a Yenesei steamer learned that some natives had discovered the perfectly preserved remains of a mammoth in latitude 67°, about a hundred versts west of the river. He announced the fact to a *savant*, who sent the intelligence to St. Petersburg. Scientific men deemed the discovery so important that they immediately commissioned Dr. Schmidt to follow it up. The doctor went to Eastern Siberia in February, and in the following month proceeded down the Yenesei to Turuhansk, where he remained four or five weeks waiting for the season of warmth and light. He was accompanied by Mr. Lopatin, a Russian geologist, and a staff of three or four assistants. They carried a photographic apparatus, and one of the sensations of their voyage was to take photographs at midnight in the light of a blazing sun.

When the Yenesei was free of ice the explorers, in a barge, descended from Turuhansk to the landing place nearest the mammoth deposit. Several Cossacks accompanied the party from Turuhansk, and assisted in its intercourse with the natives. The latter were peacefully inclined, and gladly served the men who came so recently from the emperor's dwelling place. They brought their reindeer and sledges, and guided the explorers to the object of their search. The country in the Arctic Circle has very little vegetation, and the drift wood that descends the Yenesei is an important item to the few natives along the river. The trees growing north of latitude 66° are very small, and as one nears the coast of the Frozen Ocean they disappear altogether. The principal features of the country are the wide *tundras*, or moss-covered plains, similar to those of North Eastern Siberia.

The scattered aboriginals are Tunguse and Samoyedes. Their chief employment is the chase in winter, fishing in summer, and the care of their reindeer at all seasons. Reindeer form their principal wealth, and are emphatically the circulating medium of the country. Dr. Schmidt told me he rode in a reindeer sledge from the river to within a short distance of the mammoth. It was the month of June, but the snow had not disappeared and nothing could be accomplished. A second visit several weeks later was more successful. In the interval the party embarked on the steamer which makes one or two journeys every summer to the Arctic Ocean in search of fish, furs, and ivory. A vigorous traffic is maintained during the short period that the river remains open.

On the return from the Arctic Ocean, the season was more favorable to mammoth-hunting. Unfortunately the remains were not perfect. The skeleton was a good deal broken and scattered, and some parts were altogether lacking. The chief object of the enterprise was to obtain the stomach of the mammoth so that its contents could be analyzed. It is known that the beast lived upon vegetable food, but no one has yet ascertained its exact character. Some contend that the mammoth was a native of the tropics, and his presence in the north is due to the action of an earthquake. Others think he dwelt in the Arctic regions, and never belonged in the tropics.

"If we had found his stomach," said the doctor, "and ascertained what kind of trees were in it, this question would have been decided. We could determine his residence from the character of his food."

Though making diligent search the doctor found no trace of the stomach, and the great point is still open to dispute. He brought away the under jaw of the beast, and a quantity of skin and hair. The skin was half an inch thick, and as dry and hard as a piece of sole leather. The hair was like fine long bristles, and of a reddish brown color. From the quantity obtained it is thought the animal was pretty well protected against ordinary weather. The doctor gave me a cigar tube which a Samoyede fabricated from a small bone of the mammoth. He estimated that the beast had been frozen about ten thousand years in the bank where he found him, and that his natural dwelling place was in the north. The country was evidently much warmer when the mammoth roamed over it than now, and there is a belief that some convulsion of the earth, followed by a lowering of the temperature, sealed the remains of the huge beasts in the spots where they are now discovered.

In the year 1799 a bank of frozen earth near the mouth of the Lina, in Latitude 77° broke away and revealed the body of a mammoth. Hair, skin, flesh and all, had been completely preserved by the frost. In 1806 a scientific commission visited the spot, but the lapse of seven years proved of serious consequence. There had been a famine in the surrounding region, and the natives did not scruple to feed their dogs from the store of flesh which nature had preserved. Not supposing the emperor desired the bones of the beast they carried away such as they fancied. The teeth of the bears, wolves, and foxes were worse than the tooth of Time, and finished all edible substance the natives did not take. Only the skeleton remained, and of this several bones were gone. All that could be found was taken, and is now in the Imperial collection at St. Petersburg.

The remains of the mammoth show that the beast was closely akin to the elephant, but had a longer and more compressed skull, and wore his tusks in a different manner. Tusks have been found more than nine feet long, and I am told that one discovered some years ago, exceeds ten feet in length. The skull from the Lena mammoth weighed four hundred and some odd pounds. Others have been found much larger. The mammoth was evidently an animal that commanded the respect of the elephant, and other small fry quadrupeds.

Bones of the rhinoceros and hippopotamus abound in Northern Siberia, and like those of the mammoth are found in the frozen earth. In the last century the body of a rhinoceros of an extinct species was found on the river Vilouy, a tributary of the Lena. In the museum at St. Petersburg there is a head of the Arctic rhinoceros on which the skin and tendons remain, and a foot of the same animal displays a portion of its hair. The claws of an enormous bird are also found in the north, some of them three feet long, and jointed through their whole length like the claws of an ostrich.

Captain Wrangell and other explorers say the mammoth bones are smaller on the Arctic islands than on the main land, but are wonderfully increased in quantity. For many years the natives and fur traders have brought away large cargoes, but the supply is not yet exhausted. The teeth and tusks on the islands are more fresh and white than those of the Continent. On the Lachoff Islands the principal deposit was on a low sand bank, and the natives declared that when the waves receded after an easterly wind, a fresh supply was always found. One island about latitude 80° was said to be largely composed of mammoth bones. I presume this statement should be received with a little caution.

During the doctor's expedition the supply of provisions was not always abundant, but there was no absolute scarcity. The party lived for some time on fish, and on the flesh of the reindeer. A story was told that the explorers were reduced to subsisting on the mammoth they discovered, and hence their failure to bring away portions of the flesh. Mammoth cutlets and soup were occasionally proposed for the entertainment of the *savants* on their return to Irkutsk.

One of my acquaintances had a narrow escape from death on the ice during an expedition toward Kotelnoi Island, and the chain lying to the east of it, generally known as New Siberia. It was early in the spring—somewhat later than the time of the ordinary winter journeys—that he set out from the mouth of the Lena, hoping to reach Kotelnoi Island, and return before the weather became warm. He had four dog teams, and was accompanied by a Russian servant and two Yakut natives, whom he engaged for a voyage down the Lena, and the expedition across the ice. It was known that a quantity of ivory had been gathered on the island, and was waiting for transportation to the Lena; to get this ivory was the object of the journey. I will tell the story in the words of the narrator, or as nearly as I can do so from recollection.

"We reached the island without serious trouble; the weather was clear and cold, and the traveling quite as good as we expected. Where the ice was level we got along very well, though there were now and then deep fissures caused by the frost, and which we had some difficulty in crossing. Frequently we were obliged to detach the dogs from the sleds and compel them to jump singly across the fissures. The sledges were then drawn over by hand, and once on the other side the teams were re-harnessed, and proceeded on their way. The ice was seven or eight feet thick, and some of the fissures were a yard wide at the surface, and tapered to a wedge shape at the bottom. It was not absolutely dangerous, though very inconvenient to fall into one of the crevices, and our dogs were very careful to secure a good foothold on the edges where they jumped.

"The second day out we got among a great many hummocks, or detached pieces of bergs, that caused us much

DOGS AMONG ICE.

trouble. They were so numerous that we were often shut out from the horizon, and were guided solely by the compass. Frequently we found them so thick that it was impossible to break a road through them, and after working for an hour or two, we would be compelled to retrace our steps, and endeavor to find a new route. Where they formed in ridges, and were not too high, we broke them down with our ice-hatchets; the work was very exhausting to us, and so was the task of drawing the sledges to the poor dogs.

"Just as we left the level ice, and came among these hummocks, the dogs came on the fresh track of a polar bear, and at once started to follow him. My team was ahead, and the dogs set out in full chase, too rapidly for me to stop them, though I made every effort to do so. The other teams followed close upon us, and very soon my sledge overturned, and the dogs became greatly mixed up. The team of Nicolai, my servant, was likewise upset close to mine, and we had much trouble to get them right again. Ivan and Paul, the two Yakuts, came up and assisted us. Their dogs following on our track had not caught the scent of the bear so readily as ours, and consequently were more easily brought to a stop.

"We set the sledges right, and when we were ready to start, the sharp eyes of Ivan discovered the bear looking at us from behind a hummock, and evidently debating in his mind whether to attack us or not. Leaving the teams in charge of Paul, I started with Nicolai and Ivan to endeavor to kill the bear. Nicolai and myself were armed with rifles, while Ivan carried a knife and an ice-hatchet.

"The bear stood very patiently as we approached; he was evidently unaccustomed to human visitors, and did not understand what we were about. The hummock where he stood was not very steep, and I thought it best to get a position a little above him for better safety, in case we had a sharp fight after firing our first shot. We took our stand on a little projection of ice a few feet higher than where he was, and about thirty paces distant; I arranged that Nicolai should fire first, as I was a better shot than he, and it would be best for me to have the reserve. Nicolai fired, aiming at the bear's heart, which was well protected, as we knew, by a thick hide and a heavy mass of flesh.

"The shot was not fatal. The bear gave a roar of pain, and sprang toward us. I waited until he placed his huge fore paws over the edge of the little ridge where we stood, and exposed his throat and chest. He was not more than ten feet away, and I buried the bullet exactly where I wished. But, notwithstanding both our shots, the animal was not killed, but lifted himself easily above the shelf, and sprang toward us.

"We retreated higher up to another shelf, and as the bear attempted to climb it, Nicolai struck him with the butt of his rifle, which the beast warded off with his paw, and sent whirling into the snow. But at the same instant Ivan took his opportunity to deal an effective blow with his ice-hatchet, which he buried in the skull of the animal, fairly penetrating his brain. The blow accomplished what our shots had not. Bruin fell back, and after a few convulsive struggles, lay dead at our feet.

"We hastened back to the teams, and brought them forward. We were not absent more than twenty minutes, but by the time we returned several Arctic foxes had made their appearance, and were snuffing the air, preparatory to a feast. We drove them off, and very soon the dogs were enjoying a meal of fresh meat, that we threw to them immediately on removing the skin of the bear, which the Yakuts accomplished with great alacrity. The beast was old and tough, so that most of his flesh went to the dogs, part of it being eaten on the spot, while the rest was packed on the sledges for future use.

"We had no other incidents of importance until our return from the island. The weather suddenly became cloudy, and a warm wind set in from the southward. The snow softened so that the dogs could with difficulty draw the sledges, even when relieved of our weight. We walked by their side, encouraging them in every possible way, and as the softness of the snow increased, it became necessary to throw away a part of the loads. Our safety required that we should reach the land as soon as possible, since there were many indications that the ice was about to break up. After sixteen hours of continuous dragging, we stopped, quite exhausted, though still thirty miles from land, as it was absolutely impossible for men or dogs to proceed further without rest. I was so utterly worn out that I sank upon the snow, hardly able to move. The Yakuts fed the dogs, and then lay down at their side, anxiously waiting the morning to bring us relief.

"Just as the day was opening, I was awakened by a rumbling noise, and a motion below me, followed by a shout from Ivan.

"'The ice is breaking up!'

"I sprang to my feet, and so did my companions. The dogs were no less sensible of their danger than ourselves, and stirred uneasily while giving vent to plaintive whines. The wind from the south had increased; it was blowing directly off the land, and I could see that the ice was cracking here and there under its influence, and the whole field was in motion. Dark lanes appeared, and continued to increase in width, besides growing every minute more numerous. I ordered all the loads thrown from the sledges, with the exception of a day's provisions for men and dogs, and a few of our extra garments. When this was done—and it was done very speedily—we started for the shore.

JUMPING THE FISSURES.

"We jumped the dogs over the smaller crevices without serious accident, but the larger ones gave us a great deal of trouble. On reaching them, we skirted along their edges till we could find a cake of ice large enough to ferry us over. In this way we crossed more than twenty openings, some of them a hundred yards in width. Do not suppose we did so without being thrown several times in the water, and on one occasion four of the dogs were drowned. The poor brutes became tangled in their harness, and it was impossible to extricate them. All the dogs seemed to be fully aware of their danger, and to understand that their greatest safety lay in their obeying us. I never saw them more obedient, and they rarely hesitated to do what we commanded. It grieved me greatly to see the dogs drowning when we were unable to help them, but could only listen to their cries for help, until stifled by the water.

"We toiled all day, and night found us five miles from shore, with a strip of open water between us and land. Here and there were floating cakes of ice, but the main body had been blown off by the wind and promised to be a mile or two further to the north before morning.

"I determined to wait for daylight, and then endeavor to reach the shore on cakes of ice. The attempt would be full of danger, but there was nothing else to be done. Reluctantly I proposed abandoning the dogs, but my companions appealed to me to keep them with us, as they had already saved our lives, and it would be the basest ingratitude to desert them. I did not require a second appeal, and promised that whatever we did, the dogs should go with us if possible.

"Imagine the horror of that night! We divided the little food that remained, men and dogs sharing alike, and tried to rest upon the ice. We had no means of making a fire, our clothing was soaked with water, and, during the night, the wind shifted suddenly to the northward and became cold. I was lying down, and fell asleep from utter exhaustion; though the cold was severe, I did not think it dangerous, and felt quite unable to exercise to keep warm. The Yakuts, with Nicolai, huddled among the dogs, and were less wearied than I. When they shouted to me at daybreak, I slowly opened my eyes, and found that I could not move. I was frozen fast to the ice!

"Had I been alone there would have been no escape. My companions came to my relief, but it was with much difficulty that they freed me from my unpleasant situation. When we looked about, we found that our circumstances had greatly changed during the night. The wind had ceased, and the frost had formed fresh ice over the space where there was open water the day before. It was out of the question to ferry to land, and our only hope lay in driving the sledges over the new ice. I ordered the teams to be made ready, and to keep several hundred yards apart, so as to make as little weight as possible on one spot. I took one sledge, Nicolai another, and the Yakuts the third. Our fourth sledge was lost at the time of our accident the day before.

THE TEAM.

"Our plan was to drive at full speed, to lessen the danger of breaking through. Once through the ice, there would have been no hope for us. We urged the dogs forward with loud cries, and they responded to our wishes by exerting all their strength. We went forward at a gallop. I reached the shore in safety, and so did Nicolai, but not so the poor Yakuts.

"When within a mile of the land I heard a cry. I well knew what it meant, but I could give no assistance, as a moment's pause would have seen me breaking through our frail support. I did not even dare to look around, but continued shouting to the dogs to carry them to land. Once there, I wiped the perspiration from my face, and ventured to look over the track where I came.

"The weight of the two men upon one sledge had crushed the ice, and men, dogs and sledge had fallen into the water. Unable to serve them in the least, we watched till their struggles were ended, and then turned sorrowfully away. The ice closed over them, and the bed of the Arctic Ocean became their grave."

CHAPTER XLII.

IN the morning after our departure from Krasnoyarsk we reached a third station, and experienced no delay in changing horses. The road greatly improved, but we made slow progress. When we were about two versts from the station one of our horses left the sleigh and bolted homeward. The yemshick went in pursuit, but did not overtake the runaway till he reached the station. During his absence we sat patiently, or rather impatiently, in our furs, and I improved the opportunity to go to sleep.

When we were properly reconstructed we moved forward, with my equipage in the rear. The mammoth sleigh went at a disreputably low speed. I endeavored to persuade our yemshick to take the lead, but he refused, on the ground that the smotretal would not permit it. Added to this, he stopped frequently to make pretended arrangements of the harness, where he imagined it out of order. To finish my irritation at his manœuvres, he proposed to change with a yemshick he met about half way on his route. This would bring each to his own station at the end of the drive, and save a return trip. The man had been so dilatory and obstinate that I concluded to take my opportunity, and stubbornly refused permission for the change. This so enraged him that he drove very creditably for the rest of the way.

"Both of them Jews," he said to the attendants at the station when we arrived. His theory as to our character was something like this. Of the male travelers in Siberia there are practically but two classes—officers and merchants. We could not be officers, as we wore no uniform; therefore we were merchants. The trading class in Siberia comprises Russians of pure blood and Jews, the former speaking only their own language and never using any other. As the yemshick did not understand our conversation, he at once set us down as Israelites in whom there was any quantity of guile.

We breakfasted on pilmania, bread, and tea while the horses were being changed, and I managed to increase our bill of fare with some boiled eggs. The continual jolting and the excessive cold gave me a good appetite and excellent digestion. Our food was plain and not served as at Delmonico's, but I always found it palatable. We stopped twice a day for meals, and the long interval between dinner time and breakfast generally made me ravenously hungry by morning. The village where the obstinate yemshick left us, had a bad reputation on the scale of honesty, but we suffered no loss there. At another village said to contain thieves, we did not leave the sleigh.

About noon we met a convoy of exiles moving slowly along the snowy road. The prisoners were walking in double column, but without regularity and not attempting to 'keep step.' Two soldiers with muskets and fixed bayonets marched in front and two others brought up the rear. There were thirty or more prisoners, all clad in sheepskin garments, their heads covered with Russian hoods, and their hands thrust into heavy mittens. Behind the column there were four or five sleighs containing baggage and foot-sore prisoners, half a dozen soldiers, and two women. The extreme rear was finished by two soldiers, with muskets and fixed bayonets, riding on an open sledge. The rate of progress was regulated by the soldiers at the head of the column. Most of the prisoners eyed us as we drove past, but there were several who did not look up.

At nearly every village there is an *ostrog*, or prison, for the accommodation of exiles. It is a building, or several buildings, enclosed with a palisade or other high fence. Inside its strong gate one cannot easily escape, and I believe the attempt is rarely made. Generally the rooms or buildings nearest the gate are the residences of the officers and guards, the prisoners being lodged as far as possible from the point of egress. The distance from one station to the next varies according to the location of the villages, but is usually about twenty versts. Generally the ostrog is outside the village, but not far away. The people throughout Siberia display unvarying kindness to exiles on their march. When a convoy reaches a village the inhabitants bring whatever they can spare, whether of food or money, and either deliver it to the prisoners in the street or carry it to the ostrog. Many peasants plant little patches of turnips and beets, where runaway prisoners may help themselves at night without danger of interference if discovered by the owner.

In every party of exiles, each man takes his turn for a day in asking and receiving charity, the proceeds being for the common good. In front of my quarters in Irkutsk a party of prisoners were engaged several days in setting posts. One of the number accosted every passer by, and when he received any thing the prisoners near him echoed his 'thank you.' Many couples were engaged, under guard, in carrying water from the river to the prison. One man of each couple solicited 'tobacco money' for both. The soldiers make no objection to charity toward prisoners. I frequently observed that when any person approached with the evident intention of giving something to the water carriers, the guards halted to facilitate the donation.

Very often on my sleigh ride I met convoys of exiles. On one occasion as we were passing an ostrog the gate suddenly opened, and a dozen sleighs laden with prisoners emerged and drove rapidly to the eastward. Five-sixths of the exiles I met on the road were riding, and did not appear to suffer from cold. They were well wrapped in sheepskin clothing, and seated, generally three together, in the ordinary sleighs of the country. Formerly most exiles walked the entire distance from Moscow to their destination, but of late years it has been found better economy to allow them to ride. Only certain classes of criminals are now required to go on foot.

All other offenders, including 'politiques,' are transported in vehicles at government expense. Any woman can accompany or follow her husband into exile.

Those on foot go from one station to the next for a day's march. They travel two days and rest one, and unless for special reasons, are not required to break the Sabbath. Medical officers are stationed in the principal towns, to look after the sanitary condition of the emigrants. The object being to people the country, the government takes every reasonable care that the exiles do not suffer in health while on the road. Of course those that ride do not require as much rest as the pedestrians. They usually stop at night at the ostrogs, and travel about twelve or fourteen hours a day. Distinguished offenders, such as the higher class of revolutionists, officers convicted of plotting against the state or robbing the Treasury, are generally rushed forward night and day. To keep him secure from escape, an exile of this class is sometimes chained to a soldier who rides at his side.

One night, between Irkutsk and Krasnoyarsk, I was awakened by an unusual motion of the sleigh. We were at the roadside passing a column of men who marched slowly in our direction. As I lifted our curtain and saw the undulating line of dark forms moving silently in the dim starlight, and brought into relief against the snow hills, the scene appeared something more than terrestrial. I thought of the array of spectres that beleaguered the walls of Prague, if we may trust the Bohemian legend, and of the shadowy battalions described by the old poets of Norseland, in the days when fairies dwelt in fountains, and each valley was the abode of a good or evil spirit. But my fancies were cut short by my companion briefly informing me that we were passing a convoy of prisoners recently ordered from Irkutsk to Yeneseisk. It was the largest convoy I saw during my journey, and included, as I thought, not less than two hundred men.

In the afternoon of the first day from Krasnoyarsk we reached Achinsk, a town of two or three thousand inhabitants, on the bank of the Chulim river. We were told the road was so bad as to require four horses to each sleigh to the next station. We consented to pay for a horse additional to the three demanded by our padaroshnia, and were carried along at very good speed. Part of the way was upon the ice, which had formed during a wind, that left disagreeable ridges. We picked out the best places, and had not our horses slipped occasionally, the icy road would not have been unpleasant. On the bare ground which we traversed in occasional patches after leaving the river, the horses behaved admirably and made little discrimination between sand and snow. Whenever they lagged the yemshick lashed them into activity.

I observed in Siberia that whip cracking is not fashionable. The long, slender, snapping whips of Western Europe and America are unknown. The Siberian uses a short stock with a lash of hemp, leather, or other flexible substance, but never dreams of a snapper at its end. Its only use is for whipping purposes, and a practiced yemshick can do much with it in a short time.

The Russian drivers talk a great deal to their horses, and the speech they use depends much upon the character and performance of the animals. If the horse travels well he may be called the dove or brother of his driver, and assured that there is abundance of excellent hay awaiting him at home. Sometimes a neat hint is given that he is drawing a nice gentleman who will be liberal and enable the horse to have an extra feed. Sometimes the man rattles off his words as if the brute understood everything said to him. An obstinate or lazy horse is called a variety of names the reverse of endearing. I have heard him addressed as '*sabaka*,' (dog); and on frequent occasions his maternity was ascribed to the canine race in epithets quite disrespectful. Horses came in for an amount of profanity about like that showered upon army mules in America. It used to look a little out of place to see a yemshick who had shouted *chort!* and other unrefined expressions to his team, devoutly crossing himself before a holy picture as soon as his beasts were unharnessed.

A few versts from Achinsk we crossed the boundary between Eastern and Western Siberia. The Chulim is navigable up to Achinsk, and during the past two years steamers have been running between this town and Tomsk. The basin of the Ob contains nearly as many navigable streams as that of the Mississippi, and were it not for the severity of the climate, the long winter, and the northerly course of the great river, this valley might easily develop much wealth. But nature is unfavorable, and man is powerless to change her laws.

On changing at the station we again took four horses to each sleigh, and were glad we did so. The ground was more bare as we proceeded, and obliged us to leave the high road altogether and seek a track wherever it could be found. While we were dashing through a mass of rocks and stumps one of our horses fell dead, and brought us to a sudden halt. In his fall he became entangled with the others, and it required some minutes to set matters right. The yemshick felt for the pulse of the beast until fully satisfied that no pulse existed. Happily we were not far from a station, so that the reduction of our team was of no serious consequence. In this region I observed cribs like roofless log houses placed near the roadside at intervals of a few hundred yards. They were intended to hold materials for repairing the road.

On the upper waters of the Chulim there is a cascade of considerable beauty, according to the statement of some who never saw it. A few years ago a Siberian gold miner discovered a cataract on the river Hook, in the Irkutsk government, that he thought equal to Niagara, and engaged an artist to make a drawing of the curiosity. On reaching the spot, the latter individual found the cascade a very small affair. Throughout Russia, Niagara is considered one of the great wonders of the world, and nothing could have been more pleasing to the Siberians than to find its rival in their own country.

When I first began traveling in Siberia a gentleman one day expressed the hope of seeing America before long, but added, "much pleasure of my visit will be lacking now that you have lost Niagara." I could not understand him, and asked an explanation.

"Why," said he, "since Niagara has been worn away to a continuous rapid it must have lost all its grandeur and sublimity. I shall go there, but I cannot enjoy it as I should have enjoyed the great cataract."

I explained that Niagara was as perfect as ever, and had no indication of wearing itself away. It appeared that some Russian newspaper, misled, I presume, by the fall of Table Rock, announced that the whole precipice had broken down and left a long rapid in place of the cataract. Several times during my journey I was called upon to correct this impression.

At the third station beyond Achinsk we found a neat and well kept room for travelers. We concluded to dine there, and were waited upon by a comely young woman whose *coiffure* showed that she was unmarried. She brought us the samovar, cooked our pilmania, and boiled a dizaine of eggs. Among the Russians articles which we count by the dozen are enumerated by tens. "*Skolka stoit, yieetsa?*" (How much do eggs cost), was generally answered, "*Petnatzet capecka, decetu,*" (fifteen copecks for ten.) Only among the Western nations one finds the dozen in use.

While we were at dinner the cold sensibly increased, and on exposing my thermometer I found it marking –18° Fahrenheit. Schmidt wrapped himself in all his furs, and I followed his example. Thus enveloped we filled the entire breadth of our sleigh and could not turn over with facility. A sharp wind was blowing dead ahead, and we closed the front of the vehicle to exclude it. The snow whirled in little eddies and made its way through the crevices at the junction of our sleigh-boot with the hood. I wrapped a blanket in front of my face for special protection, and soon managed to fall asleep. The sleigh poising on a runner and out-rigger, caused the doctor to roll against me during the first hour of my slumber, and made me dream that I was run over by a locomotive. When I waked I found my breath had congealed and frozen my beard to the blanket. It required careful manipulation to separate the two without injury to either.

When we stopped to change horses after this experience, the stars were sparkling with a brilliancy peculiar to the Northern sky. The clear starlight, unaided by the moon, enabled us to see with great distinctness. I could discover the outline of the forest away beyond the village, and trace the road to the edge of a valley where it disappeared. Every individual star appeared endeavoring to outshine his rivals, and cast his rays to the greatest distance. Vesta, Sirius, and many others burned with a brightness that recalled my first view of the Drummond light, and seemed to dazzle my eyes when I fixed my gaze upon them.

The road during the night was rough but respectable, and we managed to enjoy a fair amount of slumber in our contracted *chambre a deux*. Before daylight we reached a station where a traveling bishop had just secured two sets of horses. Though outside the jurisdiction of General Korsackoff, I exhibited my special passport knowing it could not, at all events, do any harm. Out of courtesy the smotretal offered to supply us as soon as the bishop departed. The reverend worthy was dilatory in starting, and as we were likely to be delayed an hour or two, we economized the time by taking tea. I found opportunity for a short nap after our tea-drinking was over, and only awoke when the smotretal announced, "*loshady gotoney.*"

In the forenoon we entered upon the steppe where trees were few and greatly scattered. Frequently the vision over this Siberian prairie was uninterrupted for several miles. There was a thin covering of snow on the open ground, and the dead grass peered above the surface with a suggestion of summer fertility.

Shortly after noon I looked through the eddies of snow that whirled in the frosty air, and distinguished the outline of a church. Another and another followed, and very soon the roofs and walls of the more prominent buildings in Tomsk were visible. As we entered the eastern gate of the city, and passed a capacious powder-magazine, our yemshick tied up his bell-tongues in obedience to the municipal law. Our arrival inside the city limits was marked by the most respectful silence.

We named a certain hotel but the yemshick coolly took us to another which he assured us was "*acleechny*" (excellent). As the exterior and the appearance of the servants promised fairly, we made no objection, and allowed our baggage unloaded. The last I saw of our yemshick he was receiving a subsidy from the landlord in consideration of having taken us thither. The doctor said the establishment was better than the one he first proposed to patronize, so that we had no serious complaint against the management of the affair. Hotel keepers in Siberia are obliged to pay a commission to whoever brings them patrons, a practice not unknown, I believe, in American cities.

We engaged two rooms, one large, and the other of medium size. The larger apartment contained two sofas, ten or twelve chairs, three tables, a boy, a bedstead, and a chamber-maid. The boy and the maid disappeared with a quart or so of dirt they had swept from the floor. We ordered dinner, and took our ease in our inn. Our baggage piled in one corner of the room would have made a creditable stock for an operator in the "Elbow Market" at Moscow. We thawed our beards, washed, changed our clothing, and pretended we felt none the worse for our jolting over the rough road from Krasnoyarsk.

The hotel, though Asiatic, was kept on the European plan. The landlord demanded our passports before we removed our outer garments, and apologized by saying the regulations were very strict. The documents went at once to the police, and returned in the morning with the visa of the chief. Throughout Russia a hotel proprietor generally keeps the passports of his patrons until their bills are paid, but this landlord trusted in our honor, and returned the papers at once. The visa certified there were no charges against us, pecuniary or otherwise, and allowed us to remain or depart at our pleasure. It is a Russian custom for the police to be informed of claims against persons suspected of intent to run away. The individual cannot obtain authority to depart until his accounts are settled. Formerly the law required every person, native and foreign, about to leave Russia, to advertise his intention through a newspaper. This formula is now dispensed with, but the intending traveler must produce a receipt in full from his hotel keeper.

At the hotel we found a gentleman from Eastern Siberia on his way to St. Petersburg. He left Irkutsk two days behind me, passed us in Krasnoyarsk, and came to grief in a partial overturn five miles from Tomsk. He was waiting to have his broken vehicle thoroughly repaired before venturing on the steppe. He had a single vashok in which he stowed himself, wife, three children, and a governess. How the whole party could be packed into the carriage I was at a loss to imagine. Its limits must have been suggestive of the close quarters of a can of sardines.

We used our furs for bed clothing and slept on the sofas, less comfortably I must confess than in the sleigh. The close atmosphere of a Russian house is not as agreeable to my lungs as the open air, and after a long journey one's first night in a warm room is not refreshing. There was no public table at the hotel; meals were served in our room, and each item was charged separately at prices about like those of Irkutsk.

In the morning we put on our best clothes, and visited the gubernatorial mansion. The governor was at St. Petersburg, and we were received by the Vice-Governor, an amiable gentleman of about fifty years, who reminded me of General S. R. Curtis. Before our interview we waited ten or fifteen minutes at one end of a large hall. The Vice-Governor was at the other end listening to a woman whose streaming eyes and choked utterance showed that her story was one of grief. The kind hearted man appeared endeavoring to soothe her. I could not help hearing the conversation though ignorant of its purport, and, as the scene closed, I thought I had not known before the extent of pathos in the Russian language.

We had a pleasant interview with the vice-governor who gave us passports to Barnaool, on learning that we wished to visit that place. Among those who called during our stay was the golovah of Tomsk, a man whose physical proportions resembled those of the renowned Wouter Van Twiller, as described by Washington Irving. Every golovah I met in Siberia was of aldermanic proportions, and I wondered whether physical developments had any influence in selections for this office. Just before leaving the governor's residence, we were introduced to Mr. Naschinsky, of Barnaool, to whom I had a letter of introduction from his cousin, Paul Anossoff. As he was to start for home that evening, we arranged to accompany him. Our visit ended, we drove through the principal streets, and saw the chief features of the town.

Tomsk takes its name from the river Tom, on whose banks it is built. It stands on the edge of the great Baraba steppe, and has about twenty thousand inhabitants of the usual varied character of a Russian population. I saw many fine houses, and was told that in society and wealth the city was little inferior to Irkutsk. Here, as at other places, large fortunes have been made in gold mining. Several heavy capitalists were mentioned as owners of concessions in the mining districts. Many of their laborers passed the winter at Tomsk in the delights of urban life. The city is of considerable importance as it controls much of the commerce of Siberia. The site is picturesque, being partly on the low ground next the river, and partly on the hills above it. In contemplating the location, I was reminded of Quebec. I found much activity in the streets and market places, and good assortments of merchandise in the shops.

Near our hotel, over a wide ravine, was a bridge, constantly traversed by vehicles and pedestrians, and lighted at night by a double row of lamps. Some long buildings near the river, and just outside the principal market had a likeness to American railway stations, and the quantities of goods piled on their verandas aided the illusion. About noon the market-place was densely crowded, and there appeared a brisk traffic in progress. There was a liberal array of articles to eat, wear, or use, with a very fair quantity for which no use could be imagined.

In summer there is a waterway from Tomsk to Tumen, a thousand miles to the westward, and a large amount of freight to and from Siberia passes over it. Steamers descend the Tom to the Ob, which they follow to the Irtish. They then ascend the Irtish, the Tobol, and the Tura to Tumen, the head of navigation. The government proposes a railway between Perm and Tumen to unite the great water courses of Europe and Siberia. A railway from Tomsk to Irkutsk is among the things hoped for by the Siberians, and will be accomplished at some future day. The arguments urged against its construction are the length of the route, the sparseness of population, and the cheap rates at which freight is now transported. Probably Siberia would be no exception to the rule that railways create business, and sustain it, but I presume it will be many years before the locomotive has a permanent way through the country.

Some years ago it was proposed to open a complete water route between Tumen and Kiachta. The most eastern point that a steamer could attain in the valley of the Ob is on the river Ket. A canal about thirty miles long would connect the Ket with the Yenesei, whence it was proposed to follow the Angara, Lake Baikal, and the Selenga to Oust Kiachta. But the swiftness of the Angara, and its numerous rapids, seventy-eight in all, stood in the way of the project. At present no steamers can ascend the Angara, and barges can only descend when the water is high. To make the channel safely navigable would require a heavy outlay of money for blasting rocks, and digging canals. I could not ascertain that there was any probability of the scheme being realized.

In 1866 twelve steamers were running between Tumen and Tomsk. These boats draw about two feet of water, and tow one or more barges in which freight is piled. No merchandise is carried on the boats. Twelve days are consumed in the voyage with barges; without them it can be made in a week. All the steamers yet constructed are for towing purposes, the passenger traffic not being worth attention. The golovah of Tomsk is a heavy owner in these steamboats, and he proposed increasing their number and enlarging his business. A line of smaller boats has been started to connect Tomsk with Achinsk. The introduction of steam on the Siberian rivers has given an impetus to commerce, and revealed the value of certain interests of the country. An active competition in the same direction would prove highly beneficial, and bye and bye they will have the railway.

During my ride about the streets the isvoshchik pointed out a large building, and explained that it was the seminary or high school of Tomsk. I was told that the city, like Irkutsk, had a female school or "Institute," and an establishment for educating the children of the priests. The schools in the cities and large towns of Siberia have a good reputation, and receive much praise from those who patronize them. The Institute at Irkutsk is especially renowned, and had during the winter of 1866 something more than a hundred boarding pupils. The gymnasium or school for boys was equally flourishing, and under the direct control of the Superintendent of Public Instruction for Eastern Siberia. The branches of education comprise the ordinary studies of schools everywhere—arithmetic, grammar, and geography, with reading and writing. When these elementary studies are mastered the higher mathematics, languages, music, and painting follow. In the primary course the prayers of the church and the manner of crossing one's self are considered essential.

Most of those who can afford it employ private teachers for their children, and educate them at home. The large schools in the towns are patronized by the upper and middle classes, and sometimes pupils come from long distances. There are schools for the peasant children, but not sufficiently numerous to make education general. It is a lamentable fact that the peasants as a class do not appreciate the importance of knowledge. Hitherto all these peasant schools have been controlled by the church, the subordinate priests being appointed to their management.

Quite recently the Emperor has ordered a system of public instruction throughout the empire. Schools are to be established, houses built, and teachers paid by the government. Education is to be taken entirely from the hands of the priests, and entrusted to the best qualified instructors without regard to race or religion. The common school house in the land of the czars! Universal education among the subjects of the Autocrat! Well may the other monarchies of Europe fear the growing power and intelligence of Russia. May God bless Alexander, and preserve him many years to the people whose prosperity he holds so dearly at heart.

CHAPTER XLIII.

WHEN we left Tomsk in the evening, the snow was falling rapidly, and threatened to obliterate the track along the frozen surface of the river. There were no post horses at the station, and we were obliged to charter private teams at double the usual rates. The governor warned us that we might have trouble in securing horses, and requested us to refer to him if the smotretal did not honor our pada ashnia. We did not wish to trespass further on his kindness, and concluded to submit to the extortion and say nothing. The station keeper owned the horses we hired, and we learned he was accustomed to declare his regular troikas "out" on all possible occasions. Of course, a traveler anxious to proceed, would not hesitate long at paying two or three roubles extra.

We dashed over the rough ice of the Tom for a few versts and then found a road on solid earth. We intended to visit Barnaool, and for this purpose left the great road at the third station, and turned southward. The falling snow beat so rapidly into our sleigh that we closed the vehicle and ignored the outer world. Mr. Naschinsky started with us from Tomsk, but after a few stations he left us and hurried away at courier speed toward Barnaool. He proved an *avant courier* for us, and warned the station masters of our approach, so that we found horses ready.

On this side road the contract requires but three troikas at a station. Three sleighs together were an unusual number, so that the smotretals generally obtained one or both our teams from the village. On the last half of the route the yemshicks did not take us to the stations but to the houses of their friends where we promptly obtained horses at the regular rates. The peasants between Tomsk and Barnaool own many horses, and are pleased at the opportunity to earn a little cash with them.

Snow, darkness, and slumber prevented our seeing much of the road during the night. In the morning, I found we were traveling through an undulating and generally wooded country, occasionally crossing rivers and small lakes on the ice. The track was a wonderful improvement over that between Tomsk and Krasnoyarsk. The stations or peasant houses where we changed horses, were not as good as those on the great road. The rooms were frequently small and heated to an uncomfortable degree. In one house, notwithstanding the great heat, several children were seated on the top of the stove, and apparently enjoying themselves. The yemshicks and attendants were less numerous than on the great road, but we could find no fault with their service. On one course of twenty versts our sleigh was driven by a boy of thirteen, though seemingly not more than ten. He handled the whip and reins with the skill of a veteran, and earned an extra gratuity from his passengers.

The road was marked by upright poles ten or twelve feet high at distances of one or two hundred feet. There were distance posts with the usual black and white alternations, but the figures were generally indistinct, and many posts were altogether wanting. On the main road through the whole length of Siberia, there is a post at every verst, marking in large numbers the distance to the first station on either side of it. At the stations there are generally posts that show the distance to Moscow, St. Petersburg, and the provincial or 'government' capitals on either side.

For a long time I could never rid myself of a sensation of 'goneness' when I read the figures indicating the distance to St. Petersburg. Above seven thousand they were positively frightful; between six and seven thousand, they were disagreeable to say the least. Among the five thousand and odd versts, I began to think matters improving, and when I descended below four thousand, I felt as if in my teens. The proverb says, " a watched pot never boils." I can testify that these distance figures diminished very slowly, and sometimes they seemed to remain nearly the same from day to day.

The snow storm that began when we left Tomsk, continued through the night and the following day. The air was warm, and there was little wind, so that our principal inconvenience was from the snow flakes in our faces, and the gradual filling of the road. Toward sunset a wind arose. Every hour it increased, and before midnight there was good prospect of our losing our way or being compelled to halt until daybreak. The snow whirled in thick masses through the air, and utterly blinded us when we attempted to look out. The road filled with drifts, and we had much difficulty in dragging through them. The greatest personal inconvenience was the sifting of snow through the crevices of our sleigh cover. At every halt we underwent a vigorous shaking to remove the superfluous snow from our furs.

A storm with high winds in this region takes the name of *bouran*. It is analogous to the *poorga* of Northeastern Siberia and Kamchatka, and may occur at any season of the year.

Bourans are oftentimes very violent, especially in the open steppe. Any one who has experienced the norther of Texas, or the *bora* of Southern Austria, can form an idea of these Siberian storms. The worst are when the thermometer sinks to twenty-five degrees or more below zero, and the snow is dashed about with terrific fury. At such times they are almost insupportable, and the traveler who ventures to face them runs great risk of his life. Many persons have been lost in the winter storms, and all experienced voyagers are reluctant to brave their violence. In summer the wind spends its force on the earth and sand which it whirls in large clouds. A gentleman told me he had seen the dry bed of a river where there were two feet of sand, swept clean to the rock by the strength of the wind alone.

A little past daylight the sleigh came to a sudden stop despite the efforts of all concerned. The last hundred versts of our ride we had four horses to each sleigh, and their united strength was not more than sufficient for our purpose. The drift where we stopped was at least three feet deep, and pretty closely packed. We, that is to say, the horses and yemshicks, made several efforts but could not carry the sleigh through. The mammoth sleigh came up and the two yemshicks trod a path through the worst part of the drift. The doctor and I descended from the vehicle, and assisted by looking on. The sleigh thus lightened, was dragged through the obstruction but unfortunately turned on its beam ends, and filled with snow before it could be righted.

The bouran was from the south, and raised the temperature above the freezing point. The increasing heat became uncomfortable after the cold I had experienced. The horses did not turn white from perspiration as in colder days, and the exertion of travel set them panting as in summer. The drivers carefully knotted their (the horses') tails to prevent them (the tails) from filling with snow, but the precaution was not entirely successful. The snow was of the right consistency for a school boy's frolic, and would have thrown a group of American urchins into ecstacies. Whenever our pace quickened to a trot or gallop, the larboard horse threw a great many snowballs with his feet. He seemed to aim at my face, and every few minutes I received what the prize ring would call 'plumpers in the peeper, and sockdolagers on the potato-trap.'

We drove into Barnaool about forty-four hours after leaving Tomsk. At the hotel we found three rooms containing chairs and tables in profusion, but not a bed or sofa. Of course we were expected to supply our own bedding, and need not be particular about a bedstead. The worst part of the affair was the wet condition of our furs. My sheepskin sleigh robe was altogether too damp for use, and I sent it to be dried in the kitchen. Several of my fur garments went the same way. Even my shooba, which I carried in a bag, had a feeling of dampness when I unfolded it, and in fact the only dry things about us, were our throats. We set things drying as best we could, and then ordered dinner. Before our sleighs were unloaded, a policeman took our passports and saved us all trouble of going to the station.

In the evening I accompanied Dr. Schmidt on a visit to a friend and fellow member of the Academy of Science. We found a party of six or eight persons, and, as soon as I was introduced, a gentleman despatched a servant to his house. The man returned with a roll of sheet music from which our host's daughter favored us with the "Star Spangled Banner," and "Hail Columbia," as a greeting to the first American visitor to Barnaool. On our return to our lodgings we made our beds on the floor, and slept comfortably. The dampness of the furs developed a rheumatic pain in my shoulder that stiffened me somewhat inconveniently.

We breakfasted upon cakes and tea at a late hour in the morning, and then went to pay our respects to General Freeze, the Nachalnik or Director of Mines, and to Colonel Filoff, chief of the smelting works. Both these officers were somewhat past the middle age, quiet and affable, and each enjoyed himself in coloring a meerschaum. They have been engaged in mining matters during many years, and are said to be thoroughly versed in their profession. After visiting these gentlemen we called upon other official and civilian residents of the city.

Barnaool is the center of direction of the mining enterprises of the Altai mountains, and has a population of ten or twelve thousand. Almost its entire business is in someway connected with mining affairs, and there are many engineer officers constantly stationed there. I met some of these gentlemen during my stay, and was indebted to them for information concerning the manner of working mines and reducing ores. The city contains a handsome array of public buildings, including the mining bureau, the hospital, and the zavod or smelting establishment. General Freeze, the Nachalnik, is director and chief, not only of the city but of the entire mining district of which Barnaool is the center.

The first discoveries of precious metals in the Altai regions were made by one of the Demidoffs who was sent there by Peter the Great. A monument in the public square at Barnaool records his services, in ever during brass. I was shown an autograph letter from the Empress Elizabeth giving directions to the Nachalnik who controlled the mines during her reign. The letter is kept in an ivory box on the table around which the mining board holds its sessions. The mines of this region are the personal property of the Emperor, and their revenues go directly to the crown. I was told that the government desires to sell or give these mines into private hands, in the belief that the resources of the country would be more thoroughly developed. The day before my departure from Barnaool, I learned that my visit had reference to the possible purchase of the mining works by an American company. I hastened to assure my informant that I had no intention of buying the Altai mountains or any part of them.

The Nachalnik visits all mines and smelting works in his district at least once a year, and is constantly in receipt of detailed reports of operations in progress. His power is almost despotic, and like the governors of departments throughout all Siberia, he can manage affairs pretty much in his own way. There are no convict laborers in his district, the workmen at the mines and zavods being peasants subject to the orders of government. Each man in the district may be called upon to work for the Emperor at fixed wages of money and rations. I believe the daily pay of a laborer is somewhat less than forty copecks. A compromise for saints days and other festivals is made by employing the men only two weeks out of three. Relays are so arranged as to make no stoppage of the works except during the Christmas holidays.

I saw many sheets of the geological map of the Altai region, which has been a long time in preparation, and will require several years to complete. Every mountain, hill, brook, and valley is laid down by careful surveyors, and when the map is finished it will be one of the finest and best in the world. One corps is engaged in surveying and mapping while another explores and opens mines.

When the snows are melted in the spring, and the floods have receeded from the streams, the exploring parties are sent into the mountains. Each officer has a particular valley assigned him, and commands a well equipped body of men. He is expected to remain in the mountains until he has finished his work, or until compelled to leave by the approach of winter. The party procures, meat from gam,e of which there is nearly always an abundant supply.

Holes are dug at regular intervals, on the system I have already described in the mines of the Yenesei. The rocks in and around the valley are carefully examined for traces of silver, and many specimens have been collected for the geological cabinet at Barnaool. Maps are made showing the locality of each test hole in the valley, and the spot whence every specimen of rock is obtained. On the return of the party its reports and specimens are delivered to the mining bureau. The ores go to the laboratory to be assayed, and the specimens of rock are carefully sorted and examined.

Gold washings are conducted on the general plan of those in the Yeneseisk government, the details varying according to circumstances. A representation of the principal silver mine—somewhat on the plan of Barnum's "Niagara with Real Water"—was shown me in the museum. In general features the mines are not materially unlike silver mines elsewhere. There are shafts, adits, and levels just as in the mines of Colorado and California. The Russians give the name of *priesk* to a mine where gold is washed from the earth. The silver mine with its shafts in the solid rock is called a *roodnik*. As before stated, the word *zavod* is applied to foundries, smelting works, and manufactories in general.

Colonel Filoff invited the doctor and myself to visit the zavod at Barnaool on the second day after our arrival. As he spoke no language with which I was familiar, the colonel placed me in charge of a young officer fluent in French, who took great pains to explain the *modus operandi*. The zavod is on a grand scale, and employs about six hundred laborers. It is enclosed in a large yard with high walls, and reminded

IN THE MINE.

me of a Pennsylvania iron foundry or the establishment just below Detroit. A sentry at the gate presented arms as we passed, and I observed that the rule of no admittance except on business was rigidly enforced.

In the yard we were first taken to piles of ore which appeared to an unpracticed eye like heaps of old mortar and broken granite. These piles were near a stream which furnishes power for moving the machinery of the establishment. The ore was exposed to the air and snow, but the coal for smelting was carefully housed. There were many sheds for storage within easy distance of the furnaces. The latter were of brick with tall and substantial chimneys, and the outer walls that surrounded the whole were heavily and strongly built.

Charcoal is burned in consequence of the cheapness and abundance of wood. I was told that an excellent quality of stove coal existed in the vicinity, and would be used whenever it proved most economical. Nearly all the ore contains copper, silver, and lead, while the rest is deficient in the last named article. The first kind is smelted without the addition of lead, and sometimes passes through six or seven reductions. For the ore containing only copper and silver the process by evaporation of lead is employed. Formerly the lead was brought from Nerchinsk or purchased in England, the land transport in either case being very expensive. Several years ago lead was found in the Altai mountains, and the supply is now sufficient for all purposes.

The lead absorbs the silver, and leaves the copper in the refuse matter. This was formerly thrown away, but by a newly invented process the copper is extracted and saved. The production of silver in the Altai mines is about a thousand and fifty poods annually, or forty thousand pounds avoirdupois. The silver is cast into bars or cakes about ten inches square, and weighing from seventy to a hundred pounds each.

Colonel Filoff showed us into the room where the silver is stored. Two soldiers were on guard and six or eight others rested outside. A sergeant brought a sealed box which contained the key of the safe. First the box and then the safe were opened at the colonel's order, and when we had satisfied our curiosity, the safe was locked and the key restored to its place of deposit. The colonel carried the seal that closed the box, and the sergeant was responsible for the integrity of the wax.

The cakes had a dull hue, somewhat lighter than that of lead, and were of a convenient shape for handling. Each cake had its weight, and value, and result of assay stamped upon it, and I was told that it was assayed again at St. Petersburg to guard against the algebraic process of substitution. About thirty poods of gold are extracted from every thousand poods of silver after the treasure reaches St. Petersburg. The silver is extracted from the lead used to absorb it, the latter being again employed while the former goes on its long journey to the banks of the Neva.

The ore continues to pass through successive reductions until a pood of it contains no more than three-fourths a zolotink of silver; less than that proportion will not pay expenses. I was told that the annual cost of working the mines equaled the value of the silver produced. The gold contained in the silver is the only item of profit to the crown. About thirty thousand poods of copper are produced annually in this district, but none of the copper zavods are at Barnaool.

All gold produced from the mines of Siberia, with the exception of that around Nerchinsk, is sent to Barnaool to be smelted. This work is performed in a room about fifteen feet square, the furnaces being fixed in its centre like parlor stoves of unusual size. The smelting process continues four months of each year, and during this time about twelve hundred poods of gold are melted and cast into bars. This work, for 1866, was finished a few days before my arrival, and the furnaces were utterly devoid of heat. In the yard at the

STRANGE COINCIDENCE.

zavod, I saw a dozen or more sleds, and on each of them there was an iron-bound box filled with bars of gold. This train was ready to leave under strong guard for St. Petersburg.

The morning after my visit to the zavod it was reported that a soldier guarding the sled train had been killed during the night. The incident was a topic of conversation for the rest of my stay, but I obtained no clear account of the affair. All agreed that a sentinel was murdered, and one of the boxes plundered of several bars of gold, but beyond this there were conflicting statements. It was the first occurrence of the kind at Barnaool, and naturally excited the peaceful inhabitants.

The doctor trusted that the affair would not be associated with our visit, and I quite agreed with him. It is to be hoped that the future historian of Barnaool will not mention the murder and robbery in the same paragraph with the distinguished arrival of Dr. Schmidt and an American traveler.

The rich miners send their gold once a year to Barnaool, the poorer ones twice a year. Those in pressing need of money receive certificates of deposit as soon as their gold is cast into bars, and on these certificates they can obtain cash at the government banks. The opulent miners remain content till their gold reaches the capital, and is coined. Four or six months may thus elapse after gold has left Barnaool before its owner obtains returns.

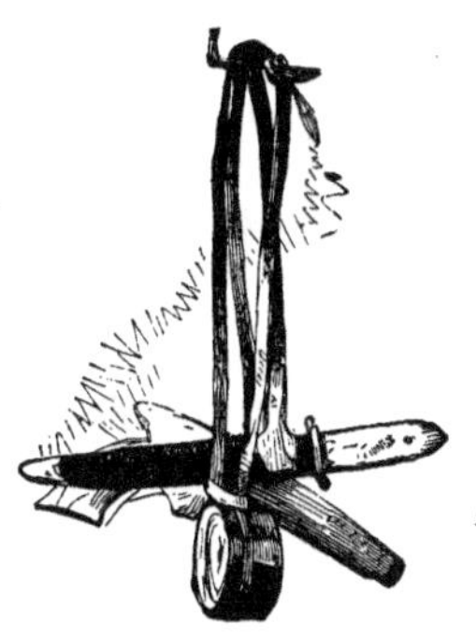

CHAPTER XLIV.

THE society of Barnaool consists of the mining and other officers, with a larger proportion of families than at Irkutsk. It had a more quiet and reserved character than the capital of Eastern Siberia, but was not the less social and hospitable. Many young officers of the mining and topographical departments pass their summers in the mountains and their winters in Barnaool. The cold season is therefore the gayest, and abounds in balls, parties, concerts, and amateur theatricals. The former theatre has been converted into a club-room.

There is a good proportion, for a Siberian town, of elegant and luxuriant houses. The furniture and adornments were quite as extensive as at Irkutsk or Tomsk, and several houses that I visited would have been creditable in Moscow or St. Petersburg. It is no little wonder to find all the comforts and luxuries of Russian life in the southern part of Siberia, on the borders of the Kirghese steppes.

The large and well arranged museum contained more than I could even glance over in a single day. There were models of machines used in gold-washing, quartz mills fifty years old, and almost identical with those of the present day; models of furnaces and zavods in various parts of Siberia, and full delineations of the principal silver mines of the Altai. There was a curious steam engine, said to have been made at Barnaool in 1764, and used for blowing the furnaces. I saw a fine collection of minerals, birds, beasts, and other curiosities of the Altai. Particular attention was called to the stuffed skins of two enormous tigers that were killed several years ago in the southern part of the district. One of them fell after a long fight, in which he killed one of his assailants and wounded two others.

The museum contains several dead specimens of the bearcoot, or eagle of the Altai. I saw a living bird of this species at the house of an acquaintance. The bearcoot is larger than the American eagle, and possesses strength enough to kill a deer or wolf with perfect ease. Dr. Duhmberg, superintendent of the hospitals, told me of an experiment with poison upon one of these birds. He began by giving half a grain of *curavar*, a poison from South America. It had no perceptible effect, the appetite and conduct of the bird being unchanged. A week later he gave four grains of strychnine, and saw the bird's feathers tremble fifteen minutes after the poison was swallowed. Five hours later the patient was in convulsions, but his head was not affected, and he recovered strength and appetite on the next day. A week later the bearcoot swallowed seven grains of curavar, and showed no change for two days. On the second evening he went into convulsions, and died during the night.

The Kirghese tame these eagles and employ them in hunting. A gentleman who had traveled among the Kirghese told me he had seen a bearcoot swoop down upon a full grown deer and kill him in a few minutes. Sometimes when a pack of wolves has killed and begun eating a deer, the feast will be interrupted by a pair of bearcoots. Two birds will attack a dozen wolves, and either kill or drive them away.

Barnaool is quite near the Kirghese steppes. One of my acquaintances had a Kirghese coachman, a tall, well formed man, with thick lips and a coppery complexion. I established a friendship with this fellow, and arranged that he should sit for his portrait, but somehow he was never ready. He brought me two of his kindred, and I endeavored to persuade the group to be photographed. There was a superstition among them that it would be detrimental to their post mortem repose if they allowed their likenesses on this earth when they themselves should leave it. I offered them one, two, three, and even five roubles, but they stubbornly refused. Their complexions were dark, and their whole physiognomy revealed the Tartar blood. They wore the Russian winter dress, but had their own costume for state occasions. In this part of Siberia Kirghese are frequently found in Russian employ, and are said to be generally faithful and industrious. A considerable number find employment at the Altai mines, and a great many are engaged in taking cattle and sheep to the Siberian markets.

The Kirghese lead a nomadic life, making frequent change of residence to find pasturage for their immense flocks and herds. The different tribes are more or less hostile to each other, and have a pleasant habit of organizing raids on a colossal scale. One tribe will suddenly swoop down upon another and steal all portable property within reach. They do not mind a little fighting, and an enterprise of this kind frequently results in a good many broken heads. The chiefs believe themselves descended from the great warriors of the ancient Tartar days, and boast loudly of their prowess. The Kirghese are brave in fighting each other, but have a respectful fear of the Russians. Occasionally they plunder Russian traders crossing the steppes, but are careful not to attack unless the odds are on their own side.

The Russians have applied their diplomacy among the Kirghese and pushed their boundaries far to the southward. They have purchased titles to districts controlled by powerful chiefs, and after being fairly settled have continued negotiations for more territory. They make use of the hostility between the different tribes, and have managed so that nearly every feud brought advantages to Russia. Under their policy of toleration they never interfere with the religion of the conquered, and are careful not to awaken prejudices. The tribes in the subjugated territory are left pretty much to their own will. Every few years the chain of frontier posts is pushed to the southward, and embraces a newly acquired region. Western Siberia is dotted over with abandoned and crumbling forts that once guarded the boundary, but are now far in the interior. Some of these defences are near the great road across the Baraba steppe.

The Kirghese do not till the soil nor engage in manufactures, except of a few articles for their own use. They sell sheep, cattle, and horses to the Russians, and frequently accompany the droves to their destination. In return for their flocks and herds they receive goods of Russian manufacture, either for their own use or for traffic with the people beyond. Their wealth consists of domestic animals and the slaves to manage them. Horses and sheep are legal tender in payment of debts, bribes, and presents.

In the last few years Russian conquest in Central Asia has moved so fast that England has taken alarm for her Indian possessions. The last intelligence from that quarter announces a victory of the Russians near Samarcand, followed by negotiations for peace. If the Muscovite power continues to extend over that part of Asia, England has very good reason to open her eyes.

I never conversed with the Emperor on this topic, and cannot speak positively of his intentions toward Asia, but am confident he has fixed his eye upon conquest as far south of the Altai as he can easily go. That his armies may sometime hoist the Russian flag in sight of the Indo-English possessions, is not at all improbable. But that they will either attempt or desire an aggressive campaign against India is quite beyond expectation.

It is but a few years ago that English travelers were killed for having made their way into Central Asia in disguise, and Vambery, the Hungarian traveler, was considered to have performed a great feat because he returned from there with his life. There is now the Tashkend *Messenger*, a Russian paper devoted to the interests of that rich province. Moscow merchants are establishing the Bank of Central Asia, having its headquarters at Tashkend and a branch at Orenburg, and Tashkend will soon be in telegraphic communication with the rest of the world.

A plan has been proposed to open Central Asia to steam.

boat navigation. The river Oxus, or Amoo-Daria, which flows through Bakhara and Khiva, emptying into the Aral sea, was once a tributary of the Caspian. Several steamers have been placed upon it, and others are promised soon. The dry bed of the old channel of the Oxus is visible in the Turcoman steppe at the present day. The original diversion was artificial, and the dikes which direct it into the Aral are said to be maintained with difficulty. It has been proposed to send an expedition to remove these barriers and turn the river into its former bed.

Coupled with this project is another to divert the course of the Syr-Daria and make it an affluent of the Oxus. This last proposition was half carried out two hundred years ago, and its completion would not be difficult.

By the first project, Russia would obtain a continuous water-way from Nijne Novgorod on the Volga to Balkh on the Amoo-Daria, within two hundred miles of British India. The second scheme carried out would bring Tashkend and all Central Asia under commercial control, and have a political effect of no secondary importance. A new route might thus be opened to British India, and European civilization carried into a region long occupied by semi-barbarian people. Afghanistan would be relieved from its anarchy and brought under wholesome rule. The geographical effect would doubtless be the drying up of the Aral sea. A railway between Balkh and Delhi would complete an inland steam route between St. Petersburg and Calcutta.

Surveys have been ordered for a Central Asiatic Railway from Orenburg or some point farther south, and it is quite possible that before many years the locomotive will be shrieking over the Tartar steppes and frightening the flocks and herds of the wandering Kalmacks and Kirghese. A railway is in process of construction from the Black Sea to the Caspian, and when this is completed, a line into Central Asia is only a question of time.

The Russians have an extensive trade with Central Asia. Goods are transported on camels, the caravans coming in season for the fairs of Irbit and Nijne Novgorod. The caravans from Bokhara proceed to Troitska, (Lat. 54° N., Lon. 61° 20′ E.,) Petropavlovsk, (Lat. 54° 30′ N., Lon. 69° E.,) and Orenburg, (Lat. 51° 46′ N., Lon. 55° 5 E.) There is also a considerable traffic to Sempolatinsk, (Lat. 50° 30′ N., Lon. 80° E.) The Russian merchandise consists of metals, iron and steel goods, beads, mirrors, cloths of various kinds, and a miscellaneous lot "too numerous to mention." Much of the country over which these caravans travel is a succession of Asiatic steppes, with occasional salt lakes and scanty supplies of fresh water.

After passing the Altai mountains and outlying chains the routes are quite monotonous. Fearful bourans are frequent, and in certain parts of the route they take the form of sand storms. A Russian army on its way to Khiva twenty-five years ago, was almost entirely destroyed in one of these desert tempests. Occasionally the caravans suffer severely.

The merchandise from Bokhara includes raw cotton, sheepskins, rhubarb, dried fruits, peltries, silk, and leather, with shawl goods of different kinds. Cotton is an important product, and in the latter part of my journey I saw large quantities going to Russian factories. Three hundred years ago a German traveler in Russia wrote an account of 'a wonderful plant beyond the Caspian sea.' "Veracious people," says the writer, "tell me that the *Borauez*, or sheep plant, grows upon a stalk larger than my thumb; it has a head, eyes, and ears like a sheep, but is without sensation. The natives use its wool for various purposes."

I heard an interesting story of an adventure in which one of the Kirghese, who was living among the Russians at the time of my visit to Barnaool, played an important part. He was a fine looking fellow, whose tribe lived between the Altai Mountains and Lake Ural, spending the winters in the low lands and the summers in the valleys of the foot-hills. He was the son of one of the patriarchs of the tribe, and was captured, during a baranta or foray, by a chief who had long been on hostile terms with his neighbors. The young man was held for ransom, but the price demanded was more than his father could pay, and so he remained in captivity.

He managed to ingratiate himself with the chief of the tribe that captured him, and as a mark of honor, and probably as an excuse for the high ransom demanded, he was appointed to live in the chief's household. He was allowed to ride with the party when they moved, and accompany the herdsmen; but a sharp watch was kept on his movements whenever he was mounted, and care was taken that the horses he rode were not very fleet. The chief had a daughter whom he expected to marry to one of his powerful neighbors, and thereby secure a permanent friendship between the tribes. She was a style of beauty highly prized among the Asiatics, was quite at home on horseback, and understood all the arts and accomplishments necessary to a Kirghese maiden of noble blood. It is nothing marvelous that the young captive, Selim, should become fond of the charming Acson, the daughter of his captor. His fondness was reciprocated, but, like prudent lovers everywhere, they concealed their feelings, and to the outer world preserved a most indifferent exterior.

Selim thought it best to elope, and broached his opinion to Acson, who readily favored it. They concluded to make the attempt when the tribe was moving to change its pasturage, and their absence would not be noticed until they had several hours start and were many miles on their way. They waited until the chief gave the order to move to another locality, where the grass was better. Acson managed to leave the tent in the night, under some frivolous pretext, and select two of her father's best horses, which she concealed in a grove not far away. By previous arrangement she appeared sullen and indignant toward Selim, who, mounted on a very sorry nag, set off with a party of men that were driving a large herd of horses. The latter were ungovernable, and the party became separated, so that it was easy for Selim to drop out altogether and make his way to the grove where the horses were concealed. In the same way Acson abandoned the party she started with, and within an hour from the time they left the *aool*, or encampment, the lovers met in the grove.

It was a long way to Selim's tribe, but he knew it was somewhere in the mountains to the north and west, having left its winter quarters in the low country. The pair said their prayers in the true Mahommedan style, and then, mounting their horses, set out at an easy pace to ascend the valley toward the higher land. Their horses were in excellent condition, but they knew it would be necessary to ride hard in case they were pursued, and they wished to reserve their strength for the final effort. An hour before nightfall, they saw, far down the valley, a party in pursuit. The party was riding rapidly, and from appearances had not caught sight of the fugitives. After a brief consultation the latter determined to turn aside at the first bend of the valley, and endeavor to cross at the next stream, while leaving the pursuers to go forward and be deceived.

THE ELOPEMENT.

They turned aside, and were gratified to see from a place of concealment the pursuing party proceed up the valley. The departure of the fugitives was evidently known some time earlier than they expected, else the pursuit would not have begun so soon. Guided by the general course of the hills, the fugitives made their way to the next valley, and, as the night had come upon them, they made a camp beneath a shady tree, picketing their horses, and eating such provisions as they had brought with them.

In the morning, just as their steeds were saddled and they

were preparing to resume their journey, they saw their pursuers enter the valley a mile or two below them, and move rapidly in their direction. Evidently they had turned back after losing the track, and found it without much delay. But their horses were more weary than those of the fleeing lovers, so that the latter were confident of winning the race.

Swift was the flight and swift the pursuit. The valley was wide and nearly straight, and the lovers steadily increased the distance between them and their pursuers. They followed no path, but kept steadily forward, with their faces toward the mountains. Their pursuers, originally half a dozen, diminished to five, then to four, and as the hours wore on Selim found that only two were in sight. But a new obstacle arose to his escape.

He knew that the valley he was ascending was abruptly enclosed in the mountains, and escape would be difficult. Further to the east was a more practicable one, and he determined to attempt to reach it. Turning from the valley,

THE FIGHT

he was followed by his two pursuers, who were so close upon him that he determined to fight them. Acson had brought away one of her father's scimetars, and with this Selim prepared to do battle. Finding a suitable place among the rocks, he concealed his horses, and with Acson made a stand where he could fight to advantage. He took his position on a rock just over the path his pursuers were likely to follow, and watched his opportunity to hurl a stone, which knocked one of them senseless. The other was dismounted by his horse taking fright, and before he could regain his saddle, Selim was upon him. A short hand-to-hand fight resulted in Selim's favor.

Leaving his adversaries upon the ground, one of them dead and the other mortally wounded, Selim called Acson and returned to his horses. Both the fugitives were thoroughly exhausted on reaching the valley, and found to their dismay that a stream they were obliged to cross was greatly swollen with recent rains in the mountains.

They were anxious to put the stream between them and their remaining pursuers, and after a brief halt they plunged in with their horses. Selim crossed safely, his horse stemming the current and landing some distance below the point where he entered the water. Acson was less fortunate.

While in the middle of the stream her horse stumbled upon a stone, and sprang about so wildly as to throw her from the saddle. Grasping the limb of a tree overhanging the water, she clung for a moment, but the horse sweeping against her, tore the support from her hand. With a loud cry to her terror-stricken lover, she sank beneath the waters and was dashed against the rocks a hundred yards below.

THE CATASTROPHE.

Day became night, the stars sparkled in the blue heavens; the moon rose and took her course along the sky; the wind sighed among the trees; morning tinged the eastern horizon, and the sun pushed above it, while Selim paced the banks of the river and watched the waters rolling, rolling, rolling, as they carried his heart's idol away from him forever, and it was not until night again approached that he mounted his steed and rode away, heart-broken and full of sadness. He ultimately made his way to his own tribe, but years passed before he recovered from the crushing weight of that blow; and when I saw him there was still upon his countenance a deep shadow which will never be removed. Such is the story of Selim and Acson. A more romantic one is hardly to be found.

CHAPTER XLV.

ONE morning while I was in Barnaool the doctor left me writing, and went out for a promenade. In half an hour he returned accompanied by a tall, well-formed man with a brunette complexion, and hair and mustache black as ebony. His dress was Russian, but the face impressed me as something strange.

"Let me introduce you," said the doctor, "to an officer of the Persian army. He has been eight years from home, and would like to talk with an American."

We shook hands, and by way of getting on familiar footing, I opened my cigar case. Dr. Schmidt translated our conversation, the Persian speaking Russian very fairly. His story was curious and interesting. He was captured in 1858 near Herat, by a party of predatory Turcomans. His captors sold him to a merchant at Balkh where he remained sometime. From Balkh he was sold to Khiva, and from Khiva to Bokhara, whence he escaped with a fellow captive. I asked if he was compelled to labor during his captivity, and received a negative reply. Soldiers and all others except officers are forced to all kinds of drudgery when captured by these barbarians. Officers are held for ransom, and their duties are comparatively light.

Russian slaves are not uncommon in Central Asia, though less numerous than formerly. The Kirghese cripple their prisoners by inserting a horse hair in a wound in the heel. A man thus treated is lamed for life. He cannot use his feet in escaping, and care is taken that he does not secure a horse.

The two fugitives traveled together from Bokhara, suffering

great hardships in their journey over the steppes. They avoided all towns through fear of capture, and subsisted upon whatever chance threw in their way. Once when near starvation they found and killed a sheep. They ate heartily of its raw flesh, and before the supply thus obtained was exhausted they reached the Russian boundary at Chuguchak. One of the twain died soon afterward, and his companion in flight came to Barnaool. The authorities would not let him go farther without a passport, and he had been in the town nearly a year at the time of my visit.

Through the Persian ambassador at St. Petersburg, he had communicated with his government at Teheran, and expected his passport in a few weeks.

During the eight years that had elapsed since his capture this gentleman heard nothing from his own country. He had learned to speak Russian but could not read it. I told him of the completion of the Indo-European telegraph by way of the Euphrates and the Persian Gulf, and the success of electric communication between England and India. Naturally he was less interested concerning the Atlantic cable than about the telegraph in his own country. We shook hands at parting, and mutually expressed a wish to meet again in Persia and America.

After his departure, the doctor commented upon the intelligent bearing and clear eye of the Persian, and then said:

"I have done several strange and unexpected things in my life, but I never dreamed I should be the interpreter between a Persian and an American at the foot of the Altai mountains."

I met at Barnaool, a Prussian gentleman Mr. Radroff, who was sent to Siberia by the Russian Academy of Science. He knew nearly all the languages of Europe, and had spent some years in studying those of Central Asia. He could converse and read in Chinese, Persian, and Mongol, and I don't know how many languages and dialects of lesser note. His special mission was to collect information about the present and past inhabitants of Central Asia, and in this endeavor he had made explorations in the country of the Kirghese and beyond Lake Balkask. He was preparing for a journey in 1867 to Kashgar.

Mr. Radroff possessed many archæological relics gathered in his researches, and exhibited drawings of many tumuli. He had a curious collection of spear heads, knives, swords, ornaments, stirrup irons, and other souvenirs of ancient days. He discoursed upon the ages of copper, gold, and iron, and told the probable antiquity of each specimen he brought out. He gave me a spear head and a knife blade taken from a burial mound in the Kirghese country. "You observe," said he, "they are of copper and were doubtless made before the discovery of iron. They are probably three thousand years old, and may be more. In these tumuli, copper is found much better preserved than iron, though the latter is more recently buried."

At this gentleman's house, I saw a Persian soldier who had been ten years in captivity among the Turcomans, where he was beaten and forced to the lowest drudgery, and often kept in chains. After long and patient waiting he escaped and reached the Siberian boundary. Having no passport, and unable to make himself understood, he was sent to Barnaool and lodged in prison where he remained nearly two years! The Persian officer above mentioned, heard of him by accident, and procured his release. Mr. Radroff had taken the man as a house servant and a teacher of the Persian language. I heard him read in a sonorous voice several passages from the Koran. His face bore the marks of deep suffering, and gave silent witness to the story of his terrible captivity in the hands of the Turcomans. His incarceration at Barnaool was referred to as an "unfortunate oversight." Escaping from barbarian slavery he fell into a civilized prison, and must have considered Christian kindness more fanciful than real. He expected to accompany his countryman on his return to Persia.

The day before our departure, we were invited to a public dinner in honor of our visit. It took place at the club rooms, the tables being set in what was once the parquet of the theatre. The officials, from General Freeze downward, were seated in the order of their rank, and the post of honor was assigned to the two strangers. No ladies were present, and the dinner, so far as its gastronomic features went, was much like a dinner at Irkutsk or Kiachta.

At the second course my attention was called to an excellent fish peculiar to the Ob and Yenesei rivers. It is a species of salmon under the name of Nalma, and ascends from the Arctic Ocean. Beef from the Kirghese steppes elicited our praise, and so did game from the region around Barnaool. At the end of the dinner I was ready to answer affirmatively the inquiry, " all full inside ?"

At the appearance of the champagne, Colonel Taskin of the mining engineers made a brief speech in English, and ended by proposing the United States of America and the health of the American stranger. Dr. Schmidt translated my response as well as my toast to the Russian empire, and especially the inhabitants of Barnaool. The doctor was then honored for his mammoth hunt, and made proper acknowledgment. Then we had personal toasts and more champagne with Russian and American music, and champagne again, and then we had some more champagne and then some champagne.

When the tables were removed, we had impromptu dancing to lively music, including several Cossack dances, some familiar and others new to me. There is one of these dances which usually commences by a woman stepping into the centre of the room and holding a kerchief in her right hand. Moving gracefully to the music, she passes around the apartment, beckoning to one, hiding her face from another, gesticulating with extended arms before a third, and skilfully manipulating the kerchief all the while. When this sentimental pantomime is ended, she selects a partner and waves the kerchief over him. He pretends reluctance, but allows himself to be dragged to the floor where the couple dance *en deux*. The dance includes a great deal of entreaty, aversion, hope, and despair, all in dumb show, and ends by the lady being led to a seat. I saw this dance introduced in a ballet at the Grand Theatre in Moscow, and wondered why it never appeared on the stage outside the Russian empire.

One of the gentlemen who danced admirably had recovered the use of his legs two years before, after being unable to walk no less than twenty-eight years. He declared himself determined to make up for lost time, and when I left the hall, he continued entertaining himself.

During the dancing, a party gathered around where I stood and I observed that every lady was assembling as if to witness some fun. "Be on your watch," a friend whispered, "they are going to give you the *polkedovate*."

The *polkedovate* is nothing more nor less than a tossing up at the hands of a dozen or twenty Russians. It has the effect of intoxicating a sober man, but I never heard that it sobered a drunken one. Major Collins was elevated in this way at Kiachta, and declares that the effect, added to the champagne he had previously taken, was not at all satisfactory. Remem-

THE POLKEDOVATE.

bering his experience, and fearing I might go too high or come too low, I was glad when a diversion was made in my favor by a gentleman coming to bid me good night.

The custom of tossing up a guest is less prevalent in Siberia than ten or twenty years ago. It was formerly a mark of high respect, but I presume few who were thus honored would have hesitated to forego the distinguished courtesy.

One of the gentlemen I met at dinner had a passion for trotting horses. He asked me many questions about the famous race horses in America, from Lady Suffolk down to the latest two-twenties. I answered to the best of my abilities, but truth required me to say I was not authority in equine matters. The gentleman treated me to a display of trotting by a Siberian horse five years old, and carefully trained. I forget the exact figures he gave me, but believe they were something like two-thirty to the mile. To my unhorsy eye, the animal was pretty, and well formed, and I doubt not he would have acquitted himself finely on the Bloomingdale Road. The best horses in Siberia are generally from European Russia, the Siberian climate being unfavorable to careful breeding. Kirghese horses are excellent under the saddle, but not well reputed for draught purposes.

I gave out some washing at Barnaool, and accidentally included a paper collar in the lot. When the laundress returned the linen, she explained with much sorrow the dissolution of the collar when she attempted to wash it. I presume it was the first of its kind that ever reached the Altai mountains.

MAKING EXPLANATION.

We arranged to leave Barnaool at the conclusion of the dinner at the club room. First we proceeded to the house of Colonel Taskin where we took 'positively the last' glass of champagne. Our preparations at our lodgings were soon completed, and the baggage carefully stowed. A party of our acquaintances assembled to witness our departure, and pass through a round of kissing as the yemshick uttered 'gotovey.' They did not make an end of hand-shaking until we were wrapped and bundled into the sleigh.

It was a keen, frosty night with the stars twinkling in the clear heavens as we drove outside the yard of our hotel. Horses, driver, and travelers were alike exhilarated in the sharp atmosphere and we dashed off at courier pace. The driver was a musical fellow, and endeavored to sing a Russian ballad while we were galloping over the glistening snow.

We had a long ride before us. The wide steppe of Baraba, or Barabinsky, lies between Barnaool and the foot of the Ural mountains. There was no town where we expected to stop before reaching Tumen, fifteen hundred versts away. As the luxuries of life are not abundant on this road we stored our sleighs with provisions, and hoped to add bread and eggs at the stations. Our farewell dinner was considered a sufficient preparation for at least a hundred and fifty versts. I nestled down among the furs and hay which formed my bed, leaned back upon the pillows and exposed only a few square inches of visage to the nipping and eager air.

A few versts from town we stuck upon an icy bank where the smooth feet of our horses could not obtain holding ground. After a while we attached one horse to a long rope, and enabled him to pull from the level snow above the bank. I expected the yemshick would ask us to lighten the sleigh by stepping out of it. An American driver would have put us ashore without ceremony, but custom is otherwise in Siberia. Horses and driver are engaged to take the vehicle and its burden to the next station, and it is the traveler's privilege to remain in his place in any emergency short of an overturn.

The track was excellent, having been well trodden since the storm. We followed our former road a hundred versts from Barnaool, and then turned to the left to strike the great post route near Kiansk. It was necessary to cross the river Ob, and as we reached the station near it during the night, we waited for daylight. The ice was sufficiently thick and firm, but the danger arose from holes and thin places that could not be readily discovered in the dark. While crossing we met a peasant who had tumbled into one of these holes, and been fished out by his friends. He looked unhappy, and no doubt felt so. His garments were frozen stiff, and altogether he resembled a bronze statue of Franklin after a freezing rain storm.

AFTER THE BATH.

The thermometer fell on the first night to fifteen degrees below zero, and to about – 20° just before sunrise. The colder it grew the better was our speed, the horses feeling the crisp air and the driver being anxious to complete his stage in the least time possible. With uniform roads and teams one can judge pretty fairly of the temperature by the rate at which he travels.

From Barnaool we did not have the horses of the post, but engaged our first troikas of a peasant who offered his services. Our yemshick took us to his friend at the first station, and this operation was regularly repeated. Occasionally our two yemshicks had different friends, and our sleighs were separately out-fitted. When this was the case the teams were speedily attached out of a spirit of rivalry. We frequently endeavored to excite the yemshicks to the noble ambition of a race by offering a few copecks to the winner. When the teams were furnished from different houses the temper of emulation roused itself spontaneously.

Twice we left the post route to make short cuts that saved thirty or forty miles travel. On those side roads we found plently of horses, and were promptly served. The inhabitants of the steppe are delighted at the opportunity to carry travelers at post rates. The latter are saved the trouble of exhibiting their *padarashnia* at every station, and generally prefer to employ private teams. The horses were small, wiry beasts of Tartar breed, and utter strangers to combs and brushes.

While at breakfast on the second morning we were accosted by an old and decrepid beggar. The fellow wore a decoration consisting of a box six or seven inches square, suspended on his breast by a strap around his neck. Though seedy enough to set up business on his own account, he explained that he was begging for the church. His honesty was evidently in question as the box was firmly locked and had an aperture in the top for receiving money. We each gave ten copecks into his hand, and I observed that he did not drop the gratuity into the box. I was reminded of the man who owed a grudge against a railroad line, and declared that the company should never have another cent of his money. A friend asked how he would prevent it, as he frequently traveled over the road.

"Easy enough," was the calm reply, "I shall hereafter pay my fare to the conductor."

The morning after reaching Barnaool, I had a fine twinge of rheumatism that adhered during my stay. Quite to my surprise it left me on the second day after our departure, and like the bad boy in the story never came back again. The medical faculty can have the benefit of my experience, and prescribe as follows for their rheumatic patients.

"st. nt. o. lg. sl. S. r.=ther. – ℥

Start at night on a long sleigh ride over a Siberian road with the thermometer below zero."

A bouran arose in the afternoon of the second day, but was neither violent nor very cold. At Barnaool I had my sleigh specially prepared to exclude drifting snow. I ordered a liberal supply of buttons and straps to fasten the boot to the hood, besides an overlapping flap of thick felt to cover the crevice between them. The precaution was well taken, and with our doors thoroughly closed we were not troubled with much snow. The drivers were exposed on the outside of the sleigh, and had the full benefit of the wind. At the end of the first drive after this storm commenced our yemshick might have passed for an animated snow statue. The road was tolerable, and a great improvement upon that from Krasnoyarsk to Tomsk.

CHAPTER XLVI.

THE great steppe of Baraba is quite monotonous, as there is very little change of scenery in traveling over it. Whoever has been south or west from Chicago, or west from Leavenworth, in winter, can form a very good idea of the steppe. The winter appearance is much like that of a western prairie covered with snow. Whether there is equal similarity in summer I am unable to say. The country is flat or slightly undulating, and has a scanty growth of timber. Sometimes there were many versts without trees, then there would be a scattered and straggling display of birches, and again the growth was dense enough to be called a forest. The principal arboreal productions are birches, and I found the houses, sheds, and fences in most of the villages constructed of birch timber. The open part of the steppe, far more extensive than the wooded portion, was evidently favorable to the growth of grass, as I saw a great deal protruding above the snow. There are many marshy and boggy places, covered in summer with a dense growth of reeds. They are a serious inconvenience to the traveler on account of the swarms of mosquitoes, gnats, and other tormenting insects that they produce. .

While crossing the Baraba swamps in summer, men and women are obliged to wear veils as a protection against these pests. Horses are sometimes killed by their bites, and frequently became thin in flesh from the constant annoyance. A gentleman told me that once when crossing the swamps one of his horses, maddened by the insects, broke from the carriage and fled out of sight among the tall reeds. The yemshicks, who knew the locality, said the animal would certainly be killed by his winged pursuers in less than twenty-four hours.

There is much game on the steppe in summer, birds being more numerous than beasts. The only winter game we saw was the white partridge, (*kurupatki*,) of which we secured several specimens.

The steppe is fertile, and in everything the soil can produce the people are wealthy. They have wheat, rye, and oats in abundance, but pay little attention to garden vegetables. In 1866 the crops were small in all parts of Siberia west of Lake Baikal, and I frequently heard the peasants complaining of high prices. They said such a season was almost unprecedented. On the steppe oats were forty copecks, and wheat and rye seventy copecks a pood; equaling about thirty cents and seventy-five cents a bushel respectively. In some years wheat has been sold for ten copecks the pood, and other products at proportionate prices. We paid twelve copecks the dizaine for eggs, which frequently sell for one-third that sum.

The fertility of the soil cannot be turned to great account, as there is no general market. Men and horses engaged in the transportation and postal service create a limited demand, but there is little sale beyond this. With so small a market there are very few rich inhabitants on the steppe; and with edibles at a cheap rate, there are few cases of extreme poverty. We rarely saw beggars, and on the other hand we found nobody who was able to dress in broadcloth and fine linen and fare sumptuously every day.

Hay is abundant, and may be cut on any unclaimed part of the steppe. I was told that in some places the farmers of a village assemble on horseback at an appointed time. At a given signal all start for the haying spots, and the first arrival has the first choice. There is enough for all, and in ordinary seasons no grass less than knee high is considered worth cutting.

At the villages we generally obtained excellent bread of unbolted wheat flour, rye being rarely used. There were many windmills of clumsy construction, the wheels having but four wings, and the whole concern turning on a pivot to bring its face to the wind. No bolting apparatus has been introduced, and the machinery is of the simplest and most primitive character. It was a period of fasting, just before Christmas, and our whole obtainable bill of fare comprised bread and eggs. As we reached a certain station we asked what we could get to eat.

"Everything," was the prompt reply of the smotretal. We were hungry, and this information was cheering.

"Give us some *schee*, if you please," said the doctor.

An inquiry in the kitchen showed this edible to be 'just out.'

"Some beef, then?"

There was no beef to be had. Cutlets were alike negatived.

"Any pilmania?" was our next inquiry.

"*Nierte; nizniu.*"

The 'everything' hunted down consisted of eggs, bread, and hot water. We brought out a boiled ham, that was generally our *piece de resistance*, and made a royal meal. If *trichina spiralis* existed in Siberian ham, it was never able to disturb us. We found no fruit as there are no orchards in Siberia. Attempts have been made to cultivate fruit, but none have succeeded. A little production about the size of a whortleberry was shown me in Eastern Siberia, where it was pickled and served up as a relish with meat. "This is the Siberian apple," said the gentleman who first exhibited it, "and it has degenerated to what you see since its introduction from Europe." On dissecting one of these little berries, I found it possessed the anatomy of the apple, with seeds smaller than pin-heads.

Kotzebue and other travelers say there are no bees in Siberia, but the assertion is incorrect. I saw native honey enough to convince me on this point, and learned that bees are successfully raised in the southern part of Asiatic Russia.

We were not greatly delayed in our team changing, though

we lost several hours in small instalments. We had two sleighs, and although there were anywhere up to a dozen men to prepare them, the harnessing of one team was generally completed before the other was led out. When the horses were ready, the driver often went to fetch his dehar and make his toilet. In this way we would lose five or ten minutes, a small matter by itself, but a large one when under heavy multiplication.

THE DRIVER'S TOILET.

We took breakfast and dinner daily in the peasants' houses, which we found very much like the stations. We carried our own tea and sugar, and with a fair supply of provisions, added what we could obtain. Tea was the great solace of the journey, and proved, above all others, the beverage which cheers. I could swallow several cups at a sitting, and never failed to find myself refreshed. It is far better than vodki or brandy for traveling purposes, and many Russians who are pretty free drinkers at home adhere quite closely to tea on the road. The merchant traveler drinks enormous quantities, and I have seen a couple of these worthies empty a twenty cup samovar with no appearance of surfeit. So much hot liquid inside generally sets them into a perspiration. Nothing but loaf sugar is used, and there is a very common practice of holding a lump in one hand and following a sip of the unsweetened tea with a nibble at the sugar. When several persons are engaged in this rasping process a curious sound is produced.

There are many Tartars living on the steppe, but we saw very little of them, as our changes were made at the Russian villages. Before the reign of Catherine II. there was but a small population between Tumen and Tomsk, and the road was more a fiction than a fact. The Governor General of Siberia persuaded Catherine to let him have all conscripts of one levy instead of sending them to the army. He settled them in villages along the route over the steppe, and the wisdom of his policy was very soon apparent. The present population is made up of the descendants of these and other early settlers, together with exiles and voluntary emigrants of the present century. Several villages have a bad reputation, and I heard stories of robbery and murder. In general the dwellers on the steppe are reputable, and they certainly impressed me favorably.

I was told by a Russian that Catherine once thought of giving the Siberians a constitution somewhat like that of the United States of America, but was dissuaded from so doing by one of her ministers.

The villages were generally built each in a single street, or at most, in two streets. The largest houses had yards, or enclosures, into which we drove when stopping for breakfast or dinner. The best windows were of glass or talc, fixed in frames, and generally made double. The poorer peasants contented themselves with windows of ox or cow stomachs, scraped thin and stretched in drying. There were no iron stoves in any house I visited, the Russian *peitcha* or brick stove being universal. Very often we found the women and girls engaged in spinning. No wheel is used for this purpose, the entire apparatus being a hand spindle and a piece of board. The flax is fast-

WOMEN SPINNING.

ened on an upright board, and the fingers of the left hand gather the fibres and begin the formation of a thread. The right hand twirls the spindle, and by skillful manipulation a good thread is formed with considerable rapidity.

A great deal of hemp and flax is raised upon the steppe, and we found rope abundant, cheap, and good. I bought ten fathoms of half-inch rope for forty copecks, a peasant bringing it to a house where we breakfasted. When I paid for it the mistress of the house quietly appropriated ten copecks, remarking that the rope maker owed her that amount. She talked louder and more continuously than any other woman I met in Siberia, and awakened my wonder by going barefooted into an open shed and remaining there several minutes. She stood in snow and on ice, but appeared quite unconcerned. Our thermometer at the time showed a temperature of 21° below zero.

The only city on the steppe is Omsk, at the junction of the Om and Irtish, and the capital of Western Siberia. It is said to contain twelve thousand inhabitants, and its buildings are generally well constructed. We did not follow the post route through Omsk, but took a cut-off that carried us to the northward and saved a hundred versts of sleigh riding. The city was founded in order to have a capital in the vicinity of the Kirghese frontier, but since its construction the frontier line has removed far away.

In 1834 a conspiracy, extending widely through Siberia, was organized at Omsk. M. Piotrowski gives an account of it, from which I abridge the following:

It was planned by the Abbe Sierosiuski, a Polish Catholic priest who had been exiled for taking part in the rebellion of 1831. He was sent to serve in the ranks of a Cossack regiment in Western Siberia, and after a brief period of military duty was appointed teacher in the military school at Omsk. His position gave him opportunity to project a rebellion. His plan was well laid, and found ready supporters among other exiles, especially the Poles. Some ambitious Russians and Tartars were in the secret. The object was to secure the complete independence of Siberia and the release of all prisoners. In the event of failure it was determined to march over the Kirghese steppes to Tashkend, and attempt to reach British India.

Everything was arranged, both in Eastern and Western Siberia. The revolt was to begin at Omsk, where most of the conspirators were stationed, and where there was an abundance of arms, ammunition, supplies, and money. The evening before the day appointed for the rising, the plot was revealed by three Polish soldiers, who confessed all they knew to Colonel Degrave, the governor of Omsk. Sierosiuski and his fellow conspirators in the city were at once arrested, and orders were despatched over the whole country to secure all accomplices and suspected persons. About a thousand arrests were made, and as soon as news of the affair reached St. Petersburg, a commission of inquiry was appointed. The

FLOGGING WITH STICKS.

investigations lasted until 1837, when they were concluded and the sentences confirmed.

Six principal offenders, including the chief, were each condemned to seven thousand blows of the *plette*, or stick, while walking the gauntlet between two files of soldiers. This is equivalent to a death sentence, as very few men can survive more than four thousand blows. Only one of the six outlived the day when the punishment was inflicted, some falling dead before the full number of strokes had been given. The minor offenders were variously sentenced, according to the extent of their guilt, flogging with the stick being followed by penal colonization or military service in distant garrisons.

It is said that the priest Sierosiuski while undergoing his punishment recited in a clear voice the Latin prayer, "Misere mei, Deus, secundum magnam misericordium tuam."

On approaching the Irtish we found it bordered by hills which presented steep banks toward the river. The opposite bank was low and quite level. It is a peculiarity of most rivers in Russia that the right banks rise into bluffs, while the opposite shores are low and flat. The Volga is a fine example of this, all the way from Tver to Astrachan, and the same feature is observable in most of the Siberian streams that reach the Arctic Ocean. Various conjectures account for it, but none are satisfactory to scientific men.

Steamboats have ascended to Omsk, but there is not sufficient traffic to make regular navigation profitable. We crossed the Irtish two hundred and seventy versts south of Tobolsk, a city familiar to American readers from its connection with the "Story of Elizabeth." The great road formerly passed through Tobolsk, and was changed when a survey of the country showed that two hundred versts might be saved. Formerly all exiles to Siberia were first sent to that city, where a "Commission of Transportation" held constant session. From Tobolsk the prisoners were told off to the different governments, provinces, districts, and 'circles,' and assigned to the penalties prescribed by their sentences.

Many prominent exiles have lived in the northern part of the government of Tobolsk, especially at Beresov on the river Ob. Menshikoff, a favorite of Peter the Great, died there in exile, and so did the Prince Dolgorouki and the count Osterman. It is said the body of Menshikoff was buried in the frozen earth at Beresov, and found perfectly preserved a hundred years after its interment. In that region the ground never thaws more than a foot or two from the surface; below to an unknown depth it is hardened by perpetual frost. Many Poles have been involuntary residents of this region, and contributed to the development of its few resources.

North of Tobolsk, the Ostiaks are the principal aboriginals, and frequently wander as far south as Omsk. Before the Russian occupation of Siberia the natives carried on a trade with the Tartars of Central Asia, and the abundance and cheapness of their furs made them attractive customers. Marco Polo mentions a people "in the dark regions of the North, who employ dogs to draw their sledges, and trade with the merchants from Bokhara." There is little doubt he referred to the Ostiaks and Samoyedes.

A Polish lady exiled to Beresov in 1839, described in her journal her sensation at seeing a herd of tame bears driven through the streets to the market place, just as cattle are driven elsewhere. She records that while descending the Irtish she had the misfortune to fall overboard. The soldier escorting her was in great alarm at the accident, and fairly wept for joy when she was rescued. He explained through his tears that her death would have been a serious calamity to him.

"I shall be severely punished," he said, "if any harm befalls you, and, for my sake, I hope you won't try to drown yourself, but will keep alive and well till I get rid of you."

Tobolsk is on the site of the Tartar settlement of Sibeer, from which the name of Siberia is derived. In the days of Genghis Khan northern Asia was overrun and wrested from its aboriginal inhabitants. Tartar supremacy was undisputed until near the close of the sixteenth century, when the Tartars lost Kazan and everything else west of the Urals. During the reign of Ivan the Cruel, a difficulty arose between the Czar and some of the Don Cossacks, and, as the Czar did not choose to emigrate, the Cossacks left their country for their country's good. Headed by one Yermak, they retired to the vicinity of the Ural mountains, where they started a marauding business with limited liability and restricted capital.

Crossing the Urals, Yermak subjugated the country west of the Irtish and founded a fortress on the site of Sibeer. He overpowered all the Tartars in his vicinity, and received a pardon for himself and men in return for his conquest. The czar, as a mark of special fondness, sent Yermak a suit of armor from his own wardrobe. Yermak went one day to dine with some Tartar chiefs, and was arrayed for the first time in his new store clothes. One tradition says he was treacherously killed by the Tartars on this occasion, and thrown in the river. Another story says he fell in by accident, and the weight of his armor drowned him. A monument at Tobolsk commemorates his deeds.

No leader rose to fill Yermak's place, and the Russians became divided into several independent bands. They had the good sense not to quarrel, and remained firm in the pursuit of conquest. They pushed eastward from the Irtish and founded Tomsk in 1604. Ten years later the Tartars united and attempted to expel the Russians. They surrounded Tomsk and besieged it for a long time. Russia was then distracted by civil commotions and the war with the Poles, and could not assist the Cossacks. The latter held out with great bravery, and at length gained a decisive victory. From that time the Tartars made no serious and organized resistance.

Subsequent expeditions for Siberian conquest generally originated at Tomsk. Cossacks pushed to the north, south, and east, forming settlements in the valley of the Yenesei and among the Yakuts of the Lena. In 1639 they reached the shores of the Ohotsk sea, and took possession of all Eastern Siberia to the Aldan mountains.

I believe history has no parallel to some features of this conquest. A robber-chieftain with a few hundred followers, —himself and his men under ban, and, literally, the first exiles to Siberia—passes from Europe to Asia. In seventy years these Cossacks and their descendants, with little aid from others, conquered a region containing nearly five million square miles. Everywhere displaying a spirit of adventure and determined bravery, they reduced the Tartars to the most perfect submission. The cost of their expeditions was entirely borne by individuals who sought remuneration in the lucrative trade they opened. The captured territory became Russian, though the government had neither paid for nor controlled the conquest.

I saw the portrait and bust of Yermak, but no one could assure me of their fidelity. The face was thoroughly Russian, and the lines of character were such as one might expect from the history of the man. He was represented in the suit of armor he wore at his death.

CHAPTER XLVII.

THE evening after we passed the Irtish, a severe bouran arose. As the night advanced the wind increased. The road was filled and apparently obliterated. The yemshicks found it difficult to keep the track, and frequently descended to look for it. Each interval of search was a little longer than the preceding one, so that we passed considerable time in impatient waiting. About midnight we reached a station, where we were urged to rest until morning, the people declaring it unsafe to proceed. A slight lull in the storm decided us and the yemshicks to go forward, but as we set out from the station it seemed like driving into the spray at the foot of Niagara. Midway between the station, we wandered from the route and appeared hopelessly lost, with the prospect of waiting until morning.

Just before nightfall, we saw three wolves on the steppe, pointing their sharp noses in our direction, and apparently estimating how many dinners our horses would make. Whether they took the mammoth into account I cannot say, but presume he was not considered. Wolves are numerous in all Siberia, and are not admired by the biped inhabitants. When our road seemed utterly lost, and our chances good for a bivouac in the steppe, we heard a dismal howl in a momentary lull of the wind.

"VOLK," (wolf,) said the yemshick, who was clearing away the snow near the sleigh.

Again we heard the sound, and saw the horses lift their ears uneasily.

An instant later the fury of the wind returned. The snow

whirled in dense clouds, and the roaring of the tempest drowned all other sounds. Had there been fifty howling wolves, within a hundred yards of us, we could have known nothing until they burst upon us through the curtain of drifting snow.

It was a time of suspense. I prepared to throw off my outer garments in case we were attacked, and roused the doctor, who had been some time asleep. At the cry of "wolf," he was very soon awake, though he did not lose that calm serenity that always distinguished him. The yemshicks continued their search for the road, one of them keeping near the sleigh and the other walking in circles in the vicinity. Our position was not enviable.

LOST IN A SNOW STORM.

To be served up *au natural* to the lupine race was never my ambition, and I would have given a small sum, in cash or approved paper, for a sudden transportation to the Astor House, but with my weight and substance, all the more desirable to the wolves, a change of base was not practicable. Our only fire-arms were a shot-gun and a pistol, the latter unserviceable, and packed in the doctor's valise. Of course the wolves would first eat the horses, and reserve us for dessert. We should have felt, during the preliminaries, much like those unhappy persons, in the French revolution, who were last in a batch of victims to the guillotine.

After long delay the road was discovered, and as the wolves did not come we proceeded. We listened anxiously for the renewal of their howling, but our ears did not catch the unwelcome sound. The doctor exhibited no alarm. As he was an old traveler, I concluded to follow his example, and go to sleep.

In ordinary seasons wolves are not dangerous to men, though they commit more or less havoc among live stock. Sheep and pigs are their favorite prey, as they are easily captured, and do not resist. Horses and cattle are overpowered by wolves acting in packs; the hungry brutes displaying considerable strategy. A gentleman told me he once watched a dozen wolves attacking a powerful bull. Some worried him in front and secured his attention while others attempted to cut his ham-strings. The effort was repeated several times, the wolves relieving each other in exposed positions. At length the bull was crippled and the first part of the struggle gained. The wolves began to lick their chops in anticipation of a meal, and continued to worry their expected prey up to the pitch of exhaustion. The gentleman shot two of them and drove the others into the forest. He could do no more than put the bull out of his misery. On departing he looked back and saw the wolves returning to their now ready feast.

The best parts of Russia for wolf-hunting are in the western governments, where there is less game and more population than in Siberia. It is in these regions that travelers are sometimes pursued by wolves, but such incidents are not frequent. It is only in the severest winters, when driven to desperation by hunger, that the wolves dare to attack men. The horses are the real objects of their pursuit, but when once a party is overtaken the wolves make no nice distinctions, and horses and men are alike devoured. Apropos of hunting I heard a story of a thrilling character.

"It had been," said the gentleman who narrated the incident, "a severe winter in Vitebsk and Vilna. I had spent several weeks at the country residence of a friend in Vitebsk, and we heard, during the latter part of my stay, rumors of the unusual ferocity of the wolves.

One day Kanchin, my host, proposed a wolf-hunt. 'We shall have capital sport,' said he, 'for the winter has made the wolves hungry, and they will be on the alert when they hear our decoy.'

We prepared a sledge, one of the common kind, made of stout withes, woven like basket-work, and firmly fastened to the frame and runners. It was wide enough for both of us and the same height all around so that we could shoot in any direction except straight forward. We took a few furs to keep us warm, and each had a short gun of large bore, capable of carrying a heavy load of buck-shot. Rifles are not desirable weapons where one cannot take accurate aim. As a precaution we stowed two extra guns in the bottom of the sledge.

The driver, Ivan, on learning the business before him, was evidently reluctant to go, but as a Russian servant has no choice beyond obeying his master, the man offered no objection. Three spirited horses were attached, and I heard Kanchin order that every part of the harness should be in the best condition.

We had a pig confined in a strong cage of ropes and withes, that he might last longer than if dragged by the legs. A rope ten feet long was attached to the cage and ready to be tied to the sledge.

We kept the pig in furs at the bottom of the sledge, and drove silently into the forest. The last order given by Kanchin was to open the gates of the courtyard and hang a bright lantern in front. I asked the reason of this, and he replied with a smile:

"If we should be going at full speed on our return, I don't wish to stop till we reach the middle of the yard."

As by mutual consent neither uttered a word as we drove along. We carried no bells, and there was no creaking of any part of the sledge. Ivan did not speak but held his reins taut and allowed the horses to take their own pace. In his secure and warm covering the pig was evidently asleep. The moon and stars were perfectly unclouded, and there was no motion of anything in the forest. The road was excellent, but we did not meet or pass a single traveler. I do not believe I ever *felt* silence more forcibly than then.

The forest in that region is not dense, and on either side of the road there is a space of a hundred yards or more entirely open. The snow lay crisp and sparkling, and as the country was but slightly undulating we could frequently see long distances. The apparent movement of the trees as we drove past them caused me to fancy the woods filled with animate forms to whom the breeze gave voices that mocked us.

About eight versts from the house we reached a cross road that led deeper into the forest. "*Na prava*," in a low voice from my companion turned us to the right into the road. Eight or ten versts further Kanchin, in the same low tone, commanded "*Stoi.*" Without a word Ivan drew harder upon his reins, and we came to a halt. At a gesture from my friend the team was turned about.

Kanchin stepped carefully from the sledge and asked me to hand him the rope attached to the cage. He tied this to the rear cross-bar, and removing his cloak told me to do the same. Getting our guns, ammunition, and ourselves in readiness, and taking our seats with our backs toward the driver, we threw out the pig and his cage and ordered Ivan to proceed.

The first cry from the pig awoke an answering howl in a dozen directions. The horses sprang as if struck with a heavy hand, and I felt my blood chill at the dismal sound. The driver with great difficulty kept his team from breaking into a gallop.

Five minutes later, a wolf came galloping from the forest on the left side where I sat.

"Don't fire till he is quite near," said Kanchin, "we shall have no occasion to make long shots."

The wolf was distinctly visible on the clean snow, and I allowed him to approach within twenty yards. I fired, and he fell. As I turned to re-load Kanchin raised his gun to shoot a wolf approaching the right of the sledge. His shot was successful, the wolf falling dead upon the snow.

I re-loaded very quickly, and when I looked up there were three wolves running toward me, while as many more were visible on Kanchin's side. My companion raised his eyes when his gun was ready and gave a start that thrilled me with horror. Ivan was immovable in his place, and holding with all his might upon the reins.

"*Poshol!*" shouted Kanchin.

The howling grew more terrific. Whatever way we looked we could see the wolves emerging from the forest;

> "With their long gallop, which can tire,
> The hounds' deep hate, the hunter's fire."

Not only behind and on either side but away to the front, I could see their dark forms. We fired and loaded and fired again, every shot telling but not availing to stop the pursuit.

The driver did not need Kanchin's shout of "*poshol!*" and the horses exerted every nerve without being urged. But with all our speed we could not outstrip the wolves that grew every moment more numerous. If we could only keep up our pace we might escape, but should a horse stumble, the harness give way, or the sledge overturn, we were hopelessly lost. We threw away our furs and cloaks keeping only our arms and ammunition. The wolves hardly paused over these things but steadily adhered to the pursuit.

Suddenly I thought of a new danger that menaced us. I grasped Kanchin's arm and asked how we could turn the corner into the main road. Should we attempt it at full speed the sledge would be overturned. If we slackened our pace the wolves would be upon us.

I felt my friend trembling in my grasp but his voice was firm.

"When I say the word," he replied, giving me his hunting knife, "lean over and cut the rope of the decoy. That will detain them a short time. Soon as you have done so lie down on the left side of the sledge and cling to the cords across the bottom."

Then turning to Ivan he ordered him to slacken speed a little, but only a little, at the corner, and keep the horses from running to either side as he turned. This done Kanchin clung to the left side of the sledge prepared to step upon its fender and counteract, if possible, our centrifugal force.

We approached the main road, and just as I discovered the open space at the crossing Kanchin shouted,—

"Strike!"

I whipped off the rope in an instant and we left our decoy behind us. The wolves stopped, gathered densely about the prize, and began quarreling over it. Only a few remained to tear the cage asunder. The rest, after a brief halt, continued the pursuit, but the little time they lost was of precious value to us.

We approached the dreaded turning. Kanchin placed his feet upon the fender and fastened his hands into the net-work of the sledge. I lay down in the place assigned me, and never did drowning man cling to a rope more firmly than I clung to the bottom of our vehicle. As we swept around the corner the sledge was whirled in air, turned upon its side and only saved from complete oversetting by the positions of Kanchin and myself.

Just as the sledge righted, and ran upon both runners, I heard a piercing cry. Ivan, occupied with his horses, was not able to cling like ourselves; he fell from his seat, and hardly struck the snow before the wolves were upon him. That one shriek that filled my ears was all he could utter.

The reins were trailing, but fortunately where they were not likely to be entangled. The horses needed no driver; all the whips in the world could not increase their speed.

FATAL RESULT.

Two of our guns were lost as we turned from the by-road, but the two that lay under me in the sledge were providentially saved. We fired as fast as possible into the dark mass that filled the road not twenty yards behind us. Every shot told but the pursuit did not lag. To-day I shudder as I think of that surging mass of gray forms with eyes glistening like fireballs, and the serrated jaws that opened as if certain of a feast.

A stern chase is proverbially a long one. If no accident happened to sledge or horses we felt certain that the wolves which followed could not overtake us.

As we approached home our horses gave signs of lagging, and the pursuing wolves came nearer. One huge beast sprang at the sledge and actually fastened his fore paws upon it. I struck him over the head with my gun and he released his hold.

A moment later I heard the barking of our dogs at the house, and as the gleam of the lantern caught my eye I fell unconscious to the bottom of the sledge. I woke an hour later and saw Kanchin pacing the floor in silence. Repeatedly I spoke to him but he answered only in monosyllables.

The next day, a party of peasants went to look for the remains of poor Ivan. A few shreds of clothing, and the cross he wore about his neck, were all the vestiges that could be found. For three weeks I lay ill with a fever and returned to St. Petersburg immediately on my recovery. Kanchin has lived in seclusion ever since, and both of us were gray-haired within six months."

Before the construction of the railway between Moscow and Nijne Novgorod there were forest guards at regular intervals to protect the road from bears and wolves. The men lived in huts placed upon scaffoldings fifteen or twenty feet high. This arrangement served a double purpose; the guards could see farther than on the ground and they were safe from nocturnal attacks of their four-footed enemies.

One evening at a dinner party, I heard several anecdotes about wolves, of which I preserve two.

"I was once," said a gentleman, "pursued by ten or twelve wolves. One horse fell and we had just time to cut the traces of the other, overturn our sleigh and get under as in a cage, before the wolves overtook us. We thought the free horse would run to the village and the people would come to rescue us. What was our surprise to see him charge upon the wolves, kill two with his hoofs and drive away the rest. When the other horse recovered we harnessed our team and drove home."

"And I," said another, "was once attacked when on foot. I wore a new pelisse of sheep-skin and a pair of reindeer-skin boots. Wolves are fond of deer and sheep, and they eat skin and all when they have a chance. The brutes stripped off my pelisse and boots without harming my skin. Just as I was preparing to give them my woolen trousers, some peasants came to my relief."

Although I feared my auditors would be incredulous, I told the story of David Crockett when treed by a hundred or more prairie wolves. "I shot away all my ammunition, and threw away my gun and knife among them, but it was no use. Finally, I thought I would try the effect of music and began to sing 'Old Hundred.' Before I finished the first verse every wolf put his fore paws to his ears and galloped off."

My story did not produce the same results upon my audience, but almost as marked a one, for all appreciated its humor, and before I had fairly finished a burst of laughter resounded through the room, and it was unanimously voted that Americans could excel in all things, not excepting Wolf Stories.

CHAPTER XLVIII

THE many vehicles in motion made a good road twelve hours after the storm ceased. The thermometer fell quite low, and the sharp frost hardened the track and enabled the horses to run rapidly. I found the temperature varying from 25° to 40° below zero at different exposures. This was cold enough, in fact, too cold for comfort, and we were obliged to put on all our furs. When fully wrapped I could have filled the eye of any match-making parent in Christendom, so far as quantity is concerned. The doctor walked as if the icy and inhospitable North had been his dwelling-place for a dozen generations, and promised to continue so a few hundred years longer. We were about as agile as a pair of prize hogs, or the fat boy in the side show of a circus.

My beard was the greatest annoyance that showed itself to my face, and I regretted keeping it uncut. It was in the way in a great many ways. When it was outside my coat I wanted it in, and when it was inside it would not stay there. It froze to my collar and seemed studying the doctrine of affinity. A sudden motion in such case would pull my chin painfully and tear away a few hairs. It was neither long nor heavy, but could hold a surprising quantity of snow and ice. It would freeze into a solid mass, and when thawing required much attention. The Russian officers shave the chin habitually, and wear their hair pretty short when traveling. I made a resolution to carry my beard inviolate to St. Petersburg, but frequently wished I had been less rash. A mustache makes a very good portable thermometer for low temperatures. After a little practice one can estimate within a few degrees any stage of cold below zero, Fahrenheit. A mustache will frost itself from the breath and stiffen slowly at zero, but it does not become solid. It needs no waxing to enable it to hold its own when the scale descends to –10° or thereabouts, and when one experiences –15° and so on downward, he will feel as if wearing an icicle on his upper lip. The estimate of the cold is to be based on the time required for a thorough hardening of this labial ornament, and of course the rule is not available if the face is kept covered.

There is a traveler's story that a freezing nose in a Russian city is seized upon and rubbed by the bystanders without explanation. In a winter's residence and travel in Russia I never witnessed that interesting incident, and am inclined to scepticism regarding it. The thermometer showed –53° while I was in St. Petersburg, and hovered near that figure for several days. Though I constantly hoped to see somebody's nose rubbed I was doomed to disappointment. I did observe several noses that might have been subjected to friction, but it is quite probable the operation would have enraged the rub*bee*.

EXCUSE MY FAMILIARITY.

During our coldest nights on the steppe we had the unclouded heavens in all their beauty. The stars shone in scintillating magnificence, and seemed nearer the earth than I ever saw them before. In the north was a brilliant aurora flashing in long beams of electric light, and forming a fiery arch above the fields of ice and snow. Oh, the splendor of those winter nights in the north! It cannot be forgotten, and it cannot be described.

Twilight is long in a Siberian winter, both at the commencement and the close of day. Morning is the best time to view it. A faint glimmer appears in the quarter where the sun is to rise, but increases so slowly that one often doubts that he has really seen it. The gleam of light grows broader; the heavens above it become purple, then scarlet, then golden, and gradually change to the whiteness of silver. When the sun peers above the horizon the whole scene becomes dazzlingly brilliant from the reflection of his rays on the snow. In the coldest mornings there is sometimes a cloud or fog-bank resting near the earth, from the congelation and falling of all watery particles in the atmosphere. When the sun strikes this cloud and one looks through it the air seems filled with millions of microscopic gems, throwing off many combinations of prismatic colors, and agitated and mingled by some unseen force. Gradually the cloud melts away as it receives the direct rays of light and heat.

FROSTED HORSES.

The intense cold upon the road affects horses by coating them with white frost. Their perspiration congeals and covers them as one may see the grass covered in a November morning. Nature has dressed these horses warmly, and very often their hair may justly be called fur. They do not appear to suffer from the cold; they are never blanketed, and their stables are little better than open sheds. One of their annoyances is the congelation of their breath, and in the coldest weather the yemshicks are frequently obliged to break away the icicles that form around their horses' mouths. I have seen a horse reach the end of a course with his nose encircled in a row of icy spikes, resembling the decoration sometimes attached to a weaning calf.

In a clear morning or evening of the coldest days the smoke from the chimneys in the villages rises very slowly. Gaining a certain height, it spreads out as if unable to ascend farther. It is always light in color and density, and when touched by the sun's rays appears faintly crimsoned or gilded. Once when we reached a small hill dominating a village, I could see the cloud of smoke below me agitated like the ground swell of the ocean. I had only a moment to look upon it ere we descended to the level of the street.

I have not recorded the incidents of each day on the steppe in chronological order, on account of their similarity and monotony. Just one week after our departure from Barnaool we observed that the houses were constructed of pine instead of birch, and the country began to change in character. At a station where a fiery-tempered woman required us to pay in advance for our horses, we were only twenty versts from Tumen.

It is but a step from the sublime to the ridiculous, and it is only a steppe (a thousand miles wide) between Tomsk and Tumen. Travelers from Irkutsk to St. Petersburg consider their journey pretty nearly accomplished on getting thus far along. The Siberians make light of distances that would frighten many Americans. "From Tumen you will have only sixteen hundred versts to the end of the railway," said a gentleman to me one day. A lady at Krasnoyarsk said I ought to wait until spring and visit her gold mines. I asked their locality, and received the reply, "Close by here; only four hundred versts away. You can go almost there in a carriage, and will have only a hundred and twenty versts on horseback."

The best portion of Tumen is on a bluff eighty or a hundred feet above the river Tura. The lower town spreads over a wide meadow, and its numerous windmills at once reminded me of Stockton, California. We happened to arrive on market day, when the peasants from the surrounding country were gathered in all their glory for purposes of traffic. How such a lot of merchandise of nearly every kind under the Siberian sun could find either buyer or seller, it is difficult to imagine. The market-place was densely thronged, but there seemed to be very little traffic in progress.

The population of Tumen is about twenty thousand, and said to be rapidly increasing. The town is prosperous, as its many new and well-built houses bear witness. It has shorn Tobolsk of nearly all her commerce, and left her to mourn her former greatness. It is about three hundred versts from the ridge of the Urals, and at the head of navigation on the Tura. Half a dozen steamers were frozen in and awaited the return of spring, their machinery being stored to prevent its rusting.

In the public square of Tumen there was a fountain, the first I saw in Siberia. Men, women, boys, and girls were filling buckets and barrels, which they dragged away on sleds.

When we returned from our drive, and were seated at dinner, the cook brought a quantity of "Tumen carpets" for sale. He used all his eloquence upon me, but in vain. These carpets were made by hand in the villages around Tumen, their material being goat's hair. From their appearance I judged that a coarse cloth was "looped" full of thread, which was afterward cut to a plush surface. Some of the figures were quite pretty. These carpets can be found in nearly every peasant house in Western Siberia, where they are used as bed and table coverings, floor mats, and carriage robes.

From Tumen to Nijne Novgorod the post is in the hands of a company, and one can buy a ticket for any distance he chooses. We bought to Ekaterineburg, 306 versts, paying nine copecks a verst for each vehicle. At the stations it is only necessary to show the ticket, which will bring horses without delay. The company has a splendid monopoly, protected by an imperial order forbidding competition. The peasants would gladly take travelers at lower rates if the practice were permitted. The only thing they can do is to charter their horses to the company at about one-third the ticket prices. Alexander would make many friends among the people by curtailing the monopoly.

From the Tura the country became undulating as we approached the Urals, but we passed no rugged hills. A great deal of the road lay between double rows of birch trees, that serve for shade in summer and do much to prevent the drifting of snow in winter. Forests of fir appeared on the slopes, and were especially pleasing after the half-desolation of the steppe.

The villages had a larger and more substantial appearance, that indicated our approach to Europe. Long trains laden with freight from Perm, blocked the way and delayed us. A few collisions made our sleigh tremble, and in two instances turned it on its beam ends. We were ahead of the tea trains that left Irkutsk with the early snows, so that we passed few sledges going in our own direction. The second night found us so near Ekaterineburg that we halted a couple of hours for the double purpose of taking tea and losing time.

At the last station, about six in the morning, we were greeted with Christmas festivities. While we waited in the traveler's room, two boys sung or chanted several minutes, and then begged for money. We gave them a few copecks, and their success brought two others, who were driven away by the smotretal. I was told that poor children have a privilege of begging in this manner on Christmas morning. There are many beggars in the towns and villages of the Urals, and in summer there is a fair supply of highwaymen. Several beggars surrounded our sleigh as we prepared to depart and seemed determined to make the most of the occasion.

The undulations of the road increased, and the fir woods became thicker as we approached Ekaterineburg, nestled on the bank of the Isset. Just outside the town we passed a large zavod, devoted to the manufacture of candles. An immense quantity of tallow from the Kirghese steppes undergoes conversion into stearine at this establishment, and the production supplies candles to all Siberia and part of European Russia.

As we entered the *slobodka* and descended rapidly toward the river, the bells were clanging loudly and the population was generally on its way to church. The men were in their best shoobas and caps, while the women displayed the latest fashions in winter cloaks. Several pretty faces, rosy from the biting frost, peered at the strangers, who returned as many glances as possible. Our yemshick took us to the Hotel de Berlin, and, for the first time in eighteen hundred versts, we unloaded our baggage from the sleighs. Breakfast, a bath, and a change of clothes prepared me for the sights of this Uralian city.

For sight-seeing, the time of my arrival was unfortunate. Every kind of work was suspended, every shop was closed, and nothing could be done until the end of the Christmas holidays. I especially desired to inspect the *Granilnoi Fabric*, or Imperial establishment for stone cutting, and the machine shop where all steam engines for Siberia are manufactured. But, as everything had yielded to the general festivities, I could not gratify my desire.

Ekaterineburg is on the Asiatic side of the Urals, though belonging to the European government of Perm. It has a beautiful situation, the Isset being dammed so as to form a small lake in the middle of the city. Many of the best houses overlook this lake, and, from their balconies, one can enjoy charming views of the city, water, and the dark forests of the Urals. The principal street and favorite drive passes at the end of the lake, and is pretty well thronged in fine weather. There are many wealthy citizens in Ekaterineburg, as the character of the houses will attest. I was told there was quite a rage among them for statuary, pictures, and other works of art. Special care is bestowed upon conservatories, some of which contain tropical plants imported at enormous expense. The population is about twenty thousand, and increases very slowly.

The city is the central point of mining enterprises of the

VIEW OF EKATERINEBURG.

Ural mountains, and the residence of the Nachalnik, or chief of mines. The general plan of management is much like that already described at Barnaool. The government mines include those of iron, copper, and gold, the latter being of least importance. Great quantities of shot, shell, and guns have been made in the Urals, as well as iron work for more peaceful purposes. Beside the government works, there are numerous foundries and manufactories of a private character. In various parts of the Ural chain some of the zavods are of immense extent, and employ large numbers of workmen. At Nijne Tagilsk, for example, there is a population of twenty-five thousand, all engaged directly or indirectly in the production of iron.

The sheet iron so popular in America for parlor stoves and stove pipe, comes from Ekaterineburg and its vicinity, and is made from magnetic ore. The bar iron of the Urals is famous the world over for its excellent qualities, and commands a higher price than any other. Great quantities of iron are floated in boats down the streams flowing into the Kama and Volga. Thence it goes to the fair at Nijne Novgorod, and to the points of shipment to the maritime markets.

The development of the wealth of the Urals has been largely due to the Demidoff family. Nikite Demidoff was sent by Peter the Great, about the year 1701, to examine the mines on both sides of the chain. He performed his work thoroughly, and was so well satisfied with the prospective wealth of the region that he established himself there permanently. In return for his services, the government granted a large tract to the Demidoffs in perpetuity. The famous malachite mines are on the Demidoff estate, but are only a small portion of the mineral wealth in the original grant. I have heard the Demidoff family called the richest in Russia —except the Romanoff. Many zavods in the Urals were planned and constructed by Nikite and his descendants, and most of them are still in successful operation and have undergone no change.

The iron works of the Urals are very extensive, and capable of supplying any reasonable demand of individual or imperial character. At Zlatoust there is a manufactory of firearms and sword blades that is said to be unsurpassed in the excellence of its products. The sabres from Zlatoust are of superior fineness and quality, rivaling the famous blades of Damascus and Toledo.

Close by the little lake in Ekaterineburg is the *Moneta Fabric*, or Imperial mint, where all the copper money of Russia is coined. It is an extensive concern, and most of its machinery was constructed in the city. The copper mines of the Urals are the richest in Russia, and possess inexhaustible wealth. Malachite—an oxide of copper—is found here in large quantities. I believe the only mines where malachite is worked are in the Urals, though small specimens of this beautiful mineral have been found near Lake Superior and in Australia.

About twenty-five years ago an enormous mass of malachite, said to weigh 400 tons, was discovered near Tagilsk. It has since been broken up and removed, its value being more than a million roubles. Sir Roderick Murchison, while exploring the Urals on behalf of the Russian government, saw this treasure while the excavations around it were in progress. According to his account it was found 280 feet below the surface. Strings of copper were followed by the miners until they unexpectedly reached the malachite. Other masses of far less importance have since been found, some of them containing sixty per cent. of copper.

The gold mines of the Ural are less extensive now than formerly, new discoveries not equaling the exhausted placers. They are principally on the Asiatic slope, in the vicinity of Kamenskoi. The Emperor Alexander First visited the mines of the Ural in 1824, and personally wielded the shovel and pickaxe nearly two hours. A nugget weighing twenty-four pounds and some ounces was afterward found about two feet below the point where His Majesty 'knocked off' work. A monument now marks the spot, and contains the tools handled by the Emperor.

CHAPTER XLIX.

I HAD several commissions to execute for the purchase of souvenirs at Ekaterineburg, and lost no time in visiting a dealer. While we were at breakfast an itinerant merchant called, and subsequently another accosted us on the street. At ordinary times, strangers are beset by men and boys who are walking cabinets of semi-precious stones. A small boy met me in the corridor of the hotel and repeated a lapidarious vocabulary that would have shamed a professor of mineralogy.

At the dealer's, I was very soon in a bewildering collection of amethyst, beryl, chalcedony, topaz, tourmaline, jasper, aquamarine, malachite, and other articles of value. The collection numbered many hundred pieces comprising seals, paper weights, beads, charms for watch chains, vases, statuettes, brooches, buttons, etc. The handles of seals were cut in a variety of ways, some representing animals or birds, while a goodly portion were plain or fluted at the sides.

The prettiest work I saw was in paper weights. There were imitations of leaves, flowers, and grapes in properly tinted stone fixed upon marble tablets either white or colored. Equal skill was displayed in arranging and cutting these stones. I saw many beautiful mosaics displaying the stones of the Ural and Altai mountains.

Natural crystals were finely arranged in the shape of miniature caves and grottoes. Beads were of malachite, crystal, topaz, and variegated marble, and seemed quite plentiful. Malachite is the most abundant of the half-precious stones of the Ural, crystal and topaz ranking next. Aquamarine was the most valuable stone offered. It is not found in the Urals but comes from Eastern Siberia.

In another establishment there were little busts of the Emperor and other high personages in Russia, cut in crystal and topaz. I saw a fine bust of Yermak, and another of the elder Demidoff, both in topaz. A crystal bust of Louis Napoleon was exhibited, and its owner told me it would be sent to the *Exposition Universelle*. Learning that I was an American, the proprietor showed me a half completed bust of Mr. Lincoln, and was gratified to learn that the likeness was good. The bust was cut in topaz, and when finished would be about six inches high.

Though no work was in progress I had opportunity to look through a private "fabric." Stone cutting is performed as by lapidaries every where with small wheels covered with diamond dust or emery. Each laborer has his bench and performs a particular part of the work under the direction of a superintendent. Wages were very low, skilled workmen being paid less than ordinary stevedores in America. For three roubles, I bought a twelve sided topaz, an inch in diameter with the signs of the zodiac neatly engraved upon it. In London or New York, the cutting would have cost more than ten times that amount. The Granilnoi Fabric employs about a hundred and fifty workmen, but no private establishment supports more than twenty-five. The Granilnoi Fabric was to be sold in 1867, and pass out of government control. The laborers there were formerly crown peasants, and became free under the abolition ukase of Alexander II. The palace and Imperial museum at St. Petersburg contain wonderful illustrations of their skill.

Diamonds have been sought in the Urals, and the region is said to resemble the diamond districts of Brazil. They have been found in but a single instance, and there is a suspicion that the few discovered on that occasion were a "plant."

We remained two days at Ekaterineburg, repairing sleighs and resting from fatigue. On account of the holidays, we paid double prices for labor, and were charged double by drosky drivers. At the hotel, the landlord wished to follow the same custom, but we emphatically objected. A theatrical performance came off during our stay, but we were too weary to witness it. Near the hotel there was a " live beast show " almost an exact counterpart of what one sees in America. Music, voluble doorkeepers, gaping crowd of youngsters, and canvas pictures of terrific combats between beasts and snakes, all were there.

According to our custom we prepared to start in the evening for another westward stride. The thermometer was low enough to give the snow that crisp, metallic sound under the runners only heard in cold weather. We took tickets for Kazan, and ordered horses at nine o'clock. As we left the city, we passed between two monument-like posts, marking the gateway.

Two or three versts away, we passed the zavod of Verkne Issetskoi, an immense concern with a population sufficient to found a score of western cities. In this establishment is made a great deal of the sheet-iron that comes to America. The material is of so fine a quality that it can be rolled to the thickness of letter paper without breaking. Every thing at the zavod is on a grand scale even to the house of the director, and his facilities for entertaining guests. All was silent at the time of our passage, the workmen being busy with their Christmas festivities.

Leaving the zavod we were once more among the forests of the Urals, and riding over the low hills that form this part of the range. The road was good, but there were more *oukhabas* than suited my fancy.

I was on constant lookout for the steep road leading over the range, but failed to find it. Before leaving New York a friend suggested that I should have a severe journey over the Ural mountains which were deeply shaded on the map we consulted. I can assure him it was no worse than a sleigh ride anywhere else on a clear, frosty night. The ascent is so gradual that one does not perceive it at all. Ekaterineburg stands eight hundred feet above the sea ; the pass, twenty-four miles distant, is only nine hundred feet higher. The range is depressed at this point, but nowhere attains sufficient loftiness to justify its prominence on the maps. In Ekaterineburg I asked for the mountains.

"There they are," said the person of whom I enquired, and he waved his hand toward a wooded ridge in the west. The designated locality appeared less difficult of passage than the hills opposite Cincinnati.

"Don't fail to tell the yemshick to stop at the boundary."

This was my injunction several times repeated as we changed horses at the first station. Eight or ten versts on our second course, the sleigh halted and the yemshick announced the highest point on the road.

I stepped from the sleigh and waded through a deep snow-drift to the granite obelisk erected by the first Alexander to mark the line between the two continents. It is a plain shaft—Bunker Hill monument in miniature—bearing the word "EUROPE" on one side, and "ASIA" on the other. Two fir trees planted by His August Majesty are on opposite sides of the monument.

EUROPE AND ASIA.

A snow-drift in the middle of a frosty night is not the place for sentimental musings. I rested a foot in each of two continents at the same moment, but could not discover any difference in their manners, customs, or climate.

Regaining the sleigh, I nestled into my furs, and soon fell asleep. I was in Europe. I had accomplished the hope and dream of my boyhood. But in my most romantic moments,

I had not expected to stand for the first time in Europe on the ridge of the Ural Mountains.

After passing the boundary, we dashed away over the undulating road, and made a steady though imperceptible descent into the valley of the Kama. As I commenced my first day in Europe, the sunbeams wavered and glistened on the frost-crystals that covered the trees, and the flood of light that poured full into my opening eyes was painfully dazzling. Where we halted for breakfast, the station was neat and commodious, and its rooms well furnished. We fared sumptuously on cutlets and eggs, with excellent bread. Just as we were seated in the sleigh, a beggar made a touching appeal, as explained by the doctor, in behalf of the prophet Elias.

A RUSSIAN BEGGAR.

The prophet's financial agent was of so unprepossessing appearance that we declined investing. Beggars often ask alms in the interest of particular saints, and this one had attached himself to Elias.

We met many sledges laden with goods *en route* to the fair which takes place every February at Irbit. This fair is of great importance to Siberia, and attracts merchants from all the region west of Tomsk. From forty to fifty million roubles worth of goods are exchanged there during the four weeks devoted to traffic. The commodities from Siberia are chiefly furs and tea, those from Europe comprise a great many articles. Irbit is on the Asiatic side of the Ural mountains, about two hundred versts northeast of Ekaterineburg. It is a place of little consequence except during the time of the fair.

After entering Europe, we relied upon the stations for our meals, carrying no provisions with us except tea and sugar. We knew the peasants would be well supplied with edibles during Christmas holidays, and were quite safe in depending upon them. A traveler in Russia must consult the calendar before starting on a journey, if he would ascertain what provision he may, or may not, find among the people.

Congour was the first town of importance, and has an unenviable reputation for its numerous thieves. They do not molest the post vehicles unless the opportunity is very favorable, their accomplishments being specially exercised upon merchandise trains. Sometimes when trains pass through Congour the natives manage to steal single vehicles and their loads. The operation is facilitated by there being only one driver to five or six teams. This town is also famous for its tanneries, the leather from Congour having a high reputation throughout Russia. Peter the Great was at much trouble to teach the art of tanning to his subjects. At present, the Russians have very little to learn from others on that score. Peter introduced tanning from Holland and Germany, and when the first piece of leather tanned in Russia was brought to him he took it between his teeth and exerted all the strength of his jaws to bite through it. The leather resisted his efforts, and so delighted the monarch that he decreed a pension to the successful tanner. The specimen, with the marks of his teeth upon it, is still preserved at St. Petersburg.

While waiting for dinner at Congour, I contemplated some engravings hanging in the public room at the station. Four of them represented scenes in "Elizabeth, or the exiles of Siberia," a story which has been translated into most modern languages. These engravings were made in Moscow several years ago, and illustrated the most prominent incidents in the narrative.

There were many things to remind me I was no longer in Siberia, and especially on the Baraba steppe. Snows were deeper, and the sky was clearer. The level country was replaced by a broken one. Forests of pine and fir displayed regular clearings, and evinced careful attention. Villages were more numerous, larger and of greater antiquity. Stations were better kept and had more the air of hotels. Churches appeared more venerable and less venerated. Beggars increased in number, and importunity. In Asia the yemshick was the only man at a station who asked "navodku," but in Europe the *chelavek* or *starost* expected to be remembered. In Asia, the gratuity was called "Navodku" or whisky money; in Europe, it was "*nachi*," tea money.

During the second night, we reached Perm and halted long enough to eat a supper that made me dream of tigers and polar bears during my first sleep. In entering, we drove along a lighted street with substantial houses on either side, but without meeting man or beast. This street and the station were all I saw of a city of 25,000 inhabitants. In summer travelers for Siberia usually leave the steamboat at this point, and begin their land journey, the Kama being navigable thus far in ordinary water. Perm is an important mining center, and contains several foundries and manufactories on an extensive scale. The doctor assured me that after the places I had visited in Siberia, there was nothing to be seen there—and I saw it.

A deep snow had been trodden into an uneven road in this part of the journey. At times it seemed to me as if the sleigh and all it contained would go to pieces in the terrific thumps we received. We descended hills as if pursued by wolves or a guilty conscience, and it was generally our fate to find a huge oukhaba just when the horses were doing their best. I think the sleigh sometimes made a clear leap of six or eight feet from the crest of a ridge to the bottom of a hollow. The leaping was not very objectionable, but the impact made everything rattle. I could say, like the Irishman who fell from a house top, "'twas not the fall, darling, that hurt me, but stopping so quick at the end."

When the roads are rough the continual jolting of the sleigh is very fatiguing to a traveler, and frequently, during the first two or three days of his journey, throws him into what is very properly designated the road fever. His pulse is quick, his blood warm, his head aches, his whole frame becomes sore and stiff, and his mind is far from being serene and amiable. In the first part of my land journey I had the satisfaction of ascertaining by practical experience the exact character of the road-fever. My brain seemed ready to burst, and appeared to my excited imagination about as large as a barrel; every fresh jolt and thump of the vehicle gave me a sensation as if somebody were driving a tenpenny nail into my skull; as for good-nature under such circumstances that was out of the question, and I am free to confess that my temper was not unlike that of a bear with a sore head.

Where the roads are good, or if the speed is not great, one can sleep very well in a Russian sleigh; I succeeded in extracting a great deal of slumber from my vehicle, and sometimes did not wake for three or four hours. Sometimes the roads are in such wretched condition that one is tossed to the height of discomfort, and can be very well likened to a lump of butter in a revolving churn. In such cases sleep is almost if not wholly, impossible, and the traveler, proceeding at courier speed, must take advantage of the few moments' halt at the stations while the horses are being changed. As he has but ten or fifteen minutes for the change he makes good use of his time and sleeps very soundly until his team is ready.

During the Crimean war, while the Emperor Nicholas was temporarily sojourning at Moscow, a courier arrived one day with important dispatches from Sebastopol. He was commissioned to deliver them to no one but His Majesty, and waited in the ante-room of the palace while his name and business were announced. Overcome by fatigue he fell asleep; when the chamberlains came to take him to the Imperial presence they were quite unable to rouse him. The attendants shook him and shouted, but to no purpose beyond making so much disturbance as to bring the Emperor to the ante-room. Nicholas ordered them to desist, and then, standing near the officer, said, in an ordinary voice, "*Vashe prevoschoditelstvo, loshadi gotovey*" (Your horses are ready, your Excellency). The officer sprang to his feet in an instant, greatly to the delight of the Emperor and to his own confusion when he discovered where he was.

The Russians have several popular songs that celebrate the glories of sleigh-riding. I give a translation of a portion of one of them, a song that is frequently repeated by the peasants in the vicinity of Moscow and Nijne Novgorod. It is proper to explain that a *troika* is a team of three horses abreast, the *douga* is the yoke above the shaft-horse's neck, and Valdai is the town on the Moscow and St. Petersburg road where the best and most famous bells of Russia are made.

A RUSSIAN SLEIGHING SONG.

Away, away, along the road
  The fiery troika bounds,
While 'neath the douga, sadly sweet,
  The Valdai bell resounds.

Away, away, we leave the town,
  Its roofs and spires behind,
The crystal snow-flakes dance around
  As o'er the steppe we wind.

Away, away, the glittering stars
  Shine greeting from above,
Our hearts beat fast as on we glide,
  Swift as the flying dove.

CHAPTER L.

WE found the road much better after leaving the government of Perm and entering that of Viatka. The yemshicks we took in this region were "Votiaks," descendants of the Finnish races that dwelt there before the Russian conquest. They had the dark physiognomy of the Finns, and spoke a mixture of their own language and Russian. They have been generally baptized and brought into the Greek churches, though they still adhere to some of their ancient forms of worship. They pay taxes to the crown, but their local administration is left to themselves.

Approaching Malmouish we had a sullen driver who insisted upon going slowly, even while descending hills. Indignantly I suggested giving the fellow a kick for his drink money. The doctor attempted to be stern and reproved the delinquent, but ended with giving him five copecks and an injunction to do better in future. I opposed making undeserved gratuities, and after this occurrence determined to say no more about rewards to drivers during the rest of the journey.

Memorandum for travelers making the Siberian tour:

An irritable disposition, (like mine,) should not be placed with an amiable one, (like the doctor's.) If misery loves company, so does anger; and a petulant man should have an associate who *can* be ruffled.

After leaving the Votiaks, we entered the country of the Tartars, the descendants of the followers of Genghis Khan, who carried the Mongol standard into Central Europe. Russia remained long under their yoke, and the Tartars of the present day live as a distinct people in various parts of the empire. They are nearly all Mohammedans, and the conversion of one of them to Christianity is a very rare occurrence. My attention was called to their mosques in the villages we passed, the construction being quite unlike that of the Russian churches. A tall spire or minaret, somewhat like the steeple of an American church, rises in the center of a Tartar mosque and generally overlooks the whole village. No bells are used, the people being called to prayer by the voice of a crier.

These Tartars have none of the warlike spirit of their ancestors, and are among the most peaceful subjects of the Russian emperor. They are industrious and enterprising, and manage to live comfortably. Their reputation for shrewdness doubtless gave rise to the story of the difficulty of catching a Tartar.

At the stations we generally found Russian smotretals with Tartar attendants. Blacksmiths, looking for jobs, carefully examined our sleighs. One found my shafts badly chafed where they touched the runners, and offered to iron the weak points for sixty copecks. I objected to the delay for preparing the irons. "*Gotovey*, *Gotovey; piet minute*," said the man, producing the ready prepared irons from one pocket and a hammer and nails from another. By the time the horses were led out the job was completed. I should have been better satisfied if one iron had not come off within two hours, and left the shaft as bare as ever.

The Tartars speak Russian very fairly, but use the Mongol language among themselves. They dress like the Russians, or very nearly so, the most distinguishing feature being a sort of skull cap like that worn by the Chinese. Their hair is cut like a prize fighter's, excepting a little tuft on the crown. Out of doors they wore the Russian cap over their Mohammedan one—unconsciously symbolizing their subjection to Muscovite rule.

These Tartars drove horses of the same race as those in the Baraba steppe. They carried us finely where the road permitted, and I had equal admiration for the powers of the horses and the skill of their drivers.

In the night, after passing Malmouish, the weather became warm. I laid aside my dehar only a half hour before the thermometer fell, and set me shivering. About daybreak it was warmer, and the increasing temperature ushered in a violent storm. It snowed and it blowed, and it was cold, frosty weather all day and all night. We closed the sleigh and attempted to exclude the snow, but our efforts were vain. The little crevices admitted enough to cover us in a short time, and we very soon concluded to let the wind have its own way. The road was filled, and in many places we had hard work to get through. How the yemshicks found the way was a mystery. Once at a station, when the smotretal announced "gotovey," I was actually unable to find the sleigh, though it stood not twenty feet from the door. The yemshicks said they were guided by the telegraph posts, which followed the line of road.

We were four hours making twenty-five versts to the last station before reaching Kazan. We took a hearty supper of soup, eggs, and bread, under a suspicion that we might remain out all night. Once the mammoth sleigh came up with us in the dark, and its shafts nearly ran us through. Collisions of this kind happened occasionally on the road, but were rarely as forcible as this one. We were twice on our beam ends and nearly overturned, and on several occasions stuck in the snow. By good luck we managed to arrive at Kazan about 2 A. M. On reaching the hotel, we were confronted by what I thought a snow statue, but which proved to be the *dvornik*, or watchman. Our baggage was taken up stairs, while we shook the snow from our furs. The samovar shortened our visages and filled our stomachs with tea. We retired to rest upon sofas and did not rise until a late hour.

It happened to be New Year's, and the fashionable society of Kazan was doing its congratulations. I drove through the principal part of the city and found an animated scene. Numberless and numbered droskies were darting through the streets, carrying gayly dressed officers making their ceremonious calls. Soldiers were parading with bands of music, and the lower classes were out in large numbers. The storm had ceased, the weather was warm, and everything was propitious for out-door exercise.

The soldiers were the first I had seen since entering Europe, and impressed me favorably with the Russian army. They wore grey uniforms, like those I saw in Siberia, and marched with a regular and steady stride. It was not till I had reached St. Petersburg that I saw the *elite* of the Emperor's military forces. The reforms of Alexander have not left the army untouched. Great improvements have been made in the last twelve or fifteen years. More attention has been paid to the private soldiers than heretofore, their pay being increased and time of service lessened. The Imperial family preserves its military character, and the present Emperor allows no laxity of discipline in his efforts to elevate the men in the ranks.

It is said of the grand duke Michel, uncle of Alexander II., that he was a most rigid disciplinarian. His great delight was in parades, and he never overlooked the least irregularity. Not a button, not a moustache even, escaped his notice, and whoever was not *en regle* was certain to be punished. He is reported to have said,—

"I detest war. It breaks the ranks, deranges the soldiers, and soils their uniforms."*

---

* The land forces of Russia are formed of two descriptions of troops—the regular troops properly so called, and the feudal militia of the Cossacks and similar tribes.

The regular army is recruited from the classes of peasants and artisans partly and principally by means of a conscription, partly by the adoption of the sons of soldiers, and partly by voluntary enlistment. Every individual belonging to these classes is, with a few exceptions, liable to compulsory service, provided he be of the proper age and stature. The nominal strength of the Russian army, according to the returns of the ministry of War, is as follows:

1. *Regular Army.*	Peace-footing.	War-footing
Infantry	364,422	694,511
Cavalry	38,306	49,183
Artillery	41,831	48,773
Engineers	13,413	16,203
Total	457,875	808,670

I had a letter to Colonel Molostoff, the brother of a Siberian friend and *compagnon du voyage*. I knew the colonel

2. *Army of First Reserve.*	Peace-footing.	War-footing.
Troops of the line	80,455	74,561
Garrison in regiments	80,455	23,470
Garrison in battalions	19,830	29,862
Total	100,285	127,925
3. *Army of Second Reserve.*		
Troops of all arms	254,036	199,380
General total	812,096	1,135,975

Among the irregular troops of Russia, the most important are the Cossacks. The country of the Don Cossacks contains from 600,000 to 700,000 inhabitants. In case of necessity, every Cossack, from 15 to 60 years, is bound to render military service. The usual regular military force, however, consists of 54 cavalry regiments, each numbering 1,044 men, making a total of 56,376. The Cossacks are reckoned in round numbers as follows:

	Heads.	In Military service.
On the Black Sea	125,000	18,000
Great Russian Cossacks on the Caucasian Line	150,000	18,000
Don Cossacks	440,000	66,000
Ural Cossacks	50,000	8,000
Orenburg Cossacks	60,000	10,000
Siberian Cossacks	50,000	9,000
Total	875,000	129,000

The Russian navy consists of two great divisions—the fleet of the Baltic and that of the Black Sea. Each of these two fleets is again subdivided into sections, of which three are in or near the Baltic and three in or near the Black Sea, to which must be added the small squadrons of galleys, gunboats, and similar vessels.

According to an official report, the Russian fleet consisted last year of 290 steamers, having 38,000 horse power, with 2,205 guns, besides 29 sailing vessels, with 65 guns. The greater and more formidable part of this navy was stationed in the Baltic. The Black Sea fleet numbered 43; the Caspian, 39; the Siberian or Pacific, 30; and the Lake Aral or Turkistan squadron, 11 vessels. The rest of the ships were either stationed at Kronstadt and Sweaborg or engaged in cruising in European waters.

The iron-clad fleet of war consisted, at the commencement of 1868, of 24 vessels, with an aggregate of 149 guns, as follows:

2 Frigates, one of 18, and one of 24 guns	42 guns.
3 Floating Batteries of 14, 16, and 27 guns	57 guns.
2 Corvettes of 8 guns	16 guns.
6 Monitors of 2 guns each,	12 guns.
11 Turret ships of 2 guns each	22 guns.
Total, 24 iron-clads with	149 guns.

The Imperial navy was manned at the beginning of 1868 by 60,230 sailors and marines, under the command of 3,791 officers, among whom are 119 admirals and generals.

would not be at home on the first day of the year, as he had many relatives and friends to visit. So I sent the letter to his house, and accompanied Schmidt on a call upon Dr. Freeze, a prominent physician of Kazan. Madam Freeze was a native of Heidelburg, and evidently loved the Rhine better than the Volga. She gave me a letter to her brother in Moscow, where she promised me an introduction to a niece of the poet Goethe.

In the evening Colonel Molostoff called at the hotel and took me to the New Year's ball of the nobility of Kazan. There was a maze of apartments belonging to the nobility club,—the dancing room being quite as elegant and as spacious as the large hall of the Fifth Avenue Hotel. I found files of English, French, and German papers in the reading-room, and spent a little while over the latest news from America. The male portion of the assemblage consisted of officers and civilians, the former in the majority. There was a perfect blaze of stars and gay uniforms, that quite outshone the evening dress of the civilians. As Kazan is old, populous, and wealthy, it is needless to add that the ladies were dressed just like those of St. Petersburg or Paris.

I was introduced to several officials, among them the governor, who had recently assumed command. Colonel Molostoff introduced me to three ladies who spoke English, but hardly had I opened conversation with the first before she was whisked away into the dance. The second and the third followed the same fate, and I began to look upon ball-room acquaintance as an uncertainty.

"Now," said the colonel, "I will introduce you to one who is not young, but she is charming, and does not dance." We went to seek her, but she was in the midst of a gay party just preparing for a visit to the lunch room.

I was so utterly wearied after my long ride that conversation was a great effort, and I could hardly keep my eyes from closing. I had promised to join a supper party at three o'clock, but midnight found me just able to stand. Fearful that I might bring discredit upon America by going to sleep during the festivities, I begged an excuse and returned to my hotel. Five minutes after entering my room I was in the land of dreams.

In the treasury of the Kremlin of Moscow the royal crown of Kazan is preserved. The descendants of Genghis Khan founded the city and made it the seat of their European power. For three centuries it remained a menace to Russia, and held the princes of Muscovy in fear and dread. But as the Russians grew in strength Kazan became weaker, and ultimately fell under the Muscovite control. Ivan the Terrible determined to drive the Tartars from the banks of the Volga. After three severe and disastrous campaigns, and a siege in which assailant and assailed displayed prodigies of valor, Kazan was stormed and captured. The kingdom was overthrown, and the Russian power extended to the Urals. The cruelties of Ivan the Terrible were partially forgiven in return for his breaking the Tartar yoke.

A pyramidal monument marks the burial place of the Russians who fell at the capture of the city, and the positions of the besiegers are still pointed out; but I believe no traces of the circumvallation are visible. The walls of the Tartar fortress form a part of the present Kremlin, but have been so rebuilt and enlarged that their distinctive character is gone.

Nicholas called Kazan the third capital of his empire, and the city is generally admitted first in importance after St. Petersburg and Moscow. Its position is well chosen on the banks of a small river, the Kazanka, which joins the Volga six versts away. On a high bluff stretching into a plateau in the rear of the city and frowning defiantly toward the west, its position is a commanding one. On the edge of this bluff is the Kremlin, with its thick and high walls enclosing the governor's palace and other public buildings, all overlooked by a lofty bell-tower. Every part of the city gives evidence of wealth.

The population is about sixty thousand, including, I presume, the military garrison. There are twelve or fifteen thousand Tartars, who live in a quarter of the city specially assigned them. They are said to be industrious and peaceful, and some of them have amassed great wealth. I saw a Tartar merchant at the ball on New Year's eve, and was told that his fortune was one of the best in Kazan. I can testify personally to the energy of Tartar peddlers. On my first morning at the hotel I was visited by itinerant dealers in hats, boots, dressing gowns, and other articles of wear. The Tartars at Moscow are no less active than their brethren of Kazan, and very shrewd in their dealings. Every one of them appears to believe that strangers visit Russia for the sole purpose of buying dressing gowns.

I took a drive through the Tartar quarter, or *Katai Gorod*, of Kazan, and inspected (but did not read) the signs over the shops. The houses are little different from those in the Russian quarter, and the general appearance of the streets was the same. I glanced at several female faces in defiance of Mohammedan law, which forbids women unveiling before strangers. On one occasion when no Tartar men were visible, a young and pretty woman removed her veil and evidently desired to be looked at. I satisfied my curiosity, and expressed admiration in all the complimentary Russian adjectives I could remember.

As we passed a butcher's shop, my isvoshchik intimated that horse meat was sold there. The Tartars are fond of equine flesh, and prefer it to beef. On the Kirghese steppes the horse is prominent in gastronomic festivities.

Kazan is famous throughout Russia for the extent and variety of its manufactures. Russians and Tartars are alike engaged in them, and the products of their industry bear a good reputation. The city has printing establishments on an extensive scale, one of them devoted to Tartar literature. Several editions of the Koran have been printed here for the faithful in Northern and Central Asia.

The University of Kazan is one of the most celebrated institutions of learning in Russia, and has an excellent board of professors. Special attention is devoted to the Asiatic languages and literature, but no other branch of knowledge is neglected. I met the Professor of Persian literature, and found him speaking English and French fluently. I was invited to look through the museum and cabinet attached to the university, but time did not permit. There is a ladies' seminary in equally good reputation for its educational facilities.

One morning, about two weeks before my arrival at Kazan, the early risers passing this seminary discovered the body of a young man hanging upon the fence. It was clad only in a shirt, and no other clothing could be found. No one recognized the features of the individual, and the occupants of the seminary professed utter ignorance of the affair. As might be expected, great excitement followed the discovery. Visits of the sterner sex were absolutely forbidden, and the young maidens in the building were placed under surveillance. The gentleman who told me the story, said:

"It is very strange, especially as the public can learn nothing about the young man's identity."

While conversing with a high official at Nijne Novgorod, a few days later, I referred to this affair and expressed my surprise that the police could not trace it out.

"That is to say," he replied, with a shrug of the shoulders, "that the police have suppressed the particulars. It is a scandalous occurrence that may as well be kept from the public."

One thing was quite certain: if the police thought proper to conceal the details of this affair, there was no likelihood of their publication. In Russia the police exercise a power much greater than in the United States. Those who have visited France and Austria can form a pretty correct idea of the Russian system, the three countries being nearly alike in this respect. The police has supervision over the people in a variety of ways; controls the fire department, looks after the general health, and provides for the well-being of society. Every man, woman, and child is considered under its surveillance, and accounted for by some member of the force. Passports are examined by the police, and if *en regle*, the owners are not likely to be troubled. Taxes are collected, quarrels adjusted, and debts paid through its agency.

Almost everybody has heard of the secret police of Russia, and many questions have been asked me about it. I cannot throw much light upon it, and if I could it would not be a secret police. I never knowingly came in contact with the shadow, neither did I have the slightest reason to fear it. If my letters were opened and read, those familiar with my manuscript will agree that the police had a hard time of it. If anybody dogged my steps or drew me into conversation to report my opinions at the *bureau secret*, I never knew it. The servants who brought my cutlets and tea, the woman who washed my linen, or the dvornik who guarded the door, may have been spies upon me; but, if so, I didn't see it. Where ignorance is bliss, 'tis folly to be wise.

People talk politics in Russia with apparent freedom, more so than I expected to find. Men and women expressed their opinions with candor (as I believe,) and criticised what they saw wrong in their government. The Russian journals possess more freedom than those of Paris, and the theatres can play pretty nearly what they like. Official tyranny or dishonesty can be shown up by the press or satirized on the stage more freely and safely than in the country of Napoleon Third, with all its boasted freedom.

I once read a story in which an Englishman in Austria is represented saying to his companion, "No gentleman meddles with the politics of the countries he visits." I made it my rule in Russia never to start the subject of politics in conversation with anybody. Very often it was started, and I then spoke as freely as I would have spoken in New York. If my opinion was asked upon any point, I gave it frankly, but never volunteered it. I believe the Golden Rule a good one for a traveler. We Americans would think it very rude for a foreigner to come here and point out to us our faults. But for all that, a great many of us visit Europe and have no hesitation in telling the subjects of the various monarchies a variety of impolite truths.

During the reign of Nicholas, the secret police was much more extensive than at present. The occurrences of 1825 and subsequent years led to a close surveillance of men in all stations of life. It was said under Nicholas that when three men were assembled, one was a spy and another might be. Doubtless the espionage was rigid, but I never heard that it affected those who said or did nothing objectionable. Under Alexander II. the stability of the throne hardly requires the aid of a detective force, and, if what I was told be true, it receives very little.

The police have a standing order to arrest any person who speaks to the Emperor in the promenade at the Public Garden. One day Nicholas recognized in the crowd a favorite comedian, and accosted him with a few words of encouragement. The actor thanked his majesty for his approval, and the two separated. A stupid policeman arrested the actor, and hurried him to prison on the charge of violating the law.

"But the emperor spoke to me first," was the apology.

"No matter," replied the policeman; "you spoke to the emperor, and must be arrested."

At the theatre that evening Nicholas was in the imperial box, utterly ignorant of what had occurred to his favorite. The performance was delayed, the audience impatient, manager frantic, and the emperor finally sent to know the cause of the curtain remaining down. The actor did not come, and after waiting some time, His Majesty went home. Next morning the prisoner was released, and during the day the emperor learned what had occurred. Sending for the victim of police stupidity, he asked what reparation could be made for his night in prison.

"I beg your majesty," was the frank request, "never to speak to me again in the Public Garden."

Nicholas promised compliance. He also made a pecuniary testimonial at the comedian's next benefit.

CHAPTER LI.

DR. SCHMIDT sold his sleigh and left Kazan by diligence the day after our arrival. I remained four days, and, when ready to start, managed to pick up a young Russian who was going to Nijne Novgorod. Each of us spoke two languages, but we had no common tongue. I brushed up all the Russian I had learned, and compelled it to perform very active service. Before our companionship ended I was astonished to find what an extensive business of conversation could be conducted with a limited capital of words.

Our communications were fragmentary and sometimes obscure, but we rarely became "hopelessly stuck." When my knowledge of spoken words failed I had recourse to a "Manual of Russian-English conversation," in which there were phrases on all sorts of topics. Examining the book at leisure one would think it abundantly fertile; but when I desired a particular phrase it was rarely to be found. As a last resource we tried Latin, but I could not remember a hundred words out of all my classics.

A regular thaw had set in, and the streets were in a condition of 'slosh' that reminded me of Broadway in spring. When we left the hotel, a crowd of attendants gathered to be remembered pecuniarily. The yemshick tied his horses' tails in the tightest of knots to prevent their filling with snow and water. At the western gate we found a jam of sleds and sleighs, where we stuck for nearly half an hour, despite the efforts of two soldier policemen. When able to proceed we traversed a high causeway spanning the Kazanka valley and emerged into a suburb containing a large foundry. A mosque and a church, side by side, symbolized the harmony between Tartar and Russian.

Passing this suburb we reached the winter station of many steamboats and barges, among which we threaded our way. Seven versts from Kazan we reached the bank of the Volga.

The first view of the road upon the river was not inviting. There were many pools of surface water, and the continuous travel had worn deep hollows in the snow and ice. Some of the pools into which our yemshick drove appeared about as safe as a mill-pond in May. As the fellow ought to know his route I said nothing, and let him have his own way. We met a great many sleds carrying merchandise, and passed a train going in our direction. One driver carelessly riding on his load was rolled overboard, and fell sidewise into a deep mass of snow and water. He uttered an imprecation, and rose dripping like a boiled cabbage just lifted out of a dinner pot.

We headed obliquely across the river toward a dozen towboats frozen in the ice. The navigation of the Volga employs more than four hundred steamers, three-fourths of which are tows. Dead walls in Kazan frequently displayed flaming announcements, that reminded me of St. Louis and New Orleans. The companies run a sharp rivalry in freight and passenger traffic, their season lasting from April to October. The gross receipts for 1866 of one company owning thirty-four boats, was one million, two hundred and fifty-three thousand, and some odd roubles. This, after deducting running expenses, would not leave a large amount of profit. The surplus in the case of that company was to be applied to paying debts. "Not a copeck," said my informant, "will the stockholders receive in the shape of dividends."

I did not obtain any full and clear information touching the navigation of the Volga. The steamboats run from Tver, on the Moscow and St. Petersburg railway, to Astrachan, at the mouth of the river. The best part of the business is the transport of goods and passengers,—chiefly the former,—to the fair at Nijne Novgorod. The river is full of shifting sand-bars, and the channel is very tortuous, especially at low water. The first company to introduce steam on the Volga was an English one. Its success induced many Russians to follow its example, so that the business is now over done.

Here, as in the Siberian rivers, the custom prevails of carrying freight in barges, which are towed by tugs. All the steamers I saw were side-wheelers.

We changed horses on the south bank of the Volga, only twelve versts from Kazan. The right bank of the river presents an unbroken line of hills or bluffs, while the opposite one is generally low. The summer road from Kazan westward follows the high ground in the vicinity of the river, but often several versts away. The winter road is over the ice of the Volga, keeping generally pretty near the bank. A double line of pine or other boughs in the ice marks the route. These boughs are placed by the Administration of Roads, under whose supervision the way is daily examined. No one is allowed to travel on the ice until the officials declare it safe.

Night came upon us soon after passing the first station. The road was a combination of pitch-holes, water, soft snow, and detours to avoid dangerous places. The most unpleasant drives were when we left the river to change horses at the villages on the high bank. It was well enough going up, but in descending the sleigh sometimes endeavored to go ahead of the horses. Once we came near going over a perpendicular bank sixty or eighty feet high. Had we done so, our establishment would have not been worth fifty cents a bushel at the bottom of the bank.

Back from the Volga on this part of the route there were many villages of Cheramess, a people of Tartar descent who preserve many of their ancient customs. They are thoroughly loyal to Russia, and keep the portrait of the emperor in nearly every cottage. In accordance with their custom of veiling women they hang a piece of gauze over the picture of the empress.

While changing horses, we were beset by many beggars, whose forlorn appearance entitled them to sympathy. I purchased a number of blessings, as each beggar made the sign of the cross over me on receiving a copeck. Russian beggars are the most devout I ever saw, and display great familiarity with the calendar of saints. One morning at Kazan I stood at my hotel window watching a beggar woman soliciting alms. Several poorly dressed peasants gave her each a copeck or two, and both giver and receiver made the sign of the cross. One decrepid old man gave her a loaf of bread, blessing it devoutly as he placed it in her hands. So far as I saw not a single well dressed person paid any attention to the mendicant. 'Only the poor can feel for the poor.'

BEGGARS IN KAZAN.

We encountered a great deal of merchandise, carried invariably upon one-horse sleds. Cotton and wool in large sacks were the principal freight going westward, while that moving toward Kazan was of a miscellaneous character. The yemshicks were the worst I found on the whole extent of my sleigh ride. They generally contented themselves with the regulation speed, and it was not often that the promise of drink-money affected them. I concluded that money was more easily obtained here than elsewhere on the route. Ten copecks were an important item to a yemshick in Siberia, but of little consequence along the Volga.

Villages were numerous along the Volga, and most of them were very liberally supplied with churches. We passed Makarief, which was for many years the scene of the great fair of European Russia. Fire and flood alike visited the place, and in 1816 the fair was transferred to Nijne Novgorod. One of the villages has a church spire that leans considerably toward the edge of the river.

THE IMMERSION.

About fifty versts from Nijne Novgorod the population of a

large village was gathered, in Sunday dress, upon the ice. A baptism was in progress, and as we drove past the assemblage we caught a glimpse of a man plunging through a freshly cut hole. Half a minute later he emerged from the crowd and ran toward the nearest house, the water dripping from his garments and hair. As we passed around the end of the village, I looked back and saw another person running in the same direction.

Converts to the Russian church are baptized by immersion, and, once received in its bosom, they continue members until death do them part. What I have said of the church in Siberia will apply throughout all Russia. The government is far more tolerant in the matter of religion than that of any Roman Catholic country in Europe, and might reprove Great Britain pretty sharply for its religious tyrannies in unhappy Ireland. Every one in Russia can worship God according to the dictates of his own conscience, provided he does not shock the moral sense of civilization in so doing. Every respectable form of Christian worship enjoys full liberty, and so does every respectable form of paganism and anti-Christianity. The Greek faith is the acknowledged religion of the government, and the priests, by virtue of their partly official character, naturally wield considerable power. The abuse or undue employment of that power is not (theoretically) permitted, however much the church may manifest its zeal. Every effort is made to convert unbelievers, but no man is forced to accept the Greek faith.

Traveling through Russia one may see many forms of worship. He will find the altars of Shamanism, the temples of Bhudha, the mosques of Islam, and the synagogues of Israel. On one single avenue of the Russian capital he will pass in succession the churches of the Greek, the Catholic, the Armenian, the Lutheran, and the Episcopal faith. He will be told that among the native Russians there are nearly fifty sects of greater or less importance. There are some advantages in belonging to the church of state, just as in England, but they are not essential. I am acquainted with officers in the military, naval, and civil service of the government who are not, and never have been, members of the Greek church. I never heard any intimation that their religion had been the least bar to their progress.

The Pope, in his encyclical of October, 1867, complains of the conduct of the Russian government toward the Catholics in Poland. No doubt Alexander has played the mischief with the Pope's faithful in that quarter, but not on account of their religion. In Warsaw a Russian officer, a Pole by birth, told me of the misfortunes that had fallen upon the Catholic monastery and college in that city. "We found in the insurrection," said the officer, "that the monks were engaged in making knives, daggers, cartridges, and other weapons. The priests were the active men of the rebellion, and did more than any other class to urge it forward, and here is a specimen of iron-mongery from the hands of the monks. We found two hundred of these in the college recently suppressed. Many more were distributed and used."

As he spoke he opened a drawer and showed me a short dagger fitting into a small handle. The point of the blade had been dipped in poison, and was carefully wrapped in paper. The instrument was used by sticking it into somebody in a crowd, and allowing it to remain. Death was pretty certain from a very slight scratch of this weapon.

If this gentleman's story is correct, and it was corroborated by others, the Russian persecution of the Polish Catholics is not entirely without reason.

Among the dissenters in the Greek church there is a body called *Staroviersty* (Old Believers). The difference between them and the adherents of the orthodox faith is more ritualistic than doctrinal. Both make the sign of the cross, though each has its own way of holding the fingers in the operation. The Staroviersty do not use tobacco in any form, and their mode of life is generally quite rigid. Under Catherine and Paul they were persecuted, and, as a matter of course, increased their numbers rapidly. For the past sixty years oppression has been removed, and they have done pretty nearly as they liked. They are found in all parts of the empire, but are most numerous in the vicinity of the Ural mountains.

Russia has its share of fanatical sects, some of whom push their religion to a wonderful extreme. One sect has a way of sacrificing children by a sort of slow torture in no way commendable. Another sect makes a burnt offering of some of its adherents, who are selected by lot. They enter a house prepared for the occasion, and begin a service of singing and prayer. After a time spent in devotions, the building is set on fire and consumed with its occupants. Another sect which is mentioned elsewhere practices the mutilation of masculine believers, and steals children for adoption into their families. Against all these fanatics the government exercises its despotic power.

RUSSIAN PRIEST.

The peasants are generally very devout, and keep all the days of the church with becoming reverence. There is a story that a moujik waylaid and killed a traveler, and while rifling the pockets of his victim found a cake containing meat. Though very hungry he would not eat the cake, because meat was forbidden in the fast then in force.

The government is endeavoring to diminish the power and influence of the priests, and the number of saints' days, when men must abstain from labor. Heretofore the priests have enjoyed the privilege of recruiting the clergy from their own members. When a village priest died his office fell to his son, and if he had no male heir the revenues went to his eldest daughter until some priest married her and took charge of the parish. By special order of the emperor any vacancy is hereafter to be filled by the most deserving candidate.

It is said that during the Crimean war the governor of Moscow notified the pastor of the English church in that city that the prayer for the success of Her Brittanic Majesty's armies must be omitted. The pastor appealed to the emperor, who replied that prayers of regular form might continue to be read, no matter what they contained. The governor made no further interference.

About three o'clock in the afternoon of the second day from Kazan, the yemshick pointed out the spires of Nijne Novgorod, on the southern bank of the Volga. A fleet of steamers, barges, and soudnas lay sealed in the ice along the shore, waiting for the moving of the waters. The road to the north bank was marked with pine boughs, that fringed the moving line of sleighs and sledges. We threaded our way among the stationary vessels, and at length came before the town. A friend had commended me to the Hotel de la Poste, and I ordered the yemshick to drive there. With an eye to his pocket the fellow carried me to an establishment of the same name on the other side of the Oka. I had a suspicion that I was being swindled, but as they blandly informed me that no other hotel with that title existed, I alighted and ordered my baggage up.

This was the end of my sleigh ride. I had passed two hundred and nine stations, with as many changes of horses and drivers. Nearly seven hundred horses had been attached to my sleigh, and had drawn me over a road of greatly varied character. Out of forty days from Irkutsk, I spent sixteen at the cities and towns on the way. I slept twenty-six nights in my sleigh with the thermometer varying from thirty-five degrees above zero to forty-five below, and encountered four severe storms and a variety of smaller ones. Including the detour to Barnaool, my sleigh ride was about thirty-six hundred miles long. From Stratensk by way of Kiachta to Irkutsk, I traveled not far from fourteen hundred miles with wheeled vehicles, and made ninety-three changes. My whole ride from steam navigation on the Amoor to the railway at Nijne Novgorod was very nearly five thousand miles.

There was a manifest desire to swindle me at the bogus Hotel de la Poste. Half a dozen attendants carried my baggage to my room, and each demanded a reward. When I gave the yemshick his "na vodka," an officious attendant suggested that the gentleman should be very liberal at the end of his ride. I asked for a bath, and they ordered a sleigh to take me to a bathing establishment several squares away. My proposition to be content for the present with a wash basin was pronounced impossible, until I finished the argument with my left boot. The waiter finally became affectionate, and when I ordered supper he suggested comforts not on the bill of fare. The landlord proposed to purchase my sleigh and superfluous furs, and we concluded a bargain at less than a twelfth of their cost.

After a night's rest I recrossed the Oka and drove to the town. Here I found the veritable Hotel de la Poste, to which I immediately changed my quarters. The house overlooked a little park enclosing a pond, where a hundred or more persons were skating. The park was well shaded, and must be quite pleasant in summer. The town hardly deserves the name of Nijne (Lower) Novgorod, as it stands on a bluff nearly two hundred feet above the river. Its lower town contains little else than small shops, storehouses, poor hotels, and steamboat offices. The Kremlin, or fortress, looks down from a very picturesque position, and its strong walls have a defiant air. From the edge of the bluff the view is wide; the low field and forest land on the opposite side of the river, the sinuous Volga and its tributary, the Oka, are all visible for a long distance. Opposite, on a tongue of land between the Volga and the Oka, is the scene of the fair of Nijne Novgorod, the greatest, I believe, in the world.

There are many fine houses in the upper town, with indications of considerable wealth. I had a letter of introduction to the Chief of Police, Colonel Kretegin, who kindly showed me the principal objects of interest in and around the Kremlin. The monument to the memory of Minin Sukhoruky possessed the greatest historical importance. This man, a peasant and butcher, believed himself called to deliver Russia from the Poles in 1612. He awakened his countrymen, and joined a Russian noble in leading them to expel the invaders. A bronze monument at Moscow represents Minin starting on his mission. The memorial at Nijne is of a less elaborate character.

We drove through the fair grounds, which were as empty of occupants as Goldsmith's deserted village. It is laid out like a regular town or city, and most of its houses are substantially built. So much has been written about this commercial center that I will not attempt its description, especially as I was not there in fair season. The population of the town—ordinarily forty thousand—becomes three hundred thousand during the fair. More than half a million persons have visited the city in a single summer, and the value of goods sold or exchanged during each fair is about two hundred millions of roubles.

Colonel Kretegin told me that the members of the Fox embassy were much astonished at finding American goods for sale at Nijne Novgorod. It would be difficult to mention any part of the civilized world where some article of our manufacture has not penetrated.

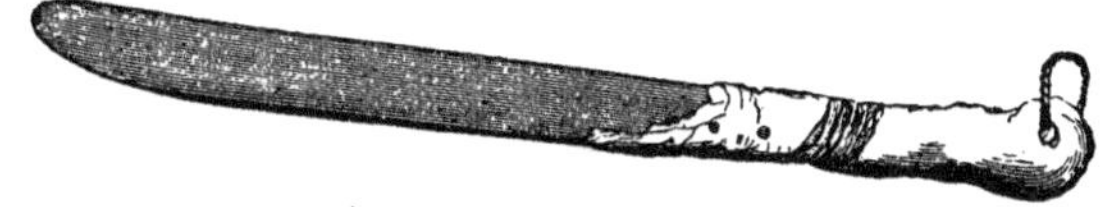

CHAPTER LII.

AT the close of the second day at Nijne Novgorod I started for Moscow. As we drove from the hotel to the railway the jackdaws, perched everywhere on the roofs, were unusually noisy. Leaving Asia and entering Europe, the magpie seemed to give place to the jackdaw. The latter bird inhabits the towns and cities east of the Ural mountains, and we frequently saw large flocks searching the debris along the Volga road. He associates freely with the pigeon, and appears well protected by public sentiment. Possibly his uneatable character and his fancied resemblance to the pigeon saves him from being knocked in the head. Pigeons are very abundant in all Russian cities, and their tameness is a matter of remark among foreign visitors.

The railway station is across the Oka and near the site of the annual fair. We went at a smashing pace down hill and over the ice to the other side, narrowly missing several collisions. At the railway I fell to the charge of two porters, who carried my baggage while I sought the ticket office. A young woman speaking French officiated at the desk, and furnished me with a *billet de voyage* to Moscow.

In the waiting room a hundred or more persons were gathered. The men were well wrapped in furs, and among the ladies hoods were more numerous than bonnets. Three-fourths of the males and a third of the females were smoking cigarettes, and there was no prohibition visible. In accordance with the national taste the chief article sold at the *buffet* was hot tea in tumblers.

Some one uttered "Sibeerski" as, clad in my dehar, I

walked past a little group. To keep up appearances and kill time I drank tea, until the door opened and a rush was made for the train. There is an adage in Germany that three kinds of people—fools, princes, and Americans—travel first class. To continue Russian pretences, and by the advice of a friend, I took a second class ticket, and found the accommodation better than the average of first class cars in America.

How strange was the sensation of railway travel! Since I last experienced it, I had journeyed more than half around the globe. I had been tossed on the Pacific and adjacent waters, had ascended the great river of northern Asia, had found the rough way of life along the frozen roads beyond the Baikal, and ended with that long, long ride over Siberian snows. I looked back through a long vista of earth and snow, storm and sunshine, starlight and darkness, rolling sea and placid river, rugged mountains and extended plains.

The hardships of travel were ended as I reached the land of railways, and our motion as we sped along the track seemed more luxurious than ever before. Contrasted with the cramped and narrow sleigh, pitching over ridges and occasionally overturning, the carriage where I sat appeared the perfection of locomotive skill. How sweet is pleasure after pain. Sunshine is brightest in the morning, and prosperity has a keener zest when it follows adversity. To be truly enjoyed, our lives must be chequered with light and shadow, and varied with different scenes.

The railway between Nijne Novgorod and Moscow is about two hundred and fifty miles in length, and was built by French and Russian capital combined. There is only one passenger train each way daily, at a speed not exceeding twenty miles an hour.

In the compartment where I sat there was a young French woman, governess in a family at Simbirsk, with a Russian female servant accompanying her. The governess was chatty, and invited me to join her in a feast of bon-bons, which she devoured at a prodigious rate. The servant was becomingly silent, and solaced herself with cigarettes. The restaurants along the road are quite well supplied, especially those where full meals are provided. Two hours after starting we halted ten minutes for tea and cigarettes. Two hours later we had thirty minutes for supper, which was all ready at our arrival. About midnight we stopped at the ancient city of Vladimir, where there is a cathedral founded in the twelfth century. Stepping from the train to get a night glimpse of the place, I found a substantial supper (or breakfast) spread for consumption. In justice to the Russians, I am happy to say very few patronized this midnight table.

At daybreak I rubbed the frost from a window and looked upon a stretch of snow and frost, with peasant cottages few and far between. An hour later, our speed slackened. Again cleaning the glass and peering through it, a large city came in sight.

It was Moscow,—" Holy Moscow,"—the city of the Czars, and beloved of every Russian. Suffering through Tartar, Polish, and French occupations, it has survived pillage, massacre, fire, and famine, and remains at this day the most thoroughly national of the great cities of the empire. The towers and domes of its many churches glittered in the morning sunlight as they glittered half a century ago, when Napoleon and his soldiers first climbed the hills that overlook the city.

It was a long drive from the station to the hotel. The morning was clear and cold, and the snow in the streets had been ground into a sand-like mass several inches deep. The solid foundation beneath was worn with hollows and ridges, that vividly recalled the oukhabas of the post road. Streets were full of sleds and sleighs, the latter dashing at a rapid rate. In the region near the station there were so many signs of '*Trakteer*,' as to suggest the possibility of one half the inhabitants selling tea, beer, and quass to the other half. Near the center of the city the best shops displayed signs in French or English, generally the former.

Of course I went early to the Kremlin. Who has ever

read or talked of Moscow without its historic fortress? Entering by the Sacred Gate, I lifted my hat in comformity to the custom, from which not even the emperor is exempt. One of my school-books contained a description of the Czar Kolokol, or Great Bell, and stated that a horse and chaise could pass through the hole where a piece was broken from one side. Possibly the miniature vehicle of Tom Thumb could be driven through, but, certainly, no ordinary one-horse shay could have any prospect of success. The hole is six feet in height, by about a yard wide at the bottom, and narrows like a wedge toward the top. The height and diameter of the bell are respectively nineteen feet four inches by twenty feet three inches. It weighs 444,000 pounds. It was cast in 1733, by order of the Empress Anne, and the hole in its side was made by the falling of some rafters during a fire in 1737. It remained buried in the ground until 1836, when it was raised and placed on its present pedestal by order of the Emperor Nicholas.

GREAT BELL OF MOSCOW.

To enumerate all the wonders of the Kremlin would consume much time and space. Somebody tells of a Yankee gazing at Niagara, and lamenting that a magnificent water power should run to waste. I could not help wondering how many miles of railway could be built from the proceeds of the mass of wealth inside the Kremlin. Diamonds, rubies, pearls, crowns, sceptres, thrones, princely and priestly robes, are gathered in such numbers that eye and brain become weary in their contemplation. The most interesting of these treasures are those around which cling historic associations. The crowns of the kingdoms of Kazan and Astrachan point to the overthrow of Tartar power in Europe, while the throne of Poland symbolizes the westward course of the Muscovite star of empire.• There are flags borne or captured in Russia's victories, from the storming of Kazan and the defence of Albazin down to the suppression of Polish revolt. Mute and dumb witnesses of the misfortunes of the *Grand Armee* are the long rows of cannon that lie near the Kremlin palace. Three hundred and sixty-five French guns tell of Napoleon's disastrous march to Moscow.

The holiest part of holy Moscow is within the Kremlin. In the church of the Assumption the czars of Russia, from John the Terrible down to the present day, have been crowned. In the Michael church, until the accession of Peter the Great, the Rurik and Romanoff dynasties were buried; while another church witnessed their baptism and marriage. What a wonderful amount of gold and jewels are visible in the churches and chapels of the Kremlin! The floor of one is of jasper and agate; pearl and amethyst and onyx adorn the inner walls of another. One has vast pillars of porphyry, and the domes and turrets of all are liberally spread or starred with gold. The pictures of the infant Saviour and his mother are hung with necklaces of jewels, each of them almost a fortune. One might easily think that the wealth of Ormuz or of Ind had been gathered to adorn the shrines of the most oriental Christian faith.

I visted the Imperial Theatre, which the Muscovites pronounce the finest in the world. To my mind it is only equaled by La Scala at Milan, or San Carlo at Naples. Outside it reminded me of our *ci-devant* Academy of Music. Inside it was gorgeous, well arranged, and spacious.

VIEW ON THE NEVSKI PROSPECT—ST. PETERSBURGH.

The *Kitai Gorod*, or Chinese town of Moscow, is close by the Kremlin and outside its walls. The only feature worthy the name of this part of the city is the number of Tartar inhabitants and the immense bazaar, or Gastinni Dvor, where the principal trade of Moscow has been centered for nearly three hundred years. The quantity of goods in the bazaar is something enormous. A Russian said to me: "If half the houses in Moscow were stripped of furniture, ornaments, and all things save the walls and roofs; if their inhabitants were plundered of all clothing and personal goods except their bank accounts,—the *gastinni dvor* could supply every deficiency within two hours. You may enter the bazaar wearing nothing but your shirt, and can depart in an hour dressed and decorated in any manner you choose, and riding in your carriage with driver and footman in livery."

The railway between St. Petersburg and Moscow is a government affair, and forms nearly a direct line from one city to the other. It is said that the emperor Nicholas placed a ruler on the map and drew a line from one capital to the other to mark the route the engineers must follow. Notwithstanding the favorable character of the country the cost of the road was enormous, in consequence of alleged peculations. There is a story that the government once wished to make a great impression upon a Persian embassy. All the marvels of St. Petersburg and Moscow were exhausted, but the oriental embassadors remained serene and unmoved.

"What shall we do to surprise them," the emperor demanded of his prime minister.

"Nothing is better, sire," replied that official, "than to tell them the cost of the Imperial railway."

One hears more about stealing and bribe taking in Russia than in any other country I ever visited. The evil is partly on account of low salaries and great expense of living, and partly due to ancient custom. The emperor has endeavored to establish a reform in this particular, but the difficulties are very great because of the secret character of "palm-greasing." It is related that a German *savant* once remarked to Nicholas that he could do Russia a great service by breaking up the system of financial corruption. "To get such a project in action," replied the emperor, "I must begin by bribing my prime minister."

Of the country between the capitals I saw very little. In the cars the double windows, covered with frost, were about as transparent as a drop curtain. We stopped at a great many capacious and well built stations, where there was abundant opportunity for feeding and drinking. The journey commenced at two in the afternoon, and was finished at ten on the following morning. The distance, according to official measurement, is four hundred and three miles.

The train halted at the station nearest St. Petersburg, and as we stood a moment upon the platform, we saw the great, gilded dome of St. Isaac's cathedral rising over the city. In St. Petersburg my first duty was to take breakfast, a bath, and a change of clothes at a hotel, and then to drive to the banker's for letters from home. I had not seen an American for five months; as I alighted from my droshky, a well-dressed individual looked at me, and not to be outdone I returned his glance. Our eyes peered over two fur collars that exposed very little of our faces. After a moment's hesitation each of us spoke the other's name, and I experienced the double pleasure of meeting in one individual a countryman and an old friend.

THE END.

MAP
to accompany
THOS. W. KNOX'S
"Overland through Asia"
ARCTIC OCEAN
PACIFIC OCEAN
RUSSIAN EMPIRE
SIBERIA
INDEPENDENT TARTARY
MONGOLIA
CHINA
THIBET
HINDOSTAN
PERSIA
AFGHANISTAN
BELOOCHISTAN
KAMCHATKA
JAPAN
COREA
LUZON
NOVA ZEMBLA
St. PETERSBURG
MOSCOW
WARSAW
Ural Mountains
Great Sandy Desert called Cobi or Shamo
LITTLE BOKHARA
LITTLE THIBET
Arctic Circle
CANTON
Longitude East from Greenwich
Latitude of England
Canada
Virginia
Louisiana
Yucatan
Guatemala
New Grenada

www.ingramcontent.com/pod-product-compliance
Lightning Source LLC
LaVergne TN
LVHW021058110826
845150LV00001B/111